Cloud Computing

With changing times, the demands on technology have changed. In response different computing models have evolved since the past decade, starting with Cluster Computing to Grid Computing and finally to Cloud Computing.

Cloud Computing has emerged as an important technique in the field of computer applications and information technology. It involves services for the storage, processing and transmission of data through shared resources, over the internet. Resources utilized for these services can be metered and the clients can be charged for the resources they utilize.

Striving to provide a dynamic understanding of the nature of cloud computing this book begins with in-depth coverage of the fundamental concepts including Virtualization, Scaling and Service Oriented Architecture. The text further discusses cloud models such as NIST Model, Cloud Deployment Model and Service Delivery Models. Associated techniques like resource pooling, load balancing, and content delivery network are also presented in detail. The book concludes with a discussion on popular, commercial cloud services and real life applications including Amazon, Google and Microsoft Azure. It helps the reader correlate theory with practically available services.

Designed for undergraduate and graduate students of computer science engineering and information technology, the book follows a structured approach to explain complex topics. A concluding chapter on mobile cloud computing and appendices on recent developments, including real-time processing and programming, in cloud computing are provided. Plenty of review questions, multiple choice questions, illustrations and comparison charts are interspersed throughout the text.

Sandeep Bhowmik works as Assistant Professor in the Department of Computer Science & Engineering at Hooghly Engineering & Technology College, West Bengal. His areas of interest include application of soft computing techniques in data processing and information security.

Cloud Computing

Sandeep Bhowmik

CAMBRIDGE
UNIVERSITY PRESS

CAMBRIDGE
UNIVERSITY PRESS

Shaftesbury Road, Cambridge CB2 8EA, United Kingdom

One Liberty Plaza, 20th Floor, New York, NY 10006, USA

477 Williamstown Road, Port Melbourne, VIC 3207, Australia

314–321, 3rd Floor, Plot 3, Splendor Forum, Jasola District Centre, New Delhi – 110025, India

103 Penang Road, #05–06/07, Visioncrest Commercial, Singapore 238467

Cambridge University Press is part of Cambridge University Press & Assessment,
a department of the University of Cambridge.

We share the University's mission to contribute to society through the pursuit of
education, learning and research at the highest international levels of excellence.

www.cambridge.org
Information on this title: www.cambridge.org/9781316638101

© Cambridge University Press & Assessment 2017

First published 2017

A catalogue record for this publication is available from the British Library

ISBN   978-1-316-63810-1   Paperback

Additional resources for this publication at www.cambridge.org/9781316638101

Cambridge University Press & Assessment has no responsibility for the persistence
or accuracy of URLs for external or third-party internet websites referred to in this
publication and does not guarantee that any content on such websites is, or will
remain, accurate or appropriate.

This book is dedicated to my mother Mrs Tapati Bhowmik,
who has passionately taken care of her family throughout her life without the slightest
negligence, in addition to being sincere towards her duties as a school teacher, involving
three hours of daily strenuous journey, for thirty-nine years till her retirement. In her
seventies now, with her husband, sons, daughters-in-law and grandchildren around her, she
still holds the key to make everyone feel the warmth of a beautiful home.

&

To God,
for allowing me the time and patience to complete this endeavor.

Contents

Figures

Tables

Preface

The future often arrives silently. In the digital world, cloud computing which emerged silently, has already made a significant place of its own and has shown enough potential to be the future of computing. The advantages it offers are plenty, and this is what makes cloud computing revolutionary.

Books on this evolving subject started appearing in the market towards the end of the last decade. A handful of books have been published so far, and they provide useful resource material. While a few among them have been written in order to discuss conceptual aspects of the subject, others have been written from research or application perspective. As the research or application oriented books serve specific purposes only, they are not appropriate for general readers of the subject.

Cloud computing is not a single technology; rather, it is a combination of multiple technologies. Hence, it is necessary to understand all those individual technologies in order to understand cloud computing as a whole. Many books have been written with their focus on some particular aspects of cloud computing, and thus, they have not been able to cover all the essential topics of cloud computing with equal importance. This book is written from conceptual perspective, for the sake of new learners of the subject, and it tries to fill the void for a book covering all the fundamentals in detail, with simplified explanations in a learner friendly manner.

The author felt the need for such a book while teaching the subject to the undergraduate engineering students, as well as software professionals who wanted to develop a basic understanding of the subject. It is either inadequate coverage or a complex approach of most books available in the market, that makes it difficult for new learners to develop a clear conception about the various aspects of these technologies, and they therefore do not satisfy the fundamental queries of students. Thus, it is a lack of books covering all the fundamentals in detail which encouraged the author to write this book.

The author is aware of the fact that computing and IT industry are fast merging into a singular cloud computing environment, and in the near future there will be a requirement for a large pool of workforce with sound insight into this subject. It will be easier for professionals to get trained in various business specific cloud applications, after gaining adequate fundamental knowledge of the subject. This book will be suitable for all people aiming to understand the basics of cloud computing. The author hopes that the readers will enjoy this book and will be able to develop an overall idea about the methodologies and technicalities involved in cloud computing.

Acknowledgments

Any technical writing task begins with gathering adequate knowledge of the domain. I offer my gratitude to all the authors of reputed books, research material and online articles, who have added value to the literature on cloud computing and its allied fields, with their resourceful publications. Their work enabled me to understand the minute technical details of the subject. Publications and other resource material from reputed cloud computing vendors were also very helpful.

I also extend my gratitude to the commissioning editors at Cambridge University Press I worked with, for their numerous suggestions and support in making this effort a success. They are wonderful people to work with, and my entire experience with them was very delightful.

Before the process of publication began, I invited a few of my students and assigned them the tedious task of individually reviewing two or three selected chapters of the manuscript, and asked for their opinions regarding the organization and presentation of the topics contained therein. I appreciate their sincere efforts, without naming them, in pointing out any complexity in the explanations, lack of elaboration or editing mistakes in the manuscript. Special thanks go to those who contributed detailed comments which helped me enhance the simplicity of presentation of the material.

I would like to thank my brother Joydeep, a computing professional and a scientist, for his valuable inputs and key interest in this venture. A highly deserved piece of appreciation also goes to my wife Sobori, an IT professional, for her efforts in thoroughly examining each and every chapter of the manuscript as a final round of review and providing her suggestions to improve its readability, before the manuscript was handed over to the publisher for publication.

Writing a technical textbook is a lengthy task that requires intense concentration of mind. Due to my professional engagements, most of the work had to be done at the end of the day and during holidays, sitting on my computer at home. The process often demanded less involvement in the day to day household affairs for long periods of time. It would never have been possible without the kind of atmosphere I enjoy at home together with all the members of my family – my parents, wife, brother, sister-in-law Chandini, along with little members Ananya and Aparna. They all kept me refreshed.

1 | Introduction

The catchword *Cloud Computing* may sound new to the arena of computing as well as information technology; although the concept behind it is not completely new. In a broad sense, it is a step (forward) to access the web-based services through Internet; or in general terms, cloud computing represents an advance in the field of computing technology where management of computing services is outsourced to greater extents and in multiple dimensions. To be specific, computing facilities are being made available as services offered by reputed vendors.

Computing technology has been evolved over the years. There have been steady developments in the field of computing hardware, software architecture, web technology and network communications over the last decade. The speed of internetworks has increased day by day and it has also become cheaper. All these developments contributed in setting the stage for the initiation of the revolutionary concept of 'cloud computing'.

Cloud computing has changed the way computation happens. It provides the means for smarter ways to do business and accordingly it makes life simpler. This chapter tries to highlight the shortcomings in the *traditional computing* approaches and it attempts to iterate how the stage was ready for the arrival of this new model of computing.

> *Cloud computing has evolved over the years and has changed the way people live and do business over the World Wide Web.*

1.1 WHAT IS THE BUZZ ABOUT

Cloud computing provides the means for users to easily avail computing facilities whenever and wherever required. They need not worry about setting up infrastructure, purchasing new equipment or investing in the procurement of licensed software. Rather they can access any volume, large or small, of computing facilities in exchange for some nominal payment. It is a new model of computing which has become possible through integration of advanced computing models, sophisticated web technologies and modern network communication technologies (especially high-speed Internet).

Cloud computing became a hot topic for large computing vendors (companies like Amazon, Google, Microsoft etc.) only from mid-2008, but the concept itself is quite old. People have different perceptions regarding this new computing model. To some, it is a new and radical innovation. Others think that it is nothing new: only the pace of modernization has been explored to obtain new uses of technologies which already existed. The fact is, like every new technology, cloud computing too has emerged from an ancestral domain of existing technology and its context.

> *Cloud computing is the delivery of computing services over the Internet.*

1.2 LIMITATIONS OF THE TRADITIONAL COMPUTING APPROACHES

Every new technology emerges with the promise to resolve the shortcomings of the existing ones. *Traditional computing* has played a pivotal role in the field of computing and communication over the past few decades. Since cloud computing is being considered as the successor of the traditional computing system, therefore, it would be wise to recognize the limitations of the traditional computing approaches before studying the contents of cloud computing.

Computing and information technology (IT) has changed the nature and scope of the human civilization in last few decades. There was a time, nearly half-of-the-decade back, when enterprises used to execute their businesses merely by the aid of the pen, paper, telephone and fax machine. Gradually, computer systems intruded manual processes and started automating them. The pen and paper were replaced by digital communication, and even the phone and faxing services started being managed by computers.

At present, businesses from local to global, are dependent on the computing systems for almost everything they do. Even individuals depend heavily on computing systems for their day-to-day activities. IT and computing are critical factors now, and life cannot be imagined without easy and all-time access to computing systems.

Easy and cheap access to computing facilities has become essential for everyone. But, a little investigation raises concerns about several issues regarding the conventional uses of computing technology. Following section focuses on problems associated with traditional computing approaches.

1.2.1 Enterprise Perspective

Enterprises have been valuable consumers of computing since inception. They have always been among the front-runners for adopting computing-based process automation for running day-to-day business activities. Table 1.1 points out the difficulties faced by enterprises with *traditional computing* approach.

Table 1.1 Difficulties faced by enterprises in traditional computing

Traditional Computing Scenario	*Problematic facts and related questions*
Business without help of computing services is beyond imagination, and the customized software packages manage business activities. Most organizations use ERP packages (implemented by some IT enterprise) to get maximum benefits from regular business operations.	To run enterprise resource planning applications, business organizations need to invest huge volumes of capital to setup the required IT infrastructure. Servers, client terminals, network infrastructure are required, and they to be put together in a proper manner. Moreover, arranging adequate power supply, cooling system and provisioning space also consume a major part of the IT budget. Are there ways to avoid this huge initial investment for computing infrastructural setup?

Traditional Computing Scenario	*Problematic facts and related questions*
Business application package implementation also over-burdens the IT enterprises with many other costs. Setting up infrastructure, installation of OS, device drivers, management of routers, firewalls, proxy servers etc. are all responsibilities of the enterprise in traditional computing approach.	Enterprises (or IT service firms) need to maintain a team of experts (system maintenance team) in order to manage the whole thing. This is a burden for HR management and incurs recurring capital investment (for salaries). Can enterprises get relief from these responsibilities and difficulties? It would help them concentrate fully on the functioning of business applications.
Even those IT enterprises whose sole business interest is developing applications are bound to setup computing infrastructure before they start any development work.	This is an extra burden for enterprises who are only interested in application development. They can outsource the management of infrastructure to some third party, but the cost and quality of such services varies quite a bit. Can IT enterprises avert such difficulties?
Computing infrastructure requires adequate hardware procurement. This procurement is costly, but it is not a one-time investment. After every few years, existing devices become outdated as more powerful devices appear.	It becomes difficult to compete in the market with outdated hardware infrastructure. Advanced software applications also require upgraded hardware in order to maximize business output. Can this process of upgrading hardware on a regular basis be eliminated from an enterprise's responsibility?
It is not unusual to find an updated version of application with new releases that is more advanced and apt to keep up with changing business scenario.	Adopting an updated version of an application requires necessary efforts from subscriber's end. Fresh installation and integration of components need to be done. Can subscribers be relieved of this difficulty of periodically upgrading the applications?
Capacity planning of computing resources is a critical task for any organization. Appropriate planning needs time, expertise and budgetary allocation since low resource volume hampers the pace of the performance of applications.	Enterprises generally plan and procure to support the maximum business load that they have anticipated. But average resource demand remains far less, most of the time. This causes resource wastage and increases the recurring cost of business. If this capacity planning task could be made less critical and resource procurement strategy more cost effective?
Resource requirements of a system may increase or decrease from time to time.	Individual enterprises cannot manage system contraction in a way that unutilized resources of a system can be utilized in some other system so that the cost of the business could be reduced. If this were somehow possible?
Many enterprise computing systems run forever without stopping. Such systems host applications which require round-the-clock availability to fulfill business demand.	When resource capacity expansion of such system becomes an absolute requirement for the respective business, an system shutdown (hence service disruption) becomes unavoidable which may cause loss in the business. If a system could be expanded without shutting it down?

Hence, an enterprise can be overburdened when handling multiple issues in the traditional way of computing. Issues like huge initial investment for setting up computing infrastructure, difficulty of managing the complex systems, difficulty in regularly replacing outdated things with latest available technology etc. have always been the matters of concern.

1.2.2 Individual User's Perspective

Individual users have also been consumers of computing since a long time. They use computing for various purposes like editing documents, developing program, playing games, watching videos, accessing Internet etc. Table 1.2 focuses on the troubles individual users of computing usually face with the *traditional computing* approach.

Table 1.2 Difficulties faced by individual users in traditional computing approach

Traditional Computing Scenario	Problematic facts and related questions
To work with software applications (like text editor, image editor, programming, games etc.), users first need to procure computing system where these software applications run.	For general users (who don't want to experiment with computer hardware devices), this initial capital investment for setting up computing infrastructure is often more than the software applications they use! If this huge unnecessary investment for procuring hardware components could be avoided?
Requirement analysis and procurement of hardware infrastructure are responsibility of the users. But, actual utilization of these resources depends on frequency of user access and the kind of software applications they run over it.	General users are usually not experts of computing systems. They are often misguided and procure unnecessary volume/capacity of hardware resources, most portions of which remain unutilized. This reduces the return on investment (ROI). If this approach could be changed; if users did not have to procure a fixed volume of hardware resource prior to its actual use or demand?
A hardware component may fail for many reasons. Maintenance of the hardware infrastructure is the users' responsibility.	Time, cost and the uncertainty are involved in the process. If users could get relief from these responsibilities and difficulties?
Computing systems (desktop, laptop etc.) procured by most users are hardly used for few hours daily on an average.	Non-utilization of procured systems results in wastage of resource with regard to total investment. If the hardware resources would be available on payment of usage basis?
Software licensing cost needs separate budgetary allocation. Licenses are sold for fixed period of time (usually for one year-duration).	If software is used for 2–5 hour per day on an average during licensing period, it depicts 8%–20% utilization of entire investment. If this cost could be reduced? If the licensing fee would be paid on hourly usage basis?
Users are burdened with installation and critical customization of software. They also troubleshoot in case the software crashes.	Professional help can be obtained against payment, or users can troubleshoot themselves, thereby investing more time. If users could get relief from these responsibilities and difficulties?

Traditional Computing Scenario	Problematic facts and related questions
Users need to have physical access to the system for using a personal computing system.	Though portable computing devices are available (like laptop, tablet etc.), it may not be possible to carry them all the time.
	Could there be a way of accessing personal computing systems remotely, from any location, any time?
Within few years, hardware systems become outdated. It becomes difficult to run advanced or new software on them.	Users have no other option but to throw out the whole setup and replace it with a new one.
	If there be a permanent solution to this wastage (from users' end)?

So, individual users also face many difficulties with traditional computing. Initial necessities of procuring expensive physical system, maintenance of the hardware, maintenance of software have always been prime concerns for general users. Moreover, within just few years of the whole investment the need for hardware up-gradation emerges.

All these limitations of traditional computing paved the way for the emergence of an alternative model of computing. Cloud computing has redefined the way computing has ever worked.

1.3 IS THERE ANY SOLUTION TO THESE WORRIES?

When an organization or an individual user needs to set up in-house IT infrastructure (small or big) for computing purpose, they have two options:

- Doing it themselves (by deploying *in-house* team, in case of an organization)
- *Outsourcing* the responsibility to some third party who are well-trained for the job

But in both of these cases, there remain concerns which bother the users, such as hardware management or software installation or application implementation etc. which are not likely to be part of the core competencies of users. Other worries have already been listed in Table 1.1 and Table 1.2. Is there a way to remove these worries from the minds of individual users or enterprises? If the answer is 'Yes' then they will be able to concentrate more on their core tasks.

IT *service outsourcing* is a popular model which has been adopted by enterprises over the last two decades, where all of the application development and implementation related activities/ responsibilities are transferred to IT service companies. But, traditional outsourcing is not the best solution to all problems mentioned above.

Traditional outsourcing may remove the worries of system or application maintenance to some extent but it cannot eliminate all of them, as different levels of computing facility subscribers have different types of requirements. For example, enterprises who only use applications to run their business activities have some kind of computing requirements, but those IT service organizations to whom they outsource the complex tasks of application development or implementation have their separate computing requirements. Application development team of an IT service organization may in turn depend on some system (physical computing system), whereas the assembling and maintenance group who need not to have knowledge of application development may have concerns that are entirely different. They will certainly have separate requirements. In brief, difficulties faced by users (of computing) depend on the layers of computing they work on.

The concerns of the users of computing vary with the layers of their computing activities.

1.4 THREE LAYERS OF COMPUTING

Computers and computing have become an integral part of our daily lives. Different people use different categories of computing facilities. These computing facilities can be segmented into three categories:

- Infrastructure
- Platform
- Application

These three categories of computing facilities form three layers in the basic architecture of computing. Figure 1.1 represents the relationships between these three entities.

1.4.1 Infrastructure

The bottom layer or the foundation is the 'computing infrastructure' facility. This includes all physical computing devices or hardware components like the processor, memory, network, storage devices and other hardware appliances. Infrastructure refers to computing resources in their bare-metal form (without any layer of software installed over them, not even the operating system). This layer needs basic amenities like electric supply, cooling system etc.

1.4.2 Platform

In computing, platform is the underlying system over which applications run. It can be said that the platform consists of the physical computing device (hardware) loaded with layer(s) of software where the program or application can run. The term 'computing platform' refers to different abstract levels. It consists of:

- Certain hardware components, only.
- Hardware loaded with an operating system (OS).
- Hardware and OS, additionally, loaded with run-time libraries.

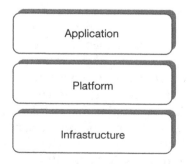

FIG 1.1: Three layers of computing facilities

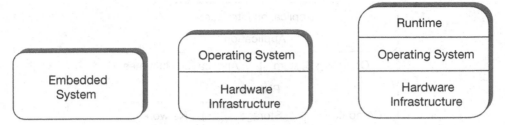

FIG 1.2: Computing platforms in different forms

Hardware alone can be considered as the platform in case of embedded systems, where physical resources can be accessed without any operating system.

A fully configured physical computer loaded with an operating system is considered as a platform for computing. Different platforms can be installed over the same computing infrastructure. Linux or Windows operating systems installed over the same physical computer (computing infrastructure) can provide two different computing platforms.

The platform layer is also the place where software developers work. Hence Integrated Development Environments (IDEs) and runtimes are part of this layer. Java Development Kit (JDK) or .NET are examples of popular computing frameworks. Software applications can be developed and run over these platforms.

Platform layer provides the platform to execute the applications; in addition it facilitates application development activities.

1.4.3 Application

Applications (application software) constitute the topmost layer of this layered architecture. This layer generally provides interfaces for interaction with external systems (human or machine) and is accessed by *end users* of computing. A user actually works on the application layer while he or she is going to edit a document, play a game or use the calculator in a computer. At this layer, organizations access enterprise applications using application interfaces to run their business.

Different types of people work at different layers of computing. They need to have different skill-sets and knowledge. Figure 1.3 shows the general users or subscribers of three different computing layers.

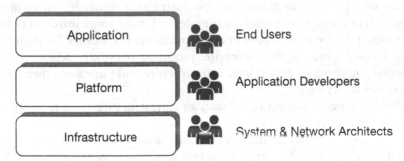

FIG 1.3: Different users/subscribers of three computing layers

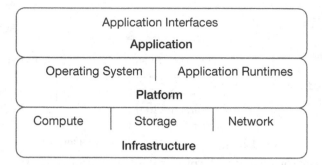

FIG 1.4: Elements of three computing layers

An upper layer in this architecture is dependent on underlying layer(s). Access to the topmost layer effectively consumes facilities from all underlying layers. Thus, a person working online or offline with some software application on a personal computing device or directly accessing the Internet basically consumes all these three facilities together.

Figure 1.4 illustrates the different constituents of the three layer of computing. In this figure, the term 'compute' refers to the set of resources required for assembling a computing system or computer, particularly processor and memory components.

1.5 THREE LAYERS IN TRADITIONAL COMPUTING

In the traditional approach, the boundaries between computing layers were not very clear to the general users. Most *end users* unknowingly had to bear the burden of being concerned about all these three computing layers, while their actual area of interest was only around the application layer. Similarly, developers had to be concerned about the infrastructure layer apart from their own layer of activities (the platform layer). This section briefly focuses on the complexities associated with these three computing layers in the traditional computing model from users' viewpoint.

1.5.1 Traditional Infrastructure Model

Traditionally enterprises arrange computing infrastructure themselves by forming an internal computing system management team or they depend upon some third-party vendors. These vendors or internal system management departments are responsible for managing the whole computing infrastructure of the enterprise, including planning, designing, assembling of physical servers, network or data storage infrastructure build ups and other services like load balancing of electricity supply.

The whole process of setting up of such an infrastructure is quite complex. For a new office, this process generally takes weeks and sometimes months. Even the purchase cycle of additional hardware to power up the infrastructure is not counted in hours or minutes, but in days or weeks. Protection and security of the infrastructure appears as an extra burden for any organization.

1.5.2 Traditional Platform Model

In the traditional model, the platform building and management tasks need special expertise. Enterprises either need to maintain an internal team or can outsource these jobs. *Computing platform* building activities involve installation of an operating system (OS), application runtimes or application development environments on computing infrastructure. For example, Java Runtime Environment (which provides a platform for the applications) is essential to run any java based application.

Traditionally the entire responsibility of platform installation, configuration, updates and other staffing at appropriate levels often fall on the shoulders of the people concerned with application development or even on users who are interested only in using applications. Thus, the actual assignments get delayed. Licensing, timebound installation of patches or maintenance of the platform cause difficulty for users (application developer or application user).

1.5.3 Traditional Application Model

At application layers, the users are the end users of computing. They need not have any knowledge about a complex computing system. Their only interests are to access or use different software applications to fulfill requirements of personal or business related works. Software applications provide solutions for various needs. In traditional model, computing infrastructure or computing platform or both often become concerns of application subscribers, which is a critical scenario. Apart from this, the traditional software applications attract fixed and prepaid licensing costs and annual support costs.

> In traditional computing model, subscribers of one computing layer cannot fully escape the responsibilities and difficulties of arranging or managing the underlying layer(s).

1.6 THE END OF TRADITIONAL COMPUTING

The limitations of traditional computing were evident for a long time and several futuristic ideas were proposed on computing techniques. But for various reasons, especially due to technological constraints, it was not possible to implement these ideas.

With technological advancement in several fields of computing and communication (i.e. in network communication), computing giants came up with a new model of computing during the second half of the last decade. The philosophy of this model says that all kind of computing facilities can be delivered as services. According to this model, the three main *layers of computing*, infrastructure, platform and application can be delivered to the consumers as ready-made stuff arranged and maintained by others, whenever they need it, relieving the consumers from the burden of arranging all the stuff themselves. This new model of computing is known as *cloud computing*.

> In traditional approach, computing subscribers were always over-burdened with many additional difficulties and cost.

1.6.1 Computing as the Utility Service

Introduction of cloud computing precipitated a significant shift in the responsibilities of managing computing resources. Computing facilities in this model are supplied in the same way as like as a civic authority supplies water or electricity in a city. Customers can use those facilities without being worried about how they are being supplied or who is managing all of these activities.

The three major aspects of computing which were represented in three-layered computing architecture in Figure 1.1 earlier, are delivered as *utility services* in cloud computing model. Hence three services corresponding to this model are:

- Infrastructure Service
- Platform Service
- Application or Software Service

Customers wanting to avail some kind of computing facilities, need not start from scratch any more. If a customer wants to work at the application level, he/she no longer needs to worry about setting up the infrastructure and platform facilities. Rather, she can directly avail the ready-made infrastructure and platform services from the cloud vendors. Again customers who want to work on platform layer of computing, get readily available infrastructure service without any difficulty.

The only thing required at customer's end to avail these readymade *computing services* (infrastructure, platform or software) are Internet connection and any basic computing device (PC, laptop, tab etc.) where software interface with cloud computing systems can run. These computing devices need not be highly configured since the local computers no longer have to do heavy tasks and cloud interface applications are fairly light-weight. If local computers are free from doing the heavy tasks that they used to do earlier, who then, is doing these on their behalf? The answer is: 'cloud' which is going to be assumed as a network of computers now onward.

> Since, cloud resides at some remote location and does all the heavy computing tasks, the hardware and software demands on the local computers at users' side decrease.

1.6.2 Who Provides the Service?

Cloud computing vendors who are Independent Software Vendors (ISV) generally provide the service. These vendors are reputed computing/IT giants. They are the owners or developers of the clouds and manage everything. Users can use cloud services by payment on use basis, just like they pay monthly bill for electricity service. This becomes profitable for both parties, the customers and the vendors. Vendors can supply the service at cheaper rates because of the large size of their business (due to, economy of scale) since the number of computing subscribers is very large.

This model of computing is much talked about because it provides a lot of flexibility compared to the traditional way of computing. For instance, it drastically reduces the cost and complexity of owning and operating computers and networks. Moreover, since specialized computing vendors manage the cloud the quality of service undoubtedly gets better.

> *Reputed computing vendors build and deliver cloud computing. Users can access any type of the capabilities served by a computer via Internet.*

1.6.3 The Concerns

Is this computing service (cloud computing) provided by others from some remote place reliable? What is the guarantee that the cloud service vendor will keep on providing reliable and uninterrupted service? Why should a user or enterprise trust a vendor when security or privacy of confidential information is involved? There are several questions raising numerous doubts and many arguments.

Adoption of cloud computing also requires entrusting another company (the *cloud vendor*) with subscriber's personal, official and confidential data. But, these threats were all along existent in traditional computing where enterprises used to depend on IT service firms to, whom they outsourced various computing activities. One thing is evident, the reliability and safeguards of cloud computing are no less if not better than the traditional computing system. Moreover, it comes with a host of other facilities and advantages.

> *Cloud computing signifies a major change in the approach how information is stored and applications can run.*

1.7 STORY OF A SIMILAR SCENARIO: A CENTURY AGO

During the 1910s, before the advent of electrical utilities, every firm and business, especially manufacturing units had to produce their own electricity and had their own infrastructural setup for electric power generation. This was a burden for the firms whose core businesses were something else. They had to maintain huge infrastructure as well as a team of people to manage the electricity production unit.

Then power grids emerged and firms slowly started taking electric supply from an outside source, who would supply them. From one perspective, firm owners saw several advantages in getting rid of those expensive electricity generation units. No more coal deliveries, no more staff to shovel the coal day-in and day-out, no more mechanical and electrical engineers to be hired. But a counter viewpoint also surfaced. The firm owners' main concern was about the reliability of the new power grids. They argued, why should a firm take chances when it is already self-sufficient?

With time, it became evident that outside firms could supply electricity at much lower cost in comparison with maintaining self-owned units. Opponents of the new idea then raised questions about the reliability of outside vendors. How can it be ensured that they will supply electricity as promised and without interruption? Who will take care of the security of those electric supply cables? What if the outside vendor shuts down business?

The concerns were all valid. But, gradually the electric utility service survived against all these odds, and for business houses sticking to the old idea of running internal power generation units the operating environment proved to be unfavourable. By 1930, the debate about choosing electric power utilities over maintaining in-house power generation units was almost over. And there is no need to mention which idea won the race. As the decades passed, the processed electric utility service from outside proved to be secure, reliable, and more importantly cheaper than the older way.

> *In the early twentieth century, before the advent of the electricity grid, industries used to build and run their own power generation plants just as many enterprises were to deploy and manage their own computing systems in traditional computing system.*

1.7.1 Moral of the Story

With computing vendors looking ready to promote their utility computing services or cloud computing capabilities, continuing with internal IT/computing infrastructural setup may prove to be a losing strategy, much like it was when firms avoided the public power grid about 100 years ago.

Cloud computing promotes the idea of *outsourcing* of *computing services*, similar to the way electricity requirements are being outsourced today. Users can avail electricity without being bothered about its generation technique, where it comes from or how it is being transported. The only thing to know is that the usage is being metered and it will be billed as per the same.

> *Cloud computing has marked the end of computing as people knew it. There is very little room for luxuries to stick with the ideology that says "we've always done it this way"!*

1.8 PEOPLE ARE ALREADY USING CLOUD COMPUTING

Individuals as well as enterprises have been using cloud computing in some form or the other, through Internet for more than a decade now. When individuals use e-mail services like Yahoo Mail, Gmail or social networking services like facebook, twitter etc., they actually use a cloud computing service. Picture or video sharing activities via mobile phones, which have been quite popular for more than a decade, are also based on the cloud computing model.

To access these services, users need not install any heavy application in local computing devices (like desktop, laptop, tablet etc.) apart from having some web browser or web-based app. For instance in earlier days, the e-mail communication needed local client applications like IBM Lotus Notes or Microsoft Outlook. But with the arrival of cloud computing, the service is available without any such local applications, and users can directly login to e-mail account remotely using the web browser. Picture or video sharing services are also accessible in similar way. The necessary software and storage for all these applications do not exist on users' computer; rather on vendors' server at some remote location.

> *Cloud computing has created the scope where consumers can rent a server on Internet and work from any place by signing-in to gain the access.*

1.9 INFLUENCES BEHIND CLOUD SERVICE ADOPTION

Individuals and enterprises are moving towards this alternative model of computing as they recognize a wide range of capabilities in it. The reasons behind adoption of cloud computing can be observed from two different perspectives, namely, technological and operational. The key drivers of cloud adoption have been discussed in this section.

1.9.1 Technological Influences

Advancements in the field of computing, software and network technology have pushed the adoption of cloud computing. The key technological influences behind cloud service adoption are discussed in the following section.

Universal Network Connectivity: Cloud computing services are generally accessed through high speed network or Internet. Well-connected digital communication network spread across the world is necessary for ubiquitous access to cloud facility. As high speed network communication infrastructure has become available around the world, access to the cloud computing facility from any location has become a reality.

High-Performance Computing: In traditional approach, high-performance computing (HPC) systems needed specialized hardware components which were costly. Affording HPC was once beyond the imagination of small enterprises and individuals. Cloud computing has made HPC affordable for everyone by aggregating computing power to produce computing performance for executing high performance tasks.

> *Cloud computing provides access to supercomputer-like power at a fraction of the traditional cost.*

Commoditization: A product or service turns into a commodity when it becomes marketable and can be interchanged with another product of same type, which should also be available in the market. This is possible when products or services from multiple vendors provide more or less same value to customers, and customers have the option of replacing one product with another product of some other vendor. Cloud offerings from different providers create the same scenario. This commoditization of cloud services has developed irrefutable marketplace for cloud adoption.

1.9.2 Operational or Business Influences

There are many business factors associated for moving into the cloud environment. Operational benefits like low initial investment, automatic service management, responsiveness of system are driving consumers to migrate into the cloud.

Low Cost Solution: With cloud computing, consumers adopt the philosophy of pay-as-you-use. This turns out more cost effective, since consumers no more need to pay for excess capacity which was very common in traditional computing. This remarkably reduces the IT budget of consumers.

Outsourcing: IT outsourcing is a common phenomenon among enterprises. Cloud computing utility services provide scope for using facilities entirely managed by others. This gives more robust solution towards IT outsourcing for the enterprises who can concentrate more on their core businesses.

Speed or Responsiveness: Responsiveness is probably the most important factor in today's business world. Cloud computing represents substantial advantages in terms of responsiveness. The time required to develop, configure, or launch new systems in cloud computing environment is much lesser in comparison with the traditional one.

Automation: Automatic availability of systems, recovery from failure, load balancing or performance monitoring of systems and applications, and auto-maintenance of computing systems are several features offered by cloud environment that provide a lots of advantages.

Small Initial Investment: Traditional computing approach had a barrier as initial investment to setup computing infrastructure was huge. Even adopting latest technology also meant considerable amount of investment for existing users. Cloud computing eliminates these barriers, as customers need to invest very small capital to start.

Less Maintenance Cost: The budget allocated for IT services in any organization has a critical influence over the performance and outcome of the business. Studies show that on an average about 70 to 80 percent of any organization's IT budgets goes to the operation and maintenance of existing systems and infrastructure. This cost has drastically reduced in the regime of the cloud computing.

Mobility: Once there was the era of personal computers when everyone used to access computing of any form using PCs from their desks, be it in a business or for personal use. But those days are far behind. It is difficult to keep pace with today's world if one needs a fixed computer (or laptop etc.) in order to use computing facility. Cloud computing provides full flexibility in this direction. Computing in any capacity can be accessed from a variety of portable devices from any location.

> The idea of cloud computing is: access anytime, from anywhere, with any device.

Flexibility: With cloud computing, it becomes very easy to change computing platform or move towards other technology without significant capital loss and with minimal effort. This flexibility was not available in traditional computing. Cloud services can also grow or shrink as needed. It can expand or shrink with business that provides the higher cost-benefit ratio. When a business needs more computing/IT support they consume more cloud services, when they need less they consume less. Since payment is on usage basis, this elasticity of cloud services provides great flexibility for the consumers.

> Business can act more dynamically with cloud computing.

With traditional computing approach, it was difficult for small enterprises to afford the budget needed to keep their computing facilities up-to-date. Cloud computing has eliminated this problem and it has become easier for anyone to avail the state-of-the-art computing facilities. Businesses can exhibit more speed and agility. *Agility* enables a system or business to exhibit quick response to changing atmosphere or situation without losing momentum. The influences

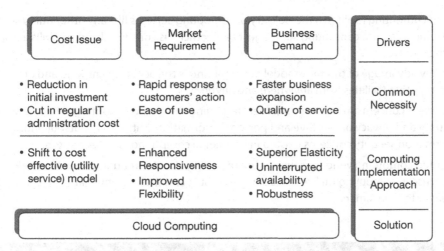

FIG 1.5: The way to opt for cloud computing

or drivers that are inspiring consumers to move towards cloud computing have been summarized in Figure 1.5.

International Data Corporation (IDC), an eminent industry research firm, defines cloud computing as "consumer and business products, services and solutions having delivered and consumed in real time over the Internet."

1.9.3 Conclusion

The adoption of cloud computing is growing, because its architecture helps customers focus more on their primary trade, and it lets reputed computing vendors take care of the required demands. This results in a vibrant usage-based cost model.

Cloud services have emerged as a lucrative option for individual users of computing as well as for most enterprises. But, along with lots of driving forces few resisting forces also exist that decide the level and speed of moving towards cloud services. How the driving forces will outweigh the resistances depends on the way restricting issues are addressed.

Cloud computing is a model, not a technology.

SUMMARY

❖ Cloud computing has emerged as a new model of computing which promises to make the planet more smart.

❖ There were many limitations in the traditional computing approaches. Those limitations used to overburden the consumers and enterprises in terms of budgetary expense and responsibility for maintaining various computing facilities.

❖ Cloud computing facilitates the delivery of computing services like any other utility service. Customers can use computing service just as electricity is consumed and pay bills at the end of the month.

❖ The key advantage of this new model of computing is the access to any kind and any volume of computing facilities from anywhere and anytime.

❖ The major concern among the customers regarding the cloud computing service is about security and privacy of sensitive and personal information. But, with IT outsourcing, information security concerns existed in traditional computing approaches too.

❖ Reputed computing vendors have started providing cloud computing services. Their expertise in computing makes these services robust and their volume of business makes it cheaper for consumers.

REVIEW QUESTIONS

What is meant by 'cloud' in cloud computing?

A cloud is combination of servers, storages, network devices (like switches etc.) networked together from where computing facilities are delivered to users. Cloud facility is developed by activating this specially designed network of commodity computing components with advanced software to power them up for the task. This powered up facility becomes capable delivering computing as utility service that user can access from any location through Internet.

Where do the clouds reside?

Globally cloud computing facilities are provided by major computing vendors. They generally develop huge infrastructure for cloud at different locations around the globe. Such arrangements are known as cloud data centers or CDCs. Apart from computing facilities, these centers have other essential amenities like uninterrupted power supply system, fire control system and cooling system. CDCs are highly protected areas where vendors set up networks of large number of computing devices like servers, storages etc. and create cloud computing utility service out of those.

How can users gain from utility computing?

Utility computing is the way of supplying computing service through an on-demand, pay-per-usage billing method. It focusses on the business model where users receive computing resources from a service provider delivered over network communication channel. The prime advantage of utility computing is its economic benefit that reduces users' computing cost.

Will cloud computing replace traditional computing devices with high-configured desktops or laptops?

In cloud computing approach, all load of computing shifts into the highly configured computing facilities provided by the cloud. People just need an interfacing device through which they can connect to the cloud using Internet. This interfacing device can be any desktop, laptop, tablet or even a mobile interface which can run the cloud interfacing application. Hence, these interfacing devices do not need to be highly configured any more. So, cloud computing is going to replace highly-configured traditional desktops or laptops with minimally-configured ones, as they will only have to act as interfacing devices to cloud.

Is cloud computing beneficial only for larger organizations?

Individual users who work in their PCs at home can avail cloud facility sitting at home itself. They can store files, install software, or run programs just like they did it in PCs. Apart from individual users, small offices that need a networked environment with a small number of terminals can easily move into the cloud. In short, cloud computing is for all those who need computing facilities in any form as well as volume.

MULTIPLE CHOICE QUESTIONS

1. Which of the following is not a limitation of traditional computing approach?

   a) Huge initial investment
   b) Hardware-system management responsibility
   c) Partial utilization of resources
   d) None of these

2. Which of the following is an advantage of cloud computing approach?

   a) It is ubiquitous
   b) Enabled by pay-for-usage model
   c) Responsiveness
   d) All of these

3. Access to a Cloud environment it costs more money compared to a traditional environment.

   a) True
   b) False

4. A Cloud environment can be accessed from anywhere in the world as long as the user has access to the Internet.

   a) True
   b) False

5. Which one of the following is the standard cloud computing pricing model?

   a) Free
   b) Pay-per-usage
   c) Licensing basis
   d) None of these

6. Cloud computing makes a business more

   a) Dynamic
   b) Strong
   c) Profitable
   d) Simple

7. Which among the following is a feature of utility service?

   a) 24×7 availability
   b) Unlimited access
   c) Metering
   d) None of these

8. A computing system is composed of three facility layers. This statement is

   a) True
   b) False

9. Which among the following is not considered as a layer in computing system?

   a) Application
   b) Server

c) Infrastructure

d) Platform

10. Computing network facility falls under which layer of computing?

   a) Application

   b) Platform

   c) Infrastructure

   d) Both b and c

11. Is the IT outsourcing model of traditional computing similar to cloud computing?

a) Yes

b) Not at all

c) To some extent

d) Depends on the requirement

12. What is the main advantage of utility computing compared to traditional computing?

   a) Less difficulty

   b) Better security

   c) Economical

   d) Availability

CHAPTER

2 | # Evolution and Enabling Technologies

Cloud computing is not an abrupt innovation. Rather, it is a series of developments that have taken place over past few decades. Progresses in computing technology, starting from its early days, has slowly metamorphosed into cloud computing in this advanced era. Although the idea of cloud computing originated long ago, the concept could not materialize due to lack of necessary technological elements.

Documentary evidence can be traced back to the 1960s, when John McCarthy (who coined the term 'artificial intelligence') wrote that 'computation may someday be organized as a *public utility.*' Since then, computing technology has gone through phases of development. Hardware and communication technology have been progressed, Internet has changed the world and at the same time, the web-based software architecture has also matured.

As advancements in all associated fields have slowly overcome the limitations of earlier approaches, it has been possible to realize the dream of computing as the new measure of public utility. This chapter focusses on the evolution of cloud computing and discusses how generations have developed through stages like centralized computing, client server computing, distributed computing and grid computing on to cloud computing.

2.1 THE EVOLUTION OF CLOUD COMPUTING

Cloud computing is not an isolated development. Cloud technology has been matured over the years with constant advancements in the field of computing. The beginning can be traced back to a time when remote access to time-shared computing system became a reality. The realization of cloud computing has been closely linked with several other subsequent developments in the domain.

> *Several decades of research, particularly in the domain of parallel and distributed computing, have paved the way for cloud computing.*

A thorough discussion about the development of cloud computing can never overlook the continuous innovations in the field of electronic and computing hardware. As the hardware technology evolved, so did the software. Beside these, with the advancements in communication protocols, network communication technology as well as Internet also played a vital role in this process. This section focusses on different phases of developments in the field of computing starting from the mainframe age and discusses how those progresses have contributed towards the growth of cloud computing.

2.1.1 Mainframe Architecture: Introduction of Time-Sharing System

The initial days of commercial usage of computing (around 1970s) started with mainframe system. At that time, organizations used such systems to automate basic data processing tasks, like payroll management and others. Mainframes were large supercomputers that required extensive cooling, and the whole system was so high-priced that it was difficult even for large business organizations to maintain more than one such system.

Solution to this problem appeared with the emergence of *time-shared* resource utilization concept. It was a major goal which technologists were trying to achieve for long time. This development opened the option of multi-users sharing the same computer resources concurrently. And with the advent of the remote access facility, the need for multiple mainframe systems disappeared.

Organizations could access a single mainframe system from different offices or departments using computer terminals to fulfill computing requirements. Such terminals did not have any processing power and were known as *dumb terminal* (non-intelligent terminal). Such terminals were only capable of transferring input-output data to communicate with the mainframe system, which was also known as the *server*.

> Multiple dumb terminals could remotely communicate with time-sharing mainframe systems simultaneously in order to fulfill several processing requirements.

2.1.2 Intelligent Terminal: Beginning of Client-Server Computing

There were limitations in the process of accessing computing resources through dumb terminals for the time-sharing mainframe systems. With centralized processing environment, the concurrent requests appearing from different terminals could not always be processed at the same time. Mainframe systems always had a number limit in regard to parallel active users. Thus users often had to wait for a long time in queue.

Solution to this problem was explored through the development of terminals with some processing capability, who could compute some minimal tasks. With the arrival of low-cost microprocessor technology during 1970s, this dream turned into reality. Technologists designed smaller computing devices which were rather cheaper. These devices had some processing capability and replaced the dumb terminals easily. They were called *intelligent terminals* (later known as *clients systems*) and they could participate in partial execution of programs along with the servers. This released load from the server to some extent and execution of tasks became faster. This was the beginning of client-server computing.

> Intelligent client systems promoted the concept of offline processing by taking part in the execution of programs along with servers.

2.1.3 The PC Revolution: Scope for Computing Everything Locally

Offline processing by intelligent terminals may have reduced load on servers for some time, but with increasing processing demand that was also proving inadequate for the performances of large organizations. During the peak hours, when client terminals were flooding the server with tasks, the response times were increasing drastically due to bottleneck problem.

The client systems had very limited processing capability and technologists were looking to take the next step ahead. Economical client systems with more processing capability could, only, solve this problem. In the mean time, microprocessor technology had been developed. Small sized powerful microprocessors along with a little main memory and limited Input/ Output (I/O) capability were embedded in chips which could be produced at relatively low cost. This invention is considered as one of the salient stepping stones towards the future age of computers.

This development created the scope for manufacturers to produce general purpose computing machines for users. Such computing machines were called *personal micro-computers* (later known as *personal computers* or PCs). Introduction of these less expensive computers revolutionized the computing world around the middle of the 1970s. The offline or local processing by *clients* combining the time-shared processing at *server* in client-server model could now be implemented together on a single system.

Everything could then be computed locally in such systems (PCs). Since these systems were not expensive, unlike mainframes, the organizations could afford many of them, and the need of maintaining expensive mainframe systems soon became less important.

> Introduction of personal computers created the scope for computing everything locally without too much capital investment like the mainframes.

2.1.4 Network of PCs: Emergence of Direct or Peer-to-Peer Communication

Big organizations installed multiple personal computers in different offices for various purposes. But one problem soon emerged as; they could not communicate directly because those machines were situated at a distance from one another. These computers installed at different offices within an organization were functioning independently. Earlier (in time-shared mainframe models) multiple computing terminals established communication through the server.

During this period, technologists working on network communication succeeded in establishing interactions between systems situated little far from one another. Data transfer rate improved, which was the main hurdle in establishing network communication between distantly situated computers. Invention of LAN (local area network) and WAN (wide area network), during this period, provided the productive insight in network communication.

> Data transfer rate was a hurdle in establishing communication between computers situated a little far from each other. Invention of LAN and then WAN solved this problem.

Meanwhile, technologists became successful in transfering data through LAN within a premises with speed at the order of Mbps (million or mega bits per second). The WAN technology also improved and data transfer among computers situated at a distance (may be in different cities or countries) became possible at speed order of kbps (kilo bits per second).

As computers placed at a distance could directly communicate with each other without hitting a server, the computing regime moved forward from the centralized network architecture of client-server era. This was the beginning of *peer-to-peer computing* (P2P computing), where each and every computer could play the role of a client as well as a server. Control became decentralized and all of the computers in a network could be assigned with equivalent responsibilities. With this, running business operations became much easier for enterprises.

> *With the development of peer-to-peer (P2P) computing, it was possible to connect one computer to another without hitting the server.*

2.1.5 Fast Network Communication: Laid the Way for Distributed Computing

Till the early 1980s, it was believed that computer performance can only be improved by producing faster and more powerful processors. Invention of *parallel processing* changed this idea. In parallel processing, multiple processors work together to solve a single computational task. The environment is like having one computer with multiple processors. This advancement in processing was followed by the introduction of the concept of distributed computing.

Distributed computing took the parallel processing concept one step forward. Here, it formed one powerful computing system by combining multiple computing systems, rather than having one computer with multiple processors. A *distributed computing* system can be roughly defined as a collection of processors interconnected by communication network in which each processor has its own local memory and other basic computing peripherals.

> *Parallel processing technology was followed by distributed processing concept.*

Distributed processing concept emerged as a powerful computing model. But, this computing model needed frequent communication among nodes of a (distributed) system during program execution. Thus higher speed in network communication was required for optimal performance.

Meanwhile, the advancements in network communication caught up and data transfer rate continued to improve during 1980s. For LAN, the speed attained neared the 100 Mbps

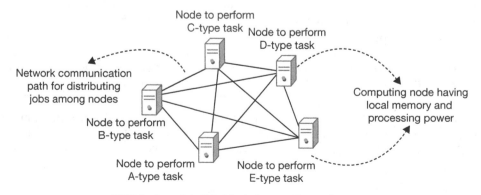

FIG 2.1: A model of distributed computing environment

mark and for WAN it went up to 64 kbps. Things were being transferred in seconds or even in fraction of second, instead of in minutes. This opened the scope for implementation of more powerful distributed computing systems.

> *Advancement of network communication technology eased the way for distributed computing. Total capacity of any distributed system can easily be increased by adding more resources to it.*

2.1.6 Cluster Computing: Creation of Resource Pool

The concept of *clustering* appeared as the next step of evolution in the field of computing. Computing clusters are made of multiple nodes (computers) connected via network which perform similar tasks. Thus, execution of a task can be faster as it can be distributed and executed in parallel across multiple machines inside a cluster. All the nodes of a cluster together give impression of a single system. A sample compute cluster is shown in Figure 2.2.

> *Each node in a simple cluster is set to perform same task or same set of tasks.*

The idea was to create a cluster (or group) of homogeneous (similar type) computer systems performing similar functionalities. In each cluster, one computer is assigned the job of controlling the cluster. That particular computer (or node) is known as *cluster head*. The head's responsibility in such a simple cluster is to divide and distribute jobs among different nodes in that cluster when matching computing tasks appear.

In an actual *cluster computing* system, multiple clusters (built to perform different type of functionalities) are linked together through a LAN (as shown in Figure 2.3). In such computing environment, when a particular job appears, the cluster head divides and distributes it among matching clusters (designated for those jobs) for faster execution. The distribution and assignment of job depends on the nature of the job. This way, the cluster head starts to utilize the resources in a clustered computing environment.

> *Computers are clustered together to achieve reliability, greater processing power and produce supercomputer like performance.*

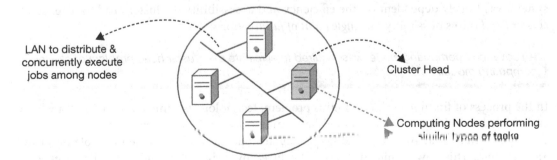

FIG 2.2: A compute cluster

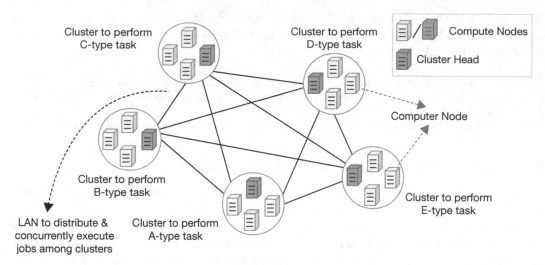

FIG 2.3: A cluster computing model

The cluster computing model emerged as a result of progress in multiple technologies and their convergence. Availability of low cost microprocessors, high speed network communication and emergence of software to manage cluster distribution made cluster computing possible.

In this computing model, a set of computers were reserved to handle specific type of task to make the system more reliable. If any node fails, other nodes in the cluster can handle the load. This was the idea behind *resource pool* that technologists were trying to implement, and clustering of nodes opened the path for creating pools of resources. With this implementation, reliability was achieved through redundancy.

> Cluster computing introduced the concept of resource pooling. The pools were made of homogeneous computing systems.

2.1.7 Grid Computing: Decentralization of Control

Cluster architecture lead to more powerful and reliable computing systems by creating resource pools, but it raised concerns regarding its dependency on the cluster head. Performance of such system was largely dependent on the efficiency and accessibility of cluster head. Existence of *cluster head* raises possibility for *single point of failure* too.

> An advanced computing model was required to eliminate the cluster head problem of cluster computing model.

In the process of finding a solution to this problem, technologists came up with an idea where each node belonging to a cluster would have same priority. It was required that all of them could perform similar functions and no particular node had to be assigned the role of 'head' among them. This new architecture was introduced in early 1990s, and was called a *grid*. A sample computing grid is shown in Figure 2.4. An analogy of this concept can be drawn with the

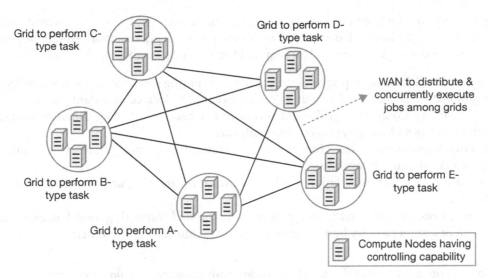

FIG 2.4: A grid computing model

electricity grid, where if connected consumers can get regular power supply. It was reasoned that subscribers just need to connect to a computing grid as a whole (not to any particular node of the grid) to avail computing resources, just like consumers plug into a power grid to avail electricity.

> *Grid computing concept introduced the idea of decentralization of control in distributed computing environment.*

Other than decentralization of control, grid computing introduced another important system feature. The computing environment could now be built with heterogeneous computing systems, that is, systems with diverse hardware configurations. This was a huge benefit as resource pools could then grow by accommodating *heterogeneous systems.*

The other major challenge that emerged as a stumbling block before setting up a large *distributed computing* environment spread around the world was establishing co-operation among systems of different administrative domains. For multiple administrative domains, the challenge was related to management of resources and security implementations of systems. Initially, grid computing was used particularly by the science and engineering community. But when enterprise applications adopted grid computing model, it became necessary to address the need for uniform security implementation and other resource management policies. Technologists focused on bringing about uniformity in these areas, during that period. Once it was done, the evolution moved on to the next level.

> *Computing grid introduced distributed computing environment, made up of heterogeneous systems which could be located at separate administrative domains.*

During that period, unlike clusters where groups of computers situated at a single location could only be connected via LAN, grid could be spread over different geographical domains by using internetwork for interaction. Software applications used in grid computing were designed specially to cope up with such distributed environments. With grid computing era, computing systems reached a stage where they had acquired the following important characteristics.

- *Large scale*: Grid concept promises to deal with computing resources going up to millions.
- *Geographical distribution*: Computing resources could be located at distant places.
- *Heterogeneity*: Computing grid could accommodate resources having different hardware characteristics and using various types of software.
- *Resource co-ordination*: Resources in a grid could coordinate among themselves to generate aggregated computing capabilities.
- *Pervasive access*: Resource failure could be handled by granting access to other available resources.
- *Unlimited resource addition (scaling)*: Being a distributed computing model, it allows easy growth of system capacity by adding more resources into an existing system.

> Grid computing is sometimes labeled as the direct predecessor of cloud computing.

Table 2.1   Characteristics of cluster and grid computing

Characteristic	Cluster Computing	Grid Computing
Ownership	Single	Multiple
System management	Centralized	Decentralized
User management	Centralized	Decentralized
Resource Pool Creation	Yes	Yes
Resource node type	Homogeneous	Heterogeneous
Resource scheduling	Centralized	Decentralized
Network connection type*	LAN	LAN/MAN (Metropolitan area network)/WAN
System architecture	Single system image	Autonomous, independent nodes
Coupling	Tight	Loose
Fault tolerance Capability	Low	High
Scaling Architecture	Scalable	Scalable, in bigger capacity
Real-time Scaling*	No	No

*During the period of consideration

2.1.8 Hardware Virtualization: Weapon for Designing Dynamic Computing System

After computing system with heterogeneous pool of resources was created with scalable system architecture, next biggest challenge was to achieve real-time scaling capability. The primary hurdle for achieving this system characteristic was to *decouple* software systems from underlying physical resources of computers.

In traditional approach, software systems (processes) were bound with hardware resources till termination of the process. This restricts application system mobility. Moreover, it is extremely critical to manage activities like resource reallocation and re-scheduling of tasks in a heterogeneous system. Some mechanism was required that would enable load shifting among computers belonging to same group.

> Heterogeneous nature of system architecture posed challenge for mobility of application.

Soon the concept of *hardware virtualization* appeared. In this, a layer of software was created over the hardware system which could simulate a whole physical system environment. In fact, virtual machines were created (in contrast to physical machines) over the simulation layer which have had all the characteristics of a physical system.

Under this approach, since application loads are assigned (to physical systems) through virtual systems, rather than directly assigned to physical systems they *decouple* software applications from hardware. Such decouplings make them easier to map and de-map tasks to resources.

Virtualization brought true essence in the scaling capability of distributed systems. Load could now be shifted to other (and stronger) set of resources without disrupting service. This provides opportunity for *real-time system scaling*. System with such characteristic is known as *scalable system*. *Scalability* is the ability of a system to accommodate growth.

Thus, virtualization coupled with resource pooling technique introduced more force and flexibility in the systems. Dynamic resource addition into system created opportunity for developing system that can grow as per business requirements.

> Virtualization technique coupled with scaling capability of distributed system introduced greater scope for real-time system scaling.

2.1.9 Advancement in Web Services: Ease in Group Collaboration

While computing technology was going through phases of evolution, users and businesses were becoming more dependent on computer systems to run their regular activities. With advancements in Internet technology, communication over web also started showing its strength. At this stage, technologists felt that group collaboration over web could be a fascinating idea.

Collaboration had always been a desire from the early days of computing, where multiple users will simultaneously work in same venture. Without collaboration capability it would not have been possible to develop a relatively large computing system spread across wide geographic location. While distributed computing provided the scope where processes could collaborate with each other, web services had to play the prime role where web applications could enable users from different geographic locations to collaborate in real time.

> As grid computing concept empowered the development of large computing system spread across wide geographic location, collaboration capability was the next need of such system where members of a team dispersed geographically could work together on a common task.

During this period, with the emergence of advanced Web Service (WS) standard, software integration became effortless. Developments in the field made it possible to glue together applications running on different platforms and combine data from various sources. The major developments in web service standards were as follows.

1. **Web 2.0:** It is the second generation in the development of the World Wide Web that appeared after 2002. Earlier technology of web was more static in its approach, although some collaboration capabilities were present in Web 1.0 as well. Web 2.0 enables collaboration by allowing sharing of user-generated content. Social networking sites, blogs, photo or video sharing sites are example of those sites which were build upon Web 2.0 technology.

> *Web 2.0 technology based development enables user collaboration over the web.*

2. **Mashup:** Mashup is a web application that can combine data from multiple web sources into a single interface. The literal meaning of 'mashup' is 'a mixture or fusion of disparate or heterogeneous elements'. In web technology, the name 'mashup' has been derived from this idea. One application or service may serve multiple functionalities. The idea behind mashup was to merge the best available web applications together effortlessly into a single application for convenience of users. This is done by calling those applications using their open *application program interfaces* (API). A common example of this is the use of Google Map in web applications. Google Map can be integrated into any web application through APIs.

> *Mashup is a web application that can use content from multiple sources to create a new service representing in a new interface.*

2.1.10 Service Oriented Architecture: Emergence of Flexible Application Architecture

With all the developments in the field of computing, communication and web services, the need for a more modular and flexible approach in IT system development was felt since the last century. Large software systems were difficult to build without language independency and *loose coupling* approach.

Emergence of service oriented concept in application or software system development bridged this gap. Service oriented architecture (SOA) is more a methodology than a technical approach. It relies on developing application components as software services as its fundamental principle. Services are independent entities: they communicate via message passing. They use standardized interfaces and can be developed based on platform as well as in a language independent way.

As systems can be developed by integrating services in SOA paradigm, they remain flexible for changes. This dynamism works well to fit with the need of ever-changing businesses and is considered as an essential foundation for cloud computing.

> *Adoption of SOA approach in IT system designing makes systems flexible to adapt changes as per business requirements.*

The SOA paradigm has been created by using web technologies like XML (Extensible Markup Language), WSDL (Web Services Description Language), SOAP (Simple Object Access Protocol), UDDI (Universal Description, Discovery and Integration). In SOA, the set of services are defined with known and described interfaces which can communicate with each other. The SOA service interfaces are specified in XML and the services are expressed in WSDL.

2.1.11   Utility Computing: Computing as Measured and Utility Service

The computing era reached a point where it was empowered with the following characteristics:

- Scalable computing infrastructure made of heterogeneous resources that can be grown as much as required in real time
- Single distributed computing environment spread across the globe, empowered by high-speed network
- Collaborative work facility from different locations, empowered by modern age web service standards
- Flexible application architecture that is easily modifiable with changing business requirements, empowered by the SOA paradigm

All these features combined with resource virtualization technique created scope for a new avenue of computing. Under this new model, the vendors could arrange all required computing facilities which users could consume on payment basis. Since, payment is calculated on use basis, and users need not take responsibility of system procurement and management related activities, that provide huge benefit from users' point of view.

    This model of computing is known as *utility computing*. The idea for such a model was first presented by John McCarthy, a professor at Massachusetts Institute of Technology (MIT) in 1961 which showed that the computing can be delivered as *utility service* much like electricity. This model possesses two important features as the service is available *on-demand* (as much computing power as required) and the *use-basis* mode of payment.

> Utility Computing is the packaging and delivery of computing resources, similar to traditional public utilities like electricity, water, or telephone. The model follows pay-per-use mode of payment and on-demand service facility.

In *utility model*, computing vendors own, build and manage the computing resources and infrastructure. They deliver any kind of computing facilities that customers can access as and when required on rental or metered basis. This sort of computing enabled small business owners to afford high-performance computing facilities, which with their limited budget they could have never dreamed of using.

> One important facilitator behind utility computing idea implementation was the virtualization concept of hardware resources like processor, memory, storage, and network.

2.1.12   Autonomic Computing: Emergence of Intelligent Infrastructure

Utility services are generally built to serve a large number of customers. When utility computing idea was established, it was evident that service providers would have to arrange and manage huge computing infrastructure. As any system grows, more human interventions are required to manage increasing number of hardware as well as to monitor the software issues. More human intervention means increasing the possibility of human errors. Manual management of such massive setup could not be a potential idea.

Autonomic computing refers to the ability of an intelligent computing system that can manage itself without any human intervention. These systems can re-configure themselves automatically with changing conditions and protect themselves from any technical failure.

> *Human intervention in system management causes service interruption and turns into a complex task as the system grows.*

Autonomy means the capacity of a system to take its own decisions about its actions. Technologists adopted the idea of autonomic computing from the concept of human nervous system that controls various physiological activities like breathing, sensing etc. without any conscious intervention.

The development of autonomic computing system could be possible through application of *artificial intelligence* (AI) concepts. Systems are controlled through pre-defined policies and rules to avoid external intervention. Run-time decisions are taken based on the policies and *knowledge base* of the system in response to collected inputs.

> *Autonomic computing concept is based on the autonomic nervous system of the human body where the system functions without external interference.*

The concept of *autonomic computing* was first presented by IBM in 2001. IBM has defined four areas of automatic computing as shown in Figure 2.5. *Self-configuration* is the ability to configure a system based on requirements without any external intervention. *Self-healing* is the capability of discovering, diagnosing and correcting errors. *Self-optimization* is the ability of a system to automatically control resources for optimal utilization while producing outcome in timely manner with changing business scenarios. *Self-protection* means the capacity to identify any occurrence of hostile behaviour and take corrective actions to make the system less vulnerable. Hostile behaviour can include virus infection, denial-of-service attack or unauthorized access etc. Thus, it takes care of security and privacy related issues.

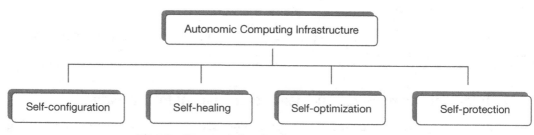

FIG 2.5: Characteristics of autonomic computing defined by IBM

Development of autonomic computing system has been possible through careful application of artificial intelligence.

Autonomic computing concept has played a very important role in developing cloud computing systems as resource management at cloud data centers is absolutely governed by this model.

2.1.13 Cloud Computing

The invention of grid computing concept was a major step towards the future age of computing. But one major advantage of cloud is its capability of real-time *scaling*. Unlike grids, computing resources in cloud can be added in real time to meet demand of computing. This has become possible as resource virtualization restricts (decouples) applications from direct access to physical resources.

Delivery of the distributed (grid) computing (power) based on *utility service* model generated from autonomic computing infrastructure has introduced the new era of computing known as cloud computing. The step-by-step development towards cloud computing era from the early age of computing is shown in Figure 2.6.

Cloud computing evolution has been an outcome based purely on the technological advancements in different fields of computing. Developments in the fields like computing hardware, distributed computing, communication technology, web technology, application

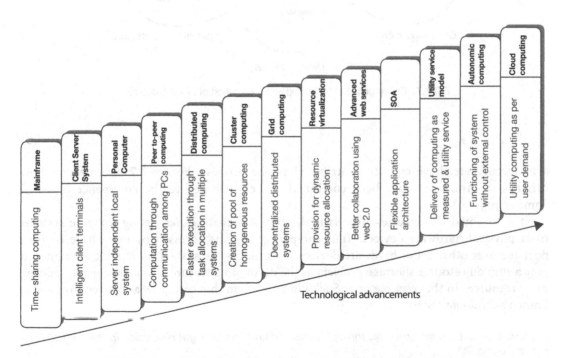

FIG 2.6: Technological advancements towards maturity of cloud computing

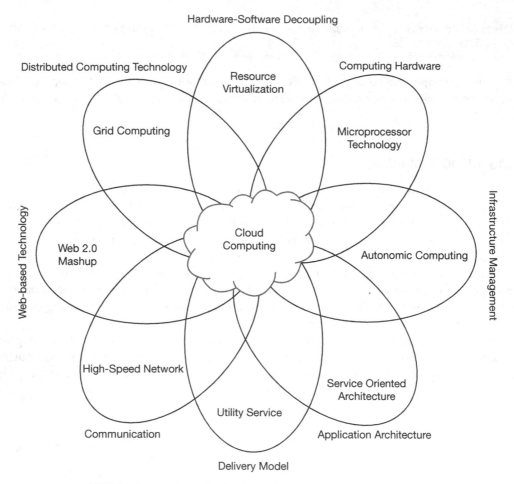

FIG 2.7: Convergence of technologies for evolution of cloud computing

architecture etc. have equally contributed in the process. Figure 2.7 summarizes how different technologies have been combined and contributed to the emergence of cloud computing.

It is to noted that, the resource virtualization has enabled *decoupling* software systems from physical hardware devices. Thus computing systems accessed by users have become portable over other set of hardware devices. This makes the system more fault tolerant and puts a stop on resource shortage problem as the decoupling feature provides scope for adding more resources in the resource pool. Such kind of system that can grow as per requirement is known as *scalable system*.

Cloud computing has emerged through evolution and has brought revolution in the field of computing.

2.2 HOW PHILOSOPHIES CONVERGED INTO CLOUD COMPUTING

Cloud computing is combination of multiple philosophies. All these philosophies have matured into reality through different methodologies. The philosophies like ubiquitous presence of computing facility, collaboration facility among users, *composable design* pattern, creation of resource pool, dynamic system architecture, intelligent system infrastructure and on-demand delivery of computing have been combined together through various technological implementations. All of these together make it such a fascinating innovation. Figure 2.8 represents the cloud computing maturity from this viewpoint. It shows how all of these philosophies have matured into cloud computing with corresponding methodologies.

For instance, the *composable design* facility that cloud computing provides is achieved through the application of service oriented architecture (SOA) based system design. There are many other system characteristics of cloud computing which have been realized through combination of multiple techniques. For example, elastic nature of cloud is achieved through dynamic infrastructure and resource pooling.

2.3 COMPARISON BETWEEN CLUSTER, GRID AND CLOUD COMPUTING

Cloud computing is built over distributed computing principles. Cluster computing and grid computing are two phases of distributed computing evolution, from which the concept of cloud computing has evolved. Grid computing extends the concept of cluster computing and cloud computing inherits many attributes of grid computing. Hence, cluster and grid

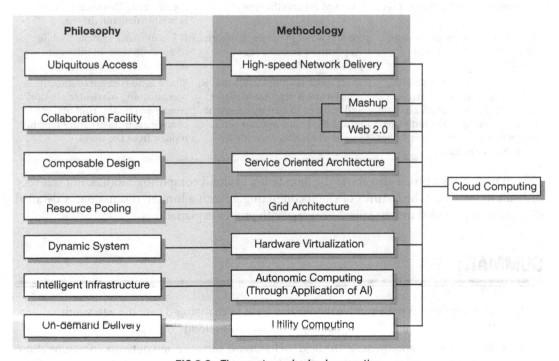

FIG 2.8: The way towards cloud computing

computing have been discussed significantly in cloud computing literature. Readers sometimes find it difficult to distinguish different characteristics of these three computing models. The following table presents a comparison between these three computing techniques.

Table 2.2   Comparison among cluster, grid and cloud computing

Cluster Computing	Grid Computing	Cloud Computing
A cluster is normally formed with computers of a single location, otherwise the system becomes complex.	Grid is inherently more distributed by its nature. The computers need not to be in the same geographical location.	It allows total distribution of resources like the grids. Hardware resources are maintained in multiple data centers spread across the globe.
Computation job takes place in one administrative domain owned by a single party.	Computation could occur over many administrative domains owned by multiple parties as connected together.	Computing resources of a cloud is usually owned by a single party. But multiple administrative domains can be combined together to perform the job.
In a cluster, all computing nodes should have similar hardware systems. That is, the system should be homogeneous in nature.	It can be heterogeneous in nature. The computers that are part of a grid can be made of different hardware architectures.	It can use heterogeneous collection of commodity hardware.
It features the centralized task management and scheduling system.	It features the distributed task management and decentralized scheduling.	It features the decentralized task management with more dynamic computing infrastructure.
Resources are generally pre-reserved for specific type of task.	Resources are generally pre-reserved for specific type of task.	Resources are not pre-reserved for specific task. Resource utilization is mainly demand-driven.
System is not dynamic in nature. Application mobility is not possible.	System is not dynamic in nature. Application mobility is not possible.	It is a dynamic system. Mobility of application is an inherent feature in this system.
One whole cluster behaves like a single system. As resources are managed by centralized resource manager, the individual computers can not be operated as separate computers.	Every node is autonomous that is, it has its own resource manager and behaves like an independent entity. So, each computer can be operated independently as distinct computer.	There is no concept of directly accessing any particular physical computing nodes. Underlying computing infrastructure remains hidden from the users.

This chapter gives a broad idea about the foundation of cloud computing models. But it is very difficult to justify all the features of cloud computing in such a limited discussion. A detailed discussion is provided in subsequent chapters with proper explanations.

SUMMARY

❖ Cloud computing is not a sudden innovation. It has been matured over the years with continuous development around different fields of computing.

❖ Technological advancements in the fields of hardware, software and network communication have contributed to the emergence of cloud computing.

❖ The introduction of distributed computing system enabled by advanced network communication technology during 1980s can be considered as the first major step towards cloud computing.

❖ Cluster computing advanced the distributed computing concept one step ahead by introducing pools of homogeneous computing resources. Resource pool is a prime necessity in creating a large and robust computing environment.

❖ Grid computing introduced during the 1990s is the successor of cluster computing. It eliminated several drawbacks of clustering. Grid system can be built using heterogeneous computing systems and allows decentralization of control.

❖ Hardware virtualization technology also emerged as a major innovation in the field of computing. It helps in designing dynamic and flexible computing system (by allowing application system mobility).

❖ Advancements in the field of web services and the introduction of service oriented architecture (SOA) emerged as tools for designing collaborative and flexible application respectively.

❖ Dynamic computing system architecture empowered by flexible application development models encouraged technologists to innovate the utility service delivery model in computing, towards the end of last century.

❖ The utility computing model gained strength through widespread efforts of researchers and technologists around the world and ultimately emerged as cloud computing within next few years.

REVIEW QUESTIONS

Why is cloud computing considered an evolution rather than as an innovation?

Cloud computing is the outcome of the convergence of research and developments in different fields of computing. Advancements in distributed computing, emergence of resource virtualization technique, developments in the field of web services and communication technology, arrival of SOA paradigm in application development, advancements in the field of AI to automatically manage computing infrastructure and related others, all of whom have contributed to realize the dream of cloud computing. This is why cloud computing is considered as the next phase of evolution in computing.

How did the introduction of distributed system revolutionize computing?

Distributed systems introduced many features those are considered as revolutionary. It took the parallel processing concept to next step where computing became faster. Faster processing results in low latency. Formation of resource pool is another feature of distributed computing model. Apart from this, distributed system opened the scope for making a system extra powerful by adding more (virtually unlimited) resources (computing nodes) into the system. Thus, computing systems got its scalable nature which turned a revolutionary feature with further developments.

Why is grid computing considered the predecessor of cloud computing?

Cloud computing is developed based on the distributed model of computing. There are several methodologies those in cloud computing have been combined together to realize itself but grid computing model was the first major breakthrough towards realizing the dream of cloud computing system. This advanced mode of computing has inherited important characteristics like creation of resource pool or system scalability from the grid computing model. This is why grid computing is considered as the predecessor of cloud computing.

How application mobility has been possible with resource virtualization?

In traditional way of computing, once an application or process was launched, it used to get attached with some physical resource(s) and fully or partially occupied the resource(s) till the completion or termination. It was impossible to move a running application to a separate set of resources. Resource virtualization decoupled application from physical computing resources. Application then did not have any direct access or could not directly occupy hardware resources too. In between them there lies the virtualized resources which can assign loads among physical resources. Thus, shifting load becomes possible.

Do enterprises need to purchase new hardware to shift into cloud?

For working in cloud, enterprises need low-configuration computing devices to be used as terminals. The existing in-house machines (which are having high configurations) are more than sufficient to be used as terminals for accessing cloud. It is likely that enterprises will have to make changes in their networks while adopting cloud computing. Every terminals need to have high speed Internet connectivity. This reorganization of the network may need some new procurement. But the organizations need not to purchase any significant volume of hardware while shifting in cloud.

MULTIPLE CHOICE QUESTIONS

1. The idea of cloud computing is entire new and surfaced at the beginning of the current century.

   a) True
   b) False, the idea was there from long back
   c) False, it didn't materialize earlier for technical constraints
   d) Both b and c

2. The concept of computing as public utility was first presented by John McCarthy in the year

   a) 1960
   b) 1970
   c) 1961
   d) 2000

3. Which of the following is an important facilitator for emergence of distributed computing?

   a) The invention of personal computers
   b) Emergence of distributed applications
   c) Fast network communication
   d) None of these

4. With which model of distributed computing, the idea of resource pool appeared?

   a) Cluster computing
   b) Grid computing
   c) Client-server computing
   d) None of these

5. Which of the following is/are advantage(s) of grid computing over cluster model?

   a) Solution of the cluster head problem
   b) Heterogeneous resource pool
   c) Co-operation between multiple administrative domains
   d) All of these

6. The difficulty of maintaining mobility of application over heterogeneous resource pool was solved with

   a) Uniform system management policy
   b) Resource virtualization
   c) Clustering
   d) None of these

7. Web based system development has been benefited with the emergence of

   a) Web 2.0
   b) Mashup
   c) SOA
   d) All of these

8. Autonomic computing is a mean for making the management of computing infrastructure

a) Automatic and faster
b) Automatic and intelligent
c) Automatic and cheaper
d) None of these

9. Cloud computing is result of the convergence of

   a) Grid computing and hardware virtualization
   b) Web technology and SOA
   c) High speed network and utility model
   d) All of these

3 Benefits and Challenges

The emergence of cloud computing provides benefits of the utility service model to the computing users. Users of computing are now being called subscribers or consumers as they move towards cloud computing. Cloud computing is delivered to its subscribers over the internetwork as well as Internet. Subscribers can access the computing facility on subscription basis, anytime and anywhere.

The scores of benefits of cloud computing are attracting users towards it. But any new innovation comes with few challenges and cloud computing is not an exception. This chapter discusses various benefits of cloud computing and also presents the challenges before it.

The biggest challenge is related to data security and compliance issue. Most of the other critical challenges are due to the absence of *open standards* where vendors develop clouds using their own proprietary standard or technology. The good aspect is that, significant efforts have been undertaken to resolve all of these issues. Apart from these, this chapter briefly presents the role of web services in cloud computing development.

3.1 ORIGIN OF THE TERM 'CLOUD COMPUTING'

The origin of the term 'cloud computing' dates back to the early 1990s. In those early days of network design, network engineers used to draw network diagrams representing different devices and connections among them. In such diagrams, they used to represent outer network arenas with cloud symbol since those details were not in their knowledge. This was known as 'network cloud' or 'cloud' in the networking industry during that period, but today we do not mean 'cloud computing' in the same sense.

With the beginning of utility computing initiatives towards the end of the last century, major software firms focussed on deliver applications over the Internet. Email services gained pace during this period as the vendors started to offer the facility to their users. And the most remarkable initiative came from Salesforce.com when they delivered business application for enterprises over the Internet in 1999. But all of these efforts were seen as part of utility computing facility development. Cloud computing did not emerge till then.

> The term 'cloud computing' appeared in the market with its present meaning in the year 2006.

During the earlier years of the current century, few industry people involved in the development of utility computing facility started to call it as 'cloud'. But it was not until 2006 that the term 'cloud computing' emerged in the commercial arena with its present meaning. The term 'cloud computing' probably was first used in an official forum by the then Google CEO Eric Schmidt in 2006 during a conference. Widespread use of the term was also observed during that time as several companies like Amazon, Microsoft, IBM started to publicize their own cloud-computing efforts. Amazon launched its revolutionary Elastic Compute Cloud (EC2) services in 2006.

The literal meaning of the word 'cloud' is fog, veil or blur. It means an obscure area, or a mass of similar particles such as dust or smoke. It is hard to say exactly on which context technologists in those days started to call it cloud computing. But the reasoning that fits best is, 'a collection of computing resources and the detail of which remains hidden from users'.

3.2 EARLY INITIATIVES

The initiative from Salesforce.com in the year of 1999 to deliver business (enterprise) applications via a 'normal' website is considered as the first-of-its-kind effort. The success of Salesforce's effort encouraged other software firms to deliver business applications via Internet. That was the breaking point, when computing technology firms started to take initiatives in developing cloud computing based business applications.

> Salesforce.com launched in 1999 was the first successful commercial initiative to deliver enterprise applications over the Internet. This was the first step towards cloud computing.

Next major initiative came from Amazon with launching of Amazon Web Service (AWS) in 2002 which delivered *computing services* over the Internet. AWS provided a suite of services including storage. Amazon played the key role in the development of utility model based computing services during that period, and soon many software firms started to modernize their data centers to support utility computing. A *data center* is an organized physical repository of computing systems and associated components, like storage and networking, which enterprises maintain to build their computing facility.

The movement slowly turned towards what is known as cloud computing today. In 2006, Amazon launched its EC2 web service, where companies and individuals could rent (virtual) computers for running their own computer applications. Soon after EC2 started attracting the attention of experts, 'Google Docs' introduced by Google (in 2006) brought cloud computing service to the public attention.

In 2007, Salesforce.com launched another service called force.com, where anyone could built applications and launch websites. 2009 saw Microsoft's commercial entry into cloud computing arena with the launch of 'Windows Azure'. The goal of Azure was to provide customers the facility of running their Windows applications over the Internet.

Apart from these commercial initiatives, many research organizations and open-source forums started their cloud computing initiatives during those years. For instance, NASA developed and launched an open-source cloud computing platform called as 'Nebula' in 2008 for its internal use.

> Elastic Compute Cloud (EC2) introduced by Amazon in 2006 is the first concrete cloud service launched in the market.

3.3 UTILITY COMPUTING

Utility computing is a computing business model in which a party called vendor or provider arranges, owns, maintains and delivers computing facilities on-demand. Use of the computing facility is metered at provider's end. Subscribers can access the computing facility as and when required on payment basis. The billing can be of two types: fixed rental or actual use-basis. In fixed rental model, a fixed amount is charged depending on subscriber's need for some fixed duration (generally counted in months). In actual use-basis approach, billing is done as per actual consumption of the service by a subscriber over a period.

> *Utility computing model is the implementation of utility model of service delivery in computing.*

Figure 3.1 describes the two important aspects of *utility model* for service delivery. The service is available as per user's demand (in little or in big volume) and it is a measured service that is metered. Service providers can impose charge on subscribers based on the metering of their usage.

In utility model, computational facilities are delivered along with computing resources (including processor, storage etc.) in packaged form that can be accessed from remote location. Computing cost reduces under this computing model as same set of resources are shared among large number of subscribers. Here, subscribers can access virtually unlimited supply of computing solutions using network communication paths or internetworks.

> *Supply of resources by provider party as per users' demand is known as 'on-demand service'.*

IBM, HP and Sun Microsystems started their utility computing initiatives towards the end of the last century. These companies invested huge capital to conduct research on on-demand computing. They were the leaders in the utility computing development initiatives. Later on, Microsoft, Google, Amazon and others joined in the race.

3.3.1 The Benefits

It has already been discussed in Chapter 1 how electric power as utility service raised concerns and doubts among people in early twentieth century. Computing as *utility service* also raises similar concerns. Debates are regular on pros and cons of outsourcing computing as utility service. There are two choices available; either to maintain own data center, or consume cloud computing service.

For electric power more than a century ago, when electricity did not come as utility service, businesses either had to maintain *in-house* team or outsource the job of maintaining and running the power generation plants inside their premises. Computing in its traditional form is maintained in similar way at organization's own data center. But what happens when an enterprise or organization outsources the job of running their own data center to some third party? Or how apt is it to run own data center by deploying in-house team, when organization does not have expertise in computing? Here comes the third choice. The cloud computing where

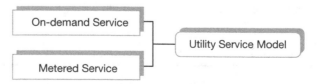

FIG 3.1: Utility model of service delivery

almost the entire computing facility is outsourced but in entirely different form. The question arose that if it would not be the safer option than earlier two choices to give the responsibilities to those reputed organizations who already did have the expertise in the field of computing. The utility model of outsourcing reduces the cost of IT operations remarkably for customers which is a big advantage in this highly challenging market. Utility computing also shifts the investment model from one time large investment to small variable payments.

This sort of the computing model also brings benefit to the providers of computing services. The capital they invest to build hardware and software infrastructures can provide multiple solutions and serve a large number of users. This ultimately leads to better *return on investment* (ROI).

> Utility service model provides the facility of very low initial investment as well as overall cost saving for subscribers.

3.4 METERING AND BILLING IN CLOUD

Actual metering of computing service has become possible in cloud computing. Earlier, in cluster computing models, few basic metering functions were available. But, those were not enough for measuring the actual service usage. The combined technological advancements adopted in cloud computing enable this capability where consumption by subscribers can be measured accurately.

Usages are measured for different types of facilities like processing, storage or network bandwidth. Subscribers are billed as per their use of computing resources. For instance, a subscriber using compute facility in cloud computing will be billed against his/her use of computing power (both processor and memory), storage usage (if any) and network bandwidth consumption over a period of time. Subscribers using storage facility in cloud are billed against the volume of actual storage used by them. The metering capability of cloud results in significant cost saving for users.

> In traditional computing, the basic metering functions were not adequate for measuring the actual use of computing. Cloud computing is empowered with this facility.

3.5 SEPARATION OF DATA CENTER OPERATION

Computing data center operation has always been a burden for most of the consumers of computing, specially enterprises. *Data center* operations involve arranging space for infrastructure development, ensuring uninterrupted electric supply, establishing cooling system and most importantly, building computing infrastructure etc. Apart from these, maintaining the system, running upgrades, recovery in case of system failure or protecting the system from network attack are all activities at the end of data center.

The cloud model of computing completely separates the data center operations from user end's computing tasks (like application development). Software developers or application users have always tried to avoid the computing infrastructure management tasks. Thus, in traditional computing model, outsourcing the management of data center was a common feature.

In cloud computing, data centers reside at some remote end and are managed by some computing vendors. The vendor arranges and manages everything. Users can simply and solely concentrate on their specific tasks. This facility comes as a huge relief for users of computing.

> *Cloud computing separates data center operations from other activities at the users' end.*

3.6 BENEFITS OF CLOUD COMPUTING

Cloud computing has introduced a real paradigm shift in the scope of computing. Unlike the conventional uses of computer technology, it facilitates computing as a utility service which is delivered on demand. The computing facility is managed by providers and can be measured in usage volume or usage time.

All these features of cloud computing provide several benefits. It has the flexibility where users can have as much or as little of it as they want at any given time. The advantages influence the adoption of cloud computing over the traditional computing process. Following section discusses different benefits that subscribers of cloud computing can enjoy.

3.6.1 Less Acquisition/Purchase Cost

In traditional computing, users have to purchase or procure computing resources in significant amount at very beginning. Cloud computing is delivered following the utility service model. Since vendor arranges all necessary resources in this model, subscribers' initial investment for acquiring hardware or software drops down drastically. They need not to arrange anything apart from client systems to access cloud services. Thus, initial capital expenditure of user gets reduced considerably.

> *The initial investment of users adopting cloud computing is very low.*

3.6.2 Reduced Operational Cost

With the outsourcing model of utility computing the cost of running any systems round the clock moves towards the provider's end. Subscribers get rid of the responsibility of system administration, maintenance, and 24×7 energy support as well as its cooling support. This is a basis for cost savings because subscribers can use the service by paying very nominal. The provider on the other hand can offer the service at nominal fee to subscribers because of their volume of business (due to large customer base).

> *Subscribers of cloud computing service need to bear nominal operational cost.*

3.6.3 Reduced System Management Responsibility

Be it a data center for enterprises or single standalone machine (PC, laptop etc.) for normal users, management of the computing setup (both hardware and software) is an extra headache for consumers of traditional computing. Cloud computing model shifts majority of the infrastructure and other system management tasks towards cloud vendors. Dedicated teams at the vendor's end takes care of all of these activities. Thus, the users can enjoy a sense of relief and can concentrate only on their area (layer) of computing interest without bothering about the management of the underlying computing layers.

> *Cloud computing releases users from the task of managing underlying computing system.*

3.6.4 Use-basis Payment Facility

Cloud computing does not charge its subscribers when they do not use it. Even the charge is not fixed; it depends on the duration of usage. Rather, any use is metered and users are charged a reasonable fee according to their consumption. This reduces the cost of computing.

3.6.5 Unlimited Computing Power and Storage

In cloud computing, users can easily access supercomputer like computing power at reasonable cost, if necessary. Earlier in traditional approach, only big corporate could afford high-end computing. Storage is another important issue for users. Cloud provides as much storage as required. It is virtually unlimited which is viewed as a big benefit for users.

3.6.6 Quality of Service

In traditional computing, enterprises often used to outsource major portion of computing related jobs to some third party. Thus, service quality was broadly dependent on the expertise of those third parties or the in-house teams managing it. Whereas in cloud computing, high quality of service (QoS) is ensured as it is provided by renowned computing vendors having well-trained staffs and expertise exclusively in the field of computing.

> *When service is provided by reputed vendors, QoS is assured and it becomes a responsibility of the vendor.*

3.6.7 Reliability

The ability to deliver the quality service and support load balancing, backup and recovery in cases of failure makes the reputed cloud vendors highly reliable which often emerges as big worry in traditional computing. In cloud computing, subscribers no more need to plan for all of these complex tasks as vendors take care of those issues and they do it better.

3.6.8 Continuous Availability

Reputed cloud vendors assure almost 24 × 7 service availability. Statistics have shown that service uptime (delivered from reputed vendors) counted for a year generally doesn't go below 99.9%. Such guaranteed continuous availability of cloud service is a big enabler for any business.

3.6.9 Locational Independence/Convenience of Access

Cloud computing is available everywhere via Internet. Users can access it through any computing device like PCs, or portable computing devices like tablet, laptop or smart phone.

Only the thing required to avail cloud computing through those devices is the access to Internet, irrespective of geographic location or time zone.

> Convenience of access and low investment make cloud computing the field with low barrier to entry.

3.6.10 High Resiliency

Resiliency is the ability of reducing the magnitude and/or period of disruptions caused by undesirable circumstances. Higher level of resiliency has great value in computing environment. Cloud computing is developed based on resilient computing infrastructure, and thus cloud services are more resilient to attacks and faults. Infrastructure resiliency is achieved through infrastructure redundancy combined with effective mechanism to anticipate, absorb and adapt. The cloud consumers can increase the reliability of their businesses by leveraging the resiliency of cloud-based IT resources.

3.6.11 Quick Deployment

Deployment time in cloud environment has significantly reduced than what is was in traditional computing environment. This is possible since resource provisioning is rapid and automatic in cloud environment. In a highly competitive market, the ability of quicker deployment gains significant business advantages.

> Quicker system or application deployment attains business advantage in competitive market.

3.6.12 Automatic Software Updates

The issue of software upgrade incurs a lot of headache in traditional computing environment. New patches are released every now and then and users need to run those patches periodically. In cloud computing environment, this upgrade happens automatically. Cloud vendors always deliver the latest available version of any software (if not asked for otherwise). Upgraded environment gets available to users almost immediately after it releases, and whenever user logs in next time.

3.6.13 No License Procurement

Application license procurement needed separate budgetary arrangements in traditional computing. Moreover, unnecessary applications used to be provided with licensed packages. Cloud computing has eliminated that problem too. Here, users need not procure any periodic license for using applications; rather, they are allowed to pay (post-payment) according to their use of any software.

> Software licensing is no more a concern for users in cloud computing.

3.6.14 Safety against Disaster

Breakdown of systems due to sudden technical failure or natural disaster is a major concern for users. Specially, any damage to physical storage devices may cause huge commercial loss. Cloud computing delivered by reputed vendors have robust recovery systems incorporated in their set up. Thus, systems and data remain more protected in cloud computing in terms of safety and security than previous ones.

3.6.15 Environment Friendly

Cloud computing promotes green computing. Proper utilization of resources minimizes overall electronic resource requirement, hence reduces generation of e-waste too. This is beneficial for environment as e-wastes are harmful for eco-system if not being processed properly. Apart from this, the reduced resource requirement results in lesser demand, hence production of computing resources. This decrease in e-production reduces carbon emissions and helps to decrease the overall carbon footprint.

> *Cloud computing is an eco-friendly computing approach.*

This long list of benefits discussed above are represented in Figure 3.2. They give some idea about the usefulness of cloud computing and why so many people are excited about it.

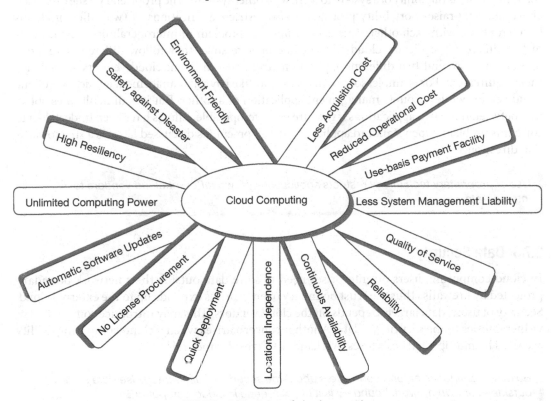

FIG 3.2: Advantages of cloud computing

3.7 CHALLENGES OF CLOUD COMPUTING

Cloud computing provides numerous benefits. But, like any new technology, this model of computing also brings some challenges with it. Following section focusses on those challenges. The promising part is that all of the concerned bodies including the cloud vendors are working rigorously to overcome these challenges.

3.7.1 Limited Portability between Cloud Providers

Cloud computing is at its early age and an overall standardization has not yet come up in the domain. Naturally different vendors are coming up with cloud computing facility for public use which is mostly proprietary to various extents. Applications developed on these proprietary clouds are difficult to move to other cloud platform due to *vendor lock-in*. This problem limits *portability* of applications. Hence, many times it becomes a challenge to move from one cloud provider to another. There various efforts are on to resolve this issue.

Presently, vendor lock-in problem limits portability of cloud applications.

3.7.2 Inter-operability Problem

Interoperability is the ability of a system to work with other systems. The proprietary issue discussed above not only raises portability problem, it also restricts applications of two different clouds to interoperate with each other. This is known as the problem of interoperability. Applications of two different proprietary clouds do not interoperate since they follow different standards. Subscribers may find two different applications from two different cloud vendors suitable for their requirement. For example, some enterprise may like payroll management application of one cloud vendor while accounts management application of another. But it is difficult to establish link between these two applications if they are not interoperable. Efforts have been undertaken to solve this problem. Open standard application development (as discussed later) is a step towards that direction.

Use of proprietary technology restricts applications of two different cloud vendors to interoperate.

3.7.3 Data Security

In cloud computing, users or enterprises need to store data outside their network boundary protected by firewalls. Thus the trust boundary of enterprises expands up to the external cloud. Security of users' data largely depends on the cloud vendors. This may introduce some extent of vulnerabilities to the security of data. Another concern arises when a cloud computing facility accessed by multiple parties causes overlapping of trust boundaries.

Building confidence among consumers about the security of user/enterprise data stored outside their own network boundary is a big challenge in cloud computing.

3.7.4 Reduced Control over Governance

Cloud computing is built and governed by the policies of computing vendor or service provider. Consumers are relieved of the tiring responsibility of managing the computing system. While this turns out as a major benefit, the low control over the *governance* or authority of computing environment sometimes raises concerns among consumers who used to enjoy full control over self-owned traditional data centers. The main concern is regarding how a vendor operates the cloud. Although low but a certain degree of operational control is given to the subscribers depending on the type of service and service level agreement plays an important role in this regard.

> Reduced control over cloud governance may sometime bother cloud computing subscribers.

3.7.5 Multi-Regional Compliance and Legal Issues

Cloud computing vendors build data centers at locations of their convenience, both geographical and economical. A vendor may even have more than one data centers dispersed over multiple geographic locations. Since subscribers remotely access cloud computing over the Internet, they may not be aware of the actual location of the resources they consume. More importantly, the storage location of subscriber's data may not be within the country or region of the subscriber. This sometimes poses serious legal concerns.

The privacy or compliance rule generally differs across different legal jurisdictions. The rules for degree of disclosure of personal data to government agencies (in cases of some official investigations) differ from country to country, or even state to state within a country. Situation may arise where the law of the country of a cloud subscriber asks for some data to be disclosed where the law of hosting region of the cloud (that is the region/country of cloud data center) does not allow such disclosure.

Most regulatory frameworks recognize cloud consumer organizations responsible for the security, integrity, and storage of data even when in reality it is held by an external cloud vendors. In such scenario, resolving the multi-regional compliance and legal issues are soaring challenges before cloud computing.

> Multi-regional legal issues raise concern over information privacy and compliance related problems in cloud computing.

3.7.6 Bandwidth Cost

This one is not as significant as the other challenges discussed above. But it is a fact that while the pay-per-use model of cloud computing cuts down costs as subscribers only pay for the resources or services they use, the model brings some associated cost along with it. That is the cost of *network bandwidth* used to access the service.

In the current age of Internet, cost of bandwidth is very low at moderate speed of access. But more bandwidth can provide higher speed which is essential for high quality service. While low cost bandwidth may often fulfill requirements of general applications, data intensive applications (those deal with critical and huge volume of data sets) demand higher bandwidth which may add a little more in the total cost of computing.

> *Cost of network bandwidth is an additional expense in cloud computing.*

3.8 HOW CLOUD COMPUTING ADDRESSES BUSINESS CHALLENGES

With a host of advantages, cloud computing has changed the way computing used to address business challenges in its way traditionally. Customers now get more flexible and robust computing environment that works in favour of businesses. Table 3.1 lists the cloud computing solutions to counter the common business challenges.

3.9 ETHICAL ISSUES IN CLOUD COMPUTING

Cloud computing implicates several ethical obligations. This is primarily caused by the fact that organizations work outside their trusted network boundary in cloud environment. Risk arises as controls are released to third party cloud vendors. The blurring network boundary raises confusion regarding accountability of participating parties.

The complicated structure of cloud may sometimes raise concern about the responsibility when some problems arise. Both the cloud computing vendors and the users must have clear ideas about their individual responsibilities. There are many instances where both parties need to work together to resolve issues.

Another important part of the ethical side falls on the cloud vendor's shoulders. This issue surfaces as cloud computing allows easy distribution of intellectual properties of other people. In cloud computing, users or enterprises have to rely their data upon cloud storages with the faith that security and privacy of information will be maintained by the cloud vendors. Cloud computing companies have total control over those data stored in their data centers. How they use those sensitive data depends on their moral. Any trusted cloud vendor must implement mechanism in order to provide unbreakable protection to its users' data.

> *Cloud computing philosophy is based upon a relationship of trustfulness between cloud computing vendor and its users.*

Table 3.1 Cloud computing solutions to business challenges

Business Challenges	Cloud Computing Solutions
Budget	It provides flexibility by maximizing utilization of available budget with the scope for future growth
Business	It reduces time to market and provides scope for rapid business growth.
Mobility of users	It enables anywhere access from a variety of devices.
Flexibility	The agile nature of cloud computing enables easier and quick changes.
Scope of Growth	The scalable (or elastic) architecture enables rapid growth.
Availability	It provides almost 24 × 7 availability round the clock.
Recovery	It integrates reliable backup and disaster recovery mechanisms.

3.10 CLOUD COMPUTING: NETWORK AS COMPUTER

The cloud can be imagined as a huge network of computers. The details of this network remain hidden from the users. Users can log-in to the cloud from their individual computing devices (as shown in Figure 3.3), but they never know in which systems they are actually working. They even do not know where their data is stored. To the individual users, the cloud is seen as a single entity.

Cloud computing environment can be described by using Sun Microsystems's popular slogan during mid 1980s, which said "The network is the computer". This philosophy can generate higher computing power by combining power of multiple computers.

> Computing cloud comprises of a vast network of computers but users visualize the entire thing as a single entity.

3.11 ROLE OF WEB SERVICE

Cloud computing environment is built of heterogeneous computing systems spread over different geographic locations. Together they all act as a single system. One important thing to learn here is how applications running on those disparate systems communicate with each other. Answer to this is the web services.

A web service is the way of establishing communication between two software systems over the internetwork. Web services use standardized way of data exchange since different software systems might be built using different programming languages and run on different platforms. Thus, this standardization is very important so that communication remains independent of programming languages or platforms.

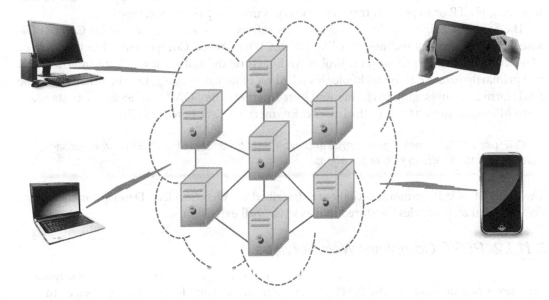

FIG 3.3: The cloud from the point of view of users

> *A critical aspect of cloud (or any other networked application) development is how processes/ threads running on systems with different platform or architecture can communicate with each other.*

3.11.1 Web Service

Web service describes the method of establishing communication between two web-based applications. World Wide Web Consortium (W3C) defines web services as "a software system designed to support interoperable machine-to-machine interaction over a network". Application of web services is an essential part of cloud computing development.

> *Web applications can communicate or publish their messages to the external world by using web services.*

Web services are generally categorized into two different classes. Based on how the service is being implemented, a web service can either be

- Simple Access Object Protocol (SOAP) based, or
- Representational State Transfer (REST) compliant.

Both these approaches of web service development are computing architecture, platform and programming language independent.

3.11.1.1 SOAP-Based Web Services

SOAP-based web services use XML format for communicating messages among web applications as XML is an open format and recognized by all kind of applications. In this approach, HTTP or hyper-text transfer protocol is used for passing messages.

The SOAP is originally developed by Microsoft as older Remote Procedure Call (RPC)-based message passing technologies like DCOM (Distributed Component Object Model) or CORBA (Common Object Request Broker Architecture) did not work well with Internet. This was primarily because those technologies relied on *binary messaging*. On the other hand, the XML format of messaging performs well over Internet. The SOAP was accepted as standard when Microsoft submitted it to the Internet Engineering Task Force (IETF).

> *SOAP uses XML as messaging format and hyper-text transfer protocol (HTTP) for message passing among various web applications.*

The rules of SOAP communications are described in Web Services Description Language (WSDL) format. The rules are stored in files with .wsdl extension.

3.11.1.2 REST: Compliant Web Services

REST represents a simpler way of communicating messages. SOAP is often considered as complex since creation of the XML structure is mandatory for passing message. In this respect, REST provides a light weight alternative. Instead of using XML to make a request,

REST relies on global identifier to locate the resources. Thus, a separate resource discovery mechanism is not needed. This 'representation' of paths of applications provides the additional power in REST.

The global identifier assigned to each resource makes the access method of the resources uniform. Any resource at a known address can be accessed by any application agents. REST allows many standard formats like XML, JavaScript Object Notation (JSON) or plain text as well as any other agreed upon formats for data exchange.

REST is an architecture style for designing networked applications. Here, simple HTTP is used to make calls between machines identified by their URLs (Uniform Resource Locators) which is simpler than other mechanisms like CORBA, DCOM or SOAP.

REST-compliant web services are known as RESTful.

3.11.1.3 SOAP versus REST

The differences between two types of web services have been summarized in Table 3.2.

Both SOAP and REST can be used for cloud computing development. The choice depends on the design and implementation requirements. Both the technologies have been used by different cloud players. But, gradually REST has gained preference over SOAP for its simplicity of use and ease of understanding. Thus, RESTful cloud APIs (Application Program Interfaces) are being more common in the market.

Both SOAP and RESTful web services can be used for developing cloud computing facilities.

Table 3.2 Differences between SOAP and REST

SOAP	REST
It is a message communication protocol that is used to build network application.	It is an architectural style for network application.
It uses XML for formatting message.	It uses simpler messaging formats like JSON. It also supports XML.
It requires the XML parsing.	Here, the XML parsing can be avoided by using JSON.
SOAP defines its own additional security over HTTPS.	It inherits security measures from the underlying transmission protocol as HTTPS.
It is a bit heavy.	It is lighter than SOAP and response time is better.
It is complex than REST.	It is simple to use and easy to understand.
It is recognized as a standard protocol.	It is not an standard, rather an architectural style.
SOAP uses services interfaces to expose the business logic.	REST uses Uniform Resource Identifier (URI) to expose business logic.
SOAP oriented development is faster since it is supported by many tools.	Development time is longer due to limited tool support.
It shows lesser flexibility in controlling resources.	It shows more flexibility in controlling resources.
It requires less knowledge in programming.	It requires rather greater knowledge in programming in comparison with SOAP system.

3.12 ROLE OF API

API (Application Program Interface) is a set of defined functions or methods which is used to compile the application. It defines the contract of communication or standard interface provided by software components for others (other software components) in order to interact with them.

APIs play important role in cloud computing. When some cloud services are released, corresponding APIs (referred as cloud API) are also released as they are critical for the usefulness and operational success of those services. Cloud services generally provide well-defined APIs for its consumers so that anyone can access and use the capabilities offered to develop application or service. Request for data or computation can be made to cloud services through cloud APIs. Cloud APIs expose their features via REST or SOAP.

For instances, the cloud APIs can be classified as IaaS (Infrastructure as a Service) API for resource configuration or workload management, PaaS (Platform as a Service) API to integrate with database service etc. and SaaS (Software as a Service) API to integrate with application services like ERP or CRM. Both vendor specific and cross platform APIs are available, but cross platform APIs are still not widespread in cloud computing arena and are available for specific functional areas only. APIs streamline the access of cloud services and enforce the adherence to compliance.

3.13 UBIQUITOUS CLOUD

The term 'ubiquitous' means as being everywhere. The idea of *ubiquitous computing* talks about making computing facility available everywhere and for all the time. The concept looks beyond personal computer like systems and involves creation of smart devices (any devices like fridge, car etc.) and connecting them to make the communication and exchange of data more efficient. The underlying technologies to support ubiquitous computing include embedded computing devices (electronic chips), networks and Internet among other things.

The *ubiquitous computing* paradigm is also known as *pervasive computing*. In comparison with desktop computing, interaction with computing environment in ubiquitous computing can happen using any devices having some computing capability of any form. Cloud computing further strengthens the idea of ubiquitous computing. *Ubiquitous cloud* refers to the use of computing resources spread over geographic locations from any place and any time.

> *Pervasive or ubiquitous means 'existing everywhere'.*

3.14 CONFUSION BETWEEN CLOUD AND INTERNET

Many people confuse Internet as cloud computing. Where however, the fact is that these two are different. The confusion arises because cloud computing is generally delivered via Internet. The actual fact is that earlier users used to access websites or web portals consisting of static and dynamic pages via Internet but now they access cloud computing too.

Cloud computing has its own characteristics. It follows utility service model and it is measurable where users can be billed as per use. More importantly, it can deliver both software and hardware to users over internetwork or Internet in special form called 'service'. Cloud computing does not mean simple static or dynamic web content; it is much more than that.

Cloud and Internet are not same. Internet is a means for accessing cloud.

SUMMARY

❖ Cloud computing developed following the utility service model. Salesforce.com first built and delivered enterprise application over Internet following utility model in 1999. Various other reputed computing firms like IBM, Amazon and others jumped into the development field of utility computing from the beginning of the current century.

❖ In utility computing model, the computing facility is delivered to users according to their demand and on payment basis. Payment is calculated as-per-usage basis. Under this model, the computing facility is built and managed by computing vendors.

❖ Utility computing model minimizes cost of computing for users as well as generates good business for vendors.

❖ The utility computing facilities became popular as 'cloud computing' around the year of 2006 after reputed computing firms like Microsoft and Amazon addressed it as 'cloud'.

❖ Cloud computing provides lots of benefits to its subscribers. It has very low initial investment compared to traditional computing, minimum system management headache, low operational cost, almost unlimited resource availability and reliable and robust service as provided by the reputed vendors.

❖ Cloud computing is also known as 'green computing' or 'eco-friendly' computing as it minimizes electronic resource wastage.

❖ Among the challenges of cloud computing the portability, interoperability, information security and privacy are some major concerns for subscribers.

❖ Roles of web services are very important in any web base development and so in cloud computing as well. A web service is the way of establishing communication between two software systems over the internetwork.

❖ Based on the implementation, web service can be divided into two categories: SOAP-based and REST-based. Among these two, earlier SOAP gained popularity among cloud vendors. But slowly they started to prefer REST since it is light-weight than SOAP.

REVIEW QUESTIONS

Justify the 'low initial investment' philosophy of cloud computing.

In cloud computing, cloud vendors develop and keep all facilities ready for its potential customers (the users). Vendors invest in large to develop the computing facilities those are essential to attract customers. Thus, investment of cloud computing vendors is very high in its initial phase.

Users on the other hand can avail those facilities on rent basis as per the requirement. They need not to procure resources or purchase software licenses any more. This reduces the initial investment of users radically. Thus, the low investment philosophy of cloud is true from users' perspective.

Why is cloud computing called variable cost computing model?

Cloud computing philosophy enables users to use computing resources on rent basis. Unlike traditional computing, users need not to invest huge capital at the beginning for developing computing infrastructure and can pay to the cloud vendors as per their usage of resources. Resource consumption is measured and billed. When use is higher, users pay accordingly and during low usage they pay less. This is why cloud computing is called a variable cost computing model.

What are the advantages of utility computing?

Utility computing brings many benefits to users. It eliminates the burden of huge initial investment from users. It allows them to pay as per their usage. Sharing of common resources among multiple users under one computing infrastructure reduces cost of computing also. Users can simply connect and use computing. In brief, users get tension-free computing facilities at much lower cost.

What is pervasive computing?

Pervasive computing refers to the computing environment having created through the use of embedded microprocessor that always remains connected with other devices via Internet. Devices those are part of pervasive computing can be anything from car, electric meter to human body. Such computing environment is generally built based on wireless communication technology, Internet and advanced electronic chips. Pervasive computing devices always remain connected.

Is it true that cloud computing ensures round the clock availability?

It can be said that cloud computing is available anywhere and anytime. But it is true that cloud computing vendors cannot generally deliver services with hundred percent service uptime assurance. Reputed cloud vendors guarantee more than 99.9% of service uptime, but till now it has not been possible for vendors to deliver 100% service uptime over a reasonable period of time. Anyway, despite of this, its service availability is still much better than the traditional computing scenario. And cloud users rarely suffer or can even feel the effect of the almost insignificant service downtime.

MULTIPLE CHOICE QUESTIONS

1. Utility model of computing is beneficial for
   a) Users of computing
   b) Vendors of computing
   c) Both b and c
   d) None

2. The term 'cloud computing' was first presented in its current meaning in the year of
   a) 1999
   b) 2006
   c) 2008
   d) 2010

3. Which among the following is/are feature(s) of utility service model?
   a) Metering
   b) Billing
   c) On-demand service availability
   d) All of these

4. Which among the following companies was first to successfully adopt utility computing model for enterprises?

   a) Amazon
   b) Salesforce.com
   c) IBM
   d) Google

5. Heterogeneous software applications communicate over the internet using

   a) HTML
   b) Message passing
   c) Web services
   d) None of these

6. Presently, the web services are categorized as

   a) SOAP & REST
   b) SOAP & RPC
   c) REST & RMI
   d) REST & CORBA

7. REST is considered as the light-weight alternative of SOAP since it can avoid

   a) the use of global identifier for resources
   b) the use of JSON for message passing
   c) the use of XML for message passing
   d) None of these

8. Use of REST-compliant web services results in longer development time than using of SOAP-based web services in cloud computing development. This statement is

   a) True
   b) False

9. REST is a/an

   a) Message communication protocol
   d) Architectural style
   c) Web architecture
   d) Cloud type

10. Which among the following is not a benefit of cloud computing?

    a) Low initial investment
    b) Fixed cost of computing
    c) Access through internet
    d) High-performance computing

11. Which among the following is not considered as an inherent nature of cloud computing?

    a) Flexibility
    b) Elasticity
    c) Scalability
    d) Portability

CHAPTER

4

Cloud Computing Model

The first three chapters of this book provide an overview of introductory cloud computing issues. Beginning with the discussion about limitations of traditional computing approach, it focused on the primary benefits of cloud computing adoption. The second chapter also explained how starting from the days of mainframe computers, cloud computing has matured over the years with continuous developments and reformations in the field of computing.

With this basic understanding of the primary concepts and knowledge regarding the technological drivers behind cloud computing, it is now time to delve further. Now, it will be appropriate to understand the architectural model of cloud computing.

In this chapter, the standard definitions and globally accepted NIST (National Institute of Standards and Technology) model of cloud computing have been explored in order to establish a baseline. NIST has identified five characteristics which have collectively revolutionized this computing model. Apart from these, different types of cloud deployments have also been discussed. Understanding the cloud deployment models is important as it is critical for making informed decisions so that appropriate cloud solution can be picked to satisfy personal or business needs.

4.1 STANDARD CLOUD MODEL

Cloud computing is a reality now and is being delivered commercially. Decades of research and several innovations have paved the way for its success. Though the concept surfaced several years back, the implementation of the concept has been possible through different phases of remodeling and renovation over the years.

During its early days, the idea was defined in many ways by different sections of people as they presented it from their respective view points. Academicians, computer engineers, system architects, software developers, and consumers had their own ideas and suggestions about the models for this new approach of computing. All these proposals had several limitations as there were many aspects which had to be considered. Formation of a complete definition which could address all of these aspects was thus felt necessary. A standard model was also required as it becomes substantive for the advancement of any technology.

Any technology needs a standard model for the conveniences of understanding uniformity.

Computing technology has relied on few institutions and organizations for standardization and guidelines since its inception. Those institutions included the National Institute of Standards and Technology (NIST) of United States, the International Organization for Standardization (ISO), the European Telecommunications Standards Institute (ETSI) and else. A number of initiatives have been taken up by these institutions and others like Cloud Security Alliance (CSA) to publish guidelines focussing to set up some standard model for cloud computing. The most acknowledged and universally accepted initiative among them has been explored in the following section.

4.1.1 The NIST Model

The most appreciated and accepted model of cloud computing was provided by the National Institute of Standards and Technology (NIST) of U.S. The model was published in a document titled as 'NIST Cloud Computing Reference Architecture' by Information Technology Laboratory of NIST in 2011. Following is the statement by the NIST:

"Cloud computing is a model for enabling ubiquitous, convenient, on-demand network access to a shared pool of configurable computing resources (e.g., networks, servers, storage, applications and services) that can be rapidly provisioned and released with minimal management effort or service provider interaction. This cloud model is comprised of five essential characteristics, three service models, and four deployment models."[1]

After analyzing this definition, we have the following salient points:

- Cloud computing is a model and not a technology.
- Cloud computing enables the users' access pools of computing resources via network.
- The resources are shared among users and made available on-demand.
- The prime benefit is the ease of use with very little management tensions for the users.

The first two among the four points are self-explanatory. The third point says that no user can hold any resource exclusively unless required for computational or associated tasks. Computing resources are delivered to a user as and when required and any user need not to own resources exclusively to use them. The last point states that the whole thing will basically be managed by a third party referred as provider party and users will simply use it without the responsibility of managing it.

The cloud computing initiative at NIST started in November 2010. The goal of the initiative was to boost the US Government's effort to incorporate cloud computing to enhance the traditional approach of information system maintenance, wherever applicable. NIST being a U.S. government organization did not limit their cloud computing works within the organization only. Rather they created the model with the intention of making it broadly usable and applicable to different organizations across the globe.

Tha NIST model of cloud computing was published by the Information Technology Laboratory at NIST in 2011.

4.1.1.1 Deployment and Service Models

The *NIST model* of cloud computing separates cloud computing in two categories. One category is based on the operational or deployment pattern of the cloud and the other one is based on the nature of service that the cloud provides.

- *Cloud modeling based on deployment*: It focusses on the access boundary and location of the cloud establishment. The access boundary defines the purpose of using the cloud to some extent. There are four categories of cloud deployment: public cloud, private cloud, community cloud and hybrid cloud.
- *Cloud modeling based on service delivery*: This model describes the type of computing service that is offered to users by the service provider. There are three prime categories of service delivery models, namely Infrastructure as a Service (IaaS), Platform as a Service (PaaS) and Software as a Service (SaaS).

Apart from cloud deployment and service models, the *NIST model* mentions five *essential characteristics* of cloud computing which are broad network access, rapid elasticity, measured service, on-demand self service and resource pooling. Figure 4.1 represents the NIST cloud model.

Thus, the NIST defines cloud computing by describing five essential attributes or characteristics, three cloud service models and four cloud deployment models. The model is a generic one and not tied to any specific reference implementation or vendor's product. In addition to this, the model defines the actors, standard activities and functions associated with the cloud computing.

> NIST defines cloud computing by describing five essential characteristics, three cloud service models and four cloud deployment models.

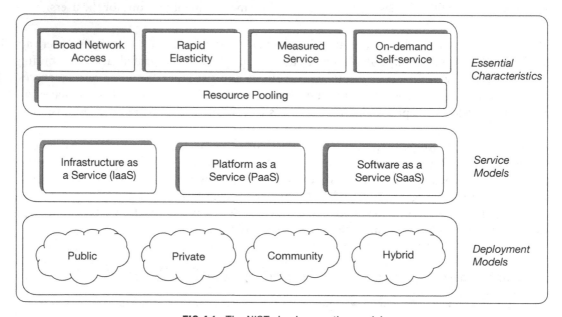

FIG 4.1: The NIST cloud computing model

4.1.1.2 Essential Characteristics

The NIST model of cloud computing comprises five essential characteristics or requirements, which differentiates the cloud model from traditional computing approach. Those characteristics are briefly discussed here.

On-demand self-service: It is the most attractive feature that users like about this computing model. The on-demand service feature refers to the ability that empowers users to consume the computing facility as much they need at any moment. Being self-service, cloud computing can arrange the on-demand facility for users without any need of human intervention at vendor's end. A user himself/herself can request cloud services as needed through some interface (generally through web forms) and resources become available within seconds. This feature is known as *self-service*. The self-service interface must be user-friendly in order to be effective and appealing.

> Cloud computing service is delivered by third-party service provider as per users' demand.

Resource pooling: Computing requires resources like processor, memory, storage and network. Cloud computing arranges these resources for users at vendor's end. Users can access and use these resources to satisfy their computing needs as and when required. Unlike traditional computing approach where every enterprise or user possesses its own physical computing resources, here pools of computing resources are maintained at remote locations by the provider which is accessed by all of the users. The resource pools must be reasonably large, flexible and capable of supporting many users simultaneously without any failure.

> Cloud vendors maintain pools of computing resources to support all users' computing need.

Broad network access: Cloud computing provides economic advantage to users as it releases them from the inconvenience of setting-up expensive in-house data centers. Instead, the cloud service facility developed and installed at the provider's end is remotely accessed by users through the network. To serve this purpose, strong network infrastructure has to be in place for effort-less and fast delivery of the computing services. Thus, high bandwidth communication links spread over the service area are the essential attributes of cloud computing so that users can access computing from any location and anytime.

> Broad network access facility makes cloud computing ubiquitous.

Rapid elasticity: Provisioning of adequate and frequently changing demand of resources for a large number of users is a major technical concern in cloud computing. Provider may not know when and how much of resources users will consume prior to actual demand. But the mechanism should be such that the required volume of resources can be arranged at the time of demand from the users. The computing environment must create an impression of limitless repository of resources to users, and they should be able to consume any volume of resources any time. Again when a user no more uses the resources, those have to be taken back immediately so that there is no wastage of valuable resources through idle possessions.

From users' point of view, the system has to be elastic enough. It should be able to grow and shrink according to the requirement. Rapid elasticity refers to this ability of the cloud where a computing system can expand or reduce itself rapidly in accordance with the actual resource requirement at runtime.

> *Rapid provisioning and release of resources is critical for building a low cost computing facility.*

Measured service: As users use computing services provided by cloud vendor, they must pay for it. In cloud computing model, this payment is determined by measuring the usages of computing resources by a user. Hence, the provider must employ some mechanism to measure the actual consumption by each individual user or organization. This means that the usage of the pooled resources has to be calculated and stated (or billed) to every user based on a metering system. Generally this is done on some known metric such as amount of processing power consumed, use of storage volume, network bandwidth used, number of network transactions etc. Any user is billed based only on the actual consumption of cloud resources or for resources which were allotted to him/her.

> *The metering of actual resource consumption dramatically reduces the cost of computing since users are no more charged for any idle resources.*

4.1.1.3 Multi-tenancy

The NIST model does not include multi-tenancy as an essential characteristic of cloud computing model. But when features like resource pooling, measured services or rapid elasticity is discussed, those implicitly refer towards the multi-tenancy concept. Although not mentioned as essential by NIST, but multi-tenancy is an important characteristic of cloud computing. For instance, Cloud Security Alliance (CSA), an industry working group that studies security issues in cloud computing, identifies multi-tenancy as a key element of cloud model.

Multi-tenancy in simple form implies that a single set of resources can have multiple tenants who are not linked with each other. This statement about multi-tenancy perfectly fits in public cloud environment but does not apply in private deployments with its full essence or ability since all of the users there are internal to a single organization or remains under a single body. This is the reason why multi-tenancy is not mentioned as an essential attribute of cloud computing by NIST. Community cloud stays in between public and private clouds in terms of supporting multi-tenancy.

> *Multi-tenancy is not called out as an essential characteristic of cloud computing, but is often discussed and considered as such.*

Unlike traditional computing model which allows users to have dedicated resources (i.e., computing facilities dedicatedly held by owner), cloud computing suggests a business model where resources are shared among isolated parties (i.e., multiple unrelated users use the same resource). The model allows several users to share computing facilities, without any user being aware of it and without compromising the privacy and security of users. From provider's perspective, multi-tenancy enables operational efficiency and makes the service economical. For more discussion on multi-tenancy, refer to Chapter 8 (Section 8.4).

> *Multi-tenancy in cloud computing allows the sharing of same computing resources by different subscribers without the subscribers being aware of it.*

Note: Multi-tenancy is an essential characteristic of any large-scale utility service to make it economical. Imagine an electricity or water-supply network that is not multi-tenant. It would imply dedicated supply lines from end to end and all the way from the provider to each and every consumer. These will not only cause exorbitant cost but also much more operating expenses associated with maintenance. Simple troubleshooting processes would be difficult and the mean time to recovery (MTTR) would be significant in case of failure. For similar reasons, without multi-tenancy the economics of cloud computing does not make financial sense.

4.1.1.4 Cluster and Grid Computing Revisited

All of three computing models as cluster, grid and cloud are distributed in nature and share many similar characteristics. The study of the five *essential characteristics* of cloud computing in cluster and grid architecture makes this new paradigm easier to be compared with former computing models. Table 4.1 summarizes the whole thing.

The first two criteria, resource pooling and broad network access are characteristics of all of these three models. Although initially, cluster and grid systems were built to be accessed through network within a relatively small area like an organization while the cloud computing system was built with the motive to facilitate access through public network, i.e., the Internet from its initial days. *Cluster computing* environment provides few basic *metering functions* which give some idea about resource usages pattern but the accurate measurement of the actual service usage is only possible in the grid and cloud computing models. The remaining two attributes rapid elasticity and on-demand self-service are not at all supported by cluster or grid models.

Table 4.1 Comparison of characteristics between cluster, grid and cloud computing models

	Cluster Model	Grid Model	Cloud Model
Resource Pooling	Yes	Yes	Yes
Broad Network Access	Yes	Yes	Yes
Measured Services	No	Yes	Yes
Rapid Elasticity	No	No	Yes
On-demand Self-service	No	No	Yes

4.1.2 The Reference Architecture

The *NIST cloud reference architecture* is a logical extension to the NIST cloud computing definition. The reference architecture was published in September 2011. The aim of the institute was to develop a neutral architectural model. They analyzed various already existing cloud reference models suggested by researchers, enterprises, and cloud vendors which had many limitations as they were either product-specific or had some other deficiencies.

The reference architecture of NIST does not model system architecture of any particular cloud. Rather it intends to simplify the conception of the operational details of cloud computing. The architecture focusses on *'what'* cloud services need to provide but not *'how to'* do that. Figure 4.2 represents the NIST reference-based architecture.

The diagram depicts a generic high-level architecture and represents an actor or role-based model. The five major *actors* of the model are *cloud consumer, cloud provider, cloud broker, cloud auditor* and *cloud carrier*. Along with the actors, the model also identifies their activities and functions. This helps in understanding the responsibilities of the actors.

> The NIST cloud computing reference architecture focusses on *'what'* cloud services must provide, not *'how to'* implement solution.

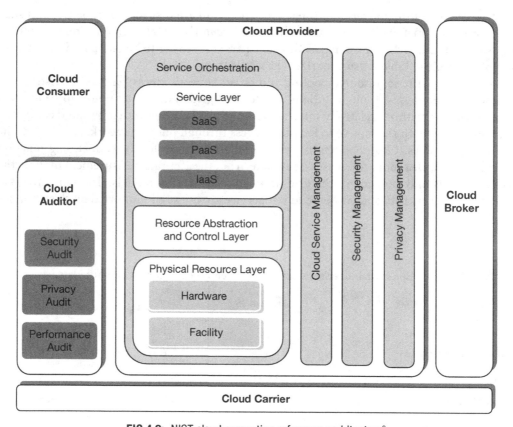

FIG 4.2: NIST cloud computing reference architecture[2]

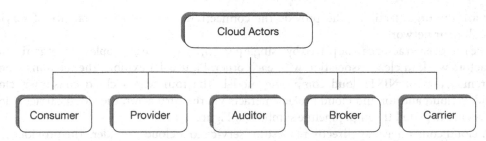

FIG 4.3: Actors of NIST cloud computing reference architecture

4.1.2.1 The Actors and Their Roles

The NIST cloud computing model describes five major *actors* as shown in Figure 4.3. These actors play key *roles* in the cloud computing business. Each actor in the reference model is actually an entity; that is, either a person or an organization. The entities perform some tasks by participating in transactions or processes.

Cloud Consumer: According to the definition of NIST, 'The cloud consumer is the principal *stakeholder* for the cloud computing service. A cloud consumer represents a person or an organization that maintains a business relationship with, and uses the service from a cloud provider.'[3] The cloud consumer uses cloud service and may be billed for the service by the provider.

Cloud Provider: According to NIST, 'A cloud provider is a person or an organization; it is the entity being responsible for making a service available to interested parties. A Cloud Provider acquires and manages the computing infrastructure required for providing the services,...'.[3] Here the interested parties who want service from cloud provider are the consumers.

Cloud Auditor: The cloud services provided by cloud provider to the cloud consumer must comply to some pre-agreed policies and regulations in terms of performance, security etc. The verification of these agreed conditions can be performed by employing a third-party auditor. The cloud auditor is a party who can conduct independent assessment of cloud services and report it accordingly.

Cloud Broker: Usually, there are enormous numbers of service providers and many similar type of services are available from different providers. This may raise confusion among the consumers regarding the uses and management of the services. Moreover, consumers may not be aware about all of the available services and their performances. Even, consumers may find two different services useful from two different providers which would have to be integrated as well. Here comes the role of the cloud broker. According to NIST, 'A cloud broker is an entity that manages the use, performance, and delivery of cloud services and negotiates the relationships between cloud providers and cloud consumers.'[3] Consumers can avoid the responsibilities of those complex tasks by requesting services from brokers instead of consuming services from providers directly.

Cloud Carrier: Cloud computing services are delivered from cloud provider to cloud consumer either directly or via some cloud broker. Cloud carrier acts as an agent in this delivery process.

They are the organizations who provide the connectivity and transport facility of services through their network.

The role of each actor can be played by a single person; by a group of people or an organization. The actors work in close association with each other. Figure 4.4 exhibits the relations among different actors of NIST cloud computing model. The four actors cloud consumer, cloud provider, cloud auditor and cloud broker interacts via the fifth actor, the cloud carrier. Cloud carriers are depicted through pipeline symbols in Figure 4.4 below.

A cloud consumer may directly request for service to a cloud provider. The provider then delivers the requested services to the consumer. This communication between consumer and provider occurs through the carriers as shown through the pipeline numbered as 1.

Instead of contacting a cloud provider directly, a cloud consumer also has the option of requesting for services to some cloud broker. Cloud broker usually integrates the required services from provider and delivers it to the consumer. The carriers involved in this communication and delivery are shown through the pipelines numbered as 2 and 3. In this case, the actual cloud providers remain invisible to the cloud consumers.

The role of cloud broker has been elaborated in Figure 4.5. Here, the broker has been linked with two providers. In such scenario, the cloud broker may create a new service by combining services of those two providers.

Figure 4.4 also represents the role of cloud auditors very clearly. For independent assessment of operations and other measures, the auditor needs to interact with the cloud provider, cloud consumer, and cloud broker too. The carriers for these interactions are shown through pipeline paths numbered as 6, 4 and 5 respectively.

> *Cloud broker establishes and eases the interaction between consumers and providers.*

4.1.2.2 Exploring the Cloud Provider

The cloud provider plays a major role in cloud computing. According to *NIST model*, cloud provider takes care of five types of activities-service deployment, service orchestration, service management, management of security and privacy. Service deployment decides the

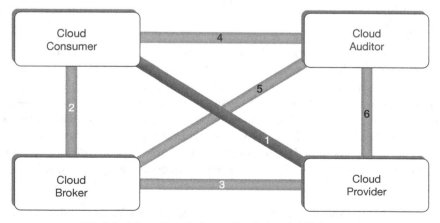

FIG 4.4: Interactions between the Actors in NIST model[4]

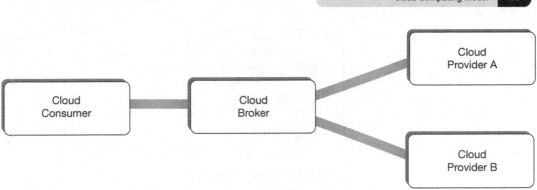

FIG 4.5: Usage Scenario of Cloud Broker[5]

deployment model (among the four models) of cloud infrastructure. Service deployment has been discussed later in this chapter.

The *Service Management* component of cloud provider takes care of the functions needed for the management and operation of cloud services. There are three modules of cloud service management as business support, provisioning/configuration and portability/interoperability. These issues have been discussed later in this book.

Security and privacy are two major concerns for building confidence and trust among the stakeholders. *Security management* in the NIST reference architecture refers towards developing a secure and reliable system. It means protecting the system and its information from unauthorized access. *Privacy management* aims to keep personal or sensitive information secret and saves them from revealing out. Security and privacy issues have been discussed in separate chapters.

Service Orchestration: *Service orchestration* is an important part for the cloud providers. According to the NIST document, service orchestration refers to the 'composition of system components to support the cloud providers' activities in arrangement, coordination and management of computing resources in order to provide cloud services to cloud consumers.'[3]

Service orchestration has three layers in it (Figure 4.6) and each layer represents a group of system components that cloud provider needs to deliver the services. At the top, there is the *service layer*. Here, cloud provider puts interfaces that enables the service consumers to access various computing services. Thus the access interfaces for different types of cloud services (SaaS, PaaS and IaaS) are represented in this layer.

The middle layer is the *resource abstraction and control layer*. At this layer, the abstraction of physical resources are implemented (through the software). Access to any hardware resources goes through this layer and the layer secures the system by controlling resource allocation and access. It also integrates underlying physical resources and monitors the resource usage by the consumers. This layer is also responsible for resource pooling and dynamic allocation of resources.

The *physical resource layer* is the lowest layer in the stack that houses all of the physical computing resources. Hardware resources include computers (with processor and memory components), storage components (hard disks), network entities (routers, firewalls, switches, network links and interfaces) and other physical computing devices. Apart from hardware

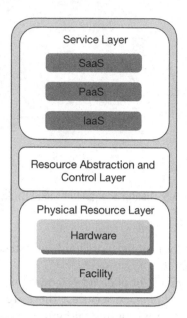

FIG 4.6: Cloud Service Orchestration[6]

resources, this layer also includes the facilities for the computing infrastructure which includes power supply, ventilation, cooling, communications and other aspects of a physical plant.

4.2 CLOUD DEPLOYMENT MODELS

Cloud services can be arranged or deployed in a number of ways. The deployment choice depends on the requirements of the consumer organization. The deployment model describes the utility of a cloud and also specifies its access boundary. The model also indicates the relative location of the cloud with respect to the location of consumer organization. The NIST definition mentions about four common *deployment models* as public, private, community and hybrid deployments. All of the clouds fall under either of these four categories.

4.2.1 Public Cloud

The *public cloud* deployment model provides the widest range of access to consumers among all cloud deployments. Anyone who subscribes it gets open access to this cloud facility. The consumer can either be an individual user or a group of people representing some organization or an enterprise. Public cloud is also referred as *external cloud* as physical location-wise it remains external or *off-premises* and the consumers can then remotely access the service.

A public cloud is hosted and managed by some *computing vendors* who establishes data centers to provide the service to consumers. The consumers under this cloud deployment model are entirely free from any tensions of infrastructure administration and system management-related issues. But, at the same time they (consumers) would have low degree of control over the cloud. Amazon Web Services, Google Cloud, Microsoft Azure and Salesforce.com are some of the popular public clouds.

Public cloud deployment promotes *multi-tenancy* at its highest degree. Same physical computing resource can be shared among multiple unrelated consumers. This provides major advantages as it becomes possible for a single *cloud vendor* to serve a large number of consumers. When a large number of consumers dispersed around the world share resources from data center of a single vendor that automatically increases resource utilization rates and decreases vendor's cost of service delivery. Thus for the consumers, the key benefit of using public cloud is its financial advantage.

The public cloud providers on the other hand, make advantage of the magnitude of their operation. Being large in volume and business, they can afford state-of-the-art technology and skilled people. This ensures better quality of service. Through this model, consumers can access potentially superior service at a lower cost. Since different consumers (from different parts of the world) have variable workload demands during a course of a day, week, month or year, a cloud provider can always support loads efficiently during high demand (which is usually raised by a section of its consumers, at any particular moment).

> Multi-tenant environment is the basic philosophy behind public cloud where multiple and a large number of unrelated customers can share resources.

4.2.2 Private Cloud

The *private cloud* deployment does not provide open access to all. It is mainly for organizational use and access to a private cloud deployment is restricted for general public. Private cloud is also referred as *internal cloud* since it is built to serve internal purpose of the organizations. While public clouds are equally useful for both individual users and organizations, private cloud generally serves the purposes of organizations only. For high-security and critical systems, like systems of defense organizations, private cloud is the suggested approach.

While a public cloud cannot physically reside at any consumer's location (*physical boundary*), private clouds may reside either inside consumer organization's premises (*on-premises*) or outside (*off-premises*) at any neutral location. On-premises private clouds physically reside under consumer organization's own physical as well as inside the network boundary. Off-premises private clouds reside outside organization's own *network boundary* but remains under the control or supervision of the consumer organization.

A private cloud may be established and managed by the consumer organization itself or they (the consumer) may outsource the responsibility to some other computing vendor. Figures 4.7 and 4.8 represent on-premises and off-premises private clouds respectively.

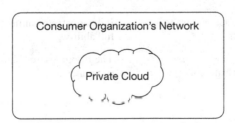

FIG 4.7: On-premises private cloud

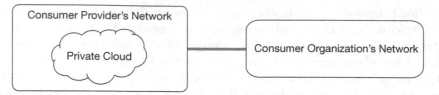

FIG 4.8: Off-premises private cloud

Private cloud may reside on-premises or off-premises.

One major difference of private cloud with public cloud is that any private cloud shares *one-to-one relationship* with consumer while a public cloud maintains *one-to-many relationship*. This depicts that the resources of a private cloud remain devoted for one consumer organization only and cannot be shared with others. Thus, the features of *multi-tenancy* (where tenants are external unrelated entities) do not apply in private cloud as it is in public cloud. But, such isolation ensures privacy and creates a more secure computing environment. However, this does not necessarily mean that public cloud is not secure enough.

The other differentiating point arises over the ability of consumer to control the cloud. Consumers have no control over a public cloud environment. But with the private cloud, consumers can benefit from most of the advantages of cloud computing and can still hold control over the environment. For consumers, the cost of availing private cloud is higher than public cloud as resources remain dedicated for a particular organization here.

Private cloud does not support multi-tenancy and thus cannot offer much in terms of cost efficiency. But, it ensures more security and privacy of data.

Table 4.2 A comparison between private cloud and public cloud

Private Cloud	Public Cloud
It can be both of types of on-premises and off-premises.	There cannot be any on-premises public cloud deployment.
On-premises private cloud can be delivered over the private network.	It can only be delivered over public network.
It does not support multi-tenancy feature for unrelated and external tenants.	It demonstrates multi-tenancy capability with its full ability.
The resources are for exclusive use of one consumer (generally an organization).	The resources are shared among multiple consumers.
A private cloud facility is accessible to a restricted number of people.	This facility is accessible to anyone.
This is for organizational use.	It can be used both by organization and the user.

Private Cloud	Public Cloud
The consumers have important roles to play in management of the cloud.	The management is entirely provider's responsibility.
The consumers have more control over the environment.	The consumers have very less control or no control.
It provides more confidence regarding security of data as remains under the control of consumer organization's security boundary.	The public cloud deployment often creates concerns regarding security and privacy of data.
The cost of computing is more in comparison to public cloud.	This is more economical as multiple unrelated consumers (tenants) share same infrastructure.
It is not an ideal scenario for promoting pay-as-you-use philosophy.	It is an ideal model for practicing pay-as-you-use philosophy.
The resource may often remain idle resulting in the resource wastage.	The resource utilization is optimum due to the presence of larger number of consumers.
It is not so environment friendly like public cloud.	It promotes green computing at its best.

4.2.3 Community Cloud

The *community cloud* deployment model allows access to a number of organizations or consumers belonging to a community and the model is built to serve some common and specific purpose. It is for the use of some community of people or organizations who share common concerns in business functionalities, security requirements etc. This model allows sharing of infrastructure and resources among multiple consumers belonging to a single community and thus becomes cheaper compared to a private cloud.

Community cloud deployment can be *on-premises* or *off-premises*. Physically it may reside on any community member's premises or it may be located in some external location. Like private cloud, this cloud can also be governed by some participating organization(s) (of the community) or can be outsourced to some external computing vendor.

This cloud deployment may be identified as a generalized form of private cloud. While a private cloud is accessible only to one consumer, one community cloud is used by multiple consumers of a community. Thus, this deployment model supports multi-tenancy although not in the same degree as public cloud which allows multiple *tenants* not related with each other. Thus, the tenancy model of community cloud falls in between that of private cloud and public cloud.

The goal of community cloud deployment is to provide the benefits of public cloud, like multi-tenancy, pay-per-use billing etc. to its consumers along with added level of privacy and security like the private cloud. One familiar example of community cloud is some services launched by government of a country with the purpose of providing cloud services to national agencies. The agencies are consumers in this case belonging to a single community (the government).

Community cloud provides advantages of public cloud deployment combining with the promise of private cloud like security and privacy of data.

Table 4.3   A comparison between private cloud and community cloud

Private Cloud	Community Cloud
One private cloud can be used by one consumer (may be an organization).	One community cloud can be used by one community.
Access is restricted among members of a single consumer.	Access is restricted among members of a single community.
Resources of a private cloud are for exclusive use of one consumer.	Resources are shared among multiple consumers of a single community.
It may reside at consumer's premises.	It may reside at some consumer's premises within the community.
The private cloud (on-premises) can be delivered over private network.	To provide access to multiple consumers (of a community), it delivers over public network.
It does not support multi-tenancy.	Here multi-tenancy is supported.
This is for organizational use.	This one is for use of the communities.

4.2.4 Hybrid Cloud

A *hybrid cloud* is generally created by combining private or community deployment with public cloud deployment together. This deployment model helps businesses to take advantage of private or community cloud by storing critical applications and data. There at the same time, it provides the cost benefit by keeping shared data and applications on the public cloud. Figure 4.9 demonstrates a hybrid cloud model combining public cloud with on-premises private cloud.

In practice, the hybrid cloud can be formed by combining two elements from a set of five different *cloud deployments* as on-premises private cloud, off-premises private cloud, on-premises community cloud, off-premises community cloud and public cloud, where one among the first four deployments is combined with the last one (public cloud). Physical locations of all of the different cloud deployments have been shown in Figure 4.10.

> *Cloud deployment states how exclusively a cloud consumer can use the computing resources.*

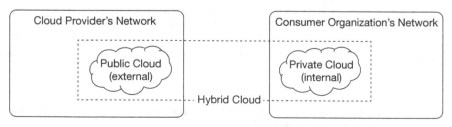

FIG 4.9: A hybrid cloud model

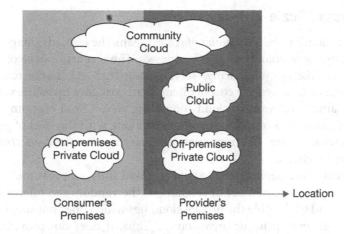

FIG 4.10: Physical locations of cloud deployments

4.3 CHOOSING THE APPROPRIATE DEPLOYMENT MODEL

The choice of appropriate *cloud deployment* depends on several factors. It largely depends on the business needs and also on the size and IT maturity of consumer organization. Consumers should analyze the pros and cons of on-premises and off-premises deployment options and must be careful before selecting a cloud deployment model as different deployments are best fitted for serving different requirements. Business need and security need (especially that of data) are two important factors which play significant role in the decision making.

For general users, any reputed public cloud service is a good option. The issue regarding the appropriate choice of cloud deployment mainly stands before organizations (and communities also). Any reputed public cloud can be a choice for them but private (or community) deployment becomes the likely option when concern is about the privacy of sensitive or importance of some vital business-related data. Even in case of setting up, an *in-house* cloud, organization (or community) must consider the capability of their in-house technical team; otherwise they have the choice of *outsourcing* the (private or community cloud) service. While outsourcing, the expertise or reputation of the service provider has to be verified.

Budget is another important issue. The cost of migration into cloud and the *total cost of ownership* have to be considered before selecting a deployment. Generally, for a critical application that has security issues, a private or hybrid cloud model may suit well. On the other hand, for a general application, the public cloud may serve the purpose better.

It is also critical to understand the business goals of consumer organization based on many functional as well as other non-functional requirements. For instance, the cost of computing and consumer's control over the computing environment directly change with the choice of deployment model. Following section discusses about two such aspects.

To select the appropriate cloud deployment model, one will have to assess the business needs, strengths and weaknesses of a model, privacy/security requirements and goals of the organization.

4.3.1 Economies of Scale

In the study of Economics, the 'economies of scale' means the cost advantages that enterprises use to obtain due to size or volume of their businesses. The scenario can be observed in various business situations, like manufacturing, service industries etc. Large scale production in manufacturing units cuts down the cost per item. Item cost goes up as the volume of business goes down. The same is relevant in cloud computing also. Cloud economy mainly depends on the number of consumers of a cloud deployment along with the level of permissible multi-tenancy of resources. Figure 4.11 represents the variations in *cost-effectiveness* offered by different cloud deployments.

Among different cloud deployments, as public cloud fully supports multi-tenancy and are generally consumed by large number of consumers, the vendors can offer services at cheaper rates. At the other end of the pole the private cloud lies which does not support multi-tenancy and is used by single enterprise or organization. Thus, it does not provide the cost benefit like public clouds because of economies of scale. The community cloud and hybrid cloud deployments stay in between these two in terms of economy of scale.

> Public cloud deployment is most economical for consumers among different deployments.

4.3.2 Consumer's Authority

Consumer's authority or control over a cloud computing environment varies with choice of cloud deployment. Figure 4.12 represents this variation for different cloud deployments. Consumers can have maximum control over a private cloud deployment. In case of private cloud, a single consumer or enterprise remains the owner of the whole thing. In off-premises private cloud, although the management of the cloud is outsourced to some third-party vendor, consumer holds the ultimate control over the cloud environment.

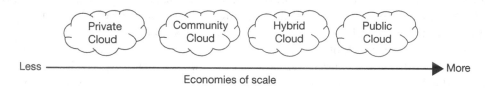

FIG 4.11: Variations of cost-effectiveness with different cloud deployments

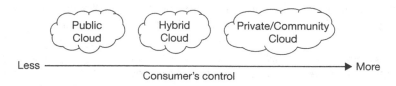

FIG 4.12: Variations in user's control over different cloud deployments

Consumers' control over cloud deployment is minimum in public cloud environment. There, the service provider is an independent body who holds authority over its cloud and hence, consumers hold very little control over the environment. Consumers can only use the service and control their part having limited functionalities.

Consumers do not gain much authority over public cloud deployments.

SUMMARY

❖ The globally-accepted definition and model for cloud computing came from the National Institute of Standards and Technology (NIST), United States. The definition divides cloud computing into two separate categories: cloud deployment and cloud service.

❖ The NIST model specifies the essential characteristics which have to be taken care of while building cloud. It says that the cloud computing should have the qualities of on-demand self-service, resource pooling, broad network access, rapid elasticity and measured services.

❖ Apart from the five characteristics identified by NIST as essential, multi-tenancy is also being considered an important feature of cloud computing, especially for public cloud.

❖ The NIST cloud reference architecture also identifies the actors of cloud and defines their roles. Five actors of cloud computing are consumer, provider, auditor, broker and carrier.

❖ Among different cloud deployments, public cloud provides financial advantages over others and it can be accessed by anyone. Private cloud is for organizational use and can only be accessed by a limited number of users belonging to a single organization. Hence, it can provide more protected or restricted computing environment.

❖ Community cloud can be used by multiple consumers belonging to a single community. Hybrid deployment combines public with private (or community) deployments to maintain a balance and take advantage of both.

❖ The choice of cloud deployment mainly depends on business as well as security needs.

❖ Public cloud is most economic among all of the types of cloud deployments. Generally, the consumers have maximum control over private cloud deployments.

REVIEW QUESTIONS

What is the importance of multi-tenancy feature in any utility service?

Utility service model eliminates the need of maintaining separate and dedicated service generation (as well as delivery) units for each and every consumer. In this model, everyone consume service from some common source being offered by some service provider. Here, resources are used as demand basis to serve consumers. A resource held by one consumer at a point of time may serve another consumer when gets released. This approach makes the utility service cost-effective. Hence, multi-tenancy is an integral part of utility service model.

Why multi-tenancy is not considered as an essential feature of cloud computing?

This is because of private cloud which does not have the scope for multi-tenancy of resources. In public cloud arena, computing resources are usually shared with consumers. One resource held by some consumer can be given to some other when it gets released from the first consumer. This increases resource utilization and decreases cost of computing. But, in private cloud, all resources get reserved for one consumer (or consumer organization), and not shared with others. This is why multi-tenancy is not treated as an essential feature of cloud computing.

'Private cloud is hosted within the security boundary of owner organization' – Justify.

Enterprises who are concerned about the protection of their business interest often choose not to share cloud environment with external organizations or external users. They work in private cloud environment. Private cloud can be deployed on-premises or off-premises both. But the cloud (which is the resources of the cloud) even if it is hosted off-premises, cannot be shared with anyone else apart from the owner enterprise. The cloud environment works as an integral part within the security boundary of the owner organization to keep the computing environment more protected.

Which one is more cost-effective: private cloud or public cloud?

Private cloud uses dedicated resources. Resources there cannot be shared with anyone else but the owner (consumer). This guarantees a secured computing environment as storage and other resources are not shared with others. But, this reservation of resources increases cost of computing. In public cloud, resources are supplied to a consumer as per actual demand. No one can forcefully hold resource without utilization and unutilized resources can be shared with any other consumers. This multi-tenancy philosophy reduces cost of computing a lot.

How can organizations benefit from hybrid cloud?

Public cloud is cost-effective but private cloud can provide more security. Hence, many organizations prefer to use private cloud. But, one problem often is being faced with private cloud during its peak hours. The reserved resources may not meet the demand during such period of time. There we can use hybrid cloud instead. In hybrid cloud, the enterprises can run the essential (or core) part of their applications in the private cloud and expand into the public cloud utility when the demand goes beyond a certain limit. Thus, they enjoy the security of private cloud by reducing the total cost.

MULTIPLE CHOICE QUESTIONS

1. Which among the following is not an essential characteristic of NIST cloud model?
   a) Rapid elasticity
   b) Multi-tenancy
   c) Resource pooling
   d) Broad network access

2. NIST definition of cloud computing was published in the year of
   a) 2007
   b) 2009
   c) 2011
   d) 2013

3. According to NIST definition, cloud computing is a

   a) Model
   b) Technology
   c) Paradigm
   d) Revolution

4. Which among the following service can only be accessed by a restricted number of people?

   a) Public cloud
   b) Community cloud
   c) Private cloud
   d) Both a & b

5. Which among the essential characteristics of cloud computing is not present in grid computing model?

   a) Rapid elasticity
   b) On-demand service
   c) Measured service
   d) Both a & b

6. Public cloud can't be deployed on-premises.

   a) False
   b) True

7. Private cloud can be deployed on-premises. This statement is

   a) False
   b) True

8. Users' control over cloud environment is maximum in

   a) Public cloud
   b) Community cloud

   c) Private cloud
   d) Hybrid cloud

9. Hybrid cloud is cheaper than private cloud. This statement is

   a) True
   b) False

10. Which among the following refers to the location and management of the cloud's infrastructure?

    a) Application
    b) Services
    c) Deployment
    d) All of these

11. Which cloud deployment is managed by provider who resides offsite and is accessible to some restricted people?

    a) Private cloud
    b) Community cloud
    c) Public cloud
    d) Hybrid cloud

12. The number of actors mentioned in the NIST cloud computing reference architecture is

    a) 4
    b) 5
    c) 6
    d) 7

CHAPTER

5

Cloud Computing Services

As discussed in the previous chapter, the NIST model of cloud computing treats the computing methodology from two perspectives as deployment and as service. While cloud can be deployed in four possible ways, the services it offers can be categorized primarily into three different types.

Apart from three primary cloud services, computing vendors deliver a number of specialized cloud services which are considered as special services under these three primary cloud services. In order to understand how cloud computing can be of value to consumers, it is important to understand the services it offers. This chapter focusses on all of these service delivery models.

There are many vendors who provide different cloud services in the market today. Along with proprietary public cloud services, many open-source initiatives are also available which mainly focus on to create private as well as hybrid cloud environments. Few among those open-source initiatives have also been discussed in this chapter.

5.1 SERVICE DELIVERY MODELS

Three categories of computing services that people consume from the days of traditional computing have been already mentioned in the first chapter. They are:

- Infrastructure Service
- Platform Service
- Software Application Service

Cloud computing talks about delivering these facilities to consumers as *computing services* through network/internetwork. The benefit for the consumers is that they can avail these facilities over Internet anytime, as much as required, sitting at their own locations in a cost-effective manner. They only need to have a simple and suitable access device (like PC, laptop, tablet, mobile etc.) to access these services. Using these simple devices anyone can access any kind of computing infrastructure, platform or software application on payment-as-per-actual-usage basis.

Cloud computing offers computing infrastructure, platform and application delivered 'as-a-service'. Those services are considered as primary *cloud computing services* and are referred to as:

- Infrastructure-as-a-Service (IaaS)
- Platform-as-a-Service (PaaS)
- Software-as-a-Service (SaaS)

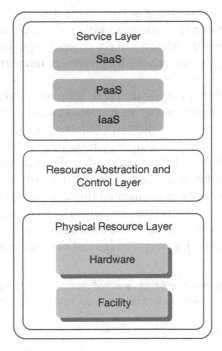

FIG 5.1: Service Layer as part of Cloud Service Orchestration[6]

These services are generally pronounced as 'i-a-a-s', 'pass', and 'saas' respectively. They are the driving forces behind the growth of cloud computing. Clubbed together these three service models are commonly referred as SPI (Service-Platform-Infrastructure) model. Cloud service providers arrange these services for the cloud consumers. The NIST reference architecture represents these services under 'service orchestration' component of the providers (Figure 5.1).

Service layer is the topmost layer of cloud service orchestration over the resource abstraction and control layer. The service layer includes three major cloud services as SaaS, PaaS and IaaS. The PaaS layer resides over IaaS and SaaS layer resides over PaaS. In this layered architecture, the service of a higher layer is built upon the capabilities offered by the underlying layers.

IaaS, PaaS and SaaS refer to the delivery of computing services to consumers over the network.

5.1.1 Infrastructure-as-a-Service

Cloud computing allows access to computing resources in a virtualized environment popularly referred as 'the Cloud'. *Infrastructure-as-a-Service* delivers virtualized-hardware (not physical, but simulated software) resources to consumers known as virtual resources or virtual components. It provides the facility of remotely using virtual processor, memory, storage and network resources to the consumers. These virtual resources can be used just like physical (hardware) resources to build any computing setup (like virtual machine or virtual network). For this reason, IaaS is also referred as *Hardware-as-a-Service* (HaaS).

Consumers no longer need to manage or control the underlying computing infrastructure that they consume as IaaS. IaaS is the bottommost layer of cloud computing service model. The IaaS component stack is shown in Figure 5.2. It is a computing solution where the complexities and expenses for managing the underlying hardware are outsourced to some cloud service providers.

Here the meaning of *outsourcing* is different from its conventional interpretation. In traditional system, outsourcing of computing hardware means some other party will provide and manage hardware resources as per the user's requirement. Users there can directly access that hardware and can utilize those resources by installing necessary software over them. In cloud computing IaaS model, provider arranges and manages hardware resources for users but users cannot access those hardware resources directly. The hardware resources are represented as simulated software components (implemented through resource virtualization technique) and are delivered to consumers via Internet (or network) using web services. Consumers can use those simulated components just like real hardware devices and can build computing system with necessary processor, memory, storage and network facilities.

> Hardware resources in cloud computing are not directly accessible to users. IaaS model provides all hardware components in virtual mode as virtual processor, virtual storage, virtual switches etc.

Thus, the simulated (or virtual) hardware component delivered as per consumers' requirement is the uniqueness of IaaS model. Consumers can access these virtual hardware resources on-demand and any time from any location over the network. They can build computers (virtual computers) using those virtual (or virtualized) hardware components and can even install operating systems and other software over that system.

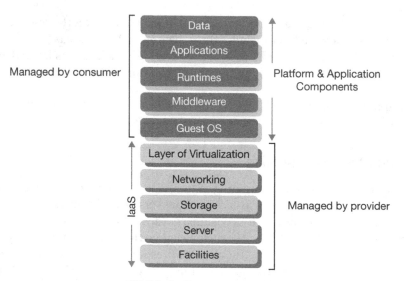

FIG 5.2: IaaS component stack

Major computing vendors like Amazon, Google, GoGrid, RackSpace provide IaaS facility. All of these vendors offer virtualized hardware resources of different types. Apart from offering resource components separately for building any computing setup, the IaaS vendors generally offer custom made *virtual machines* (made of those virtual components) for consumers. For example, Amazon EC2 and Google Compute Engine are popular server environments. Consumers can install OS and start working over these servers. Other than virtual machine, the storage is a very common IaaS offering. Amazon S3 is a popular storage service available as IaaS.

> *Cloud vendors deliver customized and ready-made virtual machines via IaaS offerings which are empty computers (even without OS) being made of virtual components.*

5.1.2 Platform-as-a-Service

In computing, platform means the underlying system on which software applications can be installed (and also developed). A computing platform comprises hardware resources, operating system, middleware (if required) and runtime libraries. Application programs are also installed over this platform.

Application development and deployment in traditional computing require the users' participation in managing hardware, operating system, middleware, web servers and other components. For instance, users must install appropriate framework (like J2EE, .NET) before working in any application platform. PaaS facility, on the other hand, relieves users from all these tensions and delivers ready-made platform to consumers via internetwork/Internet.

PaaS component stack, in addition, provides application (development and deployment) platform over IaaS component stack. A PaaS provider not only delivers fully-managed application development and deployment environment but also takes care of the lower level (infrastructure level) resource management and provisioning. As shown in Figure 5.3, PaaS comes with IaaS capability integrated into it.

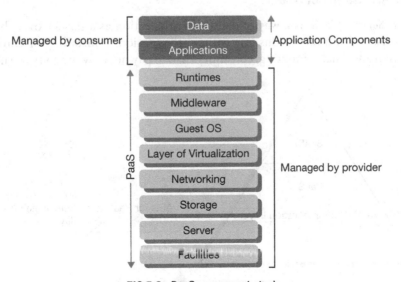

FIG 5.3: PaaS component stack

Thus, PaaS is created by adding additional layers of software over IaaS. With the use of PaaS, collaborative application development becomes easier where multiple users can work from different geographical locations. PaaS also reduces the *total cost of ownership* (TCO) as computing platform becomes available on rent basis.

> *PaaS model lets the users focus only on development and deployment of application without having the tension of arranging and managing the underlying hardware and software.*

There are many PaaS offerings available in market. Google App Engine, Microsoft Azure Platform, GoGrid Cloud Center, Force.com are very popular among them. Open-source PaaS offerings are also available in the market. *Cloud foundry* is one such which is developed by VMware.

One problem with PaaS model is that it fixes the developed applications with the platform. This causes portability problem. For instance, application developed on Google App Engine using any programming language (supported by Google PaaS) uses Google's APIs, and hence, it cannot be run over PaaS facility of other vendors. This portability issue due to *vendor lock-in* problem has been discussed later in the book with further detail.

5.1.2.1 PaaS–IaaS Integration

PaaS layer must integrate with underlying IaaS for seamless access to hardware resources. Such integration is carried out using the *application program interface* (APIs) that an IaaS layer provides to the PaaS developers. APIs are set of the functions and protocols which can be used to build the applications. IaaS developers build and offer these APIs along with their respective services so that PaaS facility can be developed above it. The integration model has been shown in Figure 5.4.

5.1.3 Software-as-a-Service

Software-as-a-Service (SaaS) is a way of delivering application as a service over the network/ Internet that users can directly consume without the tension of installing or configuring an application. In traditional computing, consumers had to pay not only the software licensing fee

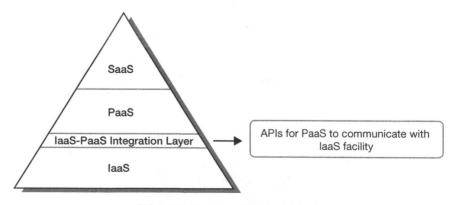

FIG 5.4: Integration of PaaS with IaaS

but also spend a large portion of their budget in setting up the infrastructure and platform over which the application would run. SaaS eliminates this problem and promises easier as well as a cheaper way of using application.

SaaS is hosted by SaaS vendors and delivered to the consumers over network/Internet. Unlike traditional packaged applications that users install on their own computing setup, SaaS vendors run it in their data centers. Customers do not need to buy software licenses or any additional computing resources to support the application and can access applications against some rental fee on usage basis. SaaS applications are sometimes referred as *web-based software*, or *hosted software*.

SaaS is built by adding layers over PaaS component stack (Figure 5.5). It is the facility of using applications administered and delivered by service provider over a cloud infrastructure. In SaaS model, everything is managed by vendor including application upgrade or updates; even the data and application acts upon are also managed (storage in database or file etc.) by SaaS. Users can access the applications through a *thin client interface* (usually a browser) from any location.

SaaS was most primitive among different types of cloud services. SaaS started to gain the popularity form the beginning of the current decade with solutions offered both for general users as well as for the enterprises. E-mail facility is one common example of SaaS application that is used by everyone. The CRM (customer relationship management) package of Salesforce.com gained popularity among enterprises since early 2000s. SAP (Systems, Application and Products) as the solution provider of Enterprise Resource Planning (ERP) entered into the SaaS CRM and ERP markets with its 'Business ByDesign' solution. Oracle launched its CRM SaaS 'On Demand'. There are also many popular SaaS offerings for general users in the market today like GoogleApps, Microsoft Office 365 and else.

> Cloud based software services (SaaS) was matured before the inception of the cloud platform or infrastructure services.

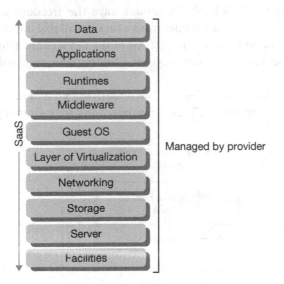

FIG 5.5: SaaS component stack

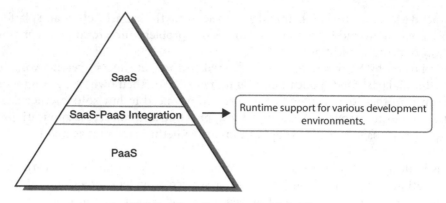

FIG 5.6: Integration of SaaS with PaaS

5.1.3.1 SaaS–PaaS Integration

The integration between PaaS and SaaS is supported by runtimes, a topmost component of PaaS stack. Runtimes are offered by PaaS to support different execution environments. These environments may include Java, .NET, Python, Ruby etc. PaaS consumers can directly run applications over these runtime environments without any system management stress.

5.2 SERVICE ABSTRACTION

The word 'abstraction' is derived from Latin words 'abs' meaning *'away from'* and *'trahere'* meaning 'to draw'. Abstraction takes away or hides the characteristics in order to reduce something into an essential utility. In computing, layer of abstraction is a way of hiding the implementation details of a particular set of functionality.

In cloud computing model, the level of *service abstraction* raises while moving from IaaS towards SaaS. At the IaaS level, consumers have the freedom of building computing infrastructure (essentially in virtual mode) from a set of available options. They can configure machines, setup network and select storages. All of the devices are available in virtual mode and consumers should have the knowledge of building the required infrastructure from the scratch.

In PaaS level, the abstraction intensifies. The underlying virtual infrastructure of IaaS level remains hidden from the consumers. They can simply work with chosen platform environment

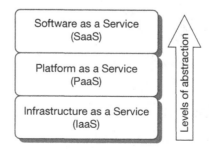

FIG 5.7: The levels of service abstraction

without knowing how the underlying system has been configured. At this level, consumers have full control over the PaaS environment and they can configure and manage the utilities like web servers, database servers, and different application development environments. This abstraction intensifies further at SaaS level where consumers remain unaware even about the technology of an application. They simply use applications without knowing anything about its implementation.

> Cloud computing abstracts the underlying computing system from the users. The degree of abstraction increases with the layers of services and abstraction is maximum at the SaaS level.

5.3 THE SPI MODEL

The three service models SaaS-PaaS-IaaS together is referred as the *SPI model* of cloud computing. In this layered architecture of *cloud service model*, by moving upward, each service layer is empowered by the capabilities of the service layer(s) beneath it. Thus, PaaS is empowered by IaaS layer and SaaS is empowered with the potentials of underlying IaaS and PaaS layers. Figure 5.8 shows the layered cloud SPI model with the mention of popular commercial services.

One point to note here is that there is no functional relation between cloud deployment models and delivery models. Any delivery model can exist in any deployment scenario and thus any delivery/deployment pairing is possible. Although, SaaS offerings are mostly public services and hence the SaaS/public combination is more common than the other combinations.

5.4 A TRADITIONAL SYSTEM vs CLOUD SYSTEM MODEL

Both in the traditional (non-cloud) and cloud computing systems, there are three layers of computing facilities where application comes on the top of the stack to operate on data. Down the stack, the two underlying layers are there as platform and infrastructure facilities.

In *traditional computing* environment, anyone working at some layer of this stack will have to take the responsibility of managing all of the underlying layers. For instance, a software-developing company needs to arrange and manage the required computing infrastructure

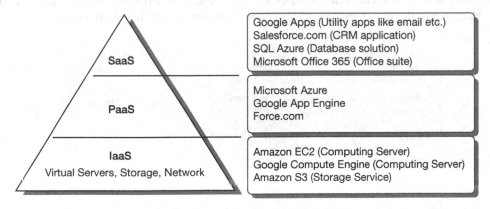

FIG 5.8: The layered cloud service model

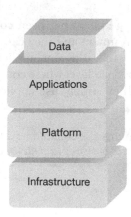

FIG 5.9: The working model of traditional computing system

along with the application developing platforms/environments. They may outsource some tasks to some third party but that does not relieve them from all headaches. The working model of traditional computing system has been shown in Figure 5.9.

> *In traditional computing environment, anyone interested to work at a layer will have the responsibility of managing everything down the stack.*

When computing facility is delivered as service, the provider takes care of a major part. Service means abstraction of a lot of complex functionalities. Figure 5.10 elaborates the modified stack structure to represent the working model at cloud computing environment. Here users' responsibility (of managing the environment) decreases as they move gradually from IaaS to SaaS.

In IaaS, the computing infrastructure is delivered to consumers by providers. Consumers can utilize this infrastructure (resources) to fulfill any type of computing requirements without worrying about the management of the infrastructure. But they only take care of platform and applications.

At PaaS level, providers not only take care of the computing infrastructure but platforms too. Consumers are free from managing anything of the platform (computing platform) on which they work. Platform is delivered as a service (PaaS) and the service provider manages everything up to the platform. The whole system remains transparent to the users.

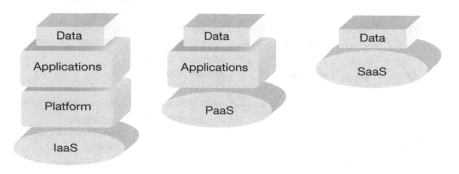

FIG 5.10: The working model of cloud computing system

The *degree of abstraction* is highest at the SaaS level where consumers can use applications without bothering about anything underlying. Consumers' responsibility in that layer is limited into managing the application's functionalities.

> Cloud computing takes responsibilities out of customer's shoulder and hides underlying complexities of computing system based on at which computing layer a customer works.

5.5 ALL APPLICATIONS DELIVERED USING WEB-SERVICES ARE NOT SAAS

It may seem that software applications delivered using web-services is SaaS. But that is not correct. A hosted application can only be treated as SaaS if that holds the basic attributes of cloud computing model. Apart from having rapid elasticity in the capability and on-demand self-service facility, it has to be a measured service.

In this context, the Application Service Provider (ASP) model that appeared in the late 1990s can be mentioned. In *ASP model*, the applications are also delivered through web. But that cannot be termed as Software-as-a-Service offering. Rather SaaS has been extended with the idea provided by the ASP model.

> ASP model of the 1990s was the first attempt for Internet-delivery of software but comparatively it was more similar to the traditional application model than the SaaS model.

5.5.1 ASP model versus SaaS model

The fundamental differences between ASP and SaaS model can be analyzed through many of their characteristics. One significant difference is that ASPs (the vendors) need not necessarily be the developer of the applications they deliver. They purchase the commercial license of applications from the developers and host them in their centrally-located servers for their customers.

The applications under *ASP model* were single-tenant and non-scalable. One hosting of an application could be used by a single customer only. The model was very much like renting a server with an application installed on it. The basic differences between the ASP and SaaS models are charted in Table 5.1.

Table 5.1 Comparison between ASP and SaaS models

	Application Service Provider (ASP)	Software-as-a-Service (SaaS)
Application development	ASPs are generally not the developer of the applications they host.	In SaaS model, the providers are the developer of the applications.
Deployment and management	ASPs deploy and manage the applications.	Service providers of the application themselves manage everything.
Multi-tenancy	One deployment can be used by a single consumer/organization only. Multi-tenancy is not supported.	Applications are designed to be used in multi-tenant environments.

(continued)

Table 5.1 (continued)

Scalability	Applications cannot grow or shrink with demand. They are not scalable.	It delivers scalable applications which can grow or shrink with changing demand.
Customization	ASPs are dependent on the commercial owner of application for any customization of the application.	Providers are the owner of the applications and hence customization is easier.
Domain knowledge	ASPs may not have much domain knowledge of application they host.	SaaS providers are specialists in their respective application domains.
Economy of cost	It incurs less cost than the traditional on-premises application model.	It is more economic because of the multi-tenancy and scaling ability.

5.5.2 Benefits of SaaS over Traditional Applications

Among all of the cloud services, SaaS is the most popular and its adoptability rate is very high. SaaS leverages all of the advantages of cloud computing. Apart from the core cloud features, SaaS applications provide visible benefits to the end users along different dimensions in comparison with traditional on-premises applications.

■ **Licensing:** In contrast to the one-time licensing approach in traditional software model, SaaS application access is sold using a subscription model with customers paying fee on the basis of the usage of the application. Consumers need not to purchase any software license for fixed period.

■ **Risks of software acquisition:** Say, for ERP or CRM application suites, deploying large-scale traditional and critical to businesses software systems are some of the major assignments. The resource, time, budget and expertise required for managing deployment of such applications are some of its critical tasks. SaaS eliminates all of these risks eventually.

■ **Business focus:** As the responsibilities of the 'overhead' activities like managing upgrades, monitoring performance etc. are transferred towards the provider's end the business organizations can focus more on high-value activities to support their own business goals.

These characteristics of SaaS have been extremely beneficial for the consumers and thus its adoptability have been increased since the early days of cloud computing.

5.6 SAAS AND PAAS: SALESFORCE.COM AND FORCE.COM

SaaS applications are developed and deployed over PaaS. PaaS provides the platform to create scalable applications those are delivered as SaaS. Salesforce.com is the pioneer among those primitive SaaS service providers. The company 'Salesforce.com' was formed in the year of 1999 by some employees of Oracle and they started to deliver a hosted customer relationship management (CRM) system.

With the popularity of Salesforce.com as SaaS utility, many consumers wanted to customize or even expand the Salesforce.com applications beyond their actual offering. Customization or expansion of application require development facility. To fulfill these requirements, Salesforce.com later introduced their PaaS platform known as Force.com.

This type of instance sometimes creates confusion regarding the classification among services, where a vendor started with SaaS offerings and then expanded its sphere by offering PaaS. Force.com is the PaaS offering platform created from Salesforce.com for developing services by consumers. Using Force.com, consumers can develop functionalities as per the requirements and add those with Salesforce.com's SaaS offerings.

5.7 OTHER CATEGORY OF CLOUD SERVICES

As cloud computing matured, vendors started sub categorizing services of SPI model and introduced new services. Some among those services dealt with specific computing issues like storage, database, backup and other services which managed business functionalities like security, compliance, identity etc. All these new '<*Something*> as a Service' fell into the category of XaaS (pronounced 'zass'), a generalization of all cloud-related services.

These new cloud services often provide great results and facilities to consumers. A particular service is managed by experts of that domain and consumers get the options of choosing more robust facilities. However, the SPI service model encompasses all of these services.

> All of the additional cloud services are part of some of three primary cloud services but many vendors offer security-management-service as a separate cloud service offering.

5.7.1 Security Management-as-a-Service

Like in traditional computing, security is a prime concern in cloud computing services too, especially in public cloud services. Adoption of cloud computing challenges the security as the consumers lose control over the computing environment. To ensure security for the environment, tasks like timely virus definition updates, maintaining logs and regular security audits are important.

Security management is an integral part of any cloud service offering like SaaS and PaaS. But, at the same time, the vendors having expertise on security management, offer the service as separate cloud service. This cloud service is known as 'Security Management-as-a-Service'. Cloud service consumers can opt for some Security Management-as-a-Service offering to delegate the responsibilities of all of the security related issues of their computing environments. Eminent vendors providing this service include Cisco, McAfee, Symantec and others.

5.7.2 Identity Management-as-a-Service (IDaaS)

Identity management in cloud computing is a critical job. Identity management for any application requires robust authentication, authorization and access control mechanisms. *Authentication* and *authorization* are maintained through some user-identification techniques and passwords respectively. Many advanced techniques like federated identity, identity governance, auditing, single sign-on etc. are used with applications nowadays for the purpose. Although, the identity management is an integral part of all of the cloud services, a number of vendors separately offer identity management-as-a-service that can be incorporated with other cloud services for managing user identity. Examples of such services include Symplified, Ping Identity and others.

5.7.3 Storage-as-a-Service

Data storage comes under IaaS offering. All of the IaaS service vendors offer storage services as an important part of their service. Data can be stored in cloud where the storage works like a disk drive and one can store files there like text, audio, video etc. Many cloud vendors offer independent storage services known as Storage-as-a-Service.

Cloud storage services of Amazon and Rackspace have gained significant popularity among others. They enable provisioning of storage space efficiently. Consumers can rent storage space on a cost-per-gigabyte-stored or cost-per-data-transfer basis. Storage-as-a-Service is seen as a good option for consumers as it is cost-effective and mitigates risks in disaster recovery.

> *Data storage service in cloud falls under IaaS service layer by definition.*

5.7.4 Database-as-a-Service

Database management has always been a significant challenge for IT enterprises. It becomes difficult for organizations to manage critical database issues where they need to focus more on application development and business matters. Issues like provisioning, configuration, performance tuning, privacy, backup and recovery in database management call for a dedicated team with significant expertise in the domain.

In cloud computing model, the database offering comes under the PaaS layer. But, the cloud service vendors have come up with exclusive cloud computing solution for database and it is called as Database-as-a-Service (DBaaS). DBaaS offers a unique platform with on-demand and self-service capability where even non-DBAs can easily fulfill their requirements. It relieves consumers from all of the worries of critical database management issues and also reduces the cost of production. Amazon RDS, Microsoft SQL Azure are example of DBaaS offerings available in the market.

> *Database-as-a-Service is considered as a special category of PaaS.*

5.7.5 Backup-as-a-Service (BaaS)

Data is core element of any business. Backing up and recovery of data is considered extremely important in computing but at the same time the system backup is also necessary to overcome uncertain circumstances like disaster and others. Backup is considered as a specialized service that asks for expertise and many cloud computing vendors offer backup-as-a-service (BaaS) that turns out to be most useful and cost-effective for the consumers.

5.7.6 Compliance-as-a-Service

Compliance is an issue of concern that appears with cloud computing. It is related with the fulfillment of the laws of the countries or regions where business is somehow linked through the cloud. Managing the compliance issues is a complex matter and needs for considerable expertise.

Some vendors offer cloud service in order to take care of these compliance issues for businesses. Such service called as Compliance-as-a-Service (CaaS) enables the organizations to meet the regulatory requirements effortlessly. A Compliance-as-a-Service provider can be a trusted third party who acts at an intermediate layer between a cloud service and its consumer. CaaS helps organizations to concentrate more on their business without worrying about violation of laws and regulations. CaaS service providers are expert in specific business domains. For this reason, CaaS service is sometime referred as 'vertical cloud' service which depicts an alternate vertical (related to some specific trade or industry) business domain.

5.7.7 Desktop-as-a-Service

Cloud services can be accessed through a suitable access devices (PC, tablet etc.) without installing the applications locally. Cloud applications remain independent of the local devices and thus consumers can access computing from any such device. Although a consumer's cloud environment remains same with change in access device but the desktop environment changes as it is local device dependent. For instance, the customized look of the desktop with shortcut icons to access applications are only stored locally.

Here comes the use of Desktop-as-a-service (DaaS). There are cloud service providers who delivers personalized desktop environments to users as service. This allows users to enjoy the benefits of their personal desktop environment irrespective of the cloud access devices. This is also referred to as *virtual desktop* or *hosted desktop*.

Readers must not get confused between SaaS and DaaS. SaaS makes applications available which are accessed through their respective interfaces. Through DaaS, the user can keep all of those interfaces together at one place (the desktop). Several well known Desktop-as-a-Service providers include Amazon, Citrix and Desktone (a VMware company).

5.7.8 Monitoring-as-a-Service

Performance monitoring is another important aspect of computing systems. Cloud vendors offer this as a service known as Monitoring-as-a-Service (MaaS). It monitors functionalities and performances of various cloud services. MaaS can be used to track some specified states of applications, storage, network etc. Enterprises even employ multiple MaaS solutions for the interest of business. Adopting performance monitoring as a service allows enterprises to take appropriate measures to maximize performance and business. For example, the average response time measured during a period might be evaluated to see if this deviates from an acceptable value. Administrators can later take action to rectify the issue or even respond in real time scenario.

5.8 OPEN CLOUD SERVICES

During its initial days, all cloud computing services were proprietary. In 1999, Salesforce.com set milestone with their SaaS services. Next Amazon launched a suite of cloud-based services in 2002. Later on Google, Microsoft, VMware and many other companies have launched one or more of the cloud computing services. Among them, Amazon is considered as pioneer in IaaS, the efforts of Google are mainly focused on SaaS and PaaS delivery and later on, Microsoft chose the PaaS and SaaS as the core of their interests.

As time passed, *open-source* communities came up with their own solutions. Unlike the public cloud services of giant facilitators like Salesforce.com, Amazon, Google, Microsoft and else, this community mainly focusses on the private cloud arena. Different open-source technologies have powered many of these solutions. Eucalyptus, Nebula, Nimbus are some eminent examples of open-source cloud solutions which can be used to create the cloud computing environment.

> Open-source cloud community generally focusses on private cloud computing arena.

5.8.1 Eucalyptus

Eucalyptus is an open-source Infrastructure-as-a-Service (IaaS) facility for building private or hybrid cloud computing environment. It is a linux-based development that enables cloud features while having installed over distributed computing resources. The name 'Eucalyptus' is an acronym for 'Elastic Utility Computing Architecture for Linking Your Programs To Useful Systems'. Eucalyptus started as a research project at the University of California, United States and the company 'Eucalyptus Systems' was formed in the year of 2009 in order to support the commercialization of the Eucalyptus cloud. In the same year, the Ubuntu 9.04 distribution of Linux OS was included Eucalyptus software into it.

Eucalyptus Systems went into an agreement with Amazon during March 2012, which allowed them to make it compatible with Amazon Cloud. This permits transferring of instances between Eucalyptus private cloud and Amazon public cloud making them a combination for building hybrid cloud environment. Such interoperable pairing allows application developers to maintain the private cloud part (deployed as Eucalyptus) as a *sandbox* for executing prominent codes. Eucalyptus also offers a storage *cloud API* emulating as Amazon's storage service (Amazon S3) API.

5.8.2 OpenNebula

OpenNebula is an open-source Infrastructure-as-a-Service (IaaS) implementation for building public, private and hybrid clouds. Nebula is a Latin word which means as 'cloud'. OpenNebula started as a research project in the year of 2005 and its first release was made during March 2008. By March 2010, the prime authors of OpenNebula founded C12G Labs with the aim of providing value-added professional services to OpenNebula and the cloud is currently managed by them.

OpenNebula is freely available, subject to the requirements of the *Apache License version 2.* Like Eucalyptus, OpenNebula is also compatible with Amazon cloud. Consequently, the distributions of Ubuntu and Red Hat Enterprise later included OpenNebula integrating into them.

5.8.3 Nebula

Nebula is another Open-source cloud computing platform that was developed by NASA and was first released in the year of 2008. It was built to solve the problem of sharing large and complex data sets produced by NASA with outside research collaborators (or with general public in some cases). Nebula is an IaaS implementation that provides compute and storage facility. The Nebula project uses a variety of free- and open-source software. During 2011, Nebula, Inc. was founded by some former NASA employees to commercially promote their products. Later on Nebula developed and released their private cloud solution Nebula One by April 2013.

5.8.4 Nimbus

Nimbus is an open-source IaaS cloud solution compatible with Amazon's cloud services. It was developed at University of Chicago in United States and implemented the Amazon cloud's APIs. The solution was specifically developed to support the scientific community. The Nimbus project has been created by an international collaboration of open-source contributors and institutions. Nimbus code is licensed under the terms of the Apache License version 2.

> *IaaS cloud is developed by installing a host of software solutions to enable IaaS facility over distributed computing system.*

5.8.5 OpenStack

OpenStack is another free and open-source IaaS solution. In July 2010, U.S.-based IaaS cloud service provider Rackspace.com and NASA jointly launched the initiative for an open-source cloud solution called 'OpenStack' to produce a ubiquitous IaaS solution for public and private clouds. NASA donated some parts of the Nebula Cloud Platform technology that it developed. Since then, more than 200 companies (including AT&T, AMD, Dell, Cisco, HP, IBM, Oracle, Red Hat) have contributed in the project. The project was later taken over and promoted by the OpenStack Foundation, a non-profit organization founded in 2012 for promoting OpenStack solution. All the code of OpenStack is freely available under the Apache 2.0 license.

5.8.6 Apache VCL

The Virtual Computing Lab (VCL) initiative was started by NC State University of United States in 2004with the objective of remotely accessing a wide range of computing resources. In November 2008, NCSU donated the source code of VCL to the Apache Software Foundation (ASF) as an incubator project in an effort to expand the VCL community and to foster Open-source development. Later, it emerged as an open-source cloud computing platform called 'Apache Virtual Computing Lab' in 2012. The solution is built with open-source technologies like Linux as OS, Apache as web server, MySQL as database server and PHP language.

5.8.7 Apache CloudStack

Apache CloudStack is another open-source IaaS cloud solution. CloudStack was initially developed by Cloud.com, a software company based in California (United States) which was later acquired by Citrix Systems, another USA based software firm, during 2011. By next year, Citrix Systems handed it over to the Apache Software Foundation and soon after this CloudStack made its first stable release. In addition to its own APIs, CloudStack also supported AWS (Amazon Web Services) APIs which facilitated hybrid cloud deployment.

5.8.8 Enomaly ECP (Elastic Computing Platform)

Enomaly Inc. offered one of the world's first solution for building IaaS platform. The company was founded in 2004 and started developing solution for cloud environment. Enomaly launched Elastic Computing Platform (ECP) in 2009 that offered IaaS facility. Initially, it was launched under open-source initiative but later it was available commercially as closed sourced. Many vendors have used ECP to operate cloud computing platforms for their consumers.

SUMMARY

- ❖ Cloud computing delivers different computing facilities to consumers as utility services. NIST model divides these services primarily into three categories: Infrastructure-as-a-Service (IaaS), Platform-as-a-Service (PaaS) and Software-as-a-Service (SaaS).

- ❖ The three service models (SaaS-PaaS-IaaS) together are known as SPI model of cloud. IaaS provides infrastructure like server, storage and network facilities; PaaS provides application development and deployment environments and SaaS delivers software applications.

- ❖ PaaS layer interacts/communicates with the underlying IaaS layer by using the set of APIs (application program interface) provided by respective IaaS solutions.

- ❖ Computing vendors have launched many other specialized cloud services which ultimately fall under these three primary services of SPI model.

- ❖ Offerings like Security Management-as-a-Service, Storage-as-a-Service, Database-as-a-Service have shown high rate of adoptability among the consumers.

- ❖ Salesforce.com is a popular commercial SaaS offering for enterprises that was pioneer among early cloud services and was launched towards the end of the last century. It delivers customer relationship management (CRM) solutions.

- ❖ Apart from proprietary cloud service offerings from vendors like Salesforce.com, Amazon, Google, many open-source communities have also come up with their own solutions.

- ❖ Eucalyptus, Nebula, Nimbus, OpenStack, CloudStack are few examples of popular open cloud solutions which are mainly used to build private cloud environments.

- ❖ Open cloud solutions which are compatible with some public cloud service systems can be used to create hybrid cloud environment. For instance, Eucalyptus or OpenNebula are compatible with Amazon cloud.

REVIEW QUESTIONS

Computing infrastructure as service: What does it mean and how is it possible?

When computing infrastructure becomes available as service that means people need not to acquire physical computing systems for getting their works done; be it about performing computational task, forming network of computers or storing data. All kinds of computing infrastructural facilities become readily available in virtual mode which users can access through a thin client interface (usually a browser) from any computing device. Users can perform all activities using these virtual computing resources just like they used to do with actual physical computers. Computing vendors arrange, manage and deliver the resources to users over internetwork/Internet. This is called as the computing infrastructure as service.

What activities can be performed by consumers of PaaS facility?

Consumers of PaaS get a computing platform which is actually an application development and deployment environment. PaaS delivers virtual machines loaded with operating system and integrated with the runtime(s) of the desired development and/or deployment platform. Consumers can develop applications over the delivered platform and debug or test them. They can also install and run supported applications over a PaaS offering.

How can a private cloud be enabled to expand into hybrid cloud environment?

For a private cloud solution to expand into hybrid cloud environment, it must be integrated with some public cloud solutions. This is only possible when the private cloud solution is compatible with the public cloud solution. There are instances where open-source cloud solutions (those are used to build private cloud) have gone into agreement with commercial public cloud providers for compatibility. Several open-source cloud solutions like Eucalyptus, OpenNebula and Nimbus implement Amazon cloud's APIs and thus can integrate with Amazon cloud in order to build hybrid cloud.

Do all service providers follow NIST model for cloud service development?

Several architectural models have been proposed for cloud computing over the years. Among them, the model proposed by NIST has been recognized as the globally accepted cloud reference architecture. Service providers generally do not disclose their cloud computing models. But major cloud computing vendors have their own cloud architectural model and it is most likely that they follow their own model.

What is the difference between elasticity and scalability in cloud computing?

One important feature of cloud computing is its scalable nature. A scalable architecture handles growing workload by increasing resource capacity in same proportion. Thus scalability of cloud architecture helps in delivering resources as per demand of application.

Elasticity of cloud facilitates resource quantity and characteristics to vary at runtime. It is associated with the commissioning and decommissioning of resources. It is determined by the relative speed by which resources are allocated (to some process) and are consumed.

MULTIPLE CHOICE QUESTIONS

1. Which cloud service is considered as the most widely used?

   a) Infrastructure-as-a-Service
   b) Platform-as-a-Service
   c) Software-as-a-Service
   d) All of these

2. Which cloud service is known as Hardware-as-a-Service also?

   a) Infrastructure-as-a-Service
   b) Platform-as-a-Service
   c) Software-as-a-Service
   d) Desktop-as-a-Service

3. Which among the following describes a distribution model in which applications are hosted by a service provider and made available to users?

   a) Infrastructure-as-a-Service
   b) Platform-as-a-Service
   c) Software-as-a-Service
   d) All of these

4. Virtual machine in Rackspace cloud is called

   a) Rackspace Server
   b) Cloud Server
   c) RackVM
   d) None of these

5. Identify the odd one

   a) Microsoft Azure
   b) Google App Engine
   c) Force.com
   d) Amazon EC2

6. In IaaS, computing resources are delivered to the consumers

   a) Through remote access
   b) Through distribution

   c) In virtualized form
   d) None of these

7. Which is not considered as one of the three main categories of cloud services?

   a) Software-as-a-Service
   b) Database-as-a-Service
   c) Platform-as-a-Service
   d) Infrastructure-as-a-Service

8. Which cloud computing service model delivers computer, storage, and network to consumers?

   a) Infrastructure-as-a-Service
   b) Platform-as-a-Service
   c) Software-as-a-Service
   d) All of these

9. Retaining with traditional computing environment costs more compared to using cloud computing.

   a) True
   b) False

10. Name of the Open-source cloud computing PaaS facility originally developed by VMWare as

    a) VMWare platform
    b) Cloud foundry
    c) VMW-PaaS
    d) None of these

11. Eucalyptus, Nebula, Nimbus, CloudStack, VLC are few examples of

    a) Open-source cloud services
    b) Closed source cloud services
    c) Proprietary cloud services
    d) Free cloud services

6

Security Reference Model

Security is one of the topmost concerns of any computing model and cloud computing is no exception. Consumers or enterprises moving into cloud need to feel secure about their computing facilities and more importantly about the data they are disclosing to service providers. This is a critical choice for enterprises accustomed to safeguarding data sitting in their own centers in the traditional way of computing. Cloud computing promotes the concept of working on proprietary data and applications outside their jurisdiction.

It is often said that, 'cloud computing is an excellent idea, but cloud security is not good'. The common perception is that the cloud services are not inherently secure. Cloud computing creates scope for scores of possibilities although like any other technology, there are some risks associated with it which can be overcome if understood correctly.

A cloud computing environment can be formed in different ways and there can be several 'cloud formations'. Each form is not suitable for every kind of business operations. Consumers must first understand which among these forms which is best-suited for their purpose. This little judgment can make the security of cloud computing even better than that of traditional in-house computing environments. This chapter focusses on these important aspects.

> If studied and designed appropriately, cloud computing causes no more threat to security than what exist in traditional computing.

6.1 THE SECURITY CONCERN IN CLOUD

Traditional computing systems used to create a security boundary by placing firewalls at the gateways through which the network used to communicate with the outer world. Firewall blocks unwanted traffic trying to access the network it protects and thus only authenticated accesses are allowed into the system. Thus, malicious accesses get blocked at firewalls in the traditional data centers in order to keep the system protected from outside threats.

But this strategy only makes sense when all applications and data reside within one network of security perimeter. Traditional data centers allow *perimeterized* (i.e. within organization's own *network boundary* or perimeter) access to computing resources. But, the *de-perimeterization* (to open-up the interaction with outer network) and erosion of *trust boundaries* that was happening in enterprise applications, have been amplified and accelerated by cloud computing.

Cloud computing model breaks this barrier for multiple benefits. It moves computing resources outside the traditional security boundaries. Resources are remotely accessed by consumers of outer network domains and hence the traditional concept of *security boundary* no more applies here. This raised the need for a new philosophy that could provide security to computing resources at data centers, accepting the necessity of de-perimeterization.

Cloud deployments often create confusion about their locations. For example, public or private clouds are often considered as off-premises/external or on-premises/internal systems respectively which may not be accurate in all situations. Hence, it is important to understand where security boundaries lie in terms of cloud computing. A new security reference model was required to address this security concern and many initiatives have been taken in this regard.

> *Cloud computing moves beyond the concept of working inside protected network boundary.*

6.2 CLOUD SECURITY WORKING GROUPS

Many organizations and groups have worked separately on developing a cloud security model over the years. They focused on different cloud security aspects and all of these efforts put together have contributed in developing a model to address security standards in cloud computing. This section discusses the efforts of two such bodies who have contributed the most in this development.

6.2.1 The Cloud Security Alliance

The Cloud Security Alliance (CSA) is an organization focused on the promotion of a secured cloud computing environment. A group of industry leaders who realized the need for establishing an appropriate guidance for the implementation and use of cloud computing formed the alliance in the last quarter of 2008. The organization is registered as a non-profit corporation in Washington in United States and has chapters across the world.

The alliance published a white paper titled 'Security Guidance for Critical Areas of Focus in Cloud Computing' which was released in 2009 focussing on different areas of concerns related to cloud computing. Updated versions of the document were released in subsequent years. This publication is regarded as an important initiative and the document works as the key source of knowledge in cloud security domain both for providers as well as for consumers.

> *Document titled 'Security Guidance for Critical Areas of Focus in Cloud Computing', released by CSA, has been considered as vital testimonial on cloud computing security.*

In the third version of the document published in 2013, CSA categorizes the cloud security related issues into fourteen different sections (earlier it was fifteen) as follows:

- Cloud Computing Architectural Framework,
- Governance and Enterprise Risk Management,
- Legal Issues: Contracts and Electronic Discovery,
- Compliance and Audit management,
- Information Management and Data Security,
- Interoperability and Portability,
- Traditional Security, Business Continuity and Disaster Recovery,
- Data Center Operations,
- Incident Response,

- Application Security,
- Encryption and Key Management,
- Identity, Entitlement and Access Management,
- Virtualization and
- Security-as-a-Service.

CSA also recommends the best practices and offers guidance for security maintenance in cloud that helps in building quality service offerings. They provide a comprehensive roadmap to consumers for building positive relationship with service providers which is very important in cloud computing. The stated missions of the Cloud Security Alliance include offering education and promoting the use of best practices for assuring security in cloud computing.

The primary objectives of CSA include the following:

- Encourage to develop a common level of understanding between cloud service providers and service consumers regarding the necessary security requirements.
- Developing best practices related to cloud computing security by promoting independent researches in the field.
- Initiate educational programs to spread awareness about proper usages of the services.
- Generate a list of issues to be agreed upon for cloud security assurance.

CSA's initiatives and expertise have enriched the cloud computing world in many ways. A cloud security certification program for users was launched by CSA in 2010 which was first of its kind. They also offered a certification program for service providers known as 'CSA Security, Trust and Assurance Registry' (STAR) for self-assessment of providers which can be conducted by several CSA-authorized third-party agencies.

> *Security certification programs offered by CSA can develop confidence among cloud service providers as well as consumers.*

6.2.2 Jericho Forum Group

The Jericho Forum was formed in 2004 as an international IT security association of companies, vendors, government groups and academics whose mission was to improve the security of global open-network computing environment.

In the early years of the current century, the corporate network boundaries were fast becoming blurred as enterprises started to work in collaboration with third-party computing vendors through Internet. In 2003, a group of concerned CISOs (Chief Information Security Officers) formed a forum to discuss this issue. This initiative later emerged as 'Jericho Forum Group'. In 2004, Jericho Forum officially announced its existence and set its office in UK. The term 'de-perimeterization' was first coined by a member of this group to describe the blurring network boundaries. The forum concentrated to find a security solution for the *collaborative computing* environment. In 2009, this forum proposed a security model for cloud computing that has been accepted as the global standard. Later, The Jericho Forum became a part of another vendor-neutral industry consortium entitled as 'The Open Group' and declared its closure in 2013 as their objectives were fulfilled.

> *Jericho Forum was an international consortium formed with the objective of addressing concerns related to de-perimeterized computing environment.*

The collaborations among different groups have contributed positively in development of cloud security framework. For instance on several occasions, Jericho Forum and the Cloud Security Alliance had worked together to promote best practices for secured collaboration in the cloud. Initiatives and recommendations from many other organizations and informal groups have also contributed in developing a standard cloud security model. Major contributions regarding this have come from National Institute of Standards and Technology (NIST), European Union Agency for Network and Information Security (ENISA), Distributed Management Task Force (DMTF), Open Cloud Consortium (OCC) and the Object Management Group (OMG).

6.3 ELEMENTS OF CLOUD SECURITY MODEL

Analyst firm Gartner published a report titled as 'Assessing the Security Risks of Cloud Computing' in 2008. The report focussed on seven security issues which should be analyzed while moving into cloud. These seven issues can be considered as the elements for designing good security policy in computing. Cloud consumers must query to the service providers regarding these issues and ensure maximum protection and security.

1. *Privileged user access*: Here, the user means 'users' at the provider's end who are managing the cloud. With cloud computing, sensitive data of enterprises go out and consumers generally loose physical control over security of data. Hence, the consumers must ask for specific information from the provider regarding the people who manage the cloud. The queries may contain as 'how much access they have over data' or 'how their accesses are being controlled' and so on.

2. *Regulatory compliance*: Service providers may store and manage data of enterprises in cloud computing but enterprises are ultimately responsible for integrity and privacy of their own data. Hence, consumers should opt for providers who have obtained security certifications to prove credentials and conduct regular audits by reputed external audit firms to check compliance. According to Gartner, the consumers must not provide their sensitive data to those service providers who deny to undergo such scrutiny.

3. *Data location*: Data in cloud are stored in data centers of the service providers spread over the globe. Consumers generally would not have any knowledge about where their data are being stored. Even they may not know in which country or region their data is hosted. In case of specific compliance requirements of consumers, providers must abide by consumer's request for storing their data in particular region or country. Gartner advices consumers to enquire regarding this as well.

4. *Data segregation*: Cloud computing is generally a shared service. Storage in cloud are also managed in shared environment where data of multiple consumers are stored in same place. This may pose security threat. Providers must implement mechanisms to logically segregate stored data of different consumers. Encryption is one such technique but providers must ensure that any of such technique being designed by the experts is tested extensively. Otherwise undesirable accidents may create problems.

5. *Recovery*: Recovery of data in case of any disaster is another crucial issue. Cloud service providers must declare what will happen to the data in such cases and how long will it take for recovery of data as well as for restoration of the services. For a complete restoration, the provider must maintain data and application infrastructure across multiple sites.

6. *Investigative support*: Investigation of inappropriate or illegal activity may be a difficult task in cloud computing. This is primarily because data are organized and stored across ever-changing set of nodes. Co-location of stored data from multiple consumers is another problem in conducting the investigations. Consumers must ask for contractual commitment from the providers for support in some particular types of investigation if required. Consumers must also check whether the concerned vendor has supported such activities in previous instances or not.

7. *Long-term viability*: Ideally, no reputed cloud service provider will shut business or will be acquired by some larger vendor. But if such thing happens, the question will be raised about the consumer data. Will it remain available? Consumers must enquire what will happen in such situations in detail.

Satisfactory outcomes of the analysis of these issues indicate towards a secured cloud computing environment. Expertise and qualifications of the cloud designer, developer, policy maker and administrator are subjects of these reviews. Aware consumers must ensure all of these activities while moving in cloud. Adoption of services of reputed vendors may eliminate these concerns to a great extent.

> Gartner advices consumers to seek utmost transparent reviews related to seven specific issues from service providers before moving into cloud.

6.4 CLOUD SECURITY REFERENCE MODEL

The cloud computing community and many organizations working in the field of network security were working for years to develop a model to address cloud security. Many among these organizations, unofficial groups and researchers proposed different models for the purpose.

The Jericho Forum group, which was working to find solution for the de-perimeterization problem, came up with a model called 'Cloud Cube Model' to address this issue. This cube model has gained global acceptance by the experts and is considered as the security reference model for cloud computing. The Cloud Cube Model suggested by Jericho Forum has considered the multi-dimensional elements of cloud computing and appropriately suggested how to approach towards its security.

6.4.1 The Cloud Cube Model

The Jericho Forum proposed Cloud Cube Model in 2009 defining a three-dimensional cube. Their purpose was to provide a basis for standardization of a secure cloud computing. The model was originally created to address the issue of de-perimeterization network which was causing the erosion of network security boundaries among collaborating businesses from beginning of the current century.

The model suggests that the consumers should not measure cloud security only depending on the narrow perspectives of 'internal' or 'external' systems. Many other factors are related with the issue like whether everything is under consumer's own network boundary, who is responsible for the management of the cloud and/or who have the access rights to the cloud and so on.

The Cloud Cube Model illustrates different permutations available in cloud offerings and presents four criteria to differentiate various types of cloud formations. The model helps to understand how security issues can be approached in cloud computing too.

> *Jericho Forum's model addresses cloud security using a three-dimensional cube.*

6.4.1.1 Primary Objectives

The cloud cube model contributes much in understanding security perspectives in any formations of cloud. The primary objectives behind building the cloud cube model can be listed as follows:

- To represent different formations of clouds.
- To highlight the key characteristics of each cloud formation.
- To represent the benefits and risks associated with each form of cloud.
- To focus that traditional non-cloud approach is not totally obsolete and may sometimes be a suitable choice for operating the particular business functions.
- To present a roadmap for more detailed study and to make the environment more secure.

6.4.1.2 The Four Criteria

The cloud cube model is designed to represent four security related criteria. Jericho Forum suggests consumers to decide about these four issues while forming cloud computing environment.

- Whether data will be stored internally within *physical boundary* of the organization or to some external location?
- Will the cloud be formed using *proprietary technology* (technology that is property of someone) of some computing firm or by using *open technology* that is open to everyone for use? It is to note that, here 'technology' means 'cloud technology' or operating standard of cloud.
- Whether the cloud will operate within organization's *network boundary* (the logical security perimeter) only or outside the boundary also?
- Will the development and maintenance of the cloud service be outsourced to some third party or will be done with in-house team?

These four criteria are represented across different dimensions of a cube. The answers of these four questions decide the nature of the cloud formation. Since there are four issues to decide upon and the question raised for each issue can have two probable answers; there can be 4^2 or 16 different forms of cloud computing environment.

According to Jericho Forum's model, there can be 16 (sixteen) different types of cloud formations.

6.4.1.3 The Dimensions

The cube model uses four security dimensions for representing different characteristics to distinguish cloud formations from each other. These dimensions are – data boundary, ownership of the cloud, cloud security boundary and sourcing pattern of the cloud.

Data Boundary: Internal (I) / External (E)

This security dimension represents the physical storage location of organization's data. Since, data is a critical element of any computing system; its storage is a vital attribute. The storage location of the data can be either Internal (I) being within the organization's *physical boundary* or External (E) as stored outside. For example, storage inside an organization's data center would be internal while Google Cloud Storage is external to them.

It is important to note that *external storage* location does not necessarily mean lesser security. Security depends on many factors especially on how it is used. The data boundary dimension divides the entire cube in two parts as shown in Figure 6.1.

Data boundary aspect determines physical storage location of organizations' own data.

Ownership: Proprietary (P) / Open (O)

This dimension determines the ownership of the technology (i.e., cloud technology) used for building the cloud. There can be two categories of technology as Proprietary (P) and Open (O). Proprietary means that the detail about the technology is a trade secret. It is owned by some individual or organization through the *patent*. Cloud services developed using such technology generally would not integrate easily with other cloud services without support from the owner.

Reputed commercial vendors generally prefer to build services using their own proprietary technologies. But, those services would not interoperate with other cloud technologies. This limits *interoperability*. Thus, it becomes difficult for consumers operating in a proprietary cloud services to move to some other cloud system if they are not satisfied with some services. On the other hand, since proprietary services do not collaborate with other services without agreement that provide an isolated and secure environment to some extent.

Open cloud services are built following some published and recognized *open standards*. Since, the open standards are not anyone's private property more numbers of vendors deliver services

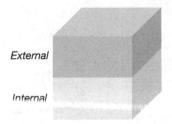

External

Internal

FIG 6.1: The External/Internal dimension

FIG 6.2: The Proprietary/Open dimensions

in this domain. Such services can easily collaborate with all other clouds that are using open cloud technology. Figure 6.2 represents these two technologies dividing the cube into two parts.

> *The ownership of technology (proprietary/open) determines the degree of interoperability among different cloud services.*

Security Boundary: Perimeterized (Per) / De-perimeterized (D-p)

Jericho Forum's model uses this third dimension to represent what they call the 'architectural mindset'. If it is necessary to operate inside the traditional network security boundary or not? If yes, then the system is Perimeterized (Per) otherwise it is to be called as De-perimeterized (D-p).

Traditional network boundaries are often indicated by network firewalls. Perimeterized approach enhances security but prevents collaboration since it does not allow other systems to access anything inside its own perimeter. In this model though collaboration can be established with external computing systems by using VPN (virtual private network) technique. VPN expands the *network boundary* but keeps the computing environment perimeterized during collaboration as it uses local networking protocols (instead of global internet protocols). At the end of collaboration the perimeter can be withdrawn back to its original form by terminating VPN.

De-perimeterized system shows the natural intent to collaborate with the systems outside its own perimeter. Jericho Forum has defined a *Collaboration Oriented Architecture* (COA) framework for secure collaboration in de-perimeterized environment. Such systems are protected by using techniques like data-level authentication, encryption etc. Figure 6.3 represents a divided cloud cube operated by this perimeterized/de-perimeterized dimensions. From Figures 6.1 and 6.3, it can be understood that a perimeterized or de-perimeterized cloud environment can use both internal and external data storages.

The above discussed three dimensions of the cube represent data boundary, ownership and security boundary of cloud. Depending on data-boundary (I/E) and ownership (P/O), there

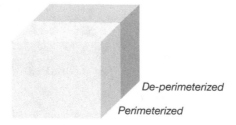

FIG 6.3: The Perimeterized / De-perimeterized dimensions

can be four types of cloud formations as IP, IO, EP and EO. Each of these forms comes with either of the two architectural mindsets as Perimeterized or De-perimeterized as per their respective security boundaries. Hence as taken together, there are total eight possible cloud formations as Per (IP, IO, EP, EO) and D-p (IP, IO, EP, EO).

> *The four basic cloud formations as Internal/Proprietary, Internal/Open, External/Proprietary and External/Open can either be Perimeterized or De-perimeterized.*

Sourcing: Insourced / Outsourced

This security dimension indicates who delivers and manages the service. Or, whom the enterprise relies on to run the cloud? If the service is delivered by (or outsourced to) some third party then it is called *outsourced*. If it is provided by organization's own/internal team, then it is *insourced*. The service sourcing is not a technical issue rather it is basically a business decision.

While insourced cloud services indicate towards private cloud (since they are built by an organization for their own exclusive usage), outsourced service can deliver both public and private cloud. Private cloud may provide better outcome in terms of information security and privacy but lot of that would depend on the expertise of the in-house team that manages the cloud. Reputed cloud service providers are often better equipped to deliver a secured service. Thus, the sourcing decision must take care of the expertise and reputation of the team that is going to deliver the cloud.

> *In-sourcing of service does not mean better security. Security of cloud service largely depends on the expertise of the delivery team.*

Sourcing can either be outsourced or insourced for each of the eight cloud forms discussed earlier. In Jericho Forum's Cloud Cube Model, this *fourth dimension* is represented by two different colours for painting the cubes. Hence the eight smaller cubes that come out after combining the first three dimensions discussed above can take either of the two colours as shown in Figure 6.4.

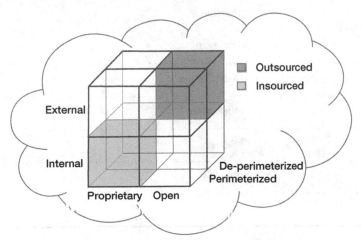

FIG 6.4: Jericho Forum's Cloud Cube Model[7]

It (figure 6.4) represents the cloud cube model after combining the four security dimensions together. In this model, the top-right-rear E / O / D-p cloud formation is considered as the 'sweet spot' where optimal flexibility and collaboration can be achieved. On the other hand, the bottom-left-front I / P / Per cloud formation is the most restricted one.

It is to note that although in the above model (Figure 6.4), the top-right cube is shown in the shade for outsourced service and bottom-left cube is shown in the shade for insourced service, those are just indicative. Any of the eight cubes can take any among those two shades.

6.5 EXAMINING CLOUD SECURITY AGAINST TRADITIONAL COMPUTING

Cloud computing may be built and delivered by providers (when the service is outsourced) but the security of the computing environment does not solely depend on the service providers. Consumers and other related actors have important role to play in securing the entire cloud computing environment.

Collaboration is the tune of cloud based business systems. Both consumers and service providers have their share of responsibilities in ensuring adequate security of a cloud system. Security perspectives have to be measured appropriately to strengthen this protection before moving into cloud. *Cloud security reference model* provides guidance in performing this analysis.

In *outsourced* service model, IaaS consumers have maximum security management responsibility among all cloud service consumers. The responsibility (of consumers) decreases as they move from IaaS service towards SaaS service. Figure 6.5 represents the security management responsibilities in both traditional and cloud-based computing environments. It can be observed

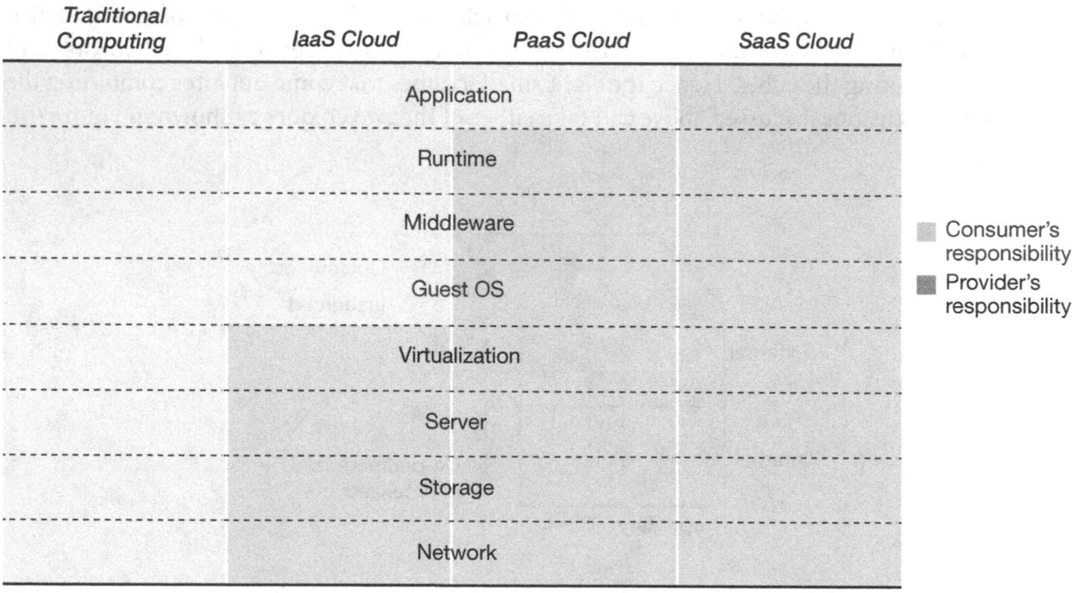

FIG 6.5: Share of security management responsibilities in traditional computing and cloud service environment

Table 6.1 Security management responsibilities in cloud by service type

Service Type	Security management responsibilities at			
	Infrastructure Level	Platform Level	Application Level	Operation Level
Outsourced/IaaS	Provider	Consumer	Consumer	Consumer
Outsourced/PaaS	Provider	Provider	Consumer	Consumer
Outsourced/SaaS	Provider	Provider	Provider	Consumer
insourced/IaaS	Consumer	Consumer	Consumer	Consumer
insourced/PaaS	Consumer	Consumer	Consumer	Consumer
insourced/SaaS	Consumer	Consumer	Consumer	Consumer

that cloud service providers protect a large part of the system depending on the type of services they offer. With a reputed service provider in place, this part becomes highly protected.

Since, consumers no more need to manage everything starting from the bottom of the stack (like in case of traditional computing as shown in the figure above), they can concentrate more on the security of a limited area. This may strengthen the system with service of reputed provider.

Thus, with appropriate selection of cloud security model for business implementation, the cloud computing environment may even provide more security than the traditional environment. Table 6.1 represents the security management responsibilities of providers and consumers for different cloud services both for insourced and outsourced cloud environments.

It can be observed that similar to *in-house* traditional computing environment, consumers have all the security management responsibility in any insourced cloud services. This opens up another opportunity where consumers can enjoy all other benefits of cloud computing without relying on anyone else regarding security of their computing environments. Thus, the argument against the security threat at cloud computing against *in-house* traditional computing stands invalid if consumer opts for on-premises, insourced (internal-perimeterized and insourced) cloud model.

In traditional computing, enterprises generally opted for outsourcing. That is similar to choosing among the internally perimeterized outsourcing and externally perimeterized and deperimeterized outsourcing models which are present in cloud computing also. Thus, it can never be said that traditional computing is more secured than cloud computing when service outsourcing is dependent on some third party.

The main security concerns are raised against the most interesting model of cloud that is, the public cloud. The actual essence of cloud computing can be experienced under this model. Questions can be raised regarding the security of this provider managed cloud computing environment where consumers have no control or authority in security management. Here, it should be remembered that in traditional computing also large part of the enterprise computing systems are/were outsourced and managed by third party vendors as several IT service companies. That also invites threat to internal system security. Rather, with adoption of standard cloud services from globally reputed service providers, the system promises to become more trustworthy.

> *Cloud computing causes no more security concerns over traditional computing. Moreover adoption of reputed public cloud services for appropriate application can be of more trustworthy.*

6.6 SECURITY POLICY

Security policies are the sets of documentations that guide for reliable security implementation in a system. Applicable standards and guidelines flow to the subsequent levels from this policy documentations defined by the highest level authority.

Cloud *security strategy* define different policies like system security policies, software policies and information system policies etc. A cloud provider must satisfy all of the security regulations and directives as per those policies to make the cloud system secure. Apart from these security policies, the cloud computing environment asks the organizations to maintain some general policies related to security as stated below.

Management Policy: This is a general, high-level policy defined by senior management of an organization. It governs security guidelines throughout the enterprise, like frequency of backup operation, selection regarding cloud deployment type and sourcing and others.

Regulatory Policy: Organizations have no role in this policy making. These policies are usually specific to the industry and/or government under which the organizations operate. Regulatory policies are important to maintain compliance, regulation and/or other legal requirements.

Advisory Policy: This security policy is not mandatory but strongly suggested. This even provides with details of consequences in case of failure to follow them. One advisory policy may suggest periodic security auditing by an external audit firm.

Informative Policy: This is about making everyone concerned about the security issues. The intended audience of these information could be certain internal (within the organization) or external parties. One such policy may try to make everyone aware about some specific situation.

> *Along with system related security policy, enterprises should take care of regulatory policy too.*

6.7 TRUSTED CLOUD COMPUTING

'Trusted Computing' is a term that refers to technologies, design and policies to develop a highly secure and reliable computing system. Though cloud computing empowers users and enterprises by providing utility computing service on-demand, a lack of trust between cloud service consumers and providers may prevent the widespread acceptance of these cloud services. To increase the adoption of cloud services, cloud service providers must establish trust initially and ensure security to ease the worries of a large number of consumers.

The uses of technology, to some extent can enhance trust, though it is more a social issue than a technical problem. Cloud service providers are making substantial efforts to gain the confidence of customers by minimizing the threat of insider and outsiders' attacks. But, concerned consumers remain unsure regarding the security of this new computing system and feel insecure to put their confidential data in cloud.

This trust should be raised to a level of consumer's faith. A certified assurance regarding the protection of the cloud system against attack is a definite way to enhance this trust relationship. To satisfy the legal and forensic requirements, a trusted cloud provider may include security information and event management (SIEM) capability that can manage records and logs in a manner that evades legal constraints.

> *Trusted cloud computing can be viewed as a way to ensure that the system acts in a predictable manner as intended.*

6.7.1 How to Make a Cloud Service Trusted

The trust building initiative in cloud computing is responsibility of the service providers. They need to identify processes to strengthen the trust between them and the consumers. Consumers may be interested in security implementation approaches but it is neither a possible option nor even feasible for the providers to share the security measures with consumers in details. However, the service consumers can query regarding their doubts to assess security risks before adopting the service.

A more appropriate and feasible option for the service providers is to secure security certification for their cloud services from one or more internationally recognized reviewer organizations. 'Security, Trust & Assurance Registry (STAR)' from CSA is one of such certification programs offered by Cloud Security Alliance (CSA). These certificates act as quality stamps and guarantee for the secured services. These give the confidence to the consumers to adopt the services.

Larger cloud providers like Google, Amazon and Microsoft have already taken steps to bring transparency regarding security management. Cloud computing is in its initial days and may bring security concerns among consumers. But, it cannot be denied that most of the users being managed by the experts of reputed service providers have been better protected in cloud environment than when they used to manage their own security.

> *Reputation or trust building is a time taking process and larger cloud providers have already taken measures to establish this trust.*

SUMMARY

- ❖ Cloud computing expands itself beyond the traditional perimeterized access to resources in computing. Here, the collaboration is the tune and thus de-perimeterization is integral.
- ❖ Apart from de-perimeterization, external or off-premises access to resources also brings security concerns for cloud service consumers.

❖ Several groups and organizations have worked over the years to introduce best practices and a standard security model for cloud computing. Cloud Security Alliance and Jericho Forum are pioneers among them.

❖ Jericho Forum's Cloud Cube Model, introduced in 2009, has been accepted as the standard model for cloud security. The model clearly distinguishes different formations of cloud and focuses on the benefits and risks associated with each form.

❖ Cloud cube model talks about four issues or dimensions while forming cloud environment and represents those four dimensions through the uses of a three-dimensional cube.

❖ The cube model represents sixteen (16) different formations of cloud. Consumers must analyze their needs and select the most suitable cloud for their requirement from those suggested by Jericho Forum.

❖ With appropriate choice of cloud for computing needs of customers and security, the outcome can be better than that of traditional computing.

❖ There can be no comparison of traditional outsourcing with cloud outsourcing when cloud service is delivered by globally reputed computing vendors, rather than by IT service companies as in traditional computing.

❖ Service providers should take appropriate measures to develop trust among consumers about their cloud environment. Acquiring security certifications through an audit conducted by some external agency may enhance this trust regarding the service among consumers.

REVIEW QUESTIONS

What is the importance of the security reference model in cloud computing?

Cloud computing is made for collaboration and accessed remotely. It allows de-perimeterization that is admission of external systems into organization's network security boundary. Users may not own a major part of the systems they work in. Accountability of service providers plays an important role in this computing model. Thus, the security erupts as a basic concern. A guideline for managing security makes the scenario easy for consumers while moving into cloud environment. The model distinguishes all of the possible formations of cloud and highlights their pros and cons both.

Were the four dimensions of cloud security model relevant in traditional computing too?

Outsourcing of computing was present in traditional computing also. Thus, the sourcing dimension (third dimension of cube model) stands relevant there. In traditional approach, data center location could either be on-premises or off-premises. Hence data storage location could be internal or external. Eventually, the data boundary dimension (first dimension of cube model) is also relevant there. The second dimension becomes relevant as the ownership of technology used in traditional computing could be both proprietary and open. Now in relation with the third dimension, it we can say that the traditional computing used to prefer the perimeterized security approach. But in special cases, de-perimeterization could be done through virtual private network. Consequently, the cloud computing is primarily created to take the advantages of de-perimeterized computing approach.

What is Cloud Security Alliance?

Cloud Security Alliance (CSA) is a non-profit organization formed by a group of industry leaders, focussing on implementation of wide range of initiatives in cloud security. CSA promotes cloud security awareness programs, regularly publishes security guidance on cloud computing and offers security certifications. The organization was formed in 2008 and registered in United States.

IT outsourcing is more secured under which model: traditional computing or cloud computing?

Outsourcing model of computing can be of two types as perimeterized and de-perimeterized. Primeterization keeps the computing environment under the network boundary of consumer enterprise. Thus, it is sometimes considered as more secured option than de-perimeterization because all resources, especially storage and others remain under the control of the enterprise. Otherwise, the security in outsourcing mainly depends on the reputation and expertise of the computing vendor. In this regard, public cloud services offered by reputed computing vendors are often considered as more secured, reliable and robust in comparison to traditional model of outsourcing.

Is there any way of enjoying facilities of cloud computing without compromising security?

This is absolutely possible with private cloud deployment model. In private cloud, consumers can get all benefits of cloud computing like resource pooling, on-demand service, elasticity etc. Only thing they do not get is multi-tenancy facility which makes public cloud services more cost-effective. Private clouds can provide traditional computing like security confidence both for insourced and outsourced services.

MULTIPLE CHOICE QUESTIONS

1. What is the name of the organization majorly helping to foster security standards for cloud computing?

   a) NIST
   b) Cloud Security WatchDog
   c) Cloud Security Alliance
   d) Open Cloud Consortium

2. 'Perimeter' in the peremeterized computing environment is represented by

   a) Organization's physical boundary
   b) In-house data center boundary
   c) IP addresses
   d) Network firewalls

3. On how many elements of cloud security model it was focused in Gartner's report titled as 'Assessing the Security Risks of Cloud Computing' published in 2008?

   a) 6
   b) 7
   c) 8
   d) None of these

4. Who proposed the globally-accepted model for cloud security?

   a) Cloud Security Alliance
   b) Jericho Forum group
   c) NIST
   d) Object Management Group (OMG)

5. Into how many visible cubes, the model cube was divided in Jericho Forum's security model?

    a) 8
    b) 16
    c) 4
    d) 32

6. How many dimensions exist in Cloud Cube Model?

    a) 1
    b) 2
    c) 3
    d) 4

7. Which among of the following security policies demands special attention in cloud computing?

    a) Data security policy
    b) Security management policy
    c) Advisory policy
    d) Regulatory policy

8. Which among of the four dimensions of the cloud cube model is represented by the colour?

    a) Data Boundary
    b) Ownership
    c) Security Boundary
    d) Sourcing

9. De-perimeterization in computing promotes

    a) Outsourcing
    b) Use of open technology
    c) Collaboration
    d) All of these

10. The statement 'Internal data source can be used in de-perimeterized computing environment' is

    a) True
    b) False

11. In traditional perimeterized computing environment, collaboration with external systems are established through

    a) Virtual private network technique
    b) Virtual drive technique
    c) De-perimeterization technique
    d) None of these

7 | Resource Virtualization

Virtualization is the most significant among several enabling technologies of cloud computing. In fact, technologist could think about the delivery of computing resources as service stepping on the concept of virtualization. Along with this, implementation of many essential features of cloud computing has been made possible by virtualization technique.

As virtualization has become an essential ingredient of cloud computing, it is important to understand the concepts of virtualization and the underlying techniques required to virtualize physical computing resources. Running multiple virtual computers simultaneously on a single set of physical resources provide great advantages in terms of optimum resource utilization making it a dynamic system in nature and enhancing security of the system through resource abstraction.

A software module called 'hypervisor' plays critical role in virtualization. Different server virtualization techniques along with hypervisor based virtualization approaches have been discussed in this chapter in detail. Apart from many advantages, the chapter also focuses on few pitfalls of virtualization which should be addressed appropriately during system designing.

7.1 WHAT IS VIRTUALIZATION

Virtualization refers to the representation of physical computing resources in simulated form having made through the software. This special layer of software (installed over active physical machines) is referred as layer of virtualization. This layer transforms the physical computing resources into virtual form which users use to satisfy their computing needs. Figure 7.1 represents the basic concept of virtualization in simplified form which has been elaborated in the subsequent sections.

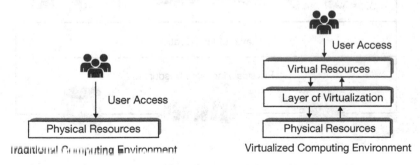

FIG 7.1: Users' interaction with computer in traditional and virtualized computing environment

In simple sense, the virtualization is the logical separation of physical resources from direct access of users to fulfill their service needs. Although, at the end, actually the physical resources are responsible to provide those services. The idea of virtualizing a computer system's resources (including processor, memory, storage etc.) has been well-established since many decades.

Virtualization provides a level of *logical abstraction* that liberates user-installed software (starting from operating system and other systems as well as application software) from being tied to a specific set of hardware. Rather, the users install everything over the logical operating environment (rather than physical ones) having created through virtualization.

> *Virtualization decouples the physical computing resources from direct access of users.*

7.2 VIRTUALIZING PHYSICAL COMPUTING RESOURCES

Any kind of computing resources can be virtualized. Apart from basic computing devices like processor, primary memory, other resources like storage, network devices (like switch, router etc.), the communication links and peripheral devices (like keyboard, mouse, printer etc.) can also be virtualized. But, it should be noted that in case of core computing resources a virtualized component can only be operational when a physical resource empowers it from the back end. For example, a virtual processor can only work when there is a physical processor linked with it.

Figure 7.2 represents a virtualized computing environment comprising of processor, memory and storage disk. The layers of virtualization transforms these physical computing devices into virtual form and presents them before user. The important thing here to be noted is that the simulated devices produced through virtualization may or may not resemble the actual physical components (in quality, architecture or in quantity). For instance, in the given figure below, users get access to three processors while there is one physical processor in reality. Or, 32-bit processor can be produced (in virtual form) from 64-bit actual physical processor.

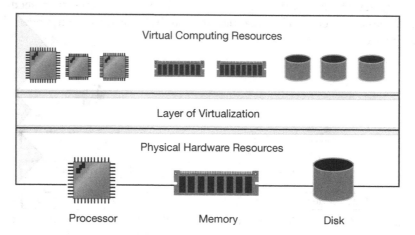

FIG 7.2: Transformation of physical resources into virtual resources through virtualization

The software for virtualization consists of a set of control programs. It offers all of the physical computing resources in custom made simulated (virtual) form which users can utilize to build virtual computing setup or *virtual computers* or *virtual machines* (VM). Users can install operating system over virtual computer just like they do it over physical computer. Operating system installed over virtual computing environment is known as *guest operating system*. When virtualization technique is in place, the guest OS executes as if it were running directly on the physical machine.

> *Virtual computers can be built using virtual computing resources produced by virtualization.*

7.3 UNDERSTANDING ABSTRACTION

The theory of virtualization is rooted around the idea of providing logical access to physical resources. Virtualization can be defined as the abstraction of different computing resources like processor, memory, storage, network etc.

Abstraction is the process of hiding the complex and non-essential characteristics of a system. Through abstraction, a system can be presented in simplified manner for some particular use after omitting unwanted details from users. In computing, abstraction is implemented through the layers of software. The layer of operating system can be treated as a layer of abstraction.

In cloud computing, resource virtualization which adds a layer of software over physical computing resources to create virtual resources, acts as a layer of abstraction. This abstraction makes it easier to offer more flexible, reliable and powerful service.

> *Virtualization creates a layer of abstraction and masks physical resources from external access.*

7.4 BUSINESS BENEFITS OF VIRTUALIZATION

Beside different technical benefits (discussed later), there are many business benefits of virtualization also. Virtualization radically improves the flexibility and availability of computing resources and organizations can gain in terms of business. In 2008, American company Ziff-Davis Inc. conducted a survey among 167 IT decision makers in order to identify the common drivers behind adopting virtualization. The survey had been sponsored by Cognizant Technology Solutions Inc.

Nearly more than seventy-five percent respondents identified both lower hardware cost and improvement in server utilization ratio as two most significant drivers of virtualization. According to the analyst firm, Gartner, more than 70 percent of any organizations' IT budgets are spent on infrastructure. This is where virtualization can help.

Although there are several kinds of virtualization technologies like server virtualization, storage virtualization, network virtualization etc. Among them, the major factor driving the move to virtualization is server virtualization which is the most important part of computing resource virtualization technology. Next part of the chapter discusses the server virtualization in detail.

7.5 MACHINE OR SERVER LEVEL VIRTUALIZATION

Machine virtualization (also called *server virtualization*) is the concept of creating virtual machine (or *virtual computer*) on actual physical machine. The parent system on which the virtual machines run is called the *host system*, and the virtual machines are themselves referred as *guest systems*.

In conventional computing system, there has always been a *one-to-one relationship* between physical computer and operating system. At a time, a single OS can run over them. Hardware virtualization eliminates this limitation of having a one-to-one relationship between physical hardware and operating system. It facilitates the running of multiple computer systems having their own operating systems on single physical machine. As shown in Figure 7.3, the OS of the guest systems running over same physical machine need not to be similar.

All these virtual machines running over a single host system, remain independent of each other. Operating systems are installed into those virtual machines. These guest systems can access the hardware of the host system and can run applications within its own operating environment.

> Virtualized physical server can host multiple virtual machines, where each one of them can have a different OS.

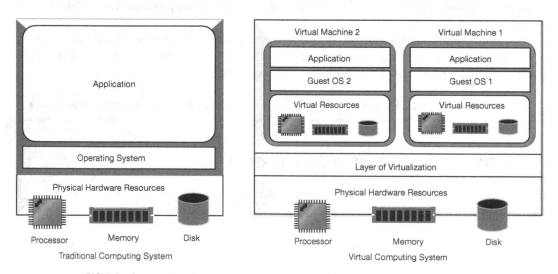

FIG 7.3: Conventional computing system versus Virtualized computing system

Table 7.1 Comparison between non-virtualized and virtualized machine environments

Non-Virtualized Machine Environment	Virtualized Machine Environment
At a moment, one single OS can run on a physical machine.	Multiple OS can run simultaneously on one physical machine.
Application and hardware system remain tightly coupled.	Virtual Machines isolates applications from the underlying hardware.

Resource utilization rate is low in most of the times.	Resource utilization improves as multiple VMs share same set of physical resources.
These increase cost of business due to low resource utilization.	They are cost-effective if planned properly.
They have the inflexible approach.	They provide lot of flexibility to system designers.

7.5.1 The Layer of Virtualization

From Figure 7.3, it can be seen that virtual machines are created over the virtualization layers. This virtualization layer is actually a set of control programs that creates the environment for the virtual machines to run on. This layer provides the access to the system resources to the virtual machines. It also controls and monitors the execution of the virtual machines over it. This software layer is referred as the *Hypervisor* or *Virtual Machine Monitor (VMM)*.

The hypervisor abstracts the underlying software and/or hardware environments and represents virtual system resources to its users. This layer also facilitates the existence of multiple VMs those are not bound to share same (underlying) OS kernel. Due to this reason, it becomes possible to run different operating systems in those virtual machines as created over a hypervisor. The hypervisor layer provides an administrative system console through which the virtual system environment (like number of virtual components to produce or capacity of the components) can be managed.

7.5.2 Machine Virtualization Techniques

There are two different techniques of server or machine virtualization as hosted approach and the bare metal approach. The techniques differ depending on the type of hypervisor used. Although the techniques are different but they have the same end or ultimate goal by creating a platform where multiple virtual machines can share same system resources. Each technique is simply a different way of achieving this goal.

7.5.2.1 Hosted Approach

In this approach, an operating system is first installed on the physical machine to activate it. This OS installed over the host machine is referred as *host operating system*. The hypervisor is then installed over this host OS. This type of hypervisor is referred to as *Type 2 hypervisor* or *Hosted hypervisor*. Figure 7.4 represents the hosted machine virtualization technique.

So, here the host OS works as the first layer of software over the physical resources. Hypervisor is the second layer of software and guest operating systems run as the third layer of software. Products like VMWare Workstation and Microsoft Virtual PC are the most common examples of *type 2 hypervisors*.

Benefits: In this approach, the host OS supplies the hardware drivers for the underlying physical resources. This eases the installation and configuration of the hypervisor. It makes the type-2 hypervisors compatible for a wide variety of hardware platform.

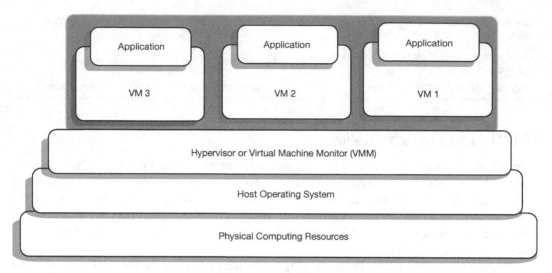

FIG 7.4: A model of hosted machine virtualization approach

Drawbacks: A hosted hypervisor does not have direct access to the hardware resources and hence, all of the requests from virtual machines must go through the host OS. This may degrade the performance of the virtual machines.

Another drawback of the hosted virtualization is the lack of support for real-time operating systems. Since the underlying host OS controls the scheduling of jobs it becomes unrealistic to run a real-time OS inside a VM using hosted virtualization.

> *Type 2 or hosted hypervisors run within an operating-system environment.*

7.5.2.2 Bare Metal Approach: Removal of the Host OS

In this approach of machine virtualization, the hypervisor is directly installed over the physical machine. Since, the hypervisor is the first layer over hardware resources, hence, the technique is referred as bare metal approach. Here, the VMM or the hypervisor communicates directly with system hardware.

In this approach, the hypervisor acts as *low-level virtual machine monitor* and also called as *Type 1 hypervisor* or *Native Hypervisor*. VMware's ESX and ESXi Servers, Microsoft's Hyper-V, solution Xen are some of the examples of *bare-metal hypervisors*.

Benefits: Since the bare metal hypervisor can directly access the hardware resources in most of the cases it provides better performance in comparison to the hosted hypervisor. For bigger application like enterprise data centers, bare-metal virtualization is more suitable because usually it provides advanced features for resource and security management. Administrators get more control over the host environment.

Drawbacks: As any hypervisor usually have limited set of device drivers built into it, so the bare metal hypervisors have limited hardware support and cannot run on a wide variety of hardware platform.

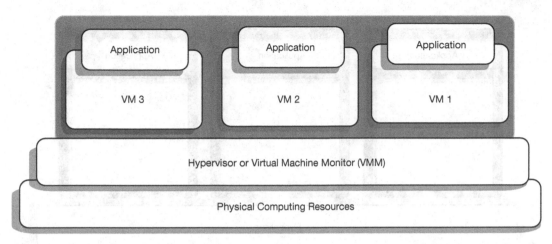

FIG 7.5: A model for the bare metal approach of machine virtualization

Type 1 or bare metal hypervisor does not use any host operating system.

7.6 EXPLORING HYPERVISOR OR VIRTUAL MACHINE MONITOR

The *hypervisor* or *virtual machine monitor* (VMM) presents a virtual operating platform before the guest systems. It also monitors and manages the execution of guest systems and the virtual machines. All of the virtual machines run as self-sufficient computers isolated from others, even though they are served by the same set of physical resources. Alternately, it can be said that a hypervisor or VMM facilitates and monitors the execution of virtual machines and allows the sharing of the underlying physical resources among them. Following section focuses on different hypervisor-based virtualization approaches.

7.6.1 Hypervisor-Based Virtualization Approaches

Hypervisor-based virtualization techniques can be divided into three categories as full virtualization, para-virtualization and hardware-assisted virtualization. The techniques being used in these three approaches are entirely different from one another.

7.6.1.1 Full Virtualization

In full virtualization (also called as *native virtualization*), the hypervisor fully simulates or emulates the underlying hardware. Virtual machines run over these virtual set of hardware. The guest operating systems assume that they are running on actual physical resources and thus remain unaware that they have been virtualized. This enables the unmodified versions of available operating systems (like Windows, Linux and else) to run as guest OS over hypervisor.

In this model, it is the responsibility of the hypervisor to handle all OS-to-hardware (i.e. guest OS to physical hardware) requests during running of guest machines. The guest OS

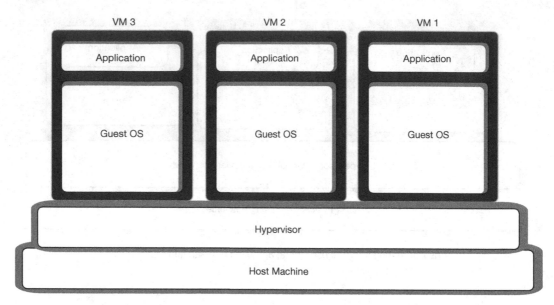

FIG 7.6: A model of full virtualization

remains completely isolated from physical resource layers by the hypervisor. This provides flexibility as almost all of the available operating systems can work as guest OS. VMware's virtualization product *VMWare ESXi Server* and *Microsoft Virtual Server* are few examples of full virtualization solution.

> *In full virtualization technique, the guest operating systems can directly run over hypervisor.*

7.6.1.2 Para-Virtualization or OS-Assisted Virtualization

'Para' is an English affix of Greek origin that means 'beside' or 'alongside'. In full virtualization, the operating systems which run in VMs as guest OSs need not to have any prior knowledge that they will run over virtualized platform. They do not need any special modification (or, functionality incorporation) for running over the hypervisors and are installed in their original form. The whole virtualization activities are managed by the hypervisor like translating instructions and establishing communication between different guest OSs and the underlying hardware platform.

In *para-virtualization*, a portion of the virtualization management task is transferred (from the hypervisor) towards the guest operating systems. Normal versions of available operating systems are not capable of doing this. They need special modification for this capability inclusion. This modification is called *porting*. Each guest OS is explicitly ported for the para-application program interface (API). A model of para-virtualization has been shown in Figure 7.7.

Thus in para-virtualization, each guest OS needs to have prior knowledge that it will run over the virtualized platform. Moreover, it also has to know on which particular hypervisor they will have to run. Depending on the hypervisor, the guest OS is modified as required to participate in the virtualization management task.

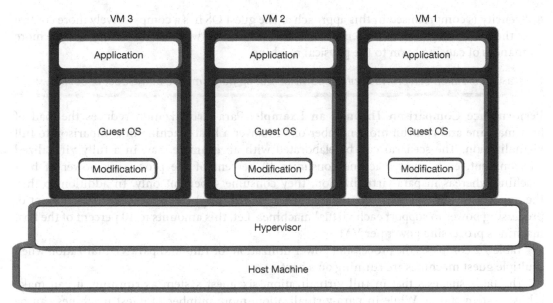

FIG 7.7: A model of para-virtualization

The unmodified versions of available operating systems (like Windows, Linux) cannot be used in para-virtualization. Since it involves modifications of the OS the para-virtualization is sometimes referred to as *OS-Assisted Virtualization* too. This technique relieves the hypervisor from handling the entire virtualization tasks to some extent. Best known example of para-virtualization hypervisor is the open-source *Xen project* which uses a customized Linux kernel.

> *Para-virtualization requires hypervisor-specific modifications of guest operating systems.*

Advantages

- Para-virtualization allows calls from guest OS to directly communicate with hypervisor (without any binary translation of instructions). The use of modified OS reduces the virtualization overhead of the hypervisor as compared to the full virtualization.
- In para-virtualization, the system is not restricted by the device drivers provided by the virtualization software layer. In fact, in para-virtualization, the virtualization layer (hypervisor) does not contain any device drivers at all. Instead, the guest operating systems contain the required device drivers.

Limitations

- Unmodified versions of available operating systems (like Windows or Linux) are not compatible with para-virtualization hypervisors. Modifications are possible in Open-source operating systems (like Linux) by the user. But for proprietary operating systems (like Windows), it depends upon the owner. If owner agrees to supply the required modified version of the OS for a hypervisor, then only that OS becomes available for the para-virtualization system.

■ Security is compromised in this approach as the guest OS has a comparatively more control of the underlying hardware. Hence, the users of some VM with wrong intentions have more chances of causing harm to the physical machine.

Para-virtualization can provide enhanced virtualization performance at the cost of security.

Performance Comparison Through an Example: Para-virtualization reduces the load of host machine and can run more number of VMs over a host machine in comparison to full virtualization. The scenario can be elaborated with an example. Say, in a fully virtualized environment, each guest machine consumes 10 percent of the processing power of host machine whereas in para-virtualization, they consume 4 percent only. In addition to this, the hypervisor (on which the virtual machines are running) consumes a certain amount of processing power to support each virtual machines. Let, this amounts to 10 percent of the host machine's processing power per VM.

Table 7.2 compares the processing power utilization for full- and para-virtualization when multiple guest machines are running on a host.

The table suggests that in full virtualization, six guest system as running, it can make a host system starve. While in para-virtualization, more number of guest machines can be accommodated which creates scope for better scaling. Here, it should be noted that data presented here are indicative in nature and much better para-virtualization performance is achieved in reality.

7.6.1.3 Hardware-Assisted Virtualization

Inspired by software-enabled virtualization, hardware vendors later started manufacturing devices tailored to support virtualization. Intel and AMD started this by including new virtualization features in their processors. The AMD-Virtualization (AMD-V) and Intel Virtualization Technology (Intel-VT) allows some privileged CPU calls from the guest OS to be directly handled by the CPU. These calls do not require to be translated by the hypervisors. This eliminates the need for binary translation or para-virtualization.

This kind of virtualization is only possible when specific combinations of hardware components are used, and that did not happen until 2006 when both Intel and AMD started to include new virtualization features in their processors. Many bare-metal hypervisors make use of this technology. Hypervisors like Xen, Microsoft's Hyper-V or VMWare ESXi Server can take the advantages of the hardware-assisted virtualization.

Table 7.2   A comparison between processing power utilization in full- and para-virtualization

	VM Instances	Resource engaged to process Virtualization Overhead	Resource engaged to process VMs	Total Processing power engaged
Full virtualization	5	10% per VM (50% of total)	10% per VM (50% of total)	100%
Para-virtualization	5	4% per VM (20% of total)	10% per VM (50% of total)	70%
Para-virtualization	7	4% per VM (28% of total)	10% per VM (70% of total)	98%

Hardware-assisted virtualization requires explicit features in the host machine's CPU.

7.6.1.4 A Side-by-Side Comparison

Table 7.3 provides a side-by-side comparison among three hypervisor-based virtualization approaches.

7.6.2 Threats to Hypervisor

In virtualization, although the hypervisor runs virtual machines and largely protects the underlying physical resources from damage, there are few pitfalls in it as well. System designers should be aware of those hitches as any threat to the hypervisor may turn the entire system vulnerable. Following section focuses the common vulnerabilities of the hypervisor.

Table 7.3 Comparison among Full Virtualization, Para-Virtualization and Hardware-Assisted Virtualization

Full Virtualization	Para-Virtualization or OS-Assisted Virtualization	Hardware-Assisted Virtualization
Guest OS has no role in virtualization.	Guest OS plays role in virtualization.	Guest OS has no role in virtualization.
Guest OS remains unaware about the virtualization.	Guest OS has to be aware about the virtualization.	Guest OS remains unaware about the virtualization.
Normal version of available OS can be used as guest OS.	Modified version of available OS is required.	Normal version of available OS can be used as guest OS.
It provides good options for guest OS.	It provides lesser options for guest OS.	It provides good options for guest OS.
Guest OS is not hypervisor-specific.	Guest OS is tailored to be hypervisor-specific.	Guest OS is not hypervisor-specific.
Here it requires no special feature in the host CPU.	Here it requires no special feature in the host CPU.	Here it requires explicit features in the host CPU.
Hardware does not play role in virtualization.	Hardware does not play role in virtualization.	Hardware plays role in virtualization.
Hypervisor takes care of all of the virtualization tasks.	Guest OS along with hypervisor take care of the virtualization tasks.	Specialized hardware device along with hypervisor take care of virtualization tasks.
Virtualization overhead of hypervisor is more.	Virtualization overhead of hypervisor is less.	Virtualization overhead of hypervisor is less.
Virtualization performance is little slow.	Virtualization performance is better.	Virtualization performance is better.
It provides high level of security as all of the virtualization controls remain with the hypervisor.	Here the security is compromised as guest OS has some control in virtualization.	Here the security is compromised as calls from guest OS can directly access the hardware.

7.6.2.1 Rogue Hypervisor

Hackers may create rogue hypervisor (hypervisor made with wrong intention) and can replace an original hypervisor with the same in order to attack a system without any knowledge of the system. Since hypervisor is the prime medium of communication between host machine and virtual machines, the rogue hypervisor can easily be used to cause damage to a system.

This is similar to a root-kit infection of a physical computer. *Rootkit* is a malicious piece of software inserted by an intruder into a computer to serve some illegal purpose without being detected. The key for rootkit is the access to the system root (in context with Unix OS). Rootkits themselves are not harmful or do not cause any harm to the system directly. They are used to hide entry of malware or worms into the system by creating some sort of hidden channels. Virtualization-based rootkits in the same way can use a rogue hypervisor to create a *covert channel* to dump unauthorized code into a system.

> Rogue hypervisor may create covert channel for malware to attack the system.

7.6.2.2 VM Escape

One advantage of running applications in virtual machine is that the applications as well as the users cannot get direct access to the hypervisor or the host operation system. Hypervisor creates isolated environments for different virtual machines running on it. So, applications running on one virtual machine cannot affect other VMs.

But, an improperly configured or manipulated virtual machine may allow codes to completely bypass this security and enable attackers to gain access to the hypervisor. Such bypass is known as *virtual machine escape* where the exploiter can directly access the hypervisor or host operating system and can even perform administrative tasks like VM creation, deletion, manipulation etc. So, VM escape may result in a complete failure to set up the security mechanism of the VM's physical host.

> Malwares must not be able to escape the VM security level and gain access to the hypervisor.

The threats as mentioned above to hypervisor can be eliminated with attentive system administration. A properly managed hypervisor can even protect virtualized system against threats cropping up from any weakness in operating system of the VMs. So, while implementing virtualization, proper measures must have to be taken against the common threats to the hypervisor.

7.7 OPERATING SYSTEM LEVEL VIRTUALIZATION: REMOVAL OF THE HYPERVISOR

Operating system level virtualization (also called as *system level virtualization*) works in totally different way than the virtualization techniques as discussed. Here, the host–guest paradigm does not work. The virtual machine terminology is also not used here. In this kind of virtualization technique, no hypervisor is used and the virtual servers are enabled by the kernel of the operating system of physical machine. The approach has been shown in Figure 7.8.

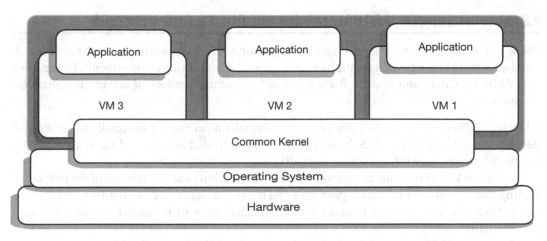

FIG 7.8. A model of operating system-level virtualization approach

Here, the kernel of the operating system installed over physical system is shared among all of the virtual servers running over it. Since all of the virtual servers share a single kernel, it is evident that all of them will have same OS as the parent system. The goal of this approach is to create multiple logically-distinct user-space instances (virtual servers) over a single instance of an OS kernel. This approach is also known as *Operating System Virtualization* or *Shared Kernel Approach.*

Virtualization solutions such as FreeBSD's jail, Linux VServer, OpenVZ are few examples of OS-level virtualization. All of them can run logically-distinct user-spaces on top of a single kernel.

Advantages: The advantages of OS level virtualization is that it is lighter in weight since all of the virtual servers share a single instance of an OS kernel. This enables a single physical system to support many others virtual servers than the number of complete virtual machines it could support.

Limitations: All virtual machines have to use the same operating system (due to sharing of OS kernel). Although different distributions (like Linux distribution) of the same system kernel are allowed.

> OS level virtualization facilitates the creation of multiple logically-distinct user-space instances rather than creating complete VMs.

7.7.1 Operating System Level Virtualization versus Machine Virtualization

Here the question differentiating the idea whether one can run different operating systems in different virtual systems running on same physical resource. In machine or server virtualization, the answer is yes. Different operating systems can be run in different virtual systems. But, this differs in case of operating system level virtualization where virtual servers share a single underlying kernel. Therefore, all of the virtual servers can only run a similar operating system.

7.8 MAJOR SERVER VIRTUALIZATION PRODUCTS AND VENDORS

There are many enterprise level server virtualization products available in the market. A number of VMMs exist which are the basis of many cloud computing environments. Companies like VMware, Citrix and Microsoft are some of the leading vendors of server virtualization products.

VMware vSphere: VMware is a pioneer in the virtualization market especially in server and desktop virtualization. This U.S.-based company was founded in 1998 and has released many products for computer infrastructure virtualization.

vSphere is VMware's enterprise-level server virtualization product. It is one of the industry's leading and reliable virtualization platforms and is used in data center virtualization for cloud computing. The vSphere was released as an enhanced suite of its earlier product VMware Infrastructure (also known as VI).

vSphere uses ESXi hypervisor which is also a product of VMware. This hypervisor is Type 1 or bare-metal hypervisor which gets installed directly on the physical server. vSphere software suite also provides a centralized management application called as vCenter Server through which virtual machines and ESXi hosts can be managed centrally.

Citrix XenServer: XenServer is one of the leading open-source server virtualization solutions offered by U.S. software company Citrix Systems. Xen hypervisor which has pioneered the para-virtualization concept, is the basis of XenServer. The Xen originated as an open-source research project at the University of Cambridge and its first release was made in 2003.

The Xen hypervisor has been used in many server virtualization solutions, both commercial and open-source. Amazon EC2, Oracle VM and XenServer are notable among them. The developer group of Xen is XenSource Inc. which later was acquired by Citrix Systems in 2007. Most of the features of Citrix XenServer are available free of cost.

Microsoft Hyper-V Server: Hyper-V Server is the server virtualization solution from Microsoft. First launched in 2008, it was formerly known as Windows Server. Now Hyper-V Server comes as a dedicated stand-alone product and also regarded as a feature of Windows Server.

Oracle VM VirtualBox: Oracle VM VirtualBox (formerly known as Sun VirtualBox) is the virtualization software package from Oracle Corporation. VirtualBox was purchased by Sun Microsystems from its developer innotek GmbH, in 2008 and now owned by Oracle. This Xen hypervisor based open-source product runs on a wide variety of host operating systems and supports a large number of guest operating systems too.

KVM: The kernel-based virtual machine (KVM) is a hypervisor built into the Linux kernel. This open-source solution was developed by Red Hat Corporation to provide virtualization services on the Linux-operating system platforms. It has been part of Linux kernel since version 2.6.20 and currently being supported by several distributions. A wide variety of guest operating systems work with KVM including several versions of Windows, Linux and UNIX.

Following table lists the different enterprise level virtualization solutions from major vendors and shows the corresponding hypervisors used by the products.

Table 7.4 Server virtualization products and corresponding hypervisors used

Manufacturers	Server Virtualization Products	Hypervisors used
VMware	vSphere	ESXi
Citrix	XenServer	Xen
Microsoft	Hyper-V Server	Hyper-V
Oracle	VirtualBox	Xen

7.9 HIGH-LEVEL LANGUAGE VIRTUAL MACHINE

The high-level language virtual machine is a concept that goes against the idea of conventional computing environment where a compiled application is firmly tied to a particular OS and ISA (instruction set architecture). Thus, in conventional computing environment, the porting of application to different computing platform requires recompilation of the application code for the targeted platform. Moreover, porting of application needs porting of the underlying compiler for the target platform first which is a tedious technical task.

The high-level language VM eases the porting of compiler by rendering HLLs to intermediate representation targeted towards *abstract machines*. The abstract machine then translates the intermediate code to physical machine's instruction set. This concept of abstract machine (as well as intermediate code representation) makes the porting of compilers less complex as only the back-end part of the compiler needs to be ported since the intermediate code representation is same for compilers of a HLL on any platform.

Thus, the intermediate representation of a HLL program having compiled over one physical computing architecture can be ported on abstract machine running over other architecture. The abstract machine then translates the intermediate code to the instruction set of underlying architecture. Such abstract machine is referred as *high-level language VM* or *HLL VM*. Java Virtual Machine (JVM) and Microsoft's Common Language Runtime (CLR) are two examples of high-level language VMs.

High-level language VM is also known as *application VM* or *process VM*. Application or process virtualization can be considered as the smaller version of machine virtualization. Instead of virtual machines, this technology decouples application software from the underlying platform on which it is executed.

The best known example of this type of virtualization is Java Virtual Machine (JVM). JVM makes the execution of java applications machine-independent as the applications do not interact with the underlying OS and hardware platform directly. Rather, the JVM (which are usually machine-dependent) creates a uniform virtual machine environment (over different operating system and hardware architecture) and makes java applications portable.

Microsoft has even adopted a similar approach in the Common Language Runtime (CLR) used by .NET applications. The concept of process virtualization was actually pioneered by the UCSD P-System (a portable operating system) during late 1970s which was developed by a team at the University of California at San Diego, United States.

Application virtual machine places a sort of software wrapper around the application running over it and this wrapper restricts the application from directly interacting with system. This is referred to as *sandboxing*. The *sandbox* technology is often used to test unverified programs which may contain malicious code in order to prevent them from damaging the underlying hardware devices.

> *Virtual machines designed to run only a single application or process written in high level language (HLL) are mentioned as process VM or application VM or HLL VM.*

7.10 EMULATION

Emulation in computing is done by making one system imitating another. This means a system having some architecture is made enable to support instruction set of some other machine architecture. For example, let a piece of software has been made for architecture 'A' and is not supported by architecture 'B'. Through emulation, it is possible to imitate the working of system 'A' (i.e. architecture 'A') on system 'B' (i.e. architecture 'B') and then the piece of software to run on system B. Emulators can be software or hardware both.

Emulation software converts binary data written for execution on one machine to an equivalent binary form suitable to execute on another machine. This is done by translating the binary instructions. There are two ways for implementation of emulations like interpretation and binary translation.

In *binary translation* (also known as *recompilation*), a total conversion of the binary data (made for the emulated platform) is done. The conversion recompiles the whole instruction into another binary form suitable to run on the actual or targeted platform. There are two types of binary translation like *static recompilation* and *dynamic recompilation*.

In *interpretation*, each instruction is interpreted by the emulator every time it is being encountered. This method is easier to implement but slower than binary translation process.

> *The principle of emulation in computing is instruction-set translation through interpretation.*

7.10.1 Simple Virtualization versus Emulation-based Virtualization

The terms *emulation-based virtualization* and *simple machine virtualization* sometimes creates the confusion. Both of them enable multiple virtual machines with different guest operating systems to run on single physical (or host) system. The key difference between these two is based on whether applications running on the virtual machines are compiled for the native instruction set of the host machine or they have been compiled for some other architecture and instruction set. In first case, it is simple virtualization and in second case it is emulation-based virtualization.

In emulation, the virtual machine (i.e. the emulation software) simulates the complete hardware in software. It can run on one hardware architecture and can create environment to support some other architecture. This allows an operating system made for one computer architecture to run on the architecture supported by the emulator. Here, the instruction sets of the virtual system (presented before users) and the actual physical system are not same. Hence, service requests received by the virtual machine can only be passed to the underlying physical system (where ultimate execution of instruction happens) after translation of the instruction sets (one architecture to another architecture).

In simple virtualization, the instruction set used by the virtual system and the actual hardware system is same. Hence, the virtual machine simply passes the service requests to the actual physical system. Here, the translations of the instruction sets are not required. Without the translation layer, the performance of a virtual machine is much faster and nearly approaches the native speed. Virtualization therefore is normally faster than the emulation.

Virtual machines can play the role of an emulator. Microsoft's VirtualPC is an example of emulation-based virtual machine. It emulates x86 architecture and can run on different other chipsets like the PowerPC (in addition to the x86 architecture). QEMU (Quick EMUlator) is another well-known open-source machine emulator which can emulate various CPU types on several host systems.

> In emulation, the main focus of a system is to pretend to be another system. In simple virtualization, the focus is to simulate the environment of native system into two or more duplicate systems.

7.11 SOME OTHER TYPES OF VIRTUALIZATIONS

Virtualization of computing infrastructure is not only about machine or server virtualization. Especially cloud-based service development requires each and every computing infrastructure in virtualized mode. In reality, virtualized network infrastructure, storage systems etc. are as important as the server virtualization.

7.11.1 Network Virtualization

Network virtualization is the process of combining network resources and network functionality into a single, software-based administrative entity called as a *virtual network*. There are two common forms of network virtualization which have been discussed below.

- *Virtual device-based virtual network*: Here, virtualized devices form the network. All virtual networking devices (including virtual computers, virtual switches, virtual routers etc.) communicate using actual (non-virtual) network protocols such as Ethernet as well as virtualization protocols such as the VLAN. This is actual network virtualization where the network is formed with all virtual components.
- *Protocol based virtual network*: Rather than virtualizing devices, it creates virtual area network. Virtual LAN (VLAN) and virtual private network (VPN) are examples of such virtualizations. These are logical local area networks (logical LANs) where the underlying physical LAN's structure is something else. Here, several physical LANs which are actually part of public network (such as the Internet) can function as a single logical LAN. This enables network devices (such as computers and switches) to send and receive data across shared or public networks as if they are part of a private network. The devices can communicate using LAN protocols which make faster and secure network communication.

7.11.2 Storage Virtualization

In traditional computing system, the storages have always been directly linked with the physical servers. With virtualization of storage, this concept has been changed. Now virtualized storage systems are linked with servers and actual (physical) storage systems remain hidden.

Like other computing resources, virtualization of storage also happens through layer of software which creates *logical abstraction* of the pooling of physical storage devices having linked together by network. Data stored in logical (virtualized) storage devices ultimately get stored in some physical storage disks. The advent of Storage Area Networks (SAN) has made the pooling (and hence the virtualization as well) of physical storage systems easier.

There are many commercial virtualized cloud storage systems available in the market. Google Cloud Storage, Microsoft's Azure Storage, Simple Storage System (S3) and Elastic Block Store (EBS) of Amazon are few to name among them.

7.11.3 Desktop Virtualization

Desktop virtualization does not fall under the core category of computing infrastructure virtualization concept. But it is the key to business as it can lower the total cost of ownership and enhances security of system, application and data. Desktop virtualization is different from remote desktop access. Through desktop virtualization technology, any computer's applications can be separated from its desktop and user can get the look and feel of some other environment while using those applications. For instance, VMware Fusion 7 solution provides Mac-like experience while running Windows applications on a Mac system. In an enterprise environment, individual virtualized desktops can be maintained in a central server and users can access those desktops by connecting to the central server.

7.12 ADVANTAGES OF VIRTUALIZATION

The advantages of virtualization provide many benefits to consumers. This section discusses the operational and financial advantages of computing infrastructure virtualization.

Better Utilization of Existing Resources: Physical computing resources have become advanced and powerful with time. In traditional computing, one machine instance runs on a physical server which hardly utilizes the whole power of the system. Thus, most of the processing power simply remain unutilized for most of the computer systems. Running multiple virtual machines on one physical server makes better utilization of the resources and this is known as *server consolidation*.

Reduction in Hardware Cost: As virtualization makes better use of physical resources by running multiple virtual machines on single set of physical resources, automatically cost of computing comes down. If server consolidation can be combined with capacity planning in planned manner, investment for hardware resources may reduce drastically as well.

Reduction in Computing Infrastructure Costs: Reduced physical computing resource requirements in turn reduces many other associated assets, like physical floor space, power requirement, cooling system and human resource to administrate the systems. Increases in the number of virtual machines over existing physical resources do not add to any of these loads.

Improved Fault Tolerance or Zero Downtime Maintenance: The decoupling of virtual machines from specific hardware resources increases the portability of system. In cases of any hardware failure, the virtual system can be migrated to another physical setup. This helps to build fault tolerant system by creating scope for *zero downtime maintenance*.

Simplified System Administration: Virtualization segments the management of the systems into two groups as physical resources management and virtual system management. Centralized monitoring package can be employed to keep track of health of the systems and raise alert in case of need. As managing virtual computing resources is less critical than physical resource and there are less physical machines, the system administration tasks become easier.

Simplified Capacity Expansion: Capacities of virtual resources are easier to increase than expanding and then synchronizing physical computing resources. This also becomes possible due to the decoupling of physical resources from virtual systems.

Simplified System Installation: Installation of a new system has become easier, cost-effective and hassle-free in virtual environment. A new system can be installed almost within no time by cloning a virtual machine instance. Fresh installation is much easier too than physical machine installation.

Support for Legacy Systems and Applications: Research institutes or other organizations sometimes need to run legacy software packages which can no longer be run on presently available operating system or hardware platforms. Virtualization is the only solution to tackle this kind of scenarios as any kind of VMs (including *legacy systems*) can easily be created to deploy required legacy applications over them.

Simplified System-Level Development: System software (like device driver) development and testing require frequent re-booting of the system. This is easier and faster in virtual environment since VM rebooting does not require physical machine to restart and can be performed with some clicks of mouse.

Simplified System and Application Testing: Performance testing of system software before its release is a rigorous job and requires to test the software on all supported platforms. This is a difficult situation since it requires all of those hardware platforms and operating systems to test the software. Virtualization eases this process by eliminating much of the time and effort required for system installation and configuration. Application or system software testing is one of the biggest beneficiaries of virtualization.

Security: Virtualization adds a layer of abstraction over physical hardware. Virtual machines cannot directly access physical resources any more. This can restrict the amount of destruction that might occur when some malicious software attempts to damage the system or corrupt data. For example, if an entire virtual hard disk gets damaged or corrupted, the actual physical disk remains unaffected.

> The benefits of virtualization directly propagate into cloud computing and have empowered it as well.

7.13 DOWNSIDES OF VIRTUALIZATION

Virtualization is an enthralling technology which has changed the world of computing system design. But every technology has its own shortcomings and virtualization is no exception of this. Any weakness in virtualized system design especially in hypervisor may cause severe threat to the whole environment. All such concerns have been discussed further. However, the positive effects of virtualization outweigh the negative ones by far.

Single Point of Failure Problem: The major benefit of virtualization is resource sharing. Multiple virtual machines can run over one physical machine. But, this has a downside. It increases the probability of failure of a number of virtual servers in cases of failure of single physical machine. Although, this situation can be handled easily by keeping backup resources and porting those virtual servers on the backup set of physical resources. Porting is not a difficult task as virtualization decouples virtual systems from physical resources.

Lower Performance Issue: There is a concern whether virtual environments have the capacity to accomplish the full performance of the actual physical system. It has been seen that virtual servers can achieve up to 85 percent to 90 percent of the performance of the actual physical server as VMs cannot get direct access to the hardware.

Difficulty in Root Cause Analysis: With virtualization, a new layer of complexity is added which can cause new problems. The main difficulty is that if something does not work as it is supposed to it may require considerable extra efforts to find the cause of the problem.

> *The positive impulse of virtualization prevails over the negatives by far.*

7.14 VIRTUALIZATION SECURITY THREATS

The traditional threats of any computing system are all applicable to virtual computing system also. In addition to this, with this new layers, several new types of vulnerabilities emerge. The additional security threats to virtualized systems include the following:

The single point host: Resource sharing makes virtualization cost-effective. A single set of physical computing resources can fulfill multiple purposes and run several virtual machines. Any security breach at this physical resource level may lead to a large number of system break-downs. So, the physical host level must be maintained at its best.

Threats to hypervisor: Security and stability of any virtualized environment immensely depend on the ability of the hypervisor to protect itself from attacks. Any security breach at the hypervisor level also makes the whole environment vulnerable.

Complex configuration: Virtualization adds another layer of abstraction as well as complexity to computing systems. These layers act as layer of protection to the system but at the same time any improper configuration greatly increases the probability of unseen vulnerabilities.

Privilege escalation: Privilege escalation attack happens when users or some applications get access to more resources or functionalities than they are entitled to due to some design flaw in the system. Like in any other software system, the privilege escalation problem may occur in virtualized system too where a hacker can attack a VM through the hypervisor.

Inactive virtual machines: Virtual machines which are no more active or are in dormant state, generally moves out of the monitoring system automatically. But, those machines may have sensitive data in storage or in their database. As those remain out of the scope of the monitoring system it becomes a threat. Thus, loss of access to the inactive virtual machines causes potential security threats.

Consolidation of different trust zones: Workloads of different trust levels from different zones consolidates onto same underlying physical system without adequate separation. This may sometime create threat for the security of highly sensitive and trusted applications.

> Any virtualization threats can be mitigated by maintaining security recommendations while designing a computing system.

7.15 VIRTUALIZATION SECURITY RECOMMENDATIONS

A fundamental requirement for a successful virtualization is to establish security mechanisms in order to deal with the loopholes of this fascinating technology. In this regard, in addition to the traditional techniques some other security measures are necessary to be taken to ensure security of virtualized systems.

Hardening Virtual Machines: In server virtualization, users have indirect access to computing resources through the virtual machines. All applications they run or any computations they perform can be done on VMs only. Robust and properly configured virtual machines will never allow any application to bypass them to directly access the hypervisor or underlying resources. So, hardening the virtual machines should be a practice as they act as the first layer of defence. The implementation may vary according to the vendor's recommendations. It is also important to keep virtual machine software updated to ensure that all known vulnerabilities have been corrected.

Hardening the Hypervisor: Hypervisor is the key player in virtualization. Any communication between the virtual machines and the underlying resources are directed through the hypervisor. So, it is inevitable to focus on the security of the hypervisor and make sure that the hypervisor is deployed steadily. This ensures that even if any pitfall arises in any of the guest systems (the virtual machines), the VMM protects the other VMs and the underlying resources from any attack or further security breach.

Hardening the Host Operating System: In hosted server virtualization technique, the host operating system plays vital role in managing the security of the physical system. While any pitfall in the configuration of guest operating system can only affect the particular virtual machine's environment any pitfall in host OS may affect the entire environment as well as all of the guest machines. Also a flawed host OS can weaken the hypervisor it is hosting to make the whole environment feeble.

Restrictive Physical Access to the Host: Any vulnerability of the host system exposes an entire virtual environment to risks. Host systems must be prevented from all external and unauthorized accesses. Any unauthorized physical access to the host system may easily make it vulnerable to attack in many ways.

Implementation of Single Primary Function Per VM: Although the virtual machines are capable of handling multiple tasks, it makes the virtualization environment more secure if prime processes are separated among different VMs. This isolation prevents the processes from being exposed and dilutes hacker's ability to damage multiple essential environmental functions when any weakness arises in one virtual machine.

Use of Secured Communications: Establishing secured communication mechanisms provide protection to computing system. Encryption techniques should be used to frustrate hackers. Techniques like Secure HTTP (HTTPS), encrypted virtual private networks (VPNs), transport layer security (TLS), secure shell (SSH) etc. help to prevent spoofed attacks and session hijacking.

Use of Separate NIC for Sensitive VM: Virtual machines which process sensitive data will attract more attention from hackers over the network. In such scenario, it is better to use separate physical network interfaces card (NIC) for this type of virtual machines rather than sharing one NIC among multiple VMs.

Apart from the above listed measures, keeping all of the software, like host operating system, hypervisor, guest operating systems and others up-to-date and timely patching, disabling unnecessary services are also very important factors to enhance the security of a virtualized environment.

> *Guest OS, hypervisor, host OS and the physical system are the four layers in the architecture of virtualized environment, and for security measures all of these should be considered separately.*

7.16 VIRTUALIZATION AND CLOUD COMPUTING

Resource pooling is one important feature of cloud computing. But users are not given direct access to that pool. Pools of resources are created at data centers and a layer of abstraction is created over the pools of various types of physical resources using virtualization. In this way, all of the resources at data center are virtualized and it is usually referred as data center virtualization. Consumers of cloud services can only access the virtual computing resources from the data center.

Apart from other advantages, data center virtualization provides a way to the cloud system for managing resources efficiently because of the mapping of virtual resources to the underlying physical resources being both dynamic and rapid. System gets the dynamic behaviour because the mapping can be easily done based on changing conditions and requirements. This process is rapid because any changes in mapping can be done instantaneously.

> *Data center virtualization is one foundation of cloud computing. Accesses to pooled resources is provided using resource virtualization.*

Virtualization laid the foundation for cloud computing. According to IT research firm, Gartner, the virtualization is the key enabler of most of the fundamental attributes of cloud computing. Those attributes of cloud are mentioned below.

- **Shared service:** Resource sharing capability among multiple users has been redefined with the introduction of virtualization. Users remain unaware about the actual physical resources and cannot occupy any specific resource unit while not doing any productive work. Thus, cloud computing delivers shared service among consumers using resource virtualization.
- **Elasticity:** With virtualized resources, the underlying capacity of actual resources can be easily altered to meet the varying demand of computation. Thus, virtual machines and other virtual resources exhibit elasticity as well as flexibility.
- **Service orientation:** Cloud computing is built upon the philosophy of service-oriented architecture for application development. The implementation of this architecture becomes easier when virtualization is in place.
- **Metered usage:** In cloud computing, the services are billed on usage basis. The accurate measurement of resource consumption has been possible due to use of virtualized resources.

> *Virtualization is considered a major step in the direction of cloud computing.*

SUMMARY

- ❖ Virtualization decouples the general purpose software applications from being tied with any specific type of hardware resources. Instead, they use virtual computing resources.
- ❖ This is done by creating a special software layer over the hardware resources, that virtualizes the whole environment.
- ❖ All computing resources like processor, memory, network, storage and others can be virtualized. These virtual components are used to assemble the virtual machines.
- ❖ Virtual machines function just like traditional computers. Operating system and applications can be installed over these machines. Moreover, multiple virtual computers can run simultaneously over a single physical computer. This enhances resource utilization.
- ❖ The layer of software that plays the central role in creating virtualized environment is called hypervisor or virtual machine monitor. Many software vendors have developed hypervisors, both proprietary and open-source.
- ❖ There are different techniques of machine or server virtualization like, hosted approach, bare-metal approach and operating system level virtualization. Software vendors like VMware, Citrix, Microsoft have their own server virtualization products in the market.
- ❖ High-level language virtual machine is a technique that decouples process or application from underlying hardware platform in contrast to decoupling the whole virtual machine. The Java virtual machine or Microsoft's common language runtime are few examples of HLL VM.
- ❖ There are few snags in virtualization but those turn out to be insignificant when the advantages of the technology are considered.

❖ Wrongly designed or configured hypervisor may cause security threats to a system. Hence, appropriate precautions should be taken while designing a virtualized system.

❖ During the development of a virtualized system, apart from maintaining the traditional security recommendations, all of the virtualization-specific security recommendations should also be maintained to make the environment secure.

❖ Virtualization is a revolutionary technology which has enormous advantages which paved the way for cloud computing.

REVIEW QUESTIONS

How virtualization enables multi-tenancy in computing?

In virtualization, the users as well as the applications can only access virtualized computing resources (like processor, memory, disk, switch etc.). These virtualized computing resources are made out of support from physical computing resources. One physical device may empower multiple virtual devices (of its own type) at same or different point of time which are consumed by users (tenants) not known to each other. This flexibility is there since applications or users are not tied with any physical resources, rather virtual resource are being allocated according to the demand of applications, thus one physical resource can support multiple tenants.

When does it become necessary to implement emulation-based virtualization?

Normal virtualization is simulation-based. Software simulates the actual hardware components into set of software-based (virtual) components. Architectural structure of these virtual components remains same as the actual physical components. Hence, software systems (operating system or applications) fit for the architecture (or instruction set) of the physical resources can be installed over the corresponding virtual resources.

When situation demands that software made for one architecture (that is written for one type of instruction set) has to be installed over hardware resources having some other architecture (made for some other instruction set); then only way is to create the required set of virtual devices through emulation-based virtualization. In emulation-based virtualization, the architecture of virtual devices and the underlying physical devices need not to match.

Why is hypervisor also called virtual machine monitor?

Hypervisor produces all of the virtual computing resources. Virtual machines are created over the layer of hypervisor using these virtual resources. It is the responsibility of the hypervisor to manage activities, monitor functionalities and provide support to the virtual machines. This is why hypervisor is also called as virtual machine monitor or VMM.

How virtualization empowers computing using resource pool?

In contrast to the fact that one physical resource can support multiple virtual devices (through multi-tenancy), it is also possible to form one powerful virtual device combining the power of multiple physical resources. One 6GB memory can be formed combining three 2GB RAMs. Again those three

RAMs can be replaced by two 3GB RAMs without disrupting the service or without any knowledge of applications using them. All of these mapping of virtual resources with underlying physical pool of resources occur dynamically to support maximum resource utilization. Decoupling of applications from hardware allows administrators to think more about aggregate computing capacity and less about individual hosts. Thus, the virtualization endorses to gain maximum benefit of pooled resources.

What is sandboxing?

In computing, a *sandbox* is a restricted or isolated environment for execution of application. This environment does not allow to execute all functionalities by prohibiting certain functions for security purpose. This environment works as virtual lab where un-trusted programming codes or applications can be tested without allowing it to cause any harm.

Virtualization and sandboxing are not same. Rather, sandboxing can be seen as a special and partial example of virtualization. But virtualization sometimes referred as sandboxing as it creates a protected enclosure that mimics a real-life computing infrastructure and thus malicious applications cannot damage the actual resources.

Cloud vendors often use sandboxing for security. For instance, Google App Engine uses sandbox feature to keep applications isolated to ensure that all App Engine applications run in a restricted environment. This also ensures the security of the applications against the attacks.

What is the difference between sandboxing and virtualization?

The objective of sandboxing and virtualization are entirely different. Sandboxing is to isolate a running program or application from the physical computing system so that the program cannot harm the system. It is used to verify untrusted applications. While virtualization is used to create entire machine environment, sandboxing software provides minimal functionalities required for application execution or testing and withheld codes that can harm the server and data.

Resource abstraction through virtualization: What does this mean?

When working in virtualized environment, no one can access physical resources directly. Applications run upon virtual machines and they can never know which physical devices are actually supporting those virtual devices or where they are located. Thus, the actual resource components, their architecture, and system configuration remain out of everyone's sight. Virtualization thus adds a layer of abstraction over physical resources.

When is operating system-level virtualization useful?

Server or machine virtualization facilitates the running of multiple virtual or guest machines on a single physical or host machine. In hypervisor-based virtualization, the different guest machines running over a host need not to run same OS as the host. They are free to run any OS and multiple VMs running over a host may run different OS simultaneously.

System level (or operating system level) virtualization is an option when it is known that all of the virtual servers will use same Linux-based operating system. In system-level virtualization, virtual servers share one single OS kernel (that of the host OS) and hence can run same operating system only.

MULTIPLE CHOICE QUESTIONS

1. Which of these attribute(s) in a system could be brought by computing infrastructure virtualization?

   a) Security
   b) Dynamic behaviour
   c) Flexibility
   d) All of these

2. The physical system on which virtual machines run is called

   a) Host machine
   b) Guest machine
   c) Primary machine
   d) Non-virtual machine

3. The software layer implementing virtualization is known as

   a) Operating system
   b) Hypervisor
   c) Application layer
   d) None of these

4. In server virtualization, the relationship between host machine and guest machine is

   a) Many-to-one
   b) One-to-one
   c) Many-to-many
   d) One-to-many

5. Is it possible to install operating system in a virtual machine?

   a) Yes
   b) No
   c) Sometimes
   d) OS is not required in virtual machine

6. Type 1 hypervisors are installed over

   a) Physical resource
   b) Host operating system

   c) Virtual resource
   d) Type 2 hypervisor

7. Type 2 hypervisors are installed over

   a) Physical resource
   b) Host operating system
   c) Virtual resource
   d) Type 1 hypervisor

8. Operating systems and applications made for one computer architecture can be installed on some other architecture in

   a) Simple server virtualization
   b) Simulation-based server virtualization
   c) Complex server virtualization
   d) Emulation-based server virtualization

9. Guest operating systems remain unaware about they are running in virtual environment in

   a) Full virtualization
   b) Para-virtualization
   c) Operating system-level virtualization
   d) Hardware-assisted virtualization

10. Hypervisor dependent (modified) versions of guest operating systems are required in

    a) Full virtualization
    b) Para-virtualization
    c) Hardware-assisted virtualization
    d) All of these

11. Virtualization overhead of hypervisor is maximum in case of

    a) Full virtualization
    b) Para-virtualization
    c) Hardware-assisted virtualization
    d) Equal for all

12. Virtual machines running over a physical host do not have different operating systems in
    a) Full virtualization
    b) Operating system-level virtualization
    c) Para-virtualization
    d) Hardware-assisted virtualization

13. The most popular open-source hypervisor available in the market is
    a) ESX
    b) ESXi
    c) Hyper-V
    d) Xen

14. Process virtual machines are made to run
    a) Operating system
    b) Operating system and applications
    c) Some specific application
    d) Any application

15. Server virtualization creates scope for
    a) Speeding up servers
    b) Fast installation of servers
    c) Server portability
    d) Both b & c

16. Resource abstraction in cloud computing is implemented through
    a) Resource management
    b) Resource virtualization
    c) Object orientation
    d) Remote access

17. Virtual machine monitor (VMM) is the other name of
    a) Guest system
    b) Host system
    c) Host operating system
    d) Hypervisor

18. In operating system level virtualization, different OS distributions of same kernel can be run in virtual servers.
    a) True
    b) False

19. Cloud computing IaaS services can be developed without implementing resource virtualization also.
    a) True
    b) False

20. Which among the following must be maintained to ensure security of virtualization?
    a) Hardening the hypervisor
    b) Restricting physical access to host machine
    c) Maintaining one function per VM
    d) All of these

21. The 'single point' in the 'single point of failure problem' of virtualization is
    a) Virtual machine
    b) Guest OS
    c) Host machine
    d) VMM

22. In 'VM escape', which among the following happens?
    a) Accessing guest OS by escaping VM
    b) Evading security of VM to access VMM
    c) Accessing host OS by escaping VM
    d) Escaping security of VMM to access host

23. Inactive virtualization machines may cause security threats to virtualization?
    a) True
    b) False

24. The benefits of infrastructure virtualization includes
    a) Better utilization of resources
    b) Cost saving for computation
    c) Easier capacity expansion
    d) All of these

8 Resource Pooling, Sharing and Provisioning

Cloud computing delivers virtualized resources. In previous chapter, it has been discussed how virtualization technology has revolutionized the computing environment. It is important to note that in reality the virtualized resources are effective representations of actual physical resources. Cloud data centers maintain a large pool of physical computing resources which is presented in virtual mode as infrastructure service. This chapter focuses on how those resource pools are organized in cloud data centers.

Resource sharing is another important feature of cloud computing. Any resource component from the pool of resources is not dedicatedly used to serve one particular user or application; rather they are shared among multiple users or applications. Through this increment in resource utilization rate, a comparatively smaller number of resources can serve a large number of users.

Resource pooling, virtualization and sharing of resources ultimately converge to produce the dynamic behaviour of cloud systems. Cloud supplies the resources dynamically to users. This dynamic resource provisioning eliminates the need of permanent procurement of computing resources. This turns out to be a very effective technique as application demands or loads during computation do not remain same over a period of time.

8.1 RESOURCE POOLING

The utility service model of cloud computing requires to maintain huge amount of all types of computing resources to provide different services to consumers. For this purpose, cloud service providers create pool of computing resources. Effective pooling or grouping of resources requires appropriate system designing and architectural planning.

Resource pooling in cloud needs setting up of strategies by provider for categorizing and managing resources. Before resource pooling concept appeared, earlier people used to maintain discrete and independent set of resources known as *silos*.

In traditional computing model, the silos are made with very little or no inter-connections. On the other hand in cloud computing, the consumers use well-connected pool of computing resources. They gain almost no knowledge or control over the locations from where physical resources are allotted to them. In its out-of-best scenario, the providers sometimes ask for choice of geographic location (country or continent) from where a consumer wants to get resources. But this choice is only possible in case of large service providers who have *data centers* at multiple geographic locations around the world.

> Unlike traditional silos, cloud computing delivers resources to consumers in transparent manner from pools of computing resources. Consumers remain unaware about the actual resource locations.

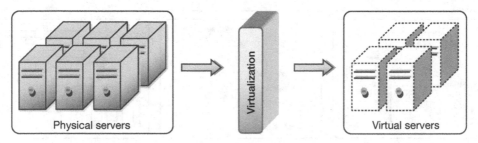

FIG 8.1: Pooling of physical and virtual servers

8.1.1 Resource Pooling Architecture

A resource pooling architecture is designed to combine multiple pools of resources where each pool groups together with identical computing resources. The challenge is to build an automated system which will ensure that all of the pools get together in synchronized manner.

Computing resources can broadly be divided into three categories as computer/server, network and storage. Hence, the physical computing resources to support these three purposes are essential to be configured in cloud data centers in good quantity. Again, a computer's capability mainly depends on two resource components like processor and memory. Thus, the resource pooling mainly concentrates on developing rich pools of four computing resources like processor, memory, network devices and storage.

8.1.1.1 Computer or Server Pool

Server pools are developed by building physical machine pools installed with operating systems and necessary system software. Virtual machines are built on these physical servers and combine into virtual machine pool. Physical processor and memory components from respective pools are later linked with these virtual servers in virtualized modes to increase capacity of the servers.

Dedicated processor pools are made of various capacity processors. Memory pools are also built in similar fashion. Processor and memory are allotted to the virtual machines as and when required. Again, they are returned to the pools of free components when load of virtual server decreases.

Figure 8.2 shows a resource pool comprising of three separate pools of resources. This is a simplified demonstration of resource pooling. In reality, the pooling is implemented with other essential resources in more structured manner.

> *The pool of virtual resources at cloud data centers are supported by pool of physical and pre-configured computing resources.*

8.1.1.2 Storage Pool

Storage is another essential resource with rapidly growing requirement, frequently accessed by applications as well as with the consumers of computing. Storage pools are made of block-based

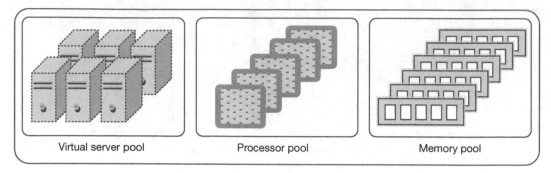

FIG 8.2: Resource pool comprising of three sub pools

storage disks. They are configured with proper portioning, formatting and are available to consumers in virtualized mode. Data having stored into those virtualized storage devices are actually saved in these pre-configured physical disks.

8.1.1.3 Network Pool

Elements of all of the resource pools and the pools themselves owned by a service provider remain well-connected with

FIG 8.3: Storage pool

each other. This networking facilitates the cloud service at provider's end.

FIG 8.4: Network pool

As the cloud computing offers the facility of creating virtualized networks to consumers, the pool of physical network devices are also maintained in data centers. Pools of networking components are composed of different pre-configured network connectivity devices like switches, routers and others. Consumers are offered virtualized versions of these components. They can configure those virtual network components in their own way to build their network.

> *Networking resource pools are made of different kind of physical networking devices and delivered in virtualized mode which consumers may use for building their own virtual network.*

8.1.1.4 Hierarchical Organization

As stated earlier, the resource pool architecture generally maintains dedicated pools for different types of computing resources. Thus, data centers usually develop separate resource pools for server, processor, memory, storage and network components respectively. A self-sufficient resource pool thus comprises of a number of smaller pools.

With a very large number of resource components, a resource pool may become very complex to manage if not organized properly. Generally hierarchical structures are established to form parent and child relationships among pools. Figure 8.5 shows a sample hierarchical organization of pools where pools A1 and A2 are comprised of similar type of sub pools. When combined, they constitute a large pool.

With such an organization, the pools eliminate the possibility of any *single point of failure* as there are multiple similar resource components which can handle load in case of failure of any component. Pools A1 and A2 may even be located at different geographic locations.

> The hierarchical pool organization with nested sub-pool architecture makes the cloud resource pool free of any single point of failure.

8.2 COMMODITIZATION OF THE DATA CENTER

In computing, commodity hardware is a device component that is widely available, relatively inexpensive and more or less inter-changeable with other hardware of similar type. Cloud computing service promises to offer *high-performance computing* (HPC) facility. Technologists have been succeeded to produce this high computing performance by combining the powers of multiple commodity computing components. This has opened up new avenues of advancement. Wide scale and planned utilization of commodity hardware has enabled the cloud service providers to achieve their operational efficiencies of scale.

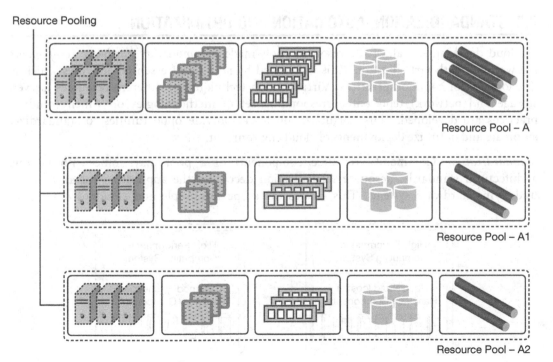

FIG 8.5: A sample resource pool organized in hierarchical manner. Each pool is comprised of five sub pools of server, processor, memory, storage and networking components.

> *Commodity hardware components are those which are inexpensive, replaceable with similar component produced by other vendors and easily available.*

Commoditization of resource pools at data centers has been an attracting feature of cloud computing, especially for the data center owners. Specialized components are not required and commodity components are used to build the pools of (high performance) servers, processors, storage disks and else. As commodity components are cheaper than specialized components, the commoditization of *data centers* is an important factor towards building of widely acceptable cloud computing facilities.

Unlike *commodity computing components*, the specialized components may not be easily available everywhere and any time. The commoditization of data centers are also inspired by the diverse physical location of data centers on which clouds operate. It is not always possible to keep the whole data center at one part of the globe for many reasons. Apart from location-wise benefits or disaster recovery issues, it is also a fact that many governments regulate the placement of physical storage of data within the jurisdiction of the business. When *commodity hardware components* are used to build such data centers, it becomes easier for computing vendors to maintain the resource pools while it requires to replace and procure further.

> *High-performance hardware components are not used to build resource pools in cloud. Rather, commodity hardware components are used to produce high-computing performance.*

8.3 STANDARDIZATION, AUTOMATION AND OPTIMIZATION

In cloud development, all of the resource pools made of *commodity hardware components* are wrapped with virtualization. This is followed by next set of essential activities which is development of common practices. Virtualization techniques of different resources (server, storage and network) represent corresponding set of methodologies on which common practices are developed. Thus, virtualization layers provide opportunities to standardize, automate and optimize deployments of cloud environment.

Standardization: Commodity resource components of a pool may come with various architectural standards. Resource virtualization decouples the application instances from underlying hardware systems. This creates the scope for simple and standardized logical

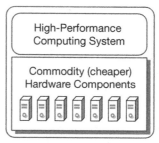

Traditional System   Cloud Data Center

FIG 8.6: Traditional system versus commoditization of cloud data center

representation of resources across the whole cloud environment. Standardization is done based on set of common criteria.

Automation: Automation is implemented for resource deployment like VM instantiation is used to bring VMs off-line back online and to remove them rapidly and automatically based on their previously set standard criteria. Thus, the automation executes operations based on criteria set during the standardization process.

Optimization: This is the process which optimizes the resource usage. Optimization is performed to get optimal resource performance with limited set of resources.

Figure 8.7 shows the layer of application of standardization, automation and optimization. At this layer, the best practices of data center design and implementation are usually followed to maintain the recommended performance as well as per its standards.

> *Standardization, automation and optimization operations are performed over the layer of virtualized pool of physical resources.*

8.4 RESOURCE SHARING

Resource sharing leads to higher resource utilization rate in cloud computing. As a large number of applications run over a pool of resources, the average utilization of each resource component can be increased by sharing them among different applications since all of the applications do not generally attain their peak demands at same time.

Cloud computing allows sharing of pooled and virtualized resources among applications, users and servers. The implementation needs appropriate architectural support. While servers are shared among users and applications the resources like storage, I/O and communication bandwidth are generally shared among several virtual machines.

Resource sharing in utility service environment does not come without its own set of challenges. The main challenge is to guarantee the Quality of Service (QoS), as *performance isolation* is a crucial condition for QoS. The sharing may affect the run-time behaviour of other applications as multiple applications compete for the same set of resources. It may

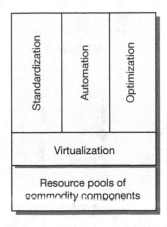

FIG 8.7: Standardization, automation and optimization at data center

also be difficult to predict the response and turnaround time. Thus, the appropriate resource management strategies like optimization and decision-based self-organization of systems are required to maintain the requisite performance of the system.

> *Resource sharing prevents performance isolation and creates the need for new resource management strategies to produce quality service in cloud computing environment.*

8.4.1 Multi-tenancy

The characteristic of a system that enables a resource component to serve different consumers (tenants), where by each of them being isolated from the other is referred to as *multi-tenancy*. This is a feature available in public cloud model in its true and complete sense. Thus, any discussion about multi-tenancy in cloud computing primarily refers to public cloud deployment by default. In multi-tenancy model, the users cannot pre-occupy any particular physical resource component. Resource is utilized by different users on temporary basis as and when required.

Multi-tenancy enables the service provider to provide computing service to multiple isolated consumers (who are not associated with each other) using single and shared set of resources. Multi-tenancy in cloud computing has been materialized based on the concepts of *ownership-free resource sharing* in virtualized mode and temporary allocation of resources from resource pool (Figure 8.8). It enables to lower computing costs and increases resource utilization which are important aspects of *utility computing*.

The pooled resource components at cloud provider's end are used to serve a large number of service consumers. Cloud computing does not allow permanent acquisition of any resource component by any consumer. Whenever a consumer needs resources, appropriate resource components are delivered to the consumer in virtualized mode. The resources again get released whenever that consumer's needs are fulfilled and been returned to the pool of available or free resources which can be used to serve some other consumer's requirements in future.

Thus, there is no *one-to-one mapping* between a consumer and a resource component in terms of resource use. Neither a resource component is dedicatedly used for some particular application. Resource components are allotted to users and applications solely on-availability basis. This increases resource utilization rate and in turn decreases investment as well. In the

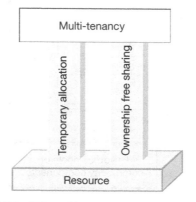

FIG 8.8: Philosophies behind the multi-tenancy

cloud computing environment where a cloud service provider uses to serve a large number of consumers, this resource-sharing model through multi-tenancy has been capable to be changed into an effective mechanism for providing quality service at low cost.

> Multi-tenancy in cloud computing is largely enabled by the ideas of resource sharing in virtualized mode and dynamic resource allocation from resource pool.

8.4.1 Types of Tenancy

Tenants of a system (multi-tenant system) can either be outsides or even insiders within an organization (like multiple departments within an organization) where each of the tenants needs their own protected zones. In cloud computing whenever *multi-tenancy* is discussed, the focus shifts towards public cloud environment as the co-tenants being mutually exclusive or unknown to each other, share same computing infrastructure ideally without compromising their individual security and privacy. However, the idea of multi-tenancy also exists in community cloud and even in private cloud to some extent in alternative sense.

Unlike the exclusiveness of the isolation and individuality of each tenant of a public cloud, the *co-tenants* in a community cloud are not mutually exclusive to each other as they belong to the same community and share similar interests. In private cloud, the concept of *multi-tenancy* is limited within the sub co-tenants internal to a single organization (or under a single tenant). The tenancy requirements of public and private clouds are almost similar irrespective of the fact that one has external co-tenants while the other has internal co-tenants.

> Multi-tenancy in its actual sense allows co-tenants external or unrelated to each other. While existence of external co-tenant is a unique feature of public cloud, the private cloud only allows sub-co-tenants under one tenant.

8.4.2 Tenancy at Different Level of Cloud Services

In a computing environment, the idea of tenancy applies at different levels from infrastructure (like storage) at the lowest layer up to application interface at the top. Similarly in cloud computing, the multi-tenancy is not limited at IaaS level, rather it covers PaaS and SaaS also. The consumers there enjoy the facility at various levels depending on the degree of multi-tenancy offered by a cloud service. However it is evident that by incorporating multi-tenancy at the infrastructure level, all layer of cloud services automatically become multi-tenant to some degree; but that should not encourage anyone to limit multi-tenancy at IaaS level only, rather it should be implemented to its highest degree.

At IaaS level, the *multi-tenancy* provides shared computing infrastructure resources like servers, storages etc. At this level, multi-tenancy is achieved through virtualization of resources and different consumers share same set of resources through their virtual representation without affecting or being aware about one another.

At PaaS level, the *multi-tenancy* means sharing of operating system by multiple applications. Applications from different vendors (tenants) can be run over same OS instance (to be offered as SaaS). This removes the need of allocating separate virtual machines per application by improving the maintenance and utilization of OS level capabilities.

At SaaS level, the multi-tenancy refers to the ability of a single application instance and/ or database instance (that is one database instance being created in some database servers) in order to serve multiple consumers. Consumers (tenants) of SaaS share same application code base as well as database tables and codes (like procedure, functions etc.). Data of multiple consumers which are stored in same set of tables are differentiated by the respective consumer numbers. Here, the separation of data is logical only although consumers get the feeling of physical separation. For application, the tenants may have the capability of customizing application functionalities or view of application interface but they cannot edit application code as the same application instance serves other consumers (tenants) also. *Multi-tenancy* eases application maintenance (like updates) and makes it economical for provider as well as for the consumers. In single-tenancy model, each consumer can be given the rights of the edit to application code as separate application instance is maintained for every consumers.

> *Not only at IaaS layer, multi-tenancy also works at all other levels of cloud services.*

8.5 RESOURCE PROVISIONING

In traditional computing, whenever a new server (or virtual server) is required to support certain workload, it takes lots of efforts and time of administrator to install and supply the server. Current age computing needs rapid infrastructure provisioning facility to meet the varying demands of the consumers. With the emergence of virtualization technology and cloud computing IaaS model, it is now just a matter of minutes to achieve the same provided required volume of resources are being available. Thus, provisioning of a new virtual machine saves lots of time and effort in cloud. One can create a virtual server through a self-service interface which is considered as one of the most attractive feature of cloud.

Flexible resource provisioning is a key requirement in cloud computing. To achieve this flexibility, it is essential to manage the available resources intelligently when required. The orchestration of resources must be performed in a way so that resources can be provisioned to applications rapidly and dynamically in a planned manner.

> *Cloud provisioning is the allocation of cloud provider's resources to the consumers.*

8.5.1 The Autonomic Way

Resource provisioning in cloud is the allocation of a cloud provider's resources directly to the consumers or to the applications. When a consumer asks for resource, cloud provider must create appropriate number of virtual machines (VMs) in order to support the demand and should also allocate physical resources accordingly. This provisioning is an automated process in cloud which is designed by applying artificial intelligence and is known as *autonomic resource provisioning*.

The purpose of autonomic resource provisioning is to automate the allocation of resources so that the overall resource demand can be managed efficiently by minimum amount of resources. One resource is allotted to different applications or consumers. This becomes possible since application loads varies with time. Through autonomic approach, computing resources can be rapidly provisioned and released with minimal management effort from a shared pool of configurable resources as on demand.

8.5.2 Role of SLA

Consumers typically enter into contract with cloud providers which describes the expected requirements of computing resource capacity being required for their applications. This contract is known as service level agreements (SLAs). A cloud provider, after combining all such SLAs, can plan for the total amount of physical resources they have to keep as prepared to support all of its consumers so that those can be allocated to users when their applications would run. This allocation is done dynamically by some provisioning algorithms that map virtual machines (VMs) running end-user applications into physical cloud infrastructure (compute nodes).

> Cloud providers estimate the resource requirements of consumers through the SLA contract that consumers make with their providers.

8.5.3 Resource Provisioning Approaches

Efficient resource provisioning is a key requirement in cloud computing. Cloud consumers do not get direct access to physical computing resources. The provisioning of resources to consumers is enabled through VM (virtual machine) provisioning. Physical resources from resource pool are made available to those VMs which in turn are made available to consumers as well as for the applications.

Physical resources can be assigned to the VMs using two types of provisioning approaches like *static* and *dynamic*. In static approach, VMs are created with specific volume of resources and the capacity of the VM does not change in its lifetime. In dynamic approach, the resource capacity per VM can be adjusted dynamically to match work-load fluctuations.

> Computing resources in cloud computing are provisioned to consumers through virtual machine provisioning.

8.5.3.1 Static Approach

Static provisioning is suitable for applications which have predictable and generally unchanging workload demands. In this approach, once a VM is created it is expected to run for long time without incurring any further resource allocation decision overhead on the system. Here, resource-allocation decision is taken only once and that too at the beginning when user's application starts running. Thus, this approach provides room for a little more time to take decision regarding resource allocation since that does not impact negatively on the performance of the system.

Although static provisioning approach does not bring about any runtime overhead it has major limitations also. This provisioning approach fails to deal with un-anticipated changes in resource demands. When resource demand crosses the limit specified in SLA document it causes trouble for the consumers. Again from provider's point of view, some resources remain unutilized forever since provider arranges for sufficient volume of resources to avoid SLA violation. So this method has drawback from the viewpoint of both provider as well as for consumer.

> *In static provisioning, resources are allocated only once during the creation of VMs. This leads to inefficient resource utilization and restricts the elasticity.*

8.5.3.2 Dynamic Approach

With *dynamic provisioning*, the resources are allocated and de-allocated as per requirement during run-time. This *on-demand resource provisioning* provides elasticity to the system. Providers no more need to keep a certain volume of resources unutilized for each and every system separately, rather they maintain a common resource pool and allocate resources from that when it is required. Resources are removed from VMs when they are no more required and returned to the pool. With this dynamic approach, the processes of billing also become as *pay-per-usage* basis.

Dynamic provisioning technique is more appropriate for cloud computing where application's demand for resources is most likely to change or vary during the execution. But this provisioning approach needs the ability of integrating newly-acquired resources into the existing infrastructure. This gives provisioning elasticity to the system.

Dynamic provisioning allows system to adapt in changed conditions at the cost of bearing run-time resource allocation decision overhead. This overhead leads some amount of delay in system but this can be minimized by putting upper limit on the complexity of provisioning algorithms.

> *In dynamic VM provisioning, resources are allocated as per application requirement during run-time.*

Table 8.1 Comparison between static and dynamic resource provisioning approaches

Static Provisioning	Dynamic Provisioning
Resource allocation decision can be made once only for an application.	For an application, resource allocation decisions can be made number of times.
Resource allocation decision should happen before starting of the application.	Decision can be taken even after starting of the application.
This approach does not provide scope for elasticity to a system.	It provides scope for elasticity to the system.
It restricts the scaling.	It enables the scaling.
It does not introduce any resource allocation decision overhead.	It incurs resource allocation decision overhead on system.
Resource once allotted cannot be returned.	Allotted resources can be returned again.
It is suitable when load pattern is predictable and more or less unchanging.	It is suitable for applications with varying workload.
It introduces under-provisioning and over-provisioning of resource problems.	It resolves the under-provisioning and over-provisioning of resource problems.

8.5.3.3 Hybrid Approach

Dynamic provisioning addresses the problems of static approac, but introduces run-time overhead. To tackle with this problem, a *hybrid provisioning approach* is suggested that combines both static and dynamic provisioning. It starts with static provisioning technique at the initial stage of VM creation and then turns it into dynamic re-provisioning of resources. This approach can often effectively address real-time scenario with changing load in cloud computing.

8.5.4 Resource Under-provision and Over-provision Problems of Traditional Computing

Traditional computing systems mostly follow static resource provisioning approach. But, it is very difficult to correctly predict the future demand of any application (and hence the resource requirement for the application) despite rigorous planning and efforts. This naturally results in under-provision or over-provision of resources in traditional environment.

When demand for computing resources crosses the limit of available resources, then a shortage of resource is created. This scenario is known as *under-provision* of resource. A simple solution to this problem is to reserve sufficient volume of resources for an application so that resource shortage can never happen. But this introduces a new problem. In such case, most of the resources will remain unutilized for majority of time. This scenario is known as *over-provision* of the resources.

> *Under-provisioning problem occurs when the reserved resources are unable to fully meet the demand.*

Figure 8.9 shows the under-provision scenario. Here, the allotted and defined volume of resource is represented by the dashed line. *Under-provisioning* problem occurs when resource demand of application is higher than this allotted volume. Under-provisioning causes application performance degradation.

The *over-provisioning* problem appears when the reserved volume of resource for an application never falls below the estimated highest-required amount of resource for the application considering the varying demand. In such case, since for most of the time, the

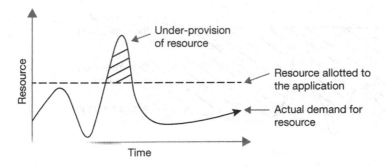

FIG 8.9: Resources under-provisioning problem in traditional system

actual resource demand remains quite lesser than the reserved amount it ultimately turns into un-utilization of valuable resource. This not only causes wastage of resource but also increases the cost of computation. Figure 8.10 represents the scenario.

> *Resource over-provisioning problem occurs when the reserved resources remain unused for most of the time.*

Figures 8.9 and 8.10 exhibit the problem of the traditional fixed-size resource allocation approach. It tends to increase cost or provides poor performance outcomes. In cloud computing, the fine-tuned dynamic or hybrid resource provisioning approaches are used to deliver high performance at low cost.

> *While over-provisioning wastes costly resources, under-provisioning degrades application performance and causes business loss.*

The static provisioning approach causes the trouble for vendors also. Vendors meet consumer's SLA requirements through resource over-provisioning in order to meet worst case demands. However, since application demand remains low most of the time resource utilization rate also remains low. This restricts the vendors to deliver services at lower cost. Cloud computing addresses this issue by dynamic provisioning of resources using virtualization.

8.5.5 Resource Provisioning Plans in Cloud

Consumers can purchase cloud resources from the provider through web form by creating the account. Cloud providers generally offer two different resource provisioning plans or pricing models to fulfill consumers' requirements. These two plans are made to serve different kind of business purposes. The plans are known as *short-term on-demand* plan and *long-term reservation* plan. Most commercial cloud providers offer both of the plans.

8.5.5.1 Short-Term On-Demand Plan

In this pricing model, resources are allotted on short-term basis as per demand. When demand rises, the resources are provisioned accordingly to meet the need. When demand

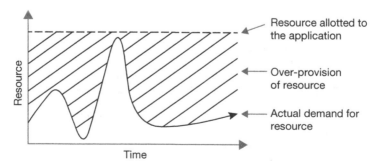

FIG 8.10: Resources over-provisioning problem in traditional systems

decreases, the allotted resources are released from the application and returned to the free resource pool. Consumers are charged on pay-per-usage basis. So, with this on-demand plan, the resource allocation follows the dynamic provisioning approach to fit the fluctuated and unpredictable demands.

In the short-term on-demand plan, it is the responsibility of the provider to ensure application performance by provisioning resources during high demand (the demand from multiple consumers at same time). This requires appropriate planning at provider's end. Estimation of resource requirements during high demand plays the vital role under this pricing model.

> Application performance under short-term on-demand plan solely depends on provider's capability in estimating overall resource demand (of all consumers) during peak hours.

8.5.5.2 Long-Term Reservation Plan

In long-term reservation plan (also known as 'advance provisioning'), a service contract is made between the consumer and the provider regarding requirement of resources. The provider then arranges in advance and keeps aside a certain volume of resources from the resource pool to support the consumer's needs in the time of urgency. This arrangement of appropriating resources is done before starting of the service. In this model of resource provisioning, pricing is not on-demand basis. Rather it is charged as a one-time fee for a fixed period of time generally counted in months or years.

At provider's end, the computational complexity as well as the cost is less under this plan in comparison to the on-demand plan. This is because the provider becomes aware about the maximum resource requirement of the consumer and keeps the resource pool ready to supply resources to meet demands. This reduces the provider's cost (of planning and implementation) and in effect the consumers may get the service in much cheaper rate (generally when long term contract is made) than the on-demand plan if hourly usage rates are considered.

The problem of the reservation plan is, since a fixed volume of resources is arranged as per the SLA there are possibilities of under-provisioning or over-provisioning of resources. It is important for the cloud consumer to estimate the requirements carefully so that those problems can be avoided and at the same time the resource provisioning cost could minimize. This goal can be achieved through an optimal resource management plan.

> Application performance under long-term reservation plan depends on consumer's ability to estimate their own resource demand in advance.

8.5.6 VM Sizing

VM sizing refers to the estimation of the amount of resources that should be allocated to a virtual machine. The estimation is made depending on various parameters extracted out of requests from consumers. In static approach of resource provisioning, the VM size is determined at the beginning of the VM creation. But in dynamic approach of resource provisioning, the VM size changes with time depending on application load. The primary objective of VM sizing is to ensure that VM capacity always remains proportionate with the workload.

> *Proper VM sizing leads to optimal system performance.*

VM sizing can be maintained in two different ways. Traditionally, VM sizing is done on a VM-by-VM basis which is known as *individual-VM based provisioning*. Here, resources are allotted to each virtual machine depending on the study of its previous workload patterns. When additional resources are required for any VM to support load beyond its initial expectation, the resources are allotted from the common resource pool.

The other way is *joint-VM provisioning* approach where resources to VMs are provisioned in combined way so that the unused resources of one VM can be allocated to other VM(s) when they are hosted over the same physical infrastructure. This approach takes advantage of the dynamic VM demand characteristics. Unutilized resources of less loaded VMs can be utilized in other VMs during their peak demand. This leads to overall resource capacity saving at provider's end. This technique is also known as *VM multiplexing*.

> *Joint-VM provisioning saves significant volume from overall resource capacity compared to individual VM-based provisioning technique.*

8.5.7 Dynamic Provisioning and Fault Tolerance

Dynamic resource provisioning brings many advantages to cloud computing over traditional computing approach. It allows runtime replacement of computing resources and helps to build reliable system. This is done by constantly monitoring over all the nodes of a system executing some of the particular tasks. Whenever some of those nodes show low reliability over a predetermined period of time, a new node is introduced into the system to replace that defective or low performing node. This little effort turns the whole cloud system being more tolerant to faults. The reliability of nodes can be measured by monitoring various parameters like finding the number of faults occurred in near past.

8.5.7.1 Zero Downtime Architecture: Advantage of Dynamic Provisioning

The dynamic resource provisioning capability of cloud systems leads to an important goal of system design which is *zero-downtime architecture*. One physical server generally facilitates or hosts multiple virtual servers. Hence, the physical server acts as the single point of failure for all of the virtual systems it creates. But the *dynamic provisioning* mechanism immediately replaces any crashing physical system with a new system instantly and thus the running virtual system gets a new physical host without halting.

Figure 8.11 demonstrates how live VM migration maintains zero downtime during failure of physical host. Here, the virtual server A1 (VM-A1) was hosted by physical server A1 and two applications were running on VM-A1. When physical server 'A1' crashes, VM-A1 is shifted to a new VM with current system status and all of the applications running in VM-A1 have been migrated to VM-A2 which is hosted by physical server 'A2'. Thus, the applications remain unaffected by the effects of zero downtime.

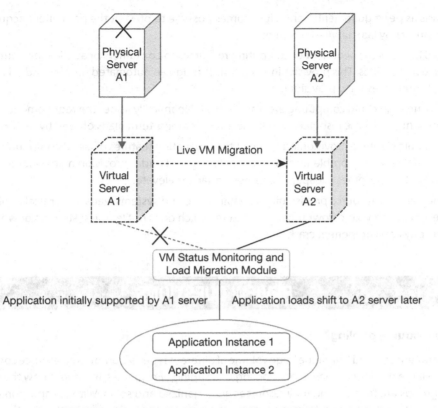

FIG 8.11: Live VM migration during failure of physical server

Dynamic VM provisioning facilitates the idea of zero-downtime architecture.

SUMMARY

❖ Cloud service providers maintain huge volumes of computing resources at data centers. These resources are organized in groups and each group has similar types of resource components. This grouping of resources in suitable structure for efficient and effective resource management is known as pooling.

❖ Cloud service providers have been able to produce high computational performance through pooled commodity computing resources. This frees any IaaS provider from the need of using costly and specialized hardware components. This is known as 'commoditization of data centers'.

❖ Virtualized pools of commodity resources then undergo standardization, system automation and optimization.

❖ Resources in cloud computing are shared among multiple users following multi-tenancy model of sharing. In this model, resources are allotted to users or applications on temporary basis as per requirement. Hence, it becomes possible to prevent the permanent acquisition of resources by IaaS service consumers.

❖ IaaS facilities the allotment of computing resources to consumers or applications through virtual machines. This provisioning happens through an automated process and is known as 'autonomic resource provisioning'.

❖ Resources in cloud computing are also allotted dynamically as per the requirement. Consumers can use resources under short-term or long-term plans offered by the providers.

❖ Dynamic resource provisioning is one of the fascinating features of cloud computing. It eliminates the key problems of over-provisioning and under-provisioning of resources. Thus, computing becomes cheaper and its performances elevate.

❖ The dynamic resource provisioning capability of cloud systems leads to a critical goal system design, namely 'zero downtime architecture' which does not let the system go down during any physical component crash.

REVIEW QUESTIONS

What is resource pooling?

Cloud data centers need to arrange huge volume of different types of computing resource components to serve a large number of consumers. Pooling is grouping of resources. It is about how the groups or nested-groups are formed, and how resources are organized and so on. Without appropriate design and organization during pool formation, computing may not function efficiently with those pooled resources.

How has commoditization helped in the growth of cloud computing?

Commodity hardware resources are cheaper and easily available all over the world. Cloud data centers require good amount of hardware resources to create resource pools. Easy availability of commodity resources and their replacements at cheaper rate makes it easy for vendors to establish and maintain data centers as they need not to look for costly and uncommon specialized (high power) resource components which are not easily available in the market.

'Servers in traditional computing also seem to support multi-tenancy' – justify.

It is true that in traditional computing, multiple users can use a server system. But more than tenants, they actually own the whole server. They permanently occupy the resources. No other people (external or unknown) can utilize the resources even when server utilization rate is low. Thus, traditional servers only support multiple users but do not support multi-tenancy. In cloud computing, the users do not permanently occupy a fixed set of physical resources. Resource allocation happens at runtime and consumers use them only as tenants.

How does 'long-term resource reservation plan' fall under dynamic provisioning category?

Unlike short-term on-demand plan, in long-term resource reservation model, the cloud providers keep aside a certain volume of computing resources in advance (depending on SLA) for consumers. Although volumes of resources are reserved under this plan, the physical resource components are still provisioned dynamically since all of the resources are delivered as virtual resources. Even, any faulty resource component can immediately be replaced dynamically. Thus, the long-term reservation plan does not confirm permanent acquisition of any physical resources and physical resources are only provisioned dynamically.

Does cloud computing entirely eliminate resource under- and over-provisioning problems?

Under on-demand resource provisioning plan, the under-provisioning and over-provisioning problems of resources are eliminated in cloud computing. But, cloud computing also keeps open a resource reservation plan for consumers which is much like owning fixed volume of resources. Under this plan, the problems of under-provisioning and over-provisioning of resources persist.

MULTIPLE CHOICE QUESTIONS

1. By which kind of hardware components makes cloud computing cost effective at the time of building resource pools?

   a) Commodity hardware
   b) Specialized hardware
   c) Both a and b
   d) None of these

2. Resource pools are organized in

   a) Heap structure
   b) Hierarchical structure
   c) Hash structure
   d) None of these

3. The traditional approach of having discrete and independent set of resources is known as

   a) Warehouse
   b) Data center
   c) Silos
   d) None of these

4. Resource pools at cloud data centers are created with

   a) Specialized hardware components
   b) Commodity hardware components
   c) Costly hardware components
   d) None of these

5. Multi-tenancy in cloud computing is powered by

   a) Ownership of free resource sharing
   b) Temporary resource allocation
   c) Resource allocation in virtual mode
   d) All of these

6. In cloud computing, resource provisioning to consumers are made through

   a) Physical servers
   b) Virtual private network
   c) Virtual machines
   d) None of these

7. In static provisioning of resources, resource allocation decision is taken

   a) Before starting of application
   b) Any time before and after starting of application
   c) Only once
   d) Both a and c

8. In dynamic provisioning of resources, the resource allocation decision can be taken

   a) After starting of application
   b) On-demand
   c) For number of times
   d) All of these

9. Dynamic resource provisioning approach eliminates the problem(s) of

   a) Resource under-provisioning
   b) Resource over-provisioning
   c) Both a and b
   d) System speed

10. Zero downtime system architecture is outcome of

    a) Dynamic provisioning
    b) Multi-tenancy
    c) Resource sharing
    d) Resource pooling

11. Standardization of cloud environment is done over the

    a) Physical resource pool
    b) Virtualized resource pool
    c) Individual physical resources
    d) None of these

Scaling in the Cloud

Resource virtualization technique creates room for the adoption of dynamic approach in computing resource provisioning. The dynamic resource provisioning approach in turn creates the scope for developing scalable computing systems and applications. Scalability of systems and applications is an essential feature of cloud computing.

Computing cost depends on the total volume of resources acquired by an application. Any acquired and unutilized resource unnecessarily increases computing cost. Again, low acquisition of resource may affect application performance during higher demand. Hence, any system must run with minimum volume of required resources and should have the ability to expand itself with growing workload which is critical from business point of view. Again, a system should also have the ability to reduce itself with declining workload in terms of acquired resources. Otherwise unnecessary resource acquisition increases the cost.

This ability of expanding and shrinking of a system as per workload is known as scaling. Dynamic resource provisioning plays a key role in building of a scalable system but that alone cannot ensure the scaling. A system should also have the ability to integrate the provisioned resources effectively into itself (or release extra resources) and still run as the same system without any interruption or hitch. This ensures smooth user experience and at the same time reduces cost of computing and improves performance of applications.

9.1 WHAT IS SCALING?

Scaling is the characteristic of a system, model or function that describes its ability of *growing* or *shrinking* whenever required. In computing, scaling represents the capability of a system or application to deal with varying workload efficiently without bringing in a situation where resource shortage hampers performance or resource surplus increases the computation cost.

In simple words, scaling is defined as the ability of being enlarged (or shrunk) for accommodating growth (or fall-off) to fulfill the business needs. A system or application architecture can be termed as *scalable* if its performance improves on adding new resources and the improvement is proportional to the capacity added.

> *A system that scales well can maintain its level of performance or efficiency when it works under larger or growing operational demands.*

The *scalability* of a scalable system is measured by the maximum workload it can competently handle at any particular moment. The point at which a system or application can not handle additional workload efficiently, any more, is known as its *limit of scalability*. Scalability reaches its limit when a system's architecture does not support scaling anymore or some critical hardware resource run out. Resource components which generally limit scalability are processor or memory of application server and disk I/O rate of database server.

9.2 SCALING IN TRADITIONAL COMPUTING

In traditional computing environment, once the resource capacity of a system is enhanced manually the status of the system is retained (ever after) till further human intervention, even if those resources do not get utilized. This under-utilization causes wastage of resources and increases the cost of computing. Yet, very little can be done about it.

The main reason behind this problem is that the infrastructure architecture is not dynamic in traditional computing system, which prevents implementation of dynamic scaling. *Static scaling* requires system shut-down (system to restart) and hence is avoided unless it becomes extremely essential. For this reason, in traditional static scaling environment, although resource capacity expansion was sometime considered a possible option, capacity contraction was beyond imagination because service disruption had to be avoided.

In contrast to the actual definition, conventionally, scalability has been about supplying additional capacity to a system. It was uncommon to reduce capacity of a system, although technically it was always possible. No one ever thought of migrating to a system of lesser capability, even when workload was reduced below the average level. System designers have built computing systems by arranging resources to meet peak demand, wasting resources and increasing cost.

> *In the traditional static scaling approach, computing system requires a 'restart' for the scaling effect to take place which causes service disruption.*

9.3 SCALING IN CLOUD COMPUTING

Scaling is one of the attractive attributes of cloud computing. Scaling in cloud is dynamic in nature and apart from a few special cases it is automatic too. In *dynamic-automatic scaling*, the system resource capacity can be altered while a system is running. Large pool of virtualized resources promises to adjust variable workload by allowing optimum resource utilization.

The *scalability* in cloud computing is offered in a transparent manner and the automatic scaling ability gives the impression of infinite resources to its consumers. Many cloud service providers even claim to offer infinite scalability although in reality that is not true. Even the largest players may at some moment face a scalability problem if cloud computing usage rate increases abruptly, beyond anticipation.

> *Dynamic scaling enables a system to keep performing consistently during times of massive demand by expanding it at pace with growing demand.*

The scaling ability provided by cloud computing is particularly helpful for applications and services to meet unpredictable business demand. If overall resource requirements are planned properly in advance at the provider's end, then on-demand resource delivery nature of cloud computing model can make it robust and economic.

Resources in cloud can be acquired in seconds through the API calls. Cloud system architecture's ability to handle a heterogeneous pool of commodity hardware components has contributed to its infinite scalability. The loosely coupled components under this architecture can scale independently of each other while enabling the system to scale to extraordinary levels.

> *Service providers can create the illusion of infinite resources during service delivery, as cloud consumers remain unaware about the transparent scaling feature.*

9.3.1 Scaling in Cloud is Reversible

Virtualization has introduced the idea of dynamic infrastructure (using virtual computing resources) which has ignited dynamic resource provisioning. *Dynamic scaling* of computing system has become a reality through the dynamic resource provisioning approach where a system can be scaled without being compelled to restart. Thus, addition and removal of resource capacity to and from a running system has become viable and it has become much simpler to exploit extra capacity in cloud computing. Any time during the running of a system, extra resource capacity can be given back to the resource pool and can be claimed again whenever it is required.

It should be noted that in any computing environment, the scaling-down is as important as scaling-up from business point of view. Cloud computing addresses both of these issues with equal priority. But downward scaling is more critical to implement than *upward scaling*. In *downward scaling*, the challenge is to maintain performance while releasing resources. The presence of downward scaling capability has made cloud computing more attractive.

> *Implementation of reversible scaling is a critical act as system performance should not be hampered while releasing the resources.*

9.4 FOUNDATION OF CLOUD SCALING

As mentioned earlier, scaling in cloud is dynamic and automatic. The *auto-scaling* facility provides enormous advantages, both to the service provider and the service consumers. They can both gain in terms of service availability (during peaks), cost and business. This auto-scaling feature in cloud computing has been achieved based on three pillars:

- *Resource virtualization*: It eases resource management tasks and reduces the complexity of system development.
- *Resource sharing*: It allows the optimal resource utilization by sharing resources among multiple users as well as applications.
- *Dynamic resource provisioning*: It supplies (or reclaims) the resources on-demand, in response to the increase (or, decrease) in workload.

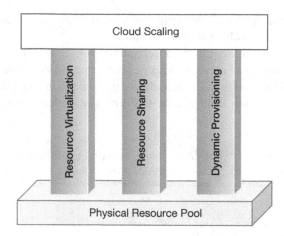

FIG 9.1: Foundations of cloud scaling

Scalability has to be kept in mind from the very beginning when sculpting the architecture of a system. A system's ability of scaling may depend on various parameters. Among them, the two important ones which are dealt meticulously in the development of scalable cloud computing system are:

■ Capacity planning on regular basis and
■ Load balancing

While topics like virtualization, resource sharing and dynamic provisioning have already been covered in Chapters 7 and 8, capacity planning and load balancing have been discussed in subsequent chapters (Chapters 10 and 11).

9.5 SCALABLE APPLICATION

Application architecture should be well-suited to scale in a scalable architectural environment. While cloud provides ideal environment for scaling, applications must also be designed accordingly, having with scaling capability. Scalable computing system architecture lays the foundation for application scalability but cannot alone ensure scalability of application if the application is not suitably designed. On the other hand, a scalable application can only scale diligently with the varying traffic load if the system on which it is running is scalable. Hence, scaling of application depends on two layers which are, scalable application architecture and scalable system architecture.

Cloud platforms provide rich auto-scaling capability to consumers. When used in combination with cloud-native applications, this capability makes the system highly effective. Sometimes, the enriched scaling characteristic of cloud computing may encourage lazy application developers to avoid the critical process of application development following scalable application architecture. But that can only result in low performance. Application's scalability depends on its design, the types of algorithms applied and on the data structures used. Scalability of application also depends on the database system architecture.

Database instances must be able to be expanded in distributed environment. Cloud native database system has been discussed in Chapter 14 of this book.

> *It is not possible to take full advantage of the scalable computing infrastructure if the application architecture is not scalable. Both have to work together to maximize the gain.*

9.6 SCALING STRATEGIES IN CLOUD

Cloud computing is empowered by its *dynamic scaling* capability. In the dynamic scaling approach, a system can be re-sized during its execution without restarting or interrupting any service. This critical task of dynamic capacity alteration can be done in two ways:

- Manually: when a system can be scaled while running by executing appropriate commands through the application interface.
- Automatically: when this type of scaling of the system can be implemented through programs that can automatically adjust system capacity by observing the actual demand.

The ability of manual capacity adjustment of a system during its operation is a huge task for any computing environment. But passing beyond this, the real power of cloud scaling lies in automatic scaling ability. Here, no human interaction is required. The system can adjust or resize itself on its own.

The dynamic auto-scaling is generally referred as *auto scaling* which is also known as *cloud scaling*. Auto-scaling can be implemented in two different ways:

- Scaling based on a predefined schedule known as *proactive scaling*.
- Scaling based on current actual demand known as *reactive scaling*.

> *Dynamic scaling of a system can be managed both manually and automatically. Auto-scaling frees a system from any manual involvement for adjusting resources.*

9.6.1 Proactive Scaling

Application demand generally varies with time. Suppose, an e-commerce site is rarely accessed in the early morning or, an enterprise application gets the majority of hits during last two hours of the day. In such cases, where the expected increase or decrease of demand is known a pre-programmed plan is placed to automatically alter the resource capacity. Such scaling strategy that does not wait for workload to change, rather alters capacity in advance based on a pre-defined schedule is known as *proactive scaling*.

These types of known situations of demand change can be categorized into two types. Separate planning is required to deal with those two types of situations. Hence, the proactive scaling schedules are implemented in two different ways as

- Proactive cyclic scaling: This type of proactive scaling event takes place at fixed regular intervals and by pre-defined times of the day, week, month or year. For example, an enterprise application may need to scale every business day from 11 AM to 3 PM which is their peak business hours.

■ Proactive event-based scaling: Major variations in traffic load may occur due to some scheduled business events like promotional campaigns or new product launch and else. For those cases, event-based proactive scaling is the best way out.

Often through business and statistical analysis, the variable pattern of application or service demand becomes predictable. When using proactive scaling, the expected standard deviation should be considered. The exact requirements may not be possible to predict but the system should be ready for slight deviation from expectations. If for an application, 5,000 page views/minute is expected during the peak hour(s) of a day and it is seen that the actual count is 5,050 it cannot be termed as unexpected. So, the provisioned resource capacity at any point of time should be able to handle the expected load with some room to spare. Understanding what comes under this 'room to spare' segment is a tricky part of capacity planning.

> *Proactive scaling strategy does not wait for demand to increase or decrease in expected circumstances. Such standard situations are handled through pre-defined plans.*

9.6.2 Reactive Scaling

In this strategy, the system reacts immediately to changing demand of resources by adding or removing capacity on its own. Here, the decision is taken based on resource utilization. When utilization of processor or memory or some other resource reaches a certain threshold, more of that resource can be added into the environment by the system itself without any external intervention. Under this scaling technique, depending on a situation where the suitable parameters are identified at first to activate the auto-scaling process. System scales in response to the changing conditions of those parameters. This eliminates the need for any pre-scheduled action to handle scaling as it always remains unknown when those conditions may change.

A *scalable system* should deal with varying workloads through proactive scaling approach as much as possible. Reactive scaling approach should be seen as a safeguard for absolutely unavoidable scenarios. Too much dependency on the reactive scaling strategy, without performing appropriate capacity planning to facilitate proactive scaling of a system may turn suicidal.

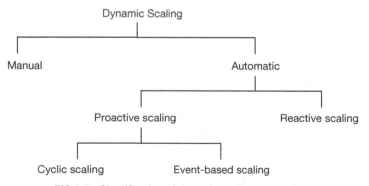

FIG 9.2: Classification of dynamic scaling approaches

One vulnerability of reactive scaling strategy is that it may create trouble if not protected properly against attacks. An attack to computing system may cause malicious consumption of all resources including whatever newly been added. In such case, reactive scaling mechanism may fire a series of failed attempts to balance the gap by launching new resources while the cost increases sharply. Such situation must be handled carefully and there should be a monitoring system in place which will govern the resource provisioning. Standard practice is to put an upper cap on the volume of resources to be provisioned for an application.

> Reactive scaling should be applied as the last layer of protection to scale a system and should not be used unless unavoidable.

9.6.3 The Combination

It is quite understandable that if an auto-scaling system only adopts reactive approach it might not scale proportionally during high spikes in demand which may turn disastrous. Therefore, the prediction-based proactive scaling is required to work together with reactive approach in order to cope up with the real-time scenarios.

A robust auto-scaling implementation needs the appropriate mixture of the two scaling approaches. For an anticipated resource requirement scenario, the system should also have properly defined schedules. For an unpredictable scenario, the system must react to environmental signals (such as sudden rises or drops in usage).

> Auto-scaling implementation requires mixture of both reactive and proactive scaling approaches.

9.7 AUTO SCALING IN CLOUD

In *auto-scaling* (also called as *cloud scaling*) mechanism, the system itself can increase the required resource capacity, automatically (and dynamically), when the demand of workload goes up. The mechanism can also release and return resources to the free pool when they are no more required. Auto-scaling facility helps to maximize resource utilization by automatically doing the work of scaling.

The working of the auto-scaling mechanism in cloud has been briefly described in Figure 9.3. Auto-scaling allows scaling of computing resources both in the predictable and unpredictable circumstances. Scaling in these two situations happens in following fashion:

- Unpredictably, based on specified conditions and
- Predictably, according to defined schedule

A set of conditions or rules can be specified based on application-specific metrics like resource utilization rates, number of simultaneous users or transactions per second etc. For example, a pre-defined condition may say that additional (same) types of resource will be launched if the overall resource utilization rate reaches 90 percent and the last added resource will be released if overall resource utilization rate of the entire system falls below 45 percent.

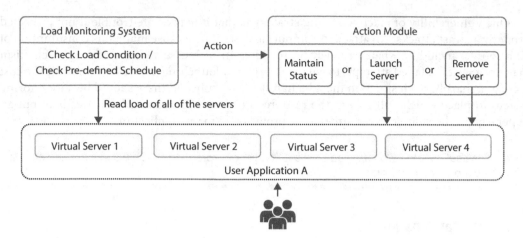

FIG 9.3: Working of the auto-scaling mechanism in cloud computing

The monitoring and the checking modules of auto-scaling unit play vital roles in the auto-scaling process. Monitoring module keeps on sending the load status to the checking module at regular intervals, while checking module decides the appropriate action depending on the current load status and stored pre-defined schedules. In the example shown in Figure 9.3, the load monitoring module launches an additional (same type of) server to support Application A, if all of the previously launched server(s) are loaded. In case of low utilization of all of the servers, the last added resource is revoked.

9.7.1 Scaling Boundaries

Implementation of auto-scaling mechanism may not always mean giving up full manual control. For tricky cases, especially where possibilities of attacks are there that may eat up all allotted resources, the scaling boundaries are set. If resource provisioning is required beyond the defined boundary, system generally raises alert asking for special attention. Then, the administrator can take decision based on various parameters and scaling is handled manually if required. Both upper and lower scaling boundaries can be added to limit the range of permitted auto-scaling. Thus auto-scaling mechanism works within those pre-defined boundaries.

> *To protect system from external attack, auto-scaling mechanism is often limited by setting boundaries. Although, beyond those boundaries the scaling is controlled manually.*

9.8 TYPES OF SCALING

A computing system can be scaled by providing additional hardware resources. There are two different ways of supplying and integrating these hardware resources into a system. Depending on this, the scaling approaches can be categorized into two types as *vertical scaling* and *horizontal scaling*.

9.8.1 Vertical Scaling or Scaling Up

One way of increasing resource capacity is to replace the existing component (processors, memory etc.) with a more powerful hardware component. Thus, the capacity can be increased (or decreased) by upgrading (or reducing) a resource quality to support raising (or falling) workload. This type of scaling where a resource component is powered up through replacement is called *scaling up* or *vertical scaling*. For example, a system with dual-processor capacity can be scaled vertically by replacing the processor with a quad-processor.

In cloud computing, increase in system capacity through vertical scaling is implemented by provisioning and integrating additional hardware resources within an existing resource node, instead of introducing new node to handle increased demand. This is shown in Figure 9.4.

Advantages: It is not a complex task to replace a component of a system since it does not require alteration in the system architecture. So, vertical scaling approach has low management complexity and is less risky.

Disadvantages: High power hardware components or specialized resources are expensive. Capacity or power of any resource component always has an upper limit. Hence, a sufficiently capable resource may not always be available or if available, the specialized hardware components may not be even affordable. On the other hand, the hardware replacement may cause interruption to the service and thereby introduce a system downtime problem.

> In vertical scaling, the overall system capacity is enhanced by replacing resource components within existing nodes.

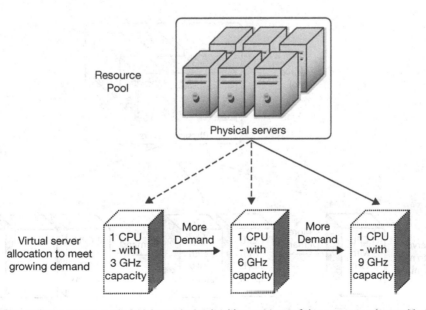

FIG 9.4: Computing resource scaled up by replacing it with more powerful resource as demand increases

9.8.2 Horizontal Scaling or Scaling Out

Resource capacity of a system can be increased by introducing additional resources (and without elimination of the existing). These new resources work together with the existing components. This type of scaling where the system is equipped with supplementary resources to expand the resource capacity is known as *scaling out* or *horizontal scaling*. For example, a system with a dual-processor capacity can be scaled horizontally by adding another dual-processor.

> In horizontal scaling, the overall system capacity is enhanced by adding more nodes.

In cloud computing, the increase in system capacity through horizontal scaling is implemented by provisioning additional resource nodes instead of replacing resource components of existing nodes with powerful components. This is shown in Figure 9.5.

Advantages: This approach does not involve any system downtime. Specialized high-end hardware components are not required to scale out a system; generally available commodity hardware are used for horizontal scaling here. And more importantly, this scaling approach is not limited by an individual component's capability as multiple similar type components (i.e. multiple processors or multiple memory units etc.) synchronize together in order to act as a powerful component. Unlike vertical scaling, no resource components are thrown out of the system (through replacement).

Disadvantages: This approach needs managing large number of distributed nodes which need to synchronize together, and hence involve complexity. Presence of heterogeneous nodes further increases the complexity. The other issue is that horizontal scaling is appropriate for running distributed software applications; hence existing applications developed to run in centralized environment are needed to be redesigned for a distributed computing environment.

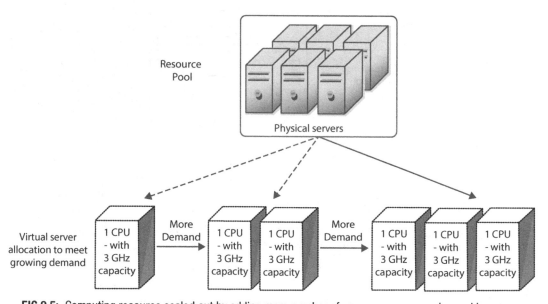

FIG 9.5: Computing resource scaled out by adding more number of same resources as demand increases

Horizontal scaling with homogeneous nodes is a significant simplification in the scaling approach. With homogeneous nodes, the associated activities for scaling like load balancing with round-robin scheduling and capacity planning becomes simple and easier.

> Horizontal scaling helps to build an economical computing system as powerful resource components can be built by combining multiple ordinary resources.

9.8.3 An Analogy

The scaling scenarios of a computing system can be described clearly through a familiar analogy. Think of the roadway communication infrastructure for automobile travel in a city. Vehicles run over the roadways just like applications run over resources. When the roadways (the hardware) becomes unable to support the desired volume of traffic, the situation can be improved in two possible ways. One way is to improve the quality of the roads (by upgrading the road materials, here it is hardware) so that traffic can be moved at a higher speed. This is vertical scaling where the vehicles (the software) can run with more speed on the same road. Alternatively, the roads can be widened to increase the number of lanes. Then more cars can run side-by-side and thus the widened road being able to support more traffic. This is horizontal scaling. To make the situation even better, it is always possible to combine vertical scaling with horizontal scaling by upgrading the quality of the existing lanes and at the same time by adding new lanes.

> There is no conflict between the two scaling strategies; nor are they mutually exclusive. Horizontal and vertical scaling approaches can work together.

9.8.4 Comparison Between Vertical and Horizontal Scaling

Horizontal scaling approach needs to manage more number of resource nodes than its vertical counterpart. Management of large number of computing resource nodes is always a complicated process. Administrating the network, managing communications and synchronizing the activities of all of the nodes are critical parts of horizontal scaling. The programming model is also different and applications need to follow the distributed computing model. On the other hand, vertical scaling involves changes in the configuration of resource node every time scaling is performed. Depending on system architecture, this may cause service interruption. Table 9.1 represents a comparison between these two models.

With increasing need of computing performance and decreasing price of commodity hardware, the cost effectiveness is always in favour of the horizontal scaling approach, in which almost unlimited high computing performance can be delivered without any service interruption.

> Horizontal scaling is, comparatively, a complex approach. Vertical scaling is simpler but limited in its usage.

Table 9.1   Comparison between vertical and horizontal scaling

Vertical Scaling	Horizontal Scaling
It is known as Scaling up.	It is known as Scaling out.
This approach involves replacement of components or resource nodes.	This approach involves introduction of additional components or resource nodes.
It can be implemented in any type of computing environment.	It can only be implemented in distributed computing environment.
It has less management complexity.	The management of larger numbers of nodes increases system complexity.
It may cause service interruption as system needs to restart after replacing component.	It does not cause service interruption. No system-restart is required.
It has less influence on application architecture.	This approach has a more fundamental influence on application architecture.
A vertically scalable application tends to run on high-end hardware.	A horizontally scalable application tends to run on low-end (commodity) hardware.
Here, the loads are concentrated.	It spreads the load.
It requires the specialized hardware components.	It can be done using normal commodity hardware components.
Upgrading the capacity of resource beyond a certain level can become very expensive in this type of scaling.	It is always less expensive and the expense is always proportional to resource capacity.
The expansion is limited by any resource's maximum capacity.	The expansion does not depend on available capacity of hardware components.
It is not a long term solution for scaling.	It provides a long term solution for scaling.

9.8.5 The Appropriate Choice

Although the architectural structures of the vertical and horizontal scaling approaches are different from one another, there are always trade-offs between the two models of scaling. The question raised here is whether it would be better to increase the power of the individual nodes or to combine the power of multiple nodes by distributing the load among them. The answer is not one. It differs on a case by case basis.

The decision depends on two aspects: the computational and business requirements. From computational viewpoint, the choice is primarily linked with factors like the architecture of the system and design architecture of application. From business stand point, the availability of requirement, cost of implementation and system performance are the decisive factors. In some cases, vertical scaling fits more appropriately and in many other cases horizontal scaling works well.

> There are always trade-offs between choosing one method for scaling versus the other. The decision depends on specific requirements.

9.9 HORIZONTAL SCALING IS MORE CLOUD-NATIVE APPROACH

Cloud computing model promises to deliver infinite scalability. Vertical scaling has limitations and it can only grow as per available resource components. Thus, the *infinite scalability* promise cannot be fulfilled with vertical scaling approach in the cloud computing environment where application load may reach the zenith on different occasions.

Horizontal scaling on the other hand can spread the load across multiple resource nodes and can thus support load unrestricted by any resource component's ability. The more resource nodes are added, the more load can be supported and thus this scaling approach is rather pertinent to deliver infinite scalability.

The other issue is that in an auto-scaling environment, replacing a component with another is not a suitable choice. Rather, adding and releasing resources to scale is much easier approach. Thus, the horizontal scaling approach becomes more cloud-native. But this does not entirely throw out vertical scaling from cloud computing, and in certain situations these scaling up process solves the issues faster.

> Infinite scalability in cloud computing can only be achieved through the horizontal scaling approach.

9.10 PERFORMANCE AND SCALABILITY

Applications are often measured by two important parameters like performance and scalability. When asked about what is scalability, many think it is about improving the performance. But that is not the case. *Performance* is what an individual user experiences but *scalability* is the number of users who happen to experience that performance.

Application performance depends on different parameters. For any application, the response time is considered the most important performance measure. Apart from this, the elapsed time for completing all of the activities determines the overall performance of any application.

Scalability refers to the number of concurrent users who have a positive (satisfactory) experience. If the application can maintain its performance with growing number of concurrent users then it is said that it scales well. Suppose, with 1000 concurrent users the average response time of an application is 1 second but as the number of concurrent users grows to 2000, the average response time becomes 2 seconds; then the application is said to be not scaling well. In an ideal scalable system, the response time should not increase with the number of the concurrent users.

An application may scale well without performing well. This may happen when the application handles many concurrent users with same performance but that performance is poor irrespective of the number of concurrent users.

Again, the performance tends to degrade with growing number of concurrent users. So there is always a clash between performance and scalability. This problem is settled by setting a threshold value which indicates the limit of scalability. The limit is determined by the maximum number of concurrent users for whom an application may perform consistently. Beyond this limit, the performance would degrade.

> Performance and scalability are different issues and both are important for a computing system.

9.11 THE RESOURCE CONTENTION PROBLEM

From one viewpoint, scalability may be about supporting growing number of concurrent users but seldom can this number limit the scalability of application. Rather, scalability often faces problems due to resource contention. In computing, *resource contention* is about the controversy over access to sufficient volume of resources. For example, when a network communication path cannot handle any more traffic towards a web application, the application suffers with scalability issue. In this case, the resource bottleneck is the network connection.

Thus, generally it is not the number of concurrent users but the resource *bottleneck problem* that limits the sequence of scalability. Different applications have different stress points. System designers must therefore analyze the expected system load patterns and carry on tests to check how different scenarios create diferent *stress points* in the infrastructure.

Here for cloud based applications, the most likely initial stress points have been mentioned below:

- Process speed of application server
- Memory capacity and speed of application server
- Speed of the disk I/O operation of database server
- Network bandwidth

Increase in stressed resource's capacity is the only way to scale a system beyond some bottleneck or stress point. But the fact remains that elimination of one bottleneck only reveals another one. Hence, the system components should be synchronized to push any such introductions of bottleneck problems as far away as possible.

9.12 CLOUD BURSTING: A SCENARIO OF FLEXIBLE SCALING

When dynamic provisioning approach is applied to provision resources from an external cloud system to support some overloaded application running on organization's internal computing environment, then this state of affairs is referred to as *cloud bursting* (or *cloud peering*). In cloud bursting architecture, initially the resources of organization's internal computing system are consumed by applications. With growing resource demand whenever a pre-defined capacity threshold is reached, the dynamic resource provisioning mechanism 'bursts out' and starts consuming essential resources from a cloud, predominantly a public cloud.

When the internal computing set-up is a private cloud facility, in such cases, the deployment becomes a hybrid application. When the existing private cloud infrastructure cannot handle the load spikes, the workload is migrated to some public cloud deployment. Again when the load of application reduces, the public-cloud-based computing resources are released and the system gets back to the on-premises environment. Thus, the workload shifts between external and internal hosting to manage the changing resource demands without any knowledge of the users.

> *Cloud burst refers to the scaling where an application primarily running on an organization's internal infrastructure or private cloud, expands into some public cloud in the event of excessive demand.*

9.12.1 Cloud Bursting Architecture

The foundation of the cloud bursting architectural model is based on two functionalities like *automated scaling listener* and *resource replicator*. The automated scaling listener decides when to redirect load to an external cloud system. Resource replication maintains the system status during load switch between on-premises system and cloud environment. Figure 9.6 represents the architectural model of cloud bursting.

> *The bursting generally erupts out to a public cloud but it may also tend to a private cloud.*

As shown in Figure 9.6, the automated scaling listener monitors the load of on-premises service 'A'. When on-premises service load exceeds the threshold value, the scaling listener redirects traffics towards the replicated implementation of service 'A' in the external cloud. In the meantime, the resource replicator copies the current state and data of on-premises service 'A' to external cloud in order to keep the systems synchronized. Service 'A' remains redundantly pre-deployed in the external cloud in an inactive mode until cloud bursting occurs.

In Figure 9.6, when the on-premises service 'A' becomes fully-loaded with traffics from service consumers 1 and 2, the automated scaling listener redirects the traffics from service consumer 3 towards the external cloud implementation of Service 'A'. When load decreases, the external cloud service is released and the system retreats to the internal on-premises system.

> *The cloud bursting architecture is suitable for internal computing systems where high volume of traffic occurs for a short period of time.*

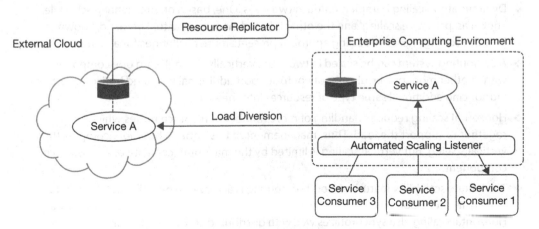

FIG 9.6: Cloud bursting architecture

9.13 SCALABILITY IS A BUSINESS CONCERN

Growth is a basic goal of any business. But infrastructural support is one primary necessity to facilitate this growth. Hence, apart from flexibility of operation, what any business looks for is scalability. Business scalability largely depends on the scalability of the computing system supporting the business. Business applications must be able to support growing workload by processing sudden traffic escalation efficiently.

Scalability is about customer satisfaction as it can process growing extent of incoming traffic with consistent performance. More customer satisfaction means more business. Studies show that a few milliseconds of delay in page load time reduce business by significant percentage. Amazon observed 1 percent decrease in retail revenue caused by 100-millisecond delay. Analysis by Google showed 20 percent decrease in traffic due to an additional 500-millisecond delay in page response time. Hence, scalability ultimately becomes a vital business concern.

In cloud computing, businesses can take advantage of nearly infinite scalability by using the right scale to deploy their applications. The automatic scaling facility to grow during traffic demands and shrink during less workload allows businesses to focus on their core business objectives.

SUMMARY

- ❖ Scaling is the ability of a system to adjust itself to changing workload. This characteristic comes handy, especially when the workload increases beyond assessment. Efficient management of such unexpected load is extremely essential for businesses.

- ❖ Cloud computing offers dynamic and automatic scaling. System can grow or shrink on its own as per requirement. The downward scaling minimizes resource wastage and thus the cost of computing, while upward scaling helps business to grow at lesser cost.

- ❖ The automatic scaling facility of cloud is built upon the foundations of virtualization, resource sharing and the concepts of dynamic resource provisioning.

- ❖ Dynamic auto-scaling is implemented in two ways. One, based on pre-defined schedule, known as 'proactive scaling' and the other is based on current actual demand, known as 'reactive scaling'. Reactive scaling approach presents more challenges for a system architect.

- ❖ A computing system can be scaled in two ways: vertically, by replacing one component with another more powerful component to support additional load; and horizontally, by introducing additional same type of resources into the system.

- ❖ Horizontal scaling requires handling of more number of resource nodes which work together to support the load. Thus, management of this approach is more complex than vertical scaling. But vertical scaling is limited by the maximum capacity of any resource component.

- ❖ The infinite scalability feature of cloud computing is achievable only through horizontal scaling. It can be done by introducing more resource nodes to support the growing load. Horizontal scaling also synchronizes well with distributed cloud architecture.

REVIEW QUESTIONS

What is auto-scaling? How does it work?

Auto-scaling is a mechanism through which resources can automatically be provisioned into a computing system during demand. Provisioned resources also get released when demand drops in auto-scaling. This can be done by keeping constant monitoring a system and by setting of certain thresholds. Whenever those thresholds are touched the automated mechanism takes necessary care to meet the demand with maximum resource utilization.

Are, dynamic scaling and automatic scaling not synonymous?

Dynamic scaling and automatic scaling are not synonymous. Dynamic scaling means scaling of a running system without any interruption. This can be done in two ways as manually or through automation. Cloud computing implements automatic dynamic scaling which is known as 'auto scaling'. In some critical situations though the manual dynamic scaling becomes unavoidable.

What is 'Auto-Scaling Group'?

'Auto-scaling group' is a feature initially been offered by Amazon cloud services. It is collection of EC2 instances. An auto-scaling group can be created to maintain the number of EC2 instances for the group. At any instance, an unhealthy Amazon EC2 instance is replaced by new one. The group can be automatically scaled up and down based on specified conditions.

Does cloud literally provide infinite scaling facility?

Infinite scalability during growth in application demand means infinite provisioning of resources which is an impractical idea. While resources are not literally infinite, the cloud computing creates the illusion of infinite resources through sharing of resources among different applications. The implementation is based on the concept that an application cannot have same resource requirements all of the time and hence the resources from a pool can be shared among applications and users. When an application demand grows, this pool of shared resources can provide support for scaling of that application as long as free resources are available there. Since public cloud computing facilities to maintain huge pool of resources it provides illusion of infinite scaling during demand.

Can resource capacity planning be avoided through auto-scaling?

Resource capacity planning has been done to estimate resource requirements so that provider can arrange resources accordingly. Through auto-scaling, a sudden traffic spike can be supported effectively. But in long run, without proper capacity planning in place, either resource shortage or resource surplus problem appears. Auto-scaling is a special characteristic of cloud computing systems but it is never a replacement for capacity planning. Moreover, for an effective implementation of auto-scaling, capacity planning should be done at each and every level of cloud service layers.

MULTIPLE CHOICE QUESTIONS

1. Which of the following is advantage of dynamic scaling?

   a) Resource capacity can be increased during run-time

   b) Resource capacity can be reduced during run-time

   c) No 'system restart' is required after resource capacity change

   d) All of these

2. Dynamic scaling facility in cloud has been achieved based on

   a) Resource virtualization

   b) Resource sharing

   c) Dynamic resource provisioning

   d) All of these

3. Can dynamic scaling approach be manual?

   a) Yes

   b) No

4. Which of the following is the most fascinating feature of dynamic scaling in cloud computing?

   a) It is prompt

   b) It is automatic

   c) It is reversible

   d) It is infinite

5. Predictable load patterns in cloud computing are managed through

   a) Dynamic scaling strategy

   b) Proactive scaling strategy

   c) Reactive scaling strategy

   d) Static scaling strategy

6. In cloud computing, auto-scaling boundaries are set for a scalable system to

   a) Make the scaling effective

   b) Protect resources from external attack

   c) Minimize cost

   d) None of these

7. Distributed computing system architecture is apt to scale

   a) Horizontally

   b) Vertically

   c) Both horizontally and vertically

   d) None of these

8. Infinite scalability can be achieved through the implementation of

   a) Reactive scaling

   b) Proactive scaling

   c) Horizontal scaling

   d) Vertical scaling

9. Better performance of a system indicates better scalability.

   a) True

   b) False

10. Which of the following is the primary factor to limit scalability?

    a) Cost of system management

    b) Resource bottleneck

    c) Growing number of users

    d) Cost of resource components

11. Which type of scaling is more apt for distributed computing environment like cloud?

    a) Horizontal scaling

    b) Vertical scaling

    c) A mixture of horizontal and vertical scaling

    d) It depends on the distributed computing architecture

CHAPTER

10 | Capacity Planning

Cloud Computing has an alluring concept about service, and that is, it has the ability to deliver infinite resources: consumers can get any kind and any volume of resources instantly as per their demands. The somewhat incorrect idea of infinite resources in cloud computing has primarily been accomplished by creating flexible resource pools. Resource virtualization technique and auto-scaling mechanism enable an uninterrupted supply of resources during the execution of system or application.

However, if not understood properly the concept of infinite computing resources may cause serious concerns about the success of a cloud service. At the physical (data center) level, it is never possible for a cloud service provider to arrange an unlimited volume of computing resources. Service providers actually create the impression of unlimited resources before their consumers by strategic arrangement and utilization of resources. This chapter will discuss these strategies.

Earlier, the safest traditional approach in capacity planning was to buy resources for an estimated maximum capacity, which resulted in resource wastage and an unprecedented increase in budget. However with the assurance of an unlimited and dynamic supply of resources, enterprises can now plan business with minimum required resources. This reduces resource wastage as well as computing costs.

Apparently, it is the responsibility of the IaaS providers to deliver all resources as per the demand of the consumers. However without the sincere participation of the upper layer service providers (PaaS and SaaS providers) IaaS providers alone cannot make this idea successful. Even end users of cloud services (application consumers) have major roles to play. The chapter focuses on these aspects also.

10.1 WHAT IS CAPACITY PLANNING

Capacity Planning in computing is basically developing a strategy which guarantees that at any moment, the available or arranged resources will be sufficient to support the actual demand for resources and that too at the minimal possible cost. The goal of capacity planning is to identify the right amount of resource requirement to meet the service demands at present and also in the future.

Resource requirement of an application generally differs with time. A cost effective *agile system* can only be developed by understanding these shifting resource needs, and with proper capacity planning in place. Appropriate capacity planning made for a system offers enormous benefits. With it, the performance of service improves while budgeting becomes more disciplined and costs come under control.

Every application is different and every user behaves in a different way. Capacity planning is required to overcome this unpredictability, and determine what volume of hardware resources are required to meet the application needs of users adequately so that they never feel a resource crunch. In a networked environment like cloud computing system, capacity planning is important both for computing as well as networking resources.

> *Capacity Planning in computing is a process that determines the future requirement of computing resources to provide desired levels of service to a given workload at the least cost.*

10.2 CAPACITY PLANNING IN COMPUTING

Similar to other resources like water, electricity, food grains, minerals etc., computing resources are also considered essential in this day and age. Capacity planning is essential for any resource to balance supply and demand, so that a system does not run into crisis.

As the computing resource management ideas have changed with time from in-house to outsourced and then to cloud, so has capacity planning. Traditionally, capacity planning in computing has been performed in *silos* (isolated storages or data centers to stock resources) or in isolated organizational structures. The other problem was that the actual stakeholders had very little control over the capacity planning process. Hence possibilities of gaps between real capacity and the actual demand were high. Also, the fixed resource capacity within a silo makes it difficult to manage varying resource needs of an application over time. In such a scenario, both over-provisioning and under-provisioning of resource ultimately turns expensive from the business point of view.

The solution to this problem only appeared with the removal of small silos and the creation of scope for the end users to regularly take part in capacity planning process. The cloud model of computing has created this scope, where end users can self-provision the resources without interacting with the provider. This increases efficiency and reduces wastage of resource.

> *In traditional computing, end users had little participation in the capacity planning process.*

10.3 CAPACITY PLANNING IN CLOUD COMPUTING

Cloud Computing as a utility service promotes multi-tenancy and resource sharing. This removes the requirement of creating small silos of computing infrastructures. A large number of consumers are served by a reputed cloud service provider through various services, and each consumer has access to a great volume of resources which are limitless as compared to their individual computing resource requirements.

This may raise doubts regarding the need of capacity planning in cloud computing. Why perform the complex task of capacity planning when cloud can supply limitless volume of resources? Is it not an unnecessary thing to do? Unfortunately, this perception is not accurate, and if not taken seriously can pose serious problems and can even derail the effectiveness of the whole computing strategy. The reality is actually different from this common perception of limitless availability of resources to individual consumers. Resources are never limitless in cloud and capacity planning is just as important in cloud computing as it was in traditional computing.

10.3.1 Infinite Resource: An Illusion, Not Reality

In reality, cloud environment gives the *illusion* of infinite computing resources available on-demand. The creation of this illusion about infinite resources marks the difference between success and failure for a service provider. The delivery model of resources in cloud computing can indeed provide what may seem to appear to be an infinite supply of resources on-demand, but it comes at a cost, and that is why we need proper capacity planning.

The illusion of infinite computing resources is possible with a business model where one service provider has many clients and an enormous number of applications to support their single or multiple connected data center(s). On different occasions, different applications raise higher resource requirements than general business hours or days. Resource demands of applications also fall in a similar fashion. The service provider needs to have a clear idea about the resource needs of all clients in advance, so that it can arrange enough resources to support all applications without a resource crunch at the time of high demand. This is the philosophy behind capacity planning in cloud computing.

For successful capacity planning the consumers must also provide a rough idea in advance to the service provider regarding their varying resource requirements throughout the year. This helps providers plan accordingly and reserve an adequate amount of resources for every application during high demand periods.

> The impression of infinite resource availability in cloud computing can only be created through proper capacity planning along with other measures.

10.3.2 Who Does the Capacity Planning in Cloud

In cloud computing, capacity planning is done at two levels. At the first level, each consumer of a cloud service does his own capacity planning. At the second level, the cloud service provider analyzes the *capacity requirements* of all consumers together and makes the ultimate overall capacity planning. In this regard, cloud service consumers can be divided into two groups.

- IaaS consumers generally plan and reserve a fixed capacity of resources they would consume for a period. This drives them to do their own capacity planning task, but only for the virtual resources they consume.
- SaaS and PaaS consumers generally opt for a dynamically metered resource use model. Hence their declaration about service requirements noted in the service level contracts (SLA contract) is considered very important for the provider in the capacity planning process.

But for all kinds/levels of service consumers in a cloud, capacity planning is totally different from the non-cloud scenario. They are not constrained with predicting the accurate physical resource needs for their applications, which is a critical task to perform. Since resource is available on demand in cloud, capacity planning is not very challenging for consumers, and they can start with a moderate estimation of resources.

But, if a service consumer at any level of cloud (be it IaaS, PaaS or SaaS) cannot estimate the future resource requirement correctly and actual demand consumes a great deal of resources than planned, the pricing model may increase the metered billing amount unexpectedly. So, consumers have to manage capacity as per their budgeting limit, and plan for their own finite demand.

At the end of the day, the bottom level capacity planning is the responsibility of IaaS provider. Cloud consumers (SaaS, PaaS or IaaS) may (and should) perform some capacity planning tasks, but all those are done either with virtual resources (by IaaS consumer), or through SLA (by IaaS, PaaS and SaaS consumers) only. They do not arrange any physical resource. The IaaS provider studies all those capacity requirements along with service level contracts to know about all service requirements of consumers and perform the actual physical capacity planning for the whole system.

The infrastructure administration team of IaaS builder, who does the ultimate capacity planning at the lowest level with physical resources, keeps a constant watch on the capacity requirements of all its consumers. They also plan for the future resource procurements and execute capacity changes wherever necessary. Thus, cloud computing provides great facility in capacity planning to its consumers; if they calculate wrong, and need more or less capacity during runtime than they planned, then cloud has the cover (from IaaS provider). This puts cloud consumers on low risk in case of critical applications.

> *Cloud Computing enables consumers to pay only for what they get. However, consumers should also manage their demands so that they consume only what they plan to pay for.*

10.3.3 Capacity Planning at Different Service Levels

One important thing that one should understand while discussing capacity planning, is the type and extent of responsibility for a designated level of service provider, as well as for a service consumer. The end users, who only use SaaS facility, are customers of the SaaS category service providers. The SaaS category service provider may in turn be customer of some PaaS category service provider, if not an *independent computing vendor*. Similarly, a PaaS category service provider is either an independent vendor, or consumer of IaaS category service provider.

To explain the whole scenario in a simple form, let us consider three different companies who are providers of different cloud services under some agreement. Company 'A' – IaaS facility provider, company 'B' – PaaS facility provider, and company 'C' – SaaS provider (Figure 10.1).

The customers of company 'C' are application users (end users of computing). They can take three ways to inform 'C' about capacity requirements. Case-1) can estimate their exact business requirement and inform 'C'. Case-2) Pass the entire responsibility of supporting their demand to company 'C'. Case-3) can take a middle path where business demand beyond a certain (estimated) level will be supported by 'C'. The choice and requirements have to

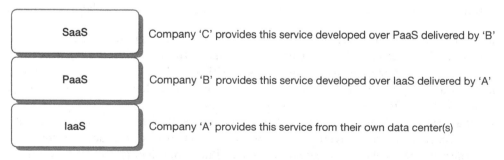

FIG 10.1: A scenario where different level of cloud services are provided by different companies

be mentioned as contract in SLA, so that 'C' can estimate capacity requirements and take appropriate measures to arrange them. Company 'C', after accumulating all SLAs made with its consumers has to estimate the future demands in a similar way. They also have the three similar choices like its consumers.

Company 'B' has two options to maintain resource capacity to support their business demand. With proper estimation, 'B' can keep few additional virtual servers (supplied by 'A') under their hold as reserved resources, to support any unexpected raise in load to manage the capacity themselves. The other option is to directly pass the ball (the responsibility of capacity planning) to company 'A' keeping faith on their capability. They can take the middle path also, by managing the capacity planning up-to a certain level by themselves and then passing the responsibility to the infrastructure service provider in extreme cases. But, a reputed service provider must handle the responsibility on their own, without depending on others.

The physical infrastructural resource management is the responsibility of the IaaS service provider 'A'. They have no option to pass the capacity planning task to other service providers as providing physical resources is the ultimate responsibility of the IaaS provider 'A'. The entire scenario has been summarized in Figure 10.2.

Hence, the capacity planning task needs appropriate estimation of future demands at each layer of cloud services. Although SaaS and PaaS consumers can not directly participate in capacity planning activity, they should estimate business demand and inform their respective underlying layers regarding future demand in advance. Each layer must remain well aware about possible future demand to keep them-self ready.

If company 'B' remains uninformed (from its upper layers) and fails to support resource demand beyond their planning, then it is likely that 'A' may fail to support the feature load in many instances, if multiple among their consumers (like 'B') fail to do so and. IaaS facility provider should be seen as the last line of defense, and the ball (the responsibility of supplying infinite resources) should be not be allowed to pass on there.

10.3.4 Role of Service Level Agreement

Service Level Agreement (SLA) contains the details of the contract made between the service provider and the consumer. The quality, and scope of the service must also include terms regarding the infinite resource provisioning arrangement when the SLA is about cloud computing. Both parties must understand the constraints and agree upon the limits of resource availability.

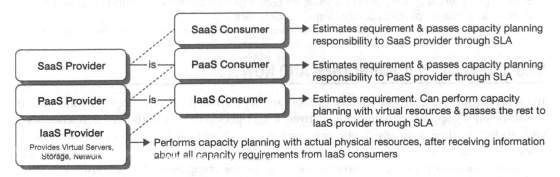

FIG 10.2: The ideal capacity planning approaches at different layers of cloud services

Consumers may declare the resource demands in the SLA to ensure availability. Apart from predictable average requirement, this should include mention of the periods when demand grows, and estimation about the amount of resources needed during those phases, so that the service provider can prepare itself. The providers on the other hand may mention the situations when supplying any more resources may become unfeasible, and what actions will be taken to tackle those situations so that the applications suffer less.

The SaaS consumers can pass the capacity planning task to SaaS provider through SLA. The SaaS provider in-turn can plan and inform about capacity requirements to the PaaS provider through SLA. The PaaS provider as an IaaS consumer can either perform capacity planning themselves with the virtual resources supplied by IaaS provider, or can again pass the capacity planning task to IaaS provider through a well-planned SAL agreement.

Thus, the service level agreements play an important role in the capacity planning process in cloud computing. All stockholders should take part in the negotiation process regarding expected and acceptable level of services before making the agreement. The document should specify all prerequisites and resource requirements.

> Service level agreement should address the expected and acceptable level of services.

10.4 CLOUD CAPACITY: CONSUMERS' VIEW vs PROVIDERS' VIEW

The cloud consumers see the cloud as an infinite source of resources that can be consumed as required. They believe that cloud can support any amount of resource demand. But, this is clearly not the actual case. From the provider's point of view this is a very tricky thing to handle. It is the responsibility of the cloud provider to create the impression of *infinite resources*.

Since service provider makes estimation about future resource requirements through appropriate capacity planning and arranges for those resources, consumers get the impression that resource is infinite. For service consumers one advantage is that, this sometimes eradicates the pains of capacity planning from their end. Detail planning can be skipped to reduce efforts and small mistakes can be corrected more easily. For service providers, arranging any amount of resource to support capacity requirement is not a difficult task due to ever declining hardware prices.

> Service providers take the pain of planning for capacity management in cloud to create the illusion of infinite resource capacity for their consumers.

10.5 CAPACITY PLANNING: THEN AND NOW

In earlier days, during the traditional model of capacity planning, resource requirements used to be estimated to support a system for a relatively longer period of time with fixed cost associated with it. But as time progressed, everyone wanted to get away with carrying the fixed costs associated with maintaining their own computing. They rather preferred variable cost pay-per-use model. Cloud computing has created the scope for the computing service consumers. Why should then any organization maintain a large computing infrastructure? The following section

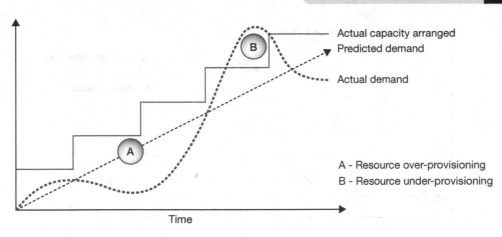

Actual capacity arranged
Predicted demand

Actual demand

A - Resource over-provisioning
B - Resource under-provisioning

Time

FIG 10.3: Traditional fixed cost computing model

focuses on the old and new model of capacity planning for computing, and describes how the new variable cost model differs from the traditional fixed cost computing model.

10.5.1 Traditional Fixed Cost Computing Model

Traditionally computing capacity planning of organizations was based on a fixed cost model. Organizations used to set up their computing infrastructure themselves or outsource it, but the investment for computing resources was fixed. In that approach, there were possibilities of occurrence of two different problematic scenarios. First one due to *over-provisioning*, and the second due to *under-provisioning* of resources (Figure 10.3).

In the traditional approach, the system architects used to estimate an average possible future requirement of resources for a reasonably longer period of time (generally a few years) and accordingly acquire resources. During the low demand of application, requirement of resources also remains low. In such a condition, the application can run smoothly, but the majority of the resources sit idle most of the time. This results in wastage of resources as well as investment. This inefficiency is illustrated in the Figure 10.3 by the region marked as 'A' in between the actual demand line and the available capacity line. This turns out to be great wastage due to the presence of a large volume of unutilized resource capacity.

During the high application demand resource requirement also increases, and it often goes beyond the limit of actual resource capacity. In such a scenario application performance degrades and business suffers. Hence, this makes it costly during the traffic spikes because suffered traffic typically means lost revenue opportunities. This scenario is illustrated in Figure 10.3 by the region marked as 'B' under the actual demand line. There the available infrastructure capacity falls below the line of actual demand. As a result, the service of application remains unavailable.

Traditional fixed cost capacity model suffers from the problem of over-provisioning and under-provisioning of resources. Both of these are costly for any business.

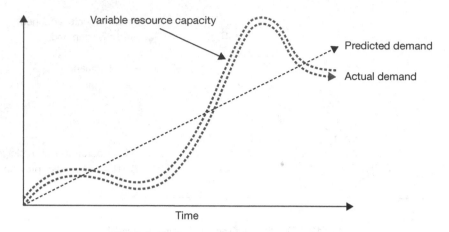

FIG 10.4: Modern variable cost computing model

10.5.2 Modern Variable Cost Computing Model

With the emergence of cloud computing, the computing service consumers now can adopt variable cost operating models rather than the fixed cost operating model. This has become possible due to the delivery of computing resources as services. Consumers under this model rarely acquire any unnecessary volume of permanent computing resources, and use resources on rent. They pay the service provider on use basis. The scenario has been shown in Figure 10.4.

Each service provider on the other hand generally has many clients, and they (the clients) have varying resource requirements over varying periods. The provider stands on the philosophy that, resource requirement of all applications generally will not rise or fall together. Hence providers can maintain a balance among all the applications they support with a pre-acquired pool of resources, which is much less than the sum of the resources required to support all applications during their peaks. They can also easily increase the pool size when business increases.

This comes as the biggest opportunity for computing service consumers today to reduce their total expenses, as they can easily move towards the variable cost operating model. With this model applications can be provisioned with additional resources only when they are needed and then resources can be released when they are no longer required.

In Figure 10.4 it can be seen that the variable resource capacity line moves up and down with the actual resource demand line, due to the dynamic provisioning of resources. Not a single instance can be found when resources sit idle due to excess capacity, or capacity is insufficient to support the demand for the application.

> *The variable cost operating model can closely match the resource capacity with actual demand and it thus decreases cost of computing by reducing resource wastage.*

10.6 APPROACHES FOR MAINTAINING SUFFICIENT CAPACITY

Capacity planning for a system is a critical job. It requires expertise, time and also adequate budget allocation to perform capacity planning. In a well-planned system, resource utilization becomes optimum, reducing the amount of idle resource. This lowers the cost of computation.

The following section discusses the traditional approach of capacity planning and the facility cloud computing provides to its consumers in the domain. The lowest level of cloud service providers or cloud infrastructure providers however, have no other way but to follow the traditional approach.

10.6.1 Traditional Approach with N+1 Rule

Dynamic resource provisioning to meet application demand is not instantaneous, as deploying and booting up a new compute node takes some time. If a smooth experience for the user is important, then rules that respond early enough have to be followed, so that the capacity remains available at the time of demand. Moreover, a system is always built on the assumption that node failures will happen in future, and by taking proactive measures to ensure that failures do not result in application downtime. The primary proactive measure is also taken by ensuring sufficient capacity.

Traditional resource capacity maintenance strategies are commonly referred to as $N + 1$ *rule*, where $N + 1$ nodes are deployed even though only N nodes are really needed to support the current requests or application demands, and '+1' is the additional capacity added in case demand exceeds supply of 'N. So, in case one node fails or gets interrupted, that won't have any impact to the application.

This '+1' node provides a buffer in case of a sudden spike in activity, and also provides extra insurance in the event of an unexpected hardware failure of a node. Without this buffer, there is the risk that incoming requests can overburden the remaining nodes, reducing their performance, and even resulting in user requests that time out or fail.

> Traditional capacity planning approach suggests maintaining one additional resource node than actually required to save the system during crisis.

10.6.2 Cloud Specific Approach

The traditional approach has obvious limitations. Depending on the business requirements, the N+1 rule may not always be sufficient. Cloud infrastructure service with virtual resources offer a more flexible and scalable approach, where auto-scaling mechanism always maintains sufficient resource capacity for applications to serve legitimate loads. *Auto-scaling* relieves the capacity planners who are cloud service consumers from the wearisome job of monitoring and maintaining sufficient capacity, and the system manages capacity itself.

Cloud infrastructure service providers (IaaS providers) build up the service with actual physical resources and hence cannot go beyond the traditional approach of capacity maintenance. But the way cloud service consumers approach capacity planning, has seen a total shift.

10.7 ROLE OF AUTO-SCALING IN CAPACITY PLANNING

One of the most useful features of cloud infrastructures is the ability to automatically scale a resource with little or no impact on the applications running in that infrastructure. This is possible for the resource sharing and multi-tenancy capability of cloud computing model.

Resources not being used by some application are released to be added to the resource pool, from where other applications get their necessary resources.

The traditional (non-cloud) approach was to maintain infrastructure keeping the peak capacity of each application in the mind and wasting resources, as most part of the resources would remain unutilized for most of the time. The shortcoming of automatic cloud scaling, however, is that the lazy application designers (who develop cloud service over service of others) can use this attribute as an opportunity to avoid the critical process of capacity planning.

10.8 CAPACITY AND PERFORMANCE: TWO IMPORTANT SYSTEM ATTRIBUTES

Many people equate capacity planning with system performance, but this is not correct. *Performance* enhancement of any system is performed through system optimization or performance tuning. Appropriate capacity planning undoubtedly improves system performance, but the main objective of *capacity planning* is to meet the future demand of workloads on a system by arranging the additional system capacity (resources) in a feasible manner.

The aim of system optimization is to get more production or output from the available system components. Capacity planning measures the maximum amount of work that can be done using the current resources and then arranges resources to do more work as needed. If system optimization is done during capacity planning phase, it is good, but capacity planning efforts focus on meeting demands.

> With capacity, the concern is about how much work a system can do, whereas with performance, the concern is the rate at which work gets done.

10.9 STEPS FOR CAPACITY PLANNING

For a service provider who provides computing as a utility service, there are three basic steps for capacity planning to add value to their system. These are also considered as the core concerns of capacity planning. The steps are mentioned below.

Step 1. Determining the expected demand – In the first step of capacity planning process the service provider must carefully examine the expected overall resource usage patterns as they vary over a course of period.

Step 2. Analyzing current response to load – Next, the service provider must analyze the available resource capacity of their system and how the applications respond to load (or overload) with current capacity, so that any requirement of additional capacity that is to be added can be identified.

Step 3. Knowing the value of the system – Finally, the service provider must be aware about the value of the systems to the business, so to know when adding more capacity provides value and when it doesn't.

Cloud providers need to maintain a balance between the financial burden of over-provisioning, and the reputation risk of under-provisioning of capacity.

10.9.1 Determining the Expected Demand

To determine the expected demand for resources of a system, capacity planners need to determine individual demands of all the applications supported by the system. Later they can aggregate those results to get idea about traffic pattern of the whole system. Understanding the demand pattern of application is important as the traffic pattern generally changes with time.

Figure 10.5 shows sample graphs plotted from the recorded number of hits in a web application viewed over a week and a year. Such statistics may give a fair idea regarding the overall workload pattern of application.

From the weekly graph it can be seen that the spikes are not always of equal demand in a single day. Sometimes it is high, sometimes low. The yearly graph provides idea about the varying demand of an application over a year. The business goal of capacity planning is to correlate these performance spikes and dips with particular events and occasions, like product launches, special campaigning or yearly festivals.

Capacity planners should evaluate these statistics on an ongoing basis. Like the weekly and yearly graphs, daily and hourly graphs also have to be analyzed. For new applications which do not have any such statistical data, the capacity planner will have to rely upon the suppositions made by business experts, until such data are recorded.

There will always be unexpected peaks in application demand beyond the expectation of capacity planner. The goal of capacity planning is not to eliminate the occurrence of such unexpected peaks. Rather it is about planning for the expected, recognizing the unexpected, and reacting appropriately to the deviation.

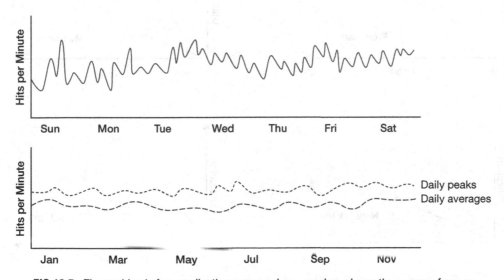

FIG 10.5: The workload of an application measured on a week, and over the course of a year

10.9.2 Analyzing Current Load

System load can be analyzed by measuring the load of different system resources. Several system metrics are used to represent these loads. In computing, the main resources used are – processor, memory, and storage and network connectivity. Hence the major system parameters are processor speed, memory access speed, disk I/O access speed and network I/O access speed. Loads on each of these resources can be measured by operating-system-specific tools.

Resource load affects system-level performance. Each of the resources has a utilization rate, and when one or more of these resources reaches the ceiling, that limits performance of the system. This limit is called *stress point*. System architects must execute tests to see how different scenarios create stress points on the infrastructure.

The ability to understand the resource usage patterns and constraints is very important in capacity planning. It may seem that simply adding another server or resource component to the pool of resources can fix the problem. In reality, it is not as simple and may even make the problem worse.

Resource utilization curve provides simple representation of resource utilization under load. To identify the stress point of the resources it is necessary to create all the resource utilization curves for a system (Figure 10.6). The *resource utilization* statistics can easily identify the *bottleneck* or the *stress point* that occurs first (also called *initial stress point*). This initial stress point depends on application and varies form system to system.

The graphs in Figure 10.6 show the resource utilization curves for the primary resources of a system. It can be seen from the graphs that the processor, memory and network bandwidth utilization rates rise with load, but do not reach their *resource ceiling*. But, the disk I/O attains

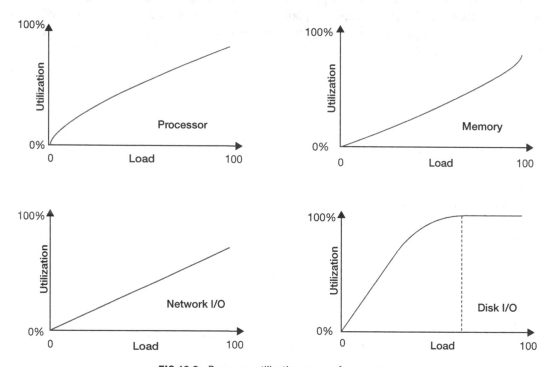

FIG 10.6: Resource utilization curves for a system

resource ceiling at around 60 percent of the tested load. This is the initial stress point for this system or the current system resource ceiling. At this point (shown by the vertical dotted line), the server is overloaded and the system begins to fail. The capacity planner must take care of this bottleneck to improve performance of the system, and repeat the load testing activity to find the next bottleneck which is supposed to appear with higher system load than the load during the occurrence of previous stress point.

> *It is the goal of a capacity planner to identify the critical resource that has resource ceiling, and resolve the problem to move the bottleneck to higher levels of demand.*

10.9.3 Value of System Capacity

Every application adds some value to the business. It is important to know how more capacity can help the business before adding any more resources to the system just because it has hit the stress point. One should have a clear idea about the outcome of the question - "How business can be benefited by supporting the additional load?" Understanding the value of the demand on the system will help to answer the question.

Two possible actions are there depending upon answer to the above question. Either add more capacity to support demands of pick hours, or wait for the existing capacity to become available again. The first strategy enhances system performance, while the second one reduces budget. Any of these two strategies is adoptable, depending on which one adds more value to the system.

> *The decision regarding capacity enhancement depends on, how much it is going to cost to add capacity against the value of that additional capacity to the business.*

SUMMARY

* ❖ Capacity planning means building a strategy that ensures the supply of adequate resources during peak demand, but at the same time reduces procurement of extra amount of resources which might have to remain idle for most of the time, in order to minimize cost.
* ❖ Capacity planning is necessary for obtaining optimal system performance at minimum cost.
* ❖ Cloud computing has changed the perception of the traditional way of capacity planning in computing. The traditional fixed cost capacity planning with N+1 approach of capacity maintenance was not a full proof system.
* ❖ The variable cost capacity maintenance approach in cloud computing eliminates the resource over-provisioning and under-provisioning problems.
* ❖ Wrong capacity planning results in huge business loss in traditional computing. Cloud service consumers are also not totally relieved of the capacity planning task; but, they are at low risk if their estimation is wrong.

❖ The cloud infrastructure service provider, after collating the service level agreements and obtaining data on resource requirements from all consumers, does the actual overall capacity planning for physical set of resources.

❖ The delivery of infinite resource in cloud is an illusion created through proper capacity planning, by cloud service providers.

❖ Cloud service provider analyzes capacity; estimates load and takes decisions about adding new resources in the pool as required, only if the additional capacity adds value to an application.

REVIEW QUESTIONS

Is the traditional N+1 rule of capacity planning applicable in cloud computing?

Cloud Computing has auto-scaling capability, through which it can grow or shrink itself according to the high and low demand of application. Hence it is not mandatory for the cloud service consumers to follow N+1 rule of capacity. They can start working exactly with as much resource they require and the cloud takes care of varying future needs. This may reduce the billing amount in the pay-per-use philosophy.

Can a cloud service consumer avoid capacity planning through auto-scaling?

The IaaS consumers (who are also PaaS provider) theoretically can avoid the capacity planning task with all virtual infrastructures, since cloud takes care of that. But sole dependency on auto-scaling may create trouble in two ways. First, with no limit governing the maximum capacity; the resource consumption may cross the allotted budget. Second, the cloud may not always be able to support sudden, unexpected resource demand hikes, if not clued-up in advance, as resources are literally not infinite.

What role does the service level agreement play in capacity planning?

Any cloud service consumers who wants to avail the variable capacity maintenance facility has to mention their resource requirement patterns in the SLA, like in which particular periods in a year the application demand increases etc. Otherwise the service provider will remain unaware about their resource requirements and may not be able to satisfy all resource demands.

How do the IaaS provider manage capacity planning?

It is important to note that, unlike PaaS or SaaS providers, IaaS providers do not have the option of building their services over some other underlying cloud services. Hence they cannot avail any facilities or features of cloud services, like unlimited resource availability; rather they are responsible for building those features. In reality, cloud infrastructure service builders maintain resource capacity following traditional approach of capacity planning. They gather requirements of all the consumers and then arrange for the capacity accordingly.

Is it always clever to add capacity to support additional application demand?

No. Additional resources should only be released to add capacity to support spikes in application demand, if that expense adds value to business. It is important to know how more capacity can help the business before adding any more resources to the system just because it has hit the stress point.

MULTIPLE CHOICE QUESTIONS

1. Cloud Computing concept of delivering infinite resource is achieved by
   a) Maintaining a huge pool of resources
   b) Workload management
   c) Proper capacity planning
   d) None of these

2. Over-provisioning of resources in traditional way of capacity planning causes
   a) Performance degradation
   b) Loss of reputation
   c) Performance enhancement
   d) Wastage of budget

3. Under-provisioning of resources in traditional way of capacity planning may cause
   a) Auto-scaling
   b) Loss of reputation
   c) Performance enhancement
   d) Budget saving

4. Availability of infinite resource on-demand in cloud computing is actually an illusion
   a) True
   b) False

5. Unlike following N + 1 rule of capacity maintenance, cloud service consumers enjoy which among the following facility in capacity maintenance
   a) N + X rule
   b) N rule
   c) Infinite resource
   d) Auto-scaling

6. Resource utilization curve represents
   a) Average resource utilization
   b) Total volume of system resources
   c) Resource utilization under load
   d) All of these

7. When resource utilization reaches ceiling, that limit is called
   a) Stress point
   b) Limiting point
   c) End point
   d) None of these

8. Unlike traditional computing, capacity planning is no more required to avail computing facility in cloud
   a) True
   b) Required, but much easier
   c) Required, but less risky
   d) Both b and c

9. Before capacity enhancement of an application, the capacity planner should know about
   a) Cost of the additional resources
   b) Value of the added capacity in business
   c) How much resource is required
   d) Both a and c

10. IaaS consumers in cloud, do the capacity planning with
    a) Virtual resources
    b) Physical resources
    c) Both physical and virtual resources
    d) None of these

11. What is the relation of capacity of system with its performance?
    a) Proportional
    b) Reverse
    c) Similar
    d) None of these

11 | Load Balancing

With appropriate capacity planning in cloud computing, the large pool of virtualized resources creates an illusion of an infinite source of computing resources. In the preceding chapters, it has been discussed how applications often need to scale to manage the varying workload and how resources are dynamically provisioned in order to meet the needs of scaling in cloud computing. It has also been discussed that horizontal scaling is more prepared for large scale scaling in distributed environment like cloud.

Upon obtaining provisioned or de-provisioned dynamic resources, the horizontal scaling provides elasticity to cloud computing. But, this flexibility comes with lots of implementation complexity. Load balancing is the mechanism through which these features are implemented. Apart from these, as there are multiple resources available to serve a particular type of service request, and in a distributed computing environment it becomes necessary to distribute proportionately those service requests among the available resources so that none of them becomes overloaded and degrades the performance of the entire system. It is the run-time logic or algorithm of distributing the service requests that has to be capable of evenly distributing the workload. This chapter discusses different types of load balancing techniques along with their pros and cons. The possible parameters for consideration while working out load balancing algorithms have also been discussed. A properly-designed workload distribution and balancing architecture reduces resource underutilization, improves the performance of a system and also brings down the cost of computation.

> Load balancing is an important ingredient for building any dynamic, flexible, scalable and robustly-distributed computing architecture.

11.1 LOAD BALANCING

Load balancing in distributed computing systems is an essential technique to distribute processing and communication activities evenly across the resources in the network so that no single computing resource gets overloaded. Among different exercises, load balancing is especially important for applications which often deal with a large and unpredictable numbers of service requests. Load balancing is a technique that distributes load evenly among multiple computing resources such as processor, memory etc.

Through *load balancing,* the incoming service requests are distributed among available computing resources. An efficient load balancing mechanism improves average resource utilization rate and therefore enhances the overall performance of a system.

The load balancing capability is created in a computing system by crafting the system with suitable architecture. Such architecture helps the system attain additional capability. For example, with load balancing architecture, the additional capacity can easily be added into computing system by introducing multiple instances of similar resources.

> Load balancing shows its real strength by making a system more productive when additional capacity is induced into the system.

A *load balancer* distributes the workloads across multiple similar types of computing resources, such as processor, memory, storage and network switches. In cloud computing, service requests can be distributed among multiple servers, either located within a data center or distributed geographically. The objectives of load balancing are to optimize resource utilization, maximize the *throughput*, minimize the *response time* and avoid overloading of any resource.

The use of multiple resources of a similar type instead of a single powerful resource also has an additional benefit. It increases the reliability of the system through the induction of redundancy. When one component fails for some reason, the load balancer can redirect the load to other operating component and thus it can avoid an injurious impact on the whole system.

In practice, load balancing techniques can be put into action either through a hardware device like a multi-layer switch system, or a software system such as domain name system server. But, hardware-based solutions generally need costly investments. Whereas, Software-based solutions on the other hand are not only cheaper, they are also easy to configure and maintain.

> The primary objective of load balancing is to obtain greater utilization of available resources.

11.2 IMPORTANCE OF LOAD BALANCING IN CLOUD COMPUTING

The goal of developing a cloud model is to provide a computing service to the consumer that is extremely reliable as well as economic. The utility service model makes cloud computing cheaper for consumers. It is economical from the business point of view. But, consistency in performance is also very important from a consumer's point of view. Irrespective of the demand and usages pattern, the service performance has to remain stable to maintain reliability.

A reliable computing system must operate efficiently under varying load conditions. The distributed architecture of the cloud computing model makes load balancing one of its essential elements in order to maintain operational efficiency. To gain optimum performance from a system, the workloads must be properly-distributed among all available resources. This also makes the system architecture scalable which is an essential attribute of cloud computing. It is because of the load balancer that the dynamic behaviour of cloud system remains non-disruptive during provisioning and de-provisioning of resources.

The load balancer acts as a layer of *abstraction* over the computing resources (physical or virtual) in a distributed environment. It can create the impression of multiple resources appearing as one, and it decouples applications running on it from (computing system's) internal implementation. This allows the system to grow or shrink without any noticeable effect on users. Cloud service consumers thus get uninterrupted service during workload fluctuation. Apart from the help in designing a scalable system, the decoupling enhances the security of the system as well.

> *Load balancing is an essential component for building scalable application architecture.*

With load balancing, multiple resources work in parallel to handle the workload. This minimizes the chance of a total system failure since it is possible to continue the service even after some components fail, providing the scope of recovery or replacement of those components without disrupting the service. Thus, load balancing is very useful to make the cloud service more *tolerant* in case of component failure. This also maximizes availability of resources reducing the amount of down-time that usually affect businesses.

Load balancing acts as the solution for more than one problem. Following points summarize the importance of balancing the load in cloud computing.

- Load balancing offers architectural flexibility and essential help in making a computing architecture scalable.
- It ensures efficient utilization of a pool of similar type resources.
- Efficient resource utilization automatically enhances the performance of the overall system.
- The technique decouples applications from its physical implementation during execution. This creates a layer of abstraction which increases application and system security.
- The *decoupling* of physical resources from direct access of applications also makes the cloud computing system more tolerant in cases of any component failure.

> *Load balancing is one key issue of cloud computing because overloading of any resource may lead to poor system performance.*

11.3 HOW LOAD BALANCING IS DONE IN CLOUD

Load balancing mechanism distributes service requests across cloud applications deployed in data centers spread around the world. Every cloud data centers themselves must have their own load balancers to schedule the incoming service requests towards appropriate resources.

A load-balancing technique can use various tactics for assigning directions to the service requests. In simple form, a load balancer listens to network ports where service requests arrive to identify the kind of application and resources has been requested for. Then, to assign the request to appropriate resource among the available resources, some *scheduling algorithm* are used.

Depending upon request type and resource requirement to serve the request, different implementations of load balancing mechanisms are required in cloud computing. Among them *service load balancing* is the most critical one. Other requirement types are load balanced virtual switch, load balanced storage mechanism and so on.

> *Among different implementations, service load balancing which distributes application service requests among resources is vital for the success of cloud computing.*

In *service load balancing*, workloads are balanced among multiple instances of each cloud service implementation. The duplicate implementations are organized into a resource pool that responds to fluctuating request volumes. The load balancers can be positioned as either an external or built-in component to allow the host servers to balance the workloads themselves.

The load balancer system in a cloud implementation that directly interfaces with clients is called the *front-end node*. All the incoming requests first arrive in this front end node at the service provider's end. This node then distributes the requests towards appropriate resources for further execution. These resources which are actually virtual machines are called as *back-end nodes*.

In cloud computing implementation, when the load balancers at the *front-end node* receive multiple requests for a particular service from clients, they distribute those requests among available virtual servers based on some defined *scheduling algorithms*. This scheduling happens depending on some policy so that all of the virtual servers stay evenly loaded. This ensures maximum as well as efficient utilization of physical and virtual resources. Figure 11.1 represents the function of a load balancer in cloud computing environment.

Here it has been assumed that all of these three virtual servers are equally loaded before six similar types of service requests appearing before the system (from same or different consumers). The incoming requests encounter the load balancer first. Load balancers use scheduling algorithm and distribute the requests among these three available virtual servers. Here, the load balancers act as the *front-end-nodes* for all of the incoming requests and the virtual servers act as the *back-end-nodes*.

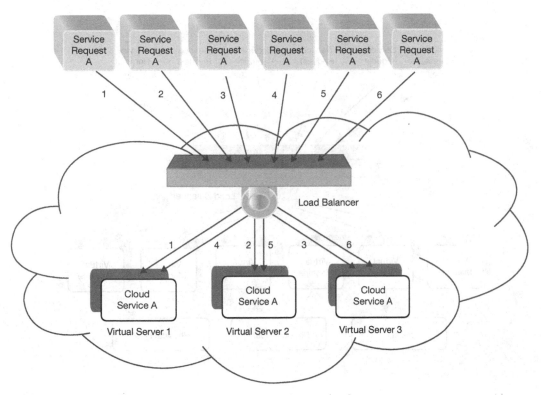

FIG 11.1: Load balancer evenly distributing service requests coming from consumers across available virtual servers

> *The use of multiple similar resources with load balancing technique incorporated, instead of a single powerful resource, increases the system's reliability through redundancy.*

11.3.1 Two Levels of Balancing: VM Provisioning and Resource Provisioning

Cloud provisioning is the technique of allocating cloud provider's resources to a customer. Earlier in this book, it has been discussed that how automated provisioning provides several advantages for cloud computing. This automated provisioning mechanism is realized through load balancing activity. Once the *front-end-node* redirects the incoming service requests, all of other activities happen at the *back-end-nodes*.

The assignments and executions of application requests at the back-end-nodes happen in two phases (Figure 11.2). In the first step, a service request is analyzed through its characteristics by the load balancer and assigned to an appropriate virtual machine instance which is called *VM provisioning*. In the second step, these requests are mapped and scheduled onto actual physical resources, and this is known as *resource provisioning*.

> *VM provisioning is the mapping of service requests with virtual machines.*

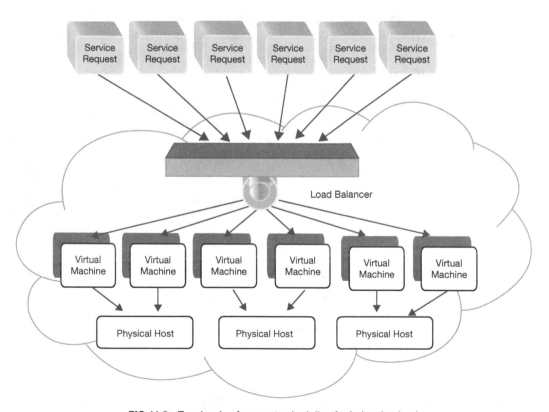

FIG 11.2: Two levels of request scheduling for balancing load

In Figure 11.2, it is assumed that for the sake of simplicity of explanation, all of the service requests from the clients are of similar type. There are six virtual machines and three physical hosts. In this case, all of them will consume similar kind and volume of resources. Again, it is also assumed that the virtual machines and the physical hosts were evenly loaded when these six service requests have appeared. Now when the six service requests happen to appear, at the first level of scheduling, the requests are distributed among those six available virtual machines. In each virtual machine, the second level of scheduling happens and the load balancers integrated into the VMs evenly distribute the load among three available physical hosts.

> Resource provisioning is the mapping of virtual machine loads with physical resources.

The ultimate goal of a load balancer is to allocate the incoming requests from clients to physical machines. If required, the load balancing technique can be built at multiple levels of a cloud computing system and those may run on physical as well as virtual systems.

11.3.2 What are to Load Balance

Following is the list of resources and services which are mainly responsible for load balancing in cloud computing environment:

- Application server instances (which include processor and memory)
- Storage resources
- Network switches
- Services such as DNS, TCP, HTTP and HTTPS

11.4 GOALS OF LOAD BALANCING

The primary goal of load balancing is to distribute service loads among resources. Apart from this, there are other objectives also. Following section briefly narrates these objectives:

To improve system performance: In a load balanced system, no resource should get overloaded when others are under-utilized. All resource components remain almost evenly loaded or uniformly free. This improves the performance and stability of the overall system.

To maximize fault tolerance: In a load balanced system, while multiple nodes work together, that enhances the tolerance of the system against the faults. If some node stops functioning due to any kind of hardware or software failure the traffic is automatically redirected among other working nodes by keeping the system up. Thus, the users of such system remain unaffected and unaware of the failure.

To accommodate scaling: An efficient computing system needs to scale as application demand grows or declines. One objective of load balancing is to support scaling by properly redirecting load to the newly introduced nodes in case of growing or by releasing load from nodes in case of shrinking.

To ensure availability of applications all the time: Another objective of load balancing is to keep the applications available all the time. As higher level of fault tolerance can be achieved and overloading of nodes can be avoided by routing traffic across the less-utilized resources this ensures availability of application all the time.

> Load balancing makes sure that all the nodes of a distributed system are assigned with almost equal load at any given instant of time. It also offers fault tolerance capability when tied with fail-over mechanism.

11.5 CATEGORIES OF LOAD BALANCING

For efficient resource utilization, as well as for effective task execution, a load balancer should have knowledge about the engagements of resources while assigning tasks to resources. For this purpose, load balancing system may maintain a knowledge base for scheduling the tasks among the resources. This knowledge base is used to keep track of the current state of the available resources. Depending upon the use of knowledge base, there are two categories of load balancing technique: *static* and *dynamic*. Following section briefly discusses these two techniques.

11.5.1 Static Approach

Static load balancing does not use any knowledge base and distributes service requests only based on the characteristics of the requests. It matches the service request characteristics to decide about suitable resource type for allocation based on some set of rules. No prior knowledge about the current state of the running system is needed to implement static load balancing. Figure 11.3 represents the static load balancing approach in simple form.

In Figure 11.3 above, it is assumed that all of the incoming service requests are similar in nature. It is further assumed that server A and server B are both able to handle those requests. Static load balancing algorithms divide the incoming traffic evenly among two available servers

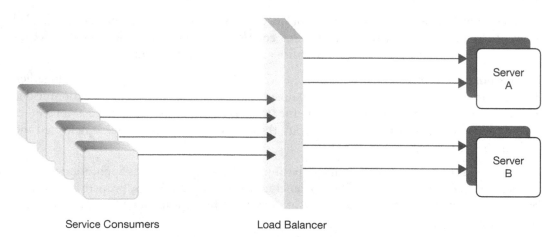

Service Consumers   Load Balancer

FIG 11.3: The Static Approach of load balancing. Here, the load balancers only consider prior knowledge base about the servers before distributing the load

being installed to handle those tasks. It only ensures that all of the servers are receiving almost equal number of service requests based on the specific features of requests. But, it does not keep knowledge base about the volume of workload each server is currently assigned with.

The static load balancing approach is easier to design and to be implemented. The scheduling algorithms are of *round robin* and *weighted round robin* categories which generally have been used with this approach to schedule the loads among resources.

> *The static approach to load balancing does not consider the current load state of the systems and allocates loads based on some fixed set of pre-configured rules related with the nature of the input traffic.*

11.5.2 Dynamic Approach

The dynamic approach of load balancing technique does not distribute loads among resources depending on any fixed set of rules. Scheduling of tasks usually happen based on the existing state of the resources or nodes. The advantage of using *dynamic load balancing* is that if any node gets fully loaded or fails, it will not halt the whole system.

This approach is implemented by applying *feedback* mechanism where the resource components are monitored continually. The nodes periodically send load and status information to the load balancer and if any node becomes non-responsive during operation, the load balancer stops sending traffic to it. This particular feature is inherited in cloud computing from grid-based platforms. However, this approach needs real-time communication via network which adds extra traffic to the system.

Figure 11.4 represents the dynamic load balancing approach in simpler form. Here, it is assumed that server A and server B can handle similar kind of requests and all of the incoming requests are within the task boundary of server A and B.

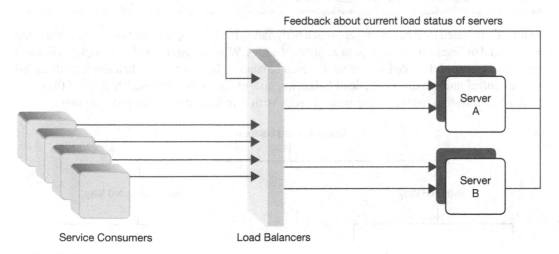

FIG 11.4: The Dynamic Approach of load balancing. Here, the load balancers consider current load information of servers as received through feedback path before distributing the load

Cloud computing is dynamic in nature. Scalability and *elasticity* of cloud is achieved via on-demand provisioning of resources in real time. Dynamic load balancing approach is one important ingredient to accomplish this dynamic nature. In next section, the concept of dynamic load balancing mechanisms has been discussed in brief.

> *Dynamic load balancing actively monitors the load levels of resources through a feedback channel and adjusts load distribution to keep all resources evenly loaded.*

11.5.3 Exploring Dynamic Load Balancing

Dynamic load balancing technique is generally used in distributed computing system and is very useful in making the behaviour of the active system. Dynamic load balancing plays a vital role in presenting the dynamic nature of cloud computing which is very important in high-performance computing model.

The implementation of the technique is done in two separate ways as distributed ways and non-distributed ways. In distributed load balancing approach, the task of load balancing is performed by all of the nodes (servers) present in the system. That is, all of the nodes of the system share the responsibility of load balancing together, through communicating among them. The sharing of the task can again happen in two ways as cooperative and non-cooperative tasks of sharing. When all of the nodes work together in parallel to attain a same goal, like improving the overall response time of the nodes, the technique is called as cooperative load balancing. Otherwise, if the nodes work separately to achieve some local goals, the technique is called as non-cooperative load balancing. In non-cooperative approach, different nodes may have different goals, like one may be concerned with response time while other one is concerned with the delivery of the system.

> *Distributed dynamic load balancing approach delegates the task of load balancing among all the nodes (servers) present in a distributed system.*

In non-distributed load balancing approach of dynamic load balancing, the task of load balancing is managed by one individual node or a cluster of nodes. When it is managed by a single/individual node, the approach is called as centralized load balancing. In this approach, a single node called as the *central node* manages the load balancing task of the entire system. Then all of the other nodes of the system must communicate directly with this central node for task allotment.

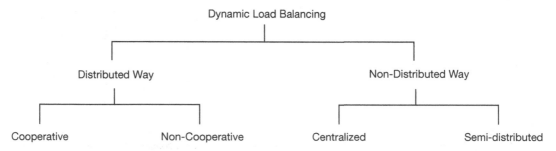

FIG 11.5: Classification of dynamic load balancing approaches

When the load balancing task is managed by a cluster of nodes, the approach is known as semi-distributed load balancing. In this approach, the whole system is partitioned into multiple parts and each has a group or cluster of nodes. In each partition or group of nodes, the load balancing task is maintained in a centralized manner. One node in each group is assigned with the task of balancing the loads within the group. Thus in each group one such node retains and all of these nodes together manage the load balancing of the entire system in a collaborative way.

> In non-distributed dynamic load balancing approach, all the nodes of a distributed system do not take part in balancing system load. One or few nodes are assigned the tasks.

The nodes engaged in balancing loads in a distributed system need to keep track of each other's status through message communication. This adds some extra traffic into the system and introduces some added load. The distributed approach of dynamic load balancing generate more messages than the non-distributed load balancing approach as there they need more interaction among the load balancer nodes in distributed approach. On the other hand, in distributed approach, the system does not suffer any major problem even if one or more load balancer nodes in the system fail since multiple load balancers work together there.

The centralized approach of load balancing exchanges very few messages to reach a decision. However, this approach may introduce other threats to a system. Since, the load balancing act of entire system is dependent on a single node that may cause *bottleneck* problem. The possibility of emergence of a *single point of failure* is also there as the load balancing process may suffer if the central node fails. Generally, in order to tackle such situations, systems keep a backup load balancer having configured to take the control over. The centralized approach is more suited for networks with small sizes.

> Distributed load balancing mechanism provides more robustness to a system at the cost of some added overhead.

Several algorithmic solutions have been used by researchers and developers for dynamic load balancing implementation. Among the algorithms as suggested based on the theory of Biased Random Sampling, Active Clustering or Honeybee Foraging Behaviour has shown satisfactory performance for large scale applications. Detailed discussion of these algorithms is out of the scope of this book.

11.6 PARAMETERS FOR CONSIDERATION

Load balancing is done to improve the performance of any distributed system, hence, in cloud computing system as well. To attain the goal of performance improvement, various factors are considered while implementing the load balancing technique.

Resource Utilization: All of the available resources have to be utilized in a planned manner, such that any single resource does not become over-utilized and could not degrade the performance of the whole system. Always a balancing has to be maintained while distributing workloads among resources to maximize an average resource utilization rate.

Response Time: It is the time required for a specific load balancing algorithm to respond. Since service requests appear in large numbers from clients in popular cloud services, the special attentions are evidently required in improving the performance of the services of the system. The first step towards this goal is to minimize the response time of the load balancer.

System health: This is related with some sort of component failure. System health should be maintained by periodically checking the efficiency of its nodes. In case of poor performance or failure of a node, a load balancer should take prompt action (by releasing or avoiding that node till recovery) to maintain the system performance.

Associated Overhead: There is always some overhead associated with load balancing activity. This overhead is introduced by the movement of tasks among nodes and *inter-processor* communications being required to execute the tasks. One criteria of designing good load balancing technique is to minimize this overhead.

Scalability: Load balancing enables scaling while the number of resource nodes in a load balanced system may increase or decrease with time to support the demand of applications. Load balancer should have the capability of handling this scalability issue efficiently.

11.7 LOAD BALANCING ALGORITHMS

The objectives of designing load balancing algorithms are to ensure that no server is overloaded either in capacity or in performance requirements. These algorithms are divided into two categories depending upon their knowledge base they use during taking the decision about service requests as appeared from the clients.

If a load balancing algorithm, executing on the load balancer at front-end node make decision about distributing the load without knowing any details about the requests, it is called *class-agnostic load balancing algorithm*. They are named so, since they remains agnostic or unsure to the nature of the request. This means that the algorithm acts without any information about the type of service request or the type of client from where the request was raised.

> Class-agnostic load balancing algorithms make decisions without considering the nature and source of incoming requests.

The other category of load balancing algorithm is called *class-aware load balancing algorithm*. This category of algorithms makes decisions with knowledge base about the nature and source of the service requests. The load balancer at front-end node then distributes service requests to appropriate back-end nodes for further processing.

Class-agnostic load balancing algorithm are simpler to design and implement. But class-aware algorithms have many advantages and are more suitable for balancing loads in critical environment like cloud computing. Depending upon awareness about received content, the class-aware algorithms can be classified in two categories. When it uses knowledge about the content type of service requests, it is called *content-aware load balancing algorithm*. When knowledge about content source (that is clients) is used in load distribution, those algorithms are known as *client-aware load balancing algorithm*.

Often, some of the clients may request for service or content in common than others. Assigning those similar types of requests received from different clients to the same (or same set of) back-end-servers minimize the need of redundant processing at different server locations. This not only decreases capacity requirements but also improves performance since content can be accessed for a single storage location. In a constrained environment, this can make the difference between meeting the capacity constraints and overflowing the system.

> *Content-aware load balancer can redirect similar kind of incoming requests to the same back-end-server to avoid duplicate processing.*

When the class-aware load balancing algorithm uses knowledge base about clients before distributing service requests to back-end servers to improve performance of system, they are called as *client-aware*. Assigning requests from similar type of clients to some particular server may often gain significant benefits in load balancing requirements due to the improved processing performance. In practice, the applications need to maintain a balance between both the *client-aware* and *content-aware* mechanisms.

Checking requests to find out its category is not simple and it needs going through some critical processing. The potential improvement in system performance through the implementation of client-aware load balancing technique largely depends on the degree of heterogeneity of the environment. If the system is almost homogeneous, much could not be gained by implementing client-aware algorithms, moreover, the overhead of dynamic client checking mechanism may degrade the performance of the system.

> *Selection of right load balancer provides opportunity for future flexibility in cloud computing.*

11.8 THE PERSISTENCE ISSUE

An important issue for load-balancer is to uniformly handle the client's requests within a session. A session is described as a sequence of associated application requests that generates from a client during a certain time period. The load balancing system must send all requests arrived within a single session to the same backend server for processing uniformity. Ensuring this consistency is important for success of a load balancer and this character is known as *persistence* or *stickiness*.

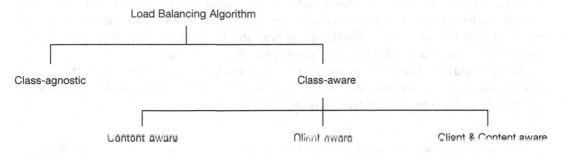

FIG 11.6: Classification of load balancing algorithms

Persistence issue is handled through appropriate tracking of sessions. *Session tracking* is implemented by storing session data in load balancer. Session tracking ensures that the client's requests are directed to the same pool of servers throughout the life of the session or even during subsequent sessions.

> Session tracking redirects all requests appearing from a single session to the same back-end server.

Ideally, the pool of servers behind the load balancer should be *session-aware*. This is generally implemented by creating an in-memory session database. In session-database approach, the session information can at first be stored in a load-balancer's database and later be replicated across the back-end servers. To redirect all of the requests appearing from a particular session to the same back-end server, the load balancer generates *session tickets*. These tickets get attached with the traffic to route them to the appropriate server.

Other simple and very common method to maintain session *persistence* is the use of *cookies*. When the client is a web browser a client-side cookie can be created to store small piece of text on a user's computer to keep track of the server at service provider's end for a session. This technique has the less overhead associated at load balancer's end since it relieves the load balancer from the job of selecting appropriate back end servers.

> Session persistency is generally maintained either by using in-memory session database or through use of session cookies.

11.9 APPLICATION DELIVERY CONTROLLER

Cloud computing does not just deliver static content they also deliver applications. Application Delivery Controller (ADC) is the advanced category of load balancers with functions and features that enhance the performance of their applications. ADCs are used to handle load balancing between the servers and also perform application acceleration.

ADC is a device that is typically placed in data centers between the firewall and one or more application servers. They can significantly improve application server's performance by off-loading many compute-intensive tasks which is known as *application acceleration*.

Major activities performed by ADCs are SSL off-loading and content compression. Processing the encryption and authentication requirements of a Secure Socket Layer (SSL) request can become a major part of the Web Server's load. The *SSL offload* feature reduces this overhead from the server. ADC has the ability of establishing safe tunnels with the clients and hence it eliminates the needs of SSL implementation for the web servers.

Compressed data can more efficiently utilize network bandwidth. By reducing the amount of data sent over the network, the compression performed by ADC allows businesses to do more while at the same time improving response times for end users.

> Cloud computing not only delivers static content, it also delivers application. ADCs are sort of advanced categories of load balancers that enhance the performance of cloud applications.

11.10 CASE STUDY: GOOGLE CLOUD

Google is one of the most popular sites on the Internet and their cloud service named as Google Cloud which has gained enormous popularity in the arena of public cloud services as well. It is quite predictable that by offering their services for millions of users, Google maintains thousands of servers in the data centers worldwide. The load balancing activity is seamlessly integrated with Google Cloud.

Google Compute Engine offers server-side load balancing facility so that incoming network traffic can be distributed across multiple virtual machine instances. For this purpose, Google Compute Engine Load Balancing defines some forwarding rules.

To process service requests initiated by the users, Google uses its Domain Name System (DNS) server to examine and find out the servers which are closer to the origin of the service request and redirects the query towards that way. Thus, the request goes to the nearest data center and then to some server in a cluster of Google servers.

At DNS, the first level of load balancing activities takes place. Later, when the service requests arrive at a Google cluster, a second level of load balancing activity starts to happen. Here, the load balancer assigns the request to some server instance based on measures of the current system load of servers in the cluster. Workload management software is used to monitor the performance of the servers, and if a server fails for some reason, the load-balancer transfers its load to another server before taking the failed server offline for recovery.

Thus, the load balancing at Google Cloud happens in two steps as first at the DNS and then at data center. DNS redirects the traffic towards appropriate data center and then load balancer at data center distributes the service requests among available servers in the cluster.

> According to Google, the Compute Engine Load Balancer is able to serve one million requests per second with a single IP address receiving the traffic.

11.11 CASE STUDY: AMAZON ELASTIC COMPUTE CLOUD (EC2)

In Amazon cloud environment, when a load balancer is created, it is configured to link with EC2 instances of an *auto-scaling group*. All of the servers of that group should be load balanced by the load balancer. The EC2 instances are registered with the load balancer using their IP addresses. Multiple load balancers can also be associated with a single auto-scaling group.

The Elastic Load Balancing (ELB) technique at Amazon EC2 has two modules like a set of load balancers and a controller service. The job of the load balancer monitors the incoming traffic and distribution of service requests. The controller service monitors the load balancers. It keeps a constant watch on the health of the load balancers and checks if they are functioning properly. If required, the controller service removes or adds more load balancers in the system.

Load balancers of EC2 cloud environment get registered under a unique domain name before it can be used. The DNS maintains those records of all of the load balancers working in the domain. When ELB scales, it updates the DNS record for the load balancers. A *time-to-live* (TTL) of few seconds remains associated with this DNS record. This ensures that the records about load balancers can get updated quickly in response to events that cause ELB to scale up or down.

When a client makes a request for some application of EC2 cloud, a DNS server returns one or more IP addresses of load balancers under the domain. The client then establishes a connection with any one among those load balancers and the load balancer then distributes the traffic to EC2 instances. Unlike with Google, here the load balancers themselves keep track of the health of those instances and when some unhealthy instances are detected, it stops sending traffics towards that instance until that is restored to a healthy state again.

Rules can be set to change the number of back-end servers dynamically by increasing or decreasing capacity to meet varying traffic loads. For instance, the condition can be defined in a load balancer to observe the latency period and when that period goes beyond a particular time limit, capacity is added automatically. Amazon Web Service (AWS) also provides a management console through which the administrators can manually add or remove EC2 instances as the capacity requirements of application change over time.

> The ELB mechanism of Amazon cloud balances the load by distributing the service requests among available Amazon EC2 instances.

SUMMARY

- ❖ The practice of improving the performance of a distributed system by distributing load among all available resources is called 'load balancing'.

- ❖ The technique of load balancing can be applied to any computing resource such as virtual server, physical server, storage device, network switch and so on.

- ❖ Load balancing improves the system performance by helping avoid a state where some of the servers are overloaded, whereas other servers are less engaged or even idle. It also creates a layer of abstraction and decouples the computing resources from direct access by an application or user.

- ❖ Load balancing permits the internal working of a system to easily scale as per requirement. It also makes a cloud computing system more tolerant in case of any component failure.

- ❖ Load balancing is implemented through scheduling of service requests. When the scheduling is done based on some fixed set of rules, it is called 'static load balancing'. Static approaches do not consider the existing state (or load) of the resources.

- ❖ If the scheduling decisions (of loads) are taken at run time, considering the current load and performance of resources at that moment, it is called 'dynamic load balancing'.

- ❖ To build an efficient and robust cloud computing system, the dynamic approach to load balancing is more apt. In the dynamic approach, the load balancer intelligently allots service requests in such a manner that all resources can operate at their maximum ability.

- ❖ In commercially available public clouds, load balancing as a method is applied across all data centers.

- ❖ The goals of balancing loads may vary with application requirements but they generally aim to minimize the execution time and response time or maximize resource utilization.

REVIEW QUESTIONS

How load balancing technique helps to build fault tolerant system?

Load balancing mechanism not only balances distribution of load among available resources, it also shifts load from one resource node to another if it be required. When some node becomes overloaded, the load balancer avoids forwarding any further load to that node. This improves system performance. But if a node fails for some reason, load balancer not only stops forwarding new tasks to that node it also withdraws all of the tasks from the failed node and re-assigns them to other working nodes. This makes a system more tolerant to faults.

How cloud scaling is linked with load balancing?

Scalability is an important characteristic of cloud computing. Scaling describes a system's ability to grow and shrink whenever required. Now, growing of a system means addition of new resources into the system. But only addition of components cannot contribute much if they are not utilized. Whenever the addition happens, the load balancer starts redirecting system loads towards those new resources and thus the new resources become active parts of the system. The opposite thing happens during the shrinking of the system. Thus, the scaling of distributed computing system is strongly dependent on the efficiency of load balancing.

For a relatively smaller and simpler system, the static load balancing approach can be more effective than dynamic approach. Justify the statement.

Dynamic load balancing technique uses a knowledge base while scheduling tasks among resources. The knowledge base is developed by collecting information about existing status of the resources. This is done by establishing feedback paths between resources and load balancer. Thus, the development of the knowledge base causes extra traffic and needs real-time communication via network. Static approach of load balancing does not use any such knowledge base and distributes service requests only by analyzing the characteristics of the incoming requests. This keeps the load balancing system simpler. This is why, for smaller and non-critical systems, the static load balancing may yield better result.

How persistence is implemented in load balancing?

Persistence ensures the assignment of all of the service requests from a client to the same server under a session, after a task from the client is assigned to some server. Persistence can be implemented based on several factors associated with a load balancing solution, but most commonly it is implemented using session cookie or source IP addresses so that the requests can be directed to the same server throughout the life of a session.

MULTIPLE CHOICE QUESTIONS

1. For which among the resource(s) the load balancing in computing is done?

   a) Processor

   b) Storage

   c) Memory

   d) All of these

2. In distributed computing environment, the load balancing is done for

   a) Servers

   b) Network Switches

   c) Storage

   d) All of these

3. Load balancing helps to implement the

   a) System over-utilization

   b) System under-utilization

   c) System scaling

   d) All of these

4. Static load balancing approach does not consider the existing states of systems. This statement is

   a) True

   b) False

5. Requests from clients in cloud environment first appear in

   a) Front-end node

   b) Back-end node

   c) Depends on type of request

   d) None of these

6. In load balancing, resource provisioning happens before VM provisioning. This statement is

   a) True

   b) False

7. In which kind of load balancing, the feedback about existing load status are required?

   a) Static

   b) Automatic

   c) Dynamic

   d) All of these

8. Which among the following problem(s) may be caused by centralized load balancing?

   a) To many messages

   b) Bottleneck

   c) No feedback

   d) None of these

9. Class-aware load balancing algorithms are more critical in nature. This statement is

   a) True

   b) False

10. Session persistency in load balancing is maintained through

    a) In-memory session database

    b) Cookies

    c) None of these

    d) Both a and b

11. Improving application server's performance by offloading compute-intensive tasks is known as

    a) Task offloading

    b) Performance tuning

    c) Application acceleration

    d) None of these

12 Service-Oriented Architecture

CHAPTER

Management of any large system turns out to be a complex task if the architecture of the system is not flexible enough. It becomes difficult to deploy new functionalities, alter existing functionalities and integrate interoperability when an immovable system grows. As a solution, any large system should be decomposed into functional primitives for efficient and flexible management and this philosophy perfectly applies to cloud computing systems too.

Clouds are generally heterogeneous and large in volume by their own nature. Hence, the flexible architecture (or flexible application architecture) is an essential criterion for making the computing system *agile* and capable of adjusting to quick changes in business strategy to take advantage in a competitive business market.

The conventional application architectures are not designed to take advantage of infrastructural agility and diversity like a cloud. In cloud computing, applications perform best when they are built based on the paradigm called as 'service-oriented architecture' or SOA. This new architectural paradigm makes cloud applications flexible and specially shows its ability when the system grows over time. This chapter focuses on the philosophy of the service orientation, discusses its advantages and indicates how business application becomes agile with SOA implementation.

12.1 THE PRE-SOA ERA

Conventional computing systems were based on centrally-administrated architecture. But, such architecture was not appropriate for quick application development, neither was it designed to support rapid changes in functionality. Moreover, the processes of developing a new application system used to become complex, time-consuming and expensive.

Then the concept of component based application development (CBD) model emerged. It had many goals similar to SOA. A component is a software object which is meant to interact with other components. Components are used to represent basic system functionalities, those which collaborate with other components. CBD promotes decomposition and reusability. It also increases productivity, quality and decreases the *time-to-market*. But interoperability is the issue that could not be handled with this system development model.

With the widespread adoption of heterogeneous distributed systems, the need for application interoperability appeared. *Heterogeneous system* refers to the ability of integrating multiple type (*cross architecture* and/or *cross vendor*) of one or more computing resources (like processor) into a single computing environment. Cloud computing system is the ultimate outcome of heterogeneity. It allows incorporation of heterogeneous hardware platforms as well as operating systems. Hence an architectural approach was required for applications that could fit into such environment. Service-oriented architectural approach for application

207

building has fulfilled the requirement. It supports interoperability along with modularity and reusability.

> *Service-oriented architecture is a paradigm for application development.*

12.2 ROLE OF SOA IN CLOUD COMPUTING

In accordance with growth in businesses, the system also grows and it becomes more and more complex gradually. Different types of systems get involved with each other (which is known as *heterogeneity*) and constant collaboration, integration and changes become inevitable. In such scenarios, the key is to improve the flexibility of a system for efficient management of the business functionalities.

Cloud computing systems are developed for large-scale business delivery and built upon the distributed heterogeneous environment. The dynamic infrastructure in cloud is developed through resource pooling and virtualization. The scalability feature of cloud infrastructure also facilitates high-performance computing.

Cloud applications are developed over a dynamic infrastructure. The role of service provider and service consumer in cloud computing applications are played by software agents on behalf of their owners. The variety of technologies (such as Java and .NET) along with multi-vendor systems, tools and solutions makes interoperation of applications challenging.

Service-oriented architecture is exactly what was needed to construct the application architecture for such a system. The role of SOA in developing flexible application architecture has already been discussed in section 2.1.10. In SOA, resources or functionalities are made available in a standardized way and thus it boosts interoperability. SOA approach helps to make applications flexible as well as scalable. SOA philosophy also maintains flexibility in large distributed systems by supporting the application's heterogeneity and the scope of decentralization.

Horizontally the applications are easily scalable if they are built using SOA. *Horizontal scaling* for an application is crucial as normal applications tend to scale vertically where limited number of functionalities individually grow bigger to handle increasing demand. Here 'horizontal' indicates the type of application scaling where any number of different functional components (known as *services*) can be integrated any time into an application effortlessly.

> *Through incorporation of a variety of disparate applications, the horizontal scaling of applications becomes effortless with SOA which are from different vendors and use different platforms.*

As shown in Figure 12.1, the flexibility of cloud environment is a collaborative effect of two layer implementation. At the lower level, flexible infrastructure is built through resource virtualization and dynamic resource provisioning. Above this, the flexible applications are built by following SOA paradigm. SOA-oriented applications and dynamic cloud infrastructure empower one another.

SOA is a way of building applications whereas 'cloud' refers to the computing infrastructure as well as the delivery model of resources and applications. The use of SOA for building services for cloud computing not only adds value to the system but also provides combined benefits for both SOA and cloud. This is primarily because many among the objectives of both SOA and cloud are common such as increased flexibility, reduced cost and easier maintenance.

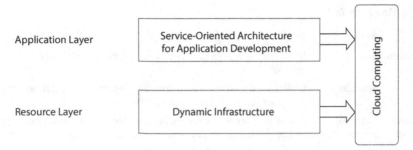

FIG 12.1: Together dynamic infrastructure and SOA result in cloud computing

Another crucial role played by SOA is the implementation of *loose coupling* (pairing of two software components). Cloud computing represents layered services of infrastructure, platform and software. Each of these services must deliver high performance. Upper level services should not be constrained by any characteristic of lower layers. This is possible through loose coupling. SOA implements loose coupling among interacting modules which makes the changes in system easier and independent of underlying infrastructure.

> *SOA and cloud computing have many similar objectives like increased flexibility, reduced cost and easier maintenance.*

12.3 SERVICE-ORIENTED ARCHITECTURE

Service-Oriented Architecture (SOA) is an approach for application development. SOA is not a tool or framework one can purchase but it is a flexible and modular approach for delivering computing applications. Software components in SOA paradigm are referred to as services. A *service* is a self-contained functional or business activity having some specific consequences. One objective of SOA is to enable the *reusability* of these software components. Applications can be built from *reusable* service components rather than as a single massive program.

With *traditional application architecture*, the process of building a service can be complex, costly and time-consuming. Moreover, as the enterprise grows, the complexity of new integrations and number of dependencies increase exponentially. This gets worse as the pace of change grows, rapid in the current business world and functional requirements change over time too.

SOA is the answer to this challenge. Application development approach based on SOA paradigm allows dynamic construction and rapid customization. Unlike *traditional application* development approach where the issue of integration of application comes as an after-thought, in SOA paradigm it comes as a before thought instead of. This improves the agility of application that enables them to respond promptly with the increasing rate of changes.

In distributed heterogeneous computing environment, the software services are developed using different programming languages over disparate computing platforms. The services are then hosted to be used by application developers. Thus, the integration of those services poses a challenge and needs standardization. SOA can be seen as a specification for using and developing language-independent as well as platform-independent service components in distributed applications.

Table 12.1 Few SOA facts

Myth	Fact
SOA is a technology.	It is a sort of design philosophy which is independent of any vendor or technology.
SOA is entirely a new idea.	CORBA, DCOM and electronic data interchange (EDI) are the examples of earlier service orientation approaches.
SOA implementation needs uses of the web services.	Use of web service is not mandatory for SOA implementation. SOA can be implemented with or without web services too.
SOA can be developed itself.	SOA cannot be developed; rather it is a mean to develop any application.

> One goal of SOA is to enable the reusability of software, where applications can be constructed from reusable software components called services.

There are some common misconceptions about SOA among people. Table 12.1 depicts some of the crucial facts about SOA.

12.3.1 The Emergence of SOA

The concept of SOA emerged from the necessity to narrow the business–IT gap while building the enterprise applications. In current world, business and IT need to go hand-in-hand. But, communication becomes difficult when business people and IT people speak in entirely different perspective. Business people and analysts know their business processes and on the other hand, the IT professionals understand computing systems and infrastructure. So there was always a need to shorten this business–IT gap.

With service-oriented architecture, a new chapter has begun in which real business-oriented processes have taken in the center stage of any type of application development. The combination of Business Process Management (BPM) and SOA has closed the gap between business management and IT implementation issues.

Service Orientation (SO) is the natural evolution of earlier software development approaches. During 1980s, the developers followed object-oriented (OO) approach. In 1990s, the *component-based development* (CBD) approach was evolved. The service-oriented approach emerged after this and was adopted as a superior approach from the beginning of the current century.

It is not known who first coined the term 'SOA'. But, several documentary evidences point towards the probability that some technologists of the reputed IT research firm, Gartner, used the term around 1995 for the first time. A report on SOA was published during 1996 by Roy W. Schulte and Yefim V. Natis, two analysts from Gartner. But the paradigm got its real momentum in the current century and at present, the architects have adopted SOA as the prime approach for application development.

> SOA is described as a way to bridge the gap between business and IT.

12.3.2 The Architecture   •

A model of the *service-oriented architecture* has been represented in Figure 12.2. With SOA approach, the applications are built through a collection of services. A *service* is an independent entity executing some functionalities. The services communicate via *message passing*. Messages have the 'schema' defining their formats like a contract is set to define the interchanges and a policy define how it should be exchanged. This makes the communication among the services effortless. Messages can be sent from one service to another without considering how the other service, handling those messages, could be implemented.

Service-oriented architecture retains the benefits of *component-based development* (CBD) model, but there is a shift in paradigm. While component-based model remotely invokes the methods on objects, SOA passes messages between the services. The *remote method invocation* (RMI) approach creates technological dependency between provider and consumer which limits flexibility as well as interoperability. The message passing schemas of SOA eliminate this dependency. They not only define the services, but also describe the message exchange patterns to establish communication with other services. Thus a service by sending message to another, need not to consider how (in which language or over which platform) the other service handling those messages could have been implemented. This promotes the *interoperability* among applications.

> SOA paradigm is based on the concept of communication through message-passing. This allows loose coupling between communicating software agents and promotes interoperability.

12.3.3 Provider and Consumer

In SOA, services interact with each other. A service component can play the role of provider or consumer or both. When being invoked by any *consumer service*, a *provider service* delivers the functionality as requested for. Here, both of the roles of provider service and consumer service are played by the agents of the software. A consumer service sends a service request to a provider service through message passing. The provider service returns a response to the consumer service containing the expected results.

> Both the roles of provider and consumer are played by the services in SOA.

12.3.4 The Interaction Model

In SOA, service providers and service consumers generally do not interact directly with each other (although it is possible); instead a software module is employed to play the role of *broker*

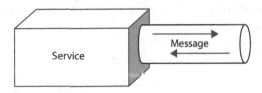

FIG 12.2: The model of SOA

who eases the interaction in between. A client service can consume a provider service only if the interface of the provider service is known. Broker does this act of assembling of all of the published interfaces (of provider services) at one place referred as *service registry* (also called as *service directory* or *service catalog*). Message exchange interaction of services happens through published interfaces of services available at broker's end.

In SOA model, there can be enormous number of services available built by different service providers. It becomes difficult for a client to gain knowledge about where to find for a required service. For this purpose, a service registry is maintained where different service providers register all of their services. A client can then query the service directory for any service and can also explore service capabilities there.

> *Middleware is a layer of software that facilitates the inter-operations of different applications. In SOA; middleware maintains list of available services in the form of registry.*

In the interaction model of services, three parties are involved: the service provider, the service requestor and the service broker. Service provider publishes service descriptions and provides the implementation of the services. Service requestors are service consumers who bind and invoke the services. Any service description can be obtained from the service brokers. The service brokers provide and maintain the service registry containing of the service interfaces. But it is also possible for a consumer to directly call a service from the provider without contacting a broker, when description of the service is quite well-known.

The service interaction model of service-oriented architecture is similar to the interaction model of cloud computing components (cloud actors) which also follow inter-connected *consumer-provider-broker model*. The SOA interaction model has been shown in Figure 12.3.

Interaction among services in SOA paradigm works in following manners:

1. A service provider registers its services in the service registry managed by the broker.
2. The service is registered accordingly in registry as per its category.
3. Service consumer looks up for services in the registry.
4. Service consumer binds itself to the service provider and uses the service.

One strength of SOA approach appears from the fact that a service logically separates its actual implementation from the declaration. The implementation remains hidden to the

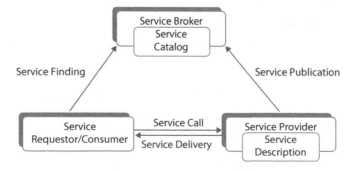

FIG 12.3: Service interaction model in SOA

outside world. This separation makes it possible to fix the changes in the implementation without affecting other services as long as the service declaration or the interface stays intact.

> In SOA, the service descriptions are separated from their implementations. Thus, any changes in service definition can be made without affecting other services which interact with it.

12.3.5 An Analogy

An interesting analogy for SOA is to think about our world of service-oriented businesses. In a city or country, different companies (or service providers) provide different services like medical service, transport service, food service and so on. When a citizen needs some service, it is convenient for him or her to search for the required service in a common market place rather than looking for it here and there. The "Yellow Pages" directory was created to solve this problem long ago where every detail of various service providers are listed in order of the categories of the services. Hence, all of service providers who register their services in the 'Yellow Pages' directory, reach the consumers without any difficulty.

In SOA terminology also, this service directory or service register is maintained. Service providers register their service interfaces in the service directory and consumers can search for required services there. Just like the 'Yellow Pages' directory interfaces the service consumers and providers in a city, SOA service directory or service registry plays the same role of middleware between consumer service and provider service in the SOA paradigm.

12.3.6 BPM and SOA

In reality, a business is the combination of multiple services. Alternatively, it can be said that services are part of any business. This is the philosophy behind service orientation and managing business processes more actively through it. Although, the business process management (BPM) is a huge topic but SOA is closely attached with BPM where lowest-level activities of a decomposed process are treated as services.

12.3.7 Event-Driven SOA

Event-driven SOA (also known as SOA 2.0) is the current and advanced form of SOA. In this approach at present, unlike the older SOA (known as SOA 1.0) approach where services used to be designed as pre-defined processes, the events generally trigger the execution of activities. SOA 2.0 appeared because SOA infrastructure should be able to address all of the requirements of dynamic and real-time businesses. In this regard, both event processing and SOA had to be combined. An SOA powered with events facilitates the agile, adaptive business process that can respond to ever-changing business modules easily.

12.4 GOAL OF SYSTEM DESIGNING

Two important goals of any superior system designing are *decoupling* and *composability*. These features make a system flexible. Cloud computing system, being regarded as a high-performing computing system has incorporated these system designing principles through the service-oriented methodology.

12.4.1 De-coupling

In software engineering terminology, coupling between pieces of software components are like the joints between metal pieces to build some structure. These joints should be tactfully designed so that they can be attached effectively and removed easily as and when required. The goal is to maximize the strength of the structure with detachable and minimum number of joints. Otherwise, the modification of the system becomes difficult, expensive, and time-consuming.

The modules or components of any software system connect with each other the same way. The more complicated these connections are, the more difficult it is to modify the whole structure or even any one module without disturbing others. Hence, the connections or coupling between software modules should also be simple and easily detachable.

SOA enables this *loose coupling* feature among applications which allows plugging or unplugging of services effortlessly. Thus, not only it becomes easier to build a new system using this philosophy, the modification of existing system also becomes less complicated. This decoupling makes the system flexible and saves time, effort and cost of system management.

> SOA enables low coupling, which is an important goal of system designing.

12.4.2 Composability

Composability is a design principle where a system can be designed to satisfy specific requirements by assembling components in various combinations. From a developer or user's perspective, the composability is a highly desirable characteristic since it makes the system implementation easier and gives solutions as more interoperable as well as portable.

The idea of building software out of independent components promotes the concept of composition. It allows incremental development of new services by adding components as on need basis. A *composable component* must have the following properties:

- Modular: This means an independent and self-contained component which is cooperative, reusable and replaceable.
- Stateless: This is a communication principle that treats each transaction separately and being independent of any other transactions.

SOA paradigm promotes composability principle where services are designed to be used in multiple solutions whereas a superior (or bigger) service itself is a composition of multiple-unit services.

> SOA promotes the concept of composable development of application/system.

12.5 SERVICE REPRESENTS BUSINESS FUNCTIONALITY

The fundamental building block of service-oriented architecture is service. A service is represented by a program that can interact with another service through exchange of messages. In the SOA paradigm, unit business functionality is represented as a service rather than an object or component of earlier paradigms.

The idea of a service comes from the world of business as the world is full of *service-oriented businesses*. Individual companies provide services and any service can generally be availed by multiple consumers. In business world, services can be classified into different categories, like medical service, transport service, packaging service and else which some individual or enterprise would offer for the benefit of other (the service consumers). Moreover, a big business can be decomposed into multiple business outlets providing different services.

This decomposition opens up the prospect for serving different business functionalities through the specialized outlets. Then, as a consumer any such business house (that is interested in providing service, not in building) gets the freedom of choosing different service providers to manage those specialized outlets from a list of the available providers.

The same idea had been adopted by technologists and thus a concept of a software service was evolved. Services in SOA deliver some results that provide value to other services (which are the consumers). A service has a provider like an individual or company that takes care for building and managing the program to produce required results. An implicit or explicit contract is also maintained between the providers and the consumers of services in regard of the specific outcome of the provider services and the constraints to be followed by the consumers.

> A service in SOA paradigm represents discrete business functionality. Software services can be accessed through web and used to compose business processes as needed.

12.5.1 Elements of a Service

Services have three main components:

- Contract
- Interface
- Implementation

A contract specifies the predicted needs of a consumer from a service and details about the service offered by the provider. A contract once published should not be changed ever as the provider never has any idea about who have already consumed the service. So the critical factors for any service are its availability and stability.

The interface defines how to access a service and make use of it. Service providers register these interfaces in service registry where consumers generally search for them. The actual realization of a service is called as implementation which remains hidden from the consumers. The other two service elements, contract and interface, are however visible to the outside world. Consumers may consider the implementation of a service as a black box entity as it is the worry of provider to implement a service for optimal performance.

The service registry (known as *service catalog*, or *service directory* too) stores the sort of information as depicted below:

- Linto of available services
- Means of using the services
- Dependencies if any

- Information about owner of the service
- The nature of service contracts

Service registry is not a constant thing and moreover the new interfaces are constantly being added in it.

> *Service orientation is a way of building distributed applications that facilitate and ensure the flexibility of loosely coupled interfaces to change.*

12.5.2 Service Implementation Approaches

The linking between a service interface and its implementation can be done in three ways as top-down, bottom-up, and meet-in-the-middle development. In *top-down approach*, the service interface is defined first and the implementation follows the same. This approach is also called as 'contract-first development'.

Bottom-up approach works in the opposite manner where the interface is generated based on an existing service implementation. In this approach, the service implementation faces less constraint and thus it is easier than the former approach. But, it may sometimes become difficult to match the exact requirement of interface and thus lack to get the full control over the service interface definition.

The *meeting in the middle approach* takes the best of both top-down and bottom-up approaches. In this approach, it is possible to get full control over the service interface definition when implementation already exists. Here a mapping of the implementation is done to the existing service interface.

> *Service implementation may follow top-down, bottom-up or meet-in-the-middle approach.*

12.5.3 Attributes of Services

A service has many attributes. However, it is not necessary that all of these attributes are always required for all of the services. Depending on the requirements, a service-oriented developmental approach may require to use some of them in appropriate places. Few of these attributes have been briefly discussed here:

Self-Contained: One objective of SOA approach is to make a service self-contained. However, on many occasions, it may not be possible to make a service fully independent. Some dependencies to one or more services may exist. The goal is to minimize the dependency to make it appropriate to run in distributed environment.

Coarse-Grained: Service granularity refers to the extent in which a system is broken down into small parts. Unlike fine-grained systems, the coarse-grained systems consist of fewer number of components which are comparatively larger in sizes. Coarse-grained service can often improve performance in networked environment by reducing switch between the service calls. It also increases security by hiding the implementation details.

Stateless: A 'stateless' service is a facility that does not maintain any state between different service calls. Hence, it becomes simple and easier to manage a stateless service than a 'state-ful' service where temporarily created local variables and objects (which store service states) cannot be thrown away immediately as service state is maintained over multiple service calls. Although use of the state-ful service cannot be avoided in some business scenarios like in the shopping cart application, the stateless services are preferred in SOA development.

Reusable: Avoiding redundancy is a general goal of any software development. Ideally each function requirements should be implemented into a service which is a one time effort. Services in SOA are reusable and just need a call to get the effect.

> A service is a software component that is self-contained and does not depend on the context or state of other services.

12.6 OPEN STANDARD IMPLEMENTATION

One important characteristic of SOA is the fact that service development follows the *open standards*. Since anyone can build service using any technology, it would have been extremely difficult to combine such services without the presence of a proper standard in service construction. The standardization was done out of this need.

The standards for service construction in SOA are developed by the Open Group, an international consortium that works to raise and enable IT standards for the implementation of business objectives through IT services. Such standards enable anyone to understand, build and adopt SOA easily. The Open Group regularly publishes the architectural standards and even periodically makes changes and/or improvements in these standards if necessary.

The Open Group publishes the *open standards* and guidelines for SOA in documented forms known as *SOA Source Books*. Enterprise architects working with service-oriented architecture may refer the Open Group's SOA Source Book as a collection of resource material. The *Open Group SOA guidelines* include the following standard documents:

- SOA Reference Architecture
- Service Integration Maturity Model
- Service-Oriented Architecture Ontology
- SOA Governance Framework
- Service-Oriented Cloud Computing Infrastructure (SOCCI) Framework

> The presence of open standard in SOA paradigm makes the integration work possible in the multi-technology and multi-vendor environment.

12.6.1 Technologies in Use

Following are the technologies used for message exchange, service interface description, service directory maintenance and message communication which have acquired the global acceptance in relation with the SOA paradigm.

Extensible markup language (XML): Unlike HTML which deals with the display of data, the purpose of XML is to transport and store data. Its flexible structure creates common formats for storing information that makes the processing of content being possible with relatively little human intervention. Message exchange among the services in SOA follows the XML formats.

Web Services Description Language (WSDL): The WSDL is an XML-based interface description language. WSDL is used to define the service interfaces in SOA. Service interfaces can be defined in a language-independent way using an interface description language (or, interface definition language) or IDL. A WSDL description of a web service provides a machine-readable component containing the details of the means to call a service, its parameters and the structures of data it returns.

Simple Object Access Protocol (SOAP): The SOAP is a platform and the language-independent communication protocol. Services in SOA paradigm communicate through this protocol. It is a XML-based protocol to let services exchange information over HTTP. The platform independence enables the SOAP to establish communication between applications running on different operating systems and the property of language independence enables it to establish communication between applications developed in different programming languages.

Universal Description, Discovery and Integration (UDDI): The UDDI is a directory service where the providers can register their web services. Consumers also search for web services using this UDDI. It uses WSDL to describe service interfaces and supports SOAP. UDDI is platform-independent and uses the open framework. A UDDI registry contains service information in categorized way depending on business functionality.

The WSDL description of service published by the providers represents everything a consumer needs to know. Consumer only deals with XML messages and need not to know how a service has been implemented to use it. This makes the coupling among services flexible and switching to different service provider becomes easier.

> SOA makes system integration easier and streamlines the data exchange activities across a collection of disparate systems by establishing a vendor-neutral communications framework.

12.7 BENEFITS OF SOA

SOA provides numerous benefits over traditional application-oriented architectural models. The benefits of service-oriented architecture can be counted from two different viewpoints like architectural and business. Following sections discuss those.

12.7.1 Architectural Benefits

The SOA paradigm was developed as a solution to the distributed software-system model. SOA brings many architectural benefits in application development like dynamic design and rapid customization of system functionalities. The most important attributes are discussed here.

Flexibility: System functionalities often need to go through changes for betterment. In monolithic application architecture, it is difficult to incorporate changes to meet new requirements. Changes can be easily implemented in service-oriented application architecture which provides greater system flexibility.

Reusability: Services are reusable. It is not only in the sense that 'write once integrate anywhere and anytime'. Moreover, one cannot throw anything away when different functionality is needed as those existing functionalities can be reused later.

Simpler integration: System integration is inevitable as multiple different solutions together may work in a system. Service-oriented approach reduces the complexity of system integration as connectivity, data exchange and process integration techniques are more simplified here. The adherence to the published contracts of services also makes it easier for future applications to connect effortlessly with existing standard-based services.

Maintainability: Service maintenance becomes easier when it can be done in isolation with help of smaller teams. Thus the maintenance of independent services in SOA becomes less complicated and incurs less cost.

12.7.2 Business Benefits

SOA enables enterprises to improve the business implementation and communication processes to deliver superior services to its end customers. Business organizations can capitalize on the following benefits through SOA implementation.

Agility: Service-orientated architecture is based on the assumption that system changes over time. Hence, a well-designed SOA-based development protects a system from the impact of this evolution. The flexibility of SOA enables a system to respond quickly to new requirements.

Cost reduction: Services once developed can be reused by disparate systems for different kind of purposes. Integration of services in a system is also easy. Therefore, the reuse of already existing assets (services) makes it cheaper as *reusability* means lower development and testing cost.

Increase in quality: Reuse of a service by multiple consumers make a service well tested and flawless. Its quality improves and thus SOA provides high performance and delivers good return-on-investment (ROI).

Quicker release to market: Service-oriented approach takes lesser time for system development or even for a system up-gradation. It thus makes the launch of a system quicker to market by diminishing the development time.

Standardization: Services in SOA are generally developed following open standards. This standardization makes services more vendor-independent and any kind of system can use a service as long as it uses the proper (standard) service interface.

Traditional application architectural approaches which once explored business opportunities, become responsible to limit the growth at present as they are no longer adaptable to changes. In contrast, systems based on SOA principles provide flexibility and agility to respond to a business environment that changes rapidly.

12.8 SOA AND CLOUD COMPUTING

SOA and the cloud have a number of common concerns like empowering distributed software assets or making improvement in *agility* and *flexibility* of system. Their focus is also on services and reusing of services. But these two things are not based on the same idea. SOA is an architectural approach that creates services which can be shared and reused; on the other hand, the cloud computing is about providing ease of access to services.

Both follow *provider-consumer-broker model* for interaction and are made to work over a robust network environment. A consumer can delegate work to services of other party (the provider) to build his/her own service without worrying about their (provider's services) implementation details. Services in SOA and cloud can be used by multiple applications or users with the goal of optimizing the resource utilization. Apart from these, the loose coupling is another issue that both SOA and cloud computing promote by allowing minimum dependencies among different parts of the system.

Capabilities of cloud are represented as services and that create the scope for SOA to play a vital role in service orientation in the domain of cloud computing. In fact, cloud computing and SOA are complementary to one another. They deliver best performance while working together. Having a service-oriented architecture already in place helps businesses to achieve value from cloud computing more quickly. But it is important to understand that while cloud computing is an approach to provide computing facilities; nothing prevents SOA applications from running on traditional non-cloud servers.

SOA particularly plays important roles at the top-most layer of cloud computing services. Cloud computing ensures availability of computing facilities to applications including hardware and software, while the SOA models the Software-as-a-Service facility. For consumers of cloud services, it is necessary to adapt SOA as application architecture in order to take full advantage of a cloud computing environment.

> *Cloud computing and SOA can be pursued concurrently or independently. But, the needs of cloud computing and its offerings provide a value-added foundation for SOA efforts.*

SUMMARY

❖ Service-oriented architecture (SOA) is an approach to building applications that provide flexibility and make it easier to incorporate changes in a system.

❖ In SOA paradigm, the applications are built through a collection of services which are software components executing some functionalities.

❖ Services are reusable components which are built and published by some providers. Consumers can get information regarding services from the service directory where providers register their services.

❖ Multiple services combine together to execute some job, communicate among themselves via message passing. This promotes loose coupling which allows plugging or unplugging of services effortlessly to make the system flexible.

❖ Loose coupling among services makes it easier to incorporate changes in a service without affecting other services of a system.

❖ Services are implemented based on open standards. This standardization streamlines the data exchange activities across disparate systems by establishing a vendor-neutral communications framework. This facilitates interoperability in distributed heterogeneous systems like cloud environment.

❖ SOA plays a significant role at the application layer of the cloud computing model. Cloud computing is empowered with the flexible applications that have been built using SOA paradigm over dynamic computing infrastructure.

❖ Cloud computing and SOA have many common concerns like loose coupling, reusability, distribution, flexibility and others. They deliver best outcome while working together.

REVIEW QUESTIONS

How SOA empowers cloud computing?

One important feature of cloud environment is its flexibility. The dynamic cloud infrastructure is achieved through implementation of resource virtualization and runtime provisioning. The services delivered through cloud computing may not accomplish the desired flexibility unless being developed using SOA paradigm. Many among the goals of cloud and SOA are similar too. Thus, the use of SOA paradigm in application development benefits the interest of cloud computing.

How loose coupling makes a system flexible?

Loose coupling means components are easily attachable and detachable from one another. This is possible when components are almost independent of one another, functionally as well as technologically, and can be developed in isolation. A business process made of loosely-coupled software components is easily modifiable, maintainable and thus it makes a system flexible as well.

'Open standard implementation of SOA promotes interoperability' – Justify.

Services are the elementary software components in SOA paradigm those are combined to compose some operative business functionality. Anyone can build service and make it available for others to use. All of such services are built using different technologies like Java, .NET etc. Now the question arises here if the services built using different technologies could be integrated with one another. 'Yes' is the answer. Any service can interoperate with another having built over any platform and this has been possible because all of the services under SOA paradigm are built following same and open standard. The standards are published by a global consortium called as 'The Open Group'.

'Integration among services through message passing promotes loose coupling' – Justify.

Variety of technologies like Java, .NET etc. are used to develop services over heterogeneous and multi-vendor systems in a distributed environment like cloud computing. It becomes difficult for one software component to invoke other because of this technological disparity, in spite of their open standard implementation. SOA model has standardized the way where these two services communicate through message passing with each other. Messages are exchanged using XML format.

Thus a service developer only needs to pass XML messages to other services for interaction and need not to know how they have been implemented to use it. This has enabled loose coupling among other services.

Discuss the complementary role of SOA and cloud computing.

Although SOA can be practiced over traditional computing environment but SOA and cloud computing are complementary to each other. The interaction model followed by the actors of cloud computing is similar to that of services in SOA. Both follow provider-broker-consumer model of interaction. The system designing goals are also similar where both promote decoupling and composability of components.

MULTIPLE CHOICE QUESTIONS

1. Which of the following design principles does SOA promote?

   a) Low coupling
   b) High coupling
   c) Low cohesion
   d) None of these

2. Which element of a service remains hidden from the consumers?

   a) Contract
   b) Interface
   c) Implementation
   d) None of these

3. Cloud computing and SOA can run separately but together they empower one another.

   a) True
   b) False

4. Benefits of using SOA paradigm include

   a) Easier maintenance
   b) Increased flexibility
   c) Reduced cost
   d) All of these

5. Service registry in SOA paradigm is maintained by

   a) Service provider
   b) Service broker
   c) Service consumer
   d) Service designer

6. Connection between services in SOA paradigm is done through

   a) Message passing
   b) Remote method invocation
   c) Functional call
   d) None of these

7. Use of variety of technologies for application development across heterogeneous systems in cloud computing makes the interoperation among the applications quite challenging without properly

   a) Designed system
   b) Standardized communication
   c) Open-source implementation
   d) None of these

8. Technological inter-dependency of two communication software agents in SOA paradigm has been eliminated by

   a) Use of SOAP
   b) Use of service registry

c) Standardized message communication technique

d) None of these

9. In cloud computing, SOA paradigm is used to

a) Build dynamic cloud infrastructure

b) Deliver the services

c) Build the application

d) All of these

10. Service contract once published should not be changed ever because

a) Provider can never know who are already using the service

b) It is a complex task

c) Service implementation is unalterable

d) All of these

13 File System and Storage

The easy access to high-performance computing resources in cloud computing has not only made the process-intensive activities smarter but the data-intensive computing activities also have taken center stage. The nature of data have radically changed with this revolutionary utility service; hence their processing and storage requirements vary. Large data-sets are generated and produced everyday are sent for processing in the high-performance computing environments.

Like the traditional storages, users can store and access multimedia files of various formats like text, image, audio and video in cloud also, but the storage requirements have been altered for efficient processing of the large data-sets which are produced in cloud every hour. The traditional enterprise level files and data storage systems were not sufficient to satisfy all of the data-intensive and high-performance computing requirements.

Efficient file handling to support parallel and distributed operations of *large data-sets* needed an entirely new file system format. Hence, researchers and computing vendors have come up with suitable storage solutions to achieve optimal performance in cloud like high-performance environment. This chapter focuses on all of these advancements made to fulfill those requirements.

> Cloud computing promises high-performance. Hence, the file system and storage to support high-performance data processing are critical requirements of cloud environment.

13.1 REQUIREMENTS OF DATA-INTENSIVE COMPUTING

Data-intensive computing presents a challenge to computing systems in terms of delivering high-performance. Large volume *complex data-sets* cannot be processed centrally in a single node and require partitioning and distribution over multiple processing nodes. Thus, *data-intensive computing* is I/O-bound and requires rapid movements of data in large numbers. This requires appropriate management of data in transaction. Data modelling, partitioning, node assignment and accumulation are some of the critical parts of this computing. Consumers' requirements and technical aspects related to the storage facility in high-performance computing environment are different from the traditional storage system in many ways. Traditional enterprise storage systems are no more sufficient to tackle those issues.

Scalability and high-performance distributed data processing are complementary to each other. Distribution of *large data-set* among as-many-nodes as required for processing promotes scalability of the application. Suitable file systems are required to support this distribution and scaling proficiently. It has been observed that data-intensive computing often involves *process-intensive computing* too. *Complex data-sets* present challenges before the computing system.

Fast and efficient processing of such data is essential along with sophisticated technique to reduce data access time.

This chapter explores two major components of the data-intensive processing for high-performance computing delivery:

1. A programming model for efficient data processing, and
2. A supporting file system.

> *The data processing model must sync with the distributed file system architecture. Sophisticated storage techniques are needed to reduce access time.*

13.2 CHALLENGES BEFORE CLOUD NATIVE FILE SYSTEM

It has already been mentioned that *cloud native file system* requirements include a high-performance data-intensive computing environment. The design goal of cloud file systems require to address the challenges those were not present in traditional distributed or network file systems. The prime considerations have been summarized below.

Multi-tenancy: Cloud system offers multi-tenancy and allows sharing of its underlying resources among multiple tenants. Especially in a public cloud, consumer share resources with others who are unknown to them. Hence, the file system in cloud must ensure that tenants (tenants' processes and data) remain isolated from one another to provide higher degree of security.

Scalability: A cloud file system must scale well so that users can rely upon the system with their growing storage needs. At the same time downward scaling is also important to minimize the resource wastage.

Unlimited storage support: File system support for unlimited data storage is another need of cloud computing for its business success. Moreover, the file system has to be extremely fault-tolerant. And, all of this needs to be achieved by building storage network out of inexpensive commodity hardware.

Efficiency: The other performance parameter to be counted over the others is the system's output. While dealing with thousands of concurrent operations issued by many clients, to achieve the requisite performance like the local file-system is a critical issue.

Compatibility: Compatibility is always an issue when new technologies are introduced. In the domain of computing file systems, backward compatibility with existing file system interfaces is important to facilitate the migration to the cloud seamlessly.

Metered Use: Metered use of resources is one of the basic requirements in cloud computing and for storage too. The file systems used in cloud have to enable and promote this capability.

Apart from these, error detection mechanism and automatic recovery have to be the integral parts of the file system. Other important ability required is constant monitoring of the health of the storage system.

Cloud native file system is one that enables the efficient implementation of cloud computing capabilities like application scaling, metering of storage usage and else.

13.3 MODEL FOR HIGH-PERFORMANCE PROCESSING OF LARGE DATA-SETS

Processing of large volume of data is often not possible in single processor and requires the parallel and distributed processing over multiple nodes for efficient outcome. The traditional models of data processing were not suitable for distributed processing of data and few distributed data processing models applied by researchers used to put a lot of burden on the application developer as they had to deal with the complex tasks of data management in the distributed environment. Thus suitable data-processing model was required for distributed processing of massive volume data sets. Such technique has direct relation with *application scalability* also as parallel distributed data processing has enabled the scaling.

13.3.1 The MapReduce Programming Model

'MapReduce' is a programming model or framework that supports developers to write those applications which could process massive amounts of unstructured data in parallel across a distributed processing environment. It was developed at Google in 2004 in order to quickly analyze the vast amount of content the search engine giant was collecting through public websites, to apply their famous PageRank algorithm aiming to decide which websites are most worthy of showing up in searches.

Development of *parallel-programming* model needs to handle the tasks like scheduling, intra-cluster communication and task monitoring by the developer. But, by using the library routines of MapReduce programming model, the developers can create parallel-programming effortlessly without worrying about all of these issues. The MapReduce model takes care of everything. MapReduce framework was inspired by the *map* and the *reduce* primitives of the 'Lisp' (List Processing) programming model. Lisp is the second oldest high-level programming language (after Fortran).

MapReduce is based on the idea for parallel processing of data-intensive applications, where data-set is split into blocks and assigned to different instances. Those instances run in parallel to process the data-set. After completing the computation works, the second phase starts where the intermediate results produced by individual instances are merged to produce the final result.

These two modules of the framework act in the following manner:

- Map, a function that divides data processing task in a distributed environment and generates the intermediate results.
- Reduce, a function that merges the intermediate results and resolves them into final result.

These functions accept data as input and then return transformed data as output. Actually, the master node takes data as input, splits it into smaller sections and sends them to other associated nodes in the cluster. These nodes may perform the same operation in turn to send those smaller sections of input to other nodes. MapReduce thus allows for massive scalability across hundreds or thousands of nodes.

> *MapReduce data processing model promotes scalability of the application.*

MapReduce model accepts input as a key-value pair and first splits those data into multiple sets of *key-value pairs*. These intermediate sets of data are then distributed across different nodes for further and parallel processing. At last, those processed data sets are reduced into the required result. The process can be described well through a simple example. Let there be a file containing data about daily minimum temperatures in five different cities over a year. The task is to find the lowest temperature of each city during that year. Such file can be broken into multiple smaller files; say in ten files and can be distributed among different nodes for processing. Here, it is to note that each smaller file may contain data about all of five cities and at the same time each file can have multiple entries for one city. Now the task of each of the ten processing nodes are reduced to find the minimum temperature of each city from the data-set as present in smaller file assigned to it. Let one processing node generates the intermediate result in the forms of following key-value pairs.

(city 1, 3) (city 2, –10) (city 3, 12) (city 4, –2) (city 5, –8)

Such intermediate result will be generated by each of other nine nodes. The next task is to accumulate all of these data for all of ten processing nodes which may look like as shown below.

(city 1, 3) (city 2, –10) (city 3, 12) (city 4, –2) (city 5, –8)

(city 1, 0) (city 2, –4) (city 3, –1) (city 4, 3) (city 5, –9)

(city 1, 6) (city 2, 2) (city 3, 5) (city 4, –7) (city 5, –1)

...

Now the task of finding the minimum temperature of each city for that year is reduced into finding the result in the above data-set which is very simple. In this way the MapReduce programming model automatically parallelize processing for large volume of data-sets.

> *Various programs written following the MapReduce model are automatically parallelized and executed on a large cluster of commodity machines.*

13.3.2 Other MapReduce-Inspired Models

MapReduce has presented revolutionary way for processing large volume of data in distributed environment but it has some limitations also. It becomes complicated to represent and process complex data-sets only in terms of *map* and *reduce* functions. To reduce effort of developers in MapReduce processing, several other modified models have been proposed by others. They have extended the MapReduce application space and presents easier interface for users.

Hadoop MapReduce, Pig and *Hive* are three such implementations by Apache. *Map-reduce-merge* is another extension of the model that introduces a third phase called as merge which allows efficient merger for portioned data after map-reduce processing. *Sphere* is another open-source programming framework for processing large volume of data-sets that exhibits similarities with MapReduce to some extent.

13.4 CLOUD NATIVE FILE SYSTEM

Any storage system builds up above a file system. Hence, to support high-performance computing for process-intensive as well as data-intensive tasks, an appropriate file system development is the first step. Such file systems meet the demand of cloud computing also as cloud computing is entirely meant for high-performance computing.

To satisfy all of these requirements of high-performance computing and with the goal of developing cloud native storage system, there a number of initiatives have been taken on behalves of different vendors and communities over the years. Few such notable efforts are discussed below. It can be noted that these files systems are applied on some virtualized computing environment (to be particular as 'virtual storage space'). The underlying systems may be built upon some traditional enterprise storage systems.

13.4.1 IBM General Parallel File System

It was one of the earliest effort towards high-performance distributed file system development. IBM's General Parallel File System (GPFS) started as the Tiger Shark file system, a research project at IBM and became available on IBM's AIX (a series of proprietary Unix operating systems developed by IBM) in 1998.

13.4.2 Google File System

The real revolution came in high-performance distributed file system development with emergence of the Google File System (GFS). It was developed during late 1990s. The file system was a result of an earlier Google effort called as *Big Files*. The main concern of the GFS designers was to ensure scalability of the system. They also enhanced reliability by working out mechanism against failures and errors. The file system was developed after detailed analyses of the characteristics of large files those are often stored in cloud environment. The access model of the system was designed in appropriate manner to minimize the storage and access time.

GFS connects a very large distributed cluster of inexpensive commodity components using high-speed network connections. GFS files are collections of fixed-size segments called as chunks. GFS uses the MapReduce programming model to split each large file into chunks of 64 MB size. Each chunk consists of 64 KB blocks. The larger chunk size increases the probability of less number of chunk being accessed to perform some operation and thus reducing the processing time.

A GFS cluster consists of two different types of nodes (Figure 13.1). One special node which is called as *master server* and a large number of other nodes known as *chunk servers*. The chunk server stores all of the GFS chunks while the master server maintains information about the associated chunks.

Chunks are distributed and replicated across multiple sites at chunk servers and are stored on Linux files systems. In Figure 13.1, two copies of every chunk is maintained. A master server maintains the metadata such as the file names, access control information and up-to-date information about locations of all of the replicas for every chunk of each file. The number of the replicas can be changed from the standard value of three, to any desired value.

GFS supports execution of distributed applications and promotes scalability of system.

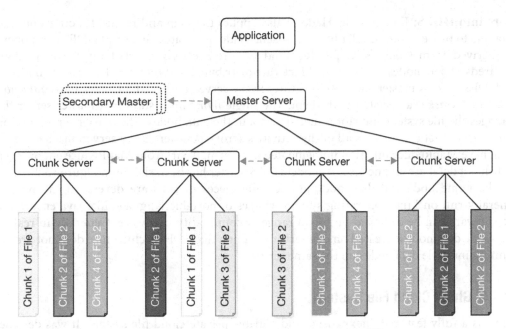

FIG 13.1: Replication and distribution of chunks in GFS

13.4.3 Hadoop Distributed File System

Hadoop Distributed File System (HDFS) is an *open-source* implementation of the Google's GFS architecture as developed by Apache Software Foundation. The development was initiated by Yahoo in 2006 being inspired by the Google's GFS and MapReduce papers and was looking to develop an open-source based system to fulfill their storage requirements. They decided to pass the storage and data processing parts of their 'Nutch' search engine project to Apache Foundation and form the Hadoop as an open-source project.

HDFS is a Java-based distributed file system that provides scalable and reliable data storage. Like GFS, HDFS is also designed to run on large clusters of commodity servers. The file system emerged as a sub-project of the Apache Hadoop project. HDFS is extremely fault-tolerant and provides high output access to application data. The file system is available for consumers on the Amazon EC2 cloud platform.

HDFS is designed to reliably store very large files across multiple machines in a large cluster. HDFS cluster contains two types of nodes as one single *master node* called as *NameNode* and other slave nodes called as *DataNodes*. Files are broken into sequence of blocks (similar to chunks in GFS) of reasonably bigger size (64 MB or 128 MB generally). These blocks are stored on DataNodes commodity servers (similar to chunk servers in GFS).

Like other distributed file systems, HDFS also assumes that nodes may fail. Hence, to increase fault tolerance of the system, it replicates blocks over multiple DataNodes. By default it uses 3 replicas. The block size and the replication factor are configurable. During read operation, data is fetched from any one of the replicas. During write operation, data is sent to all of the DataNodes containing replicas of the file. *Master node* usually stores metadata about the blocks.

HDFS is an open-source implementation of GFS and is built using the Java language.

More into HDFS: Like Google, Hadoop also applies the map and reduce functions on large data sets to process into smaller blocks. Apache Hadoop's MapReduce and HDFS components are derived from Google's MapReduce and GFS respectively. A Hadoop cluster contains hundreds of data nodes and the data blocks are distributed and replicated across the nodes.

HDFS follows master-slave architecture. Every server in a HDFS cluster have *data node* and a *task tracker* associated with them. The single *name node* stays in a master server that manages the file system and stores metadata about the data nodes. The master server also has a *job tracker* that coordinates all of the activities across a cluster. Every server, master or slave both, have MapReduce function implemented into them. Apart from MapReduce engine every node has a database engine also. A model HDFS cluster has been shown in Figure 13.2.

The name node and data node are actually pieces of software developed in Java that generally run on Linux operating system. Usages of portable language like java ensure that the software can be deployed on broad range of commodity hardware. Generally in real-life cases, one data node is created on one server although the HDFS architecture does not prevent running multiple data nodes on the same server.

13.4.4 Ghost Cloud File System

Ghost is a fully featured, inexpensive and scalable private cloud file system. It was designed to run within consumer's own Amazon web services account. Ghost Cloud Computing was founded in 2006. Its name is an acronym of **G**lobal **H**osted **O**perating **S**ystem. In 2009, it released its own cloud file system to run on AWS, known as *Ghost File System*.

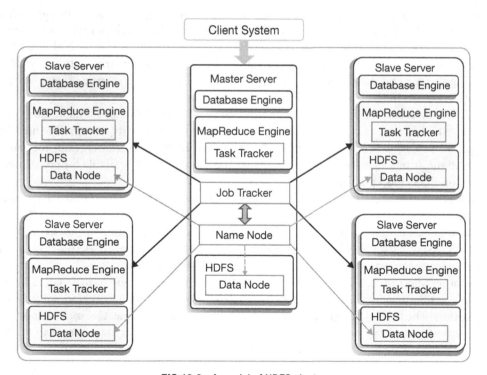

FIG 13.2: A model of HDFS cluster

13.4.5 Gluster File System

The Gluster File System (GlusterFS) is an open-source distributed file system capable of scaling. GlusterFS was developed originally by Gluster, Inc. and afterward by Red Hat, Inc., when they purchased Gluster during 2011. Like other cloud file systems, GlusterFS also allows creating a single volume of storage which spans multiple disks, multiple machines and even multiple data centers.

13.4.6 Kosmos File System

Kosmos File System (KFS) was released in 2007 as an open-source implementation of Google File System being developed in C++ programming language. It was developed by American company Kosmix for the UK Government's G-Cloud services. It paralleled the Hadoop HDFS project which is developed in the Java. Currently the file system is known as *CloudStore*.

Apart from these, 'Sector Distributed File System' is another cloud native file system which is an open-source implementation inspired by Google's GFS and uses MapReduce inspired 'Sphere' data processing framework.

> Cloud native storage systems are built over several cloud native file systems.

13.5 STORAGE DEPLOYMENT MODELS

Depending on the deployment locations, cloud storages can be categorized into three models as public, private and hybrid. This is just similar to the standard cloud computing deployment models.

Public cloud storage as the name specifies can be accessed by anyone. It is provided by reputed service providers. In this model, the consumer enterprise and storage service provider are two different organizations.

Private cloud storage is arranged by the consumer enterprise itself with help of some service providers. This type of storage can be set up both on-premises and off-premises. In this model, the consumer enterprise and storage service provider integrate each other at enterprise's data center or provider's data center.

The hybrid storage model is the combination of both public and private storages as its name implies. In this model, the enterprises get the opportunity of storing critical and active data in private cloud storage while public storage can be used for archiving data.

13.6 STORAGE TYPES

Storage needs of general users (people who simply store files into storage) are not similar to that of system developers who deploy or develop the applications. Their requirements vary in type of uses, frequency of access, data transfer rate and others. Cloud services deliver storage systems to fulfill requirements of both types of users.

General users (who are actually end users of computing) want to store their files and folders in ready-to-use storage spaces (like formatted pen drive or external hard disk). Their requirements can be fulfilled through *personal file hosting* services where users can store their files.

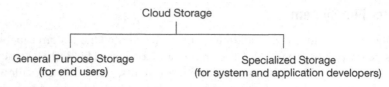

FIG 13.3: Types of cloud storage delivery

Specialized users or developers need different kind of storage services where they would be able to control the storage system on their own. Simple file hosting facility would not serve their purpose as they will deploy applications or even perform application development tasks using the storage service. So, they would like to have full control over the system. Unlike *general purpose storage system* (the file hosting storage) where files once stored remain unaltered for a long period of time, this kind of *specialized storage* system is accessed frequently by the users.

> *Cloud storage is categorized according to the purpose of use such as general storage purpose or computing system development purpose.*

13.6.1 Managed and Unmanaged Cloud Storage

The general purpose and the specialized cloud storage systems are also characterized as unmanaged and managed storages respectively. They are managed and unmanaged in the sense whether users or consumers get the chance of managing the storage or not. *Managed storage* system provides raw disk like facility to users. User can divide or format the storage spaces as per their requirements and can also install the software. This type of storages is mainly meant for computing system developers.

Unmanaged cloud storage is like ready-to-use disk drive. Users directly get storage capacity available for use. All of the primary disk management tasks like partitioning, formatting and else are managed by the vendors or service providers. Since users of such storage need not to worry about managing the storage space, it is called as *unmanaged storage*. Here, users have very little control. Storage provider decides the nature of the storage and applications through which the space can be accessed.

Unlike managed storages which provide raw storage space, the unmanaged storages provide pre-configured storage space. User can use it, but cannot separate or format as they like, or cannot even install any application in it. The other attributes or capabilities of the storage space (like encryption or compression) are also pre-configured and set by the provider. However, unmanaged storage is easy to work with and relatively cheap. Users can utilize unmanaged storage service for file hosting purpose where they can store their files. Unmanaged storages are used independently irrespective of any virtual machines. But managed cloud storage can function as a part of some virtual machine owned by the consumers.

> *Managed cloud storages are delivered as Infrastructure-as-a-Service, whereas unmanaged storages are delivered as Software-as-a-Service.*

Note: It may be little misleading as the terms *managed* and *unmanaged* often are used to recognize two different types of cloud storages. They do not go along with the cloud computing jargons where the service delivery models are generally identified as fully-managed offerings. Any facility offered directly as cloud service to the consumer is considered as fully-managed since consumers need not to worry about the back-end administration of the service and is fully-managed by the provider. On the contrary, the term 'managed storage' represents the storage type that users can manage on their own.

13.7 POPULAR CLOUD STORAGES FOR DEVELOPERS

There are many cloud storage services available for developers of computing provided by reputed service providers. Elastic Block Store (EBS) and Simple Storage Service (S3) provided by Amazon, Cloud Storage Service offered by Google and Cloud Block Storage of Rackspace are few examples of such services which provide reliable and high-performance storage service. These are called as 'managed storage services' in the sense that consumers have greater control over the storage spaces and they need to manage the storage as per their requirements. Following are brief descriptions about few such storages.

13.7.1 Amazon's Elastic Block Store

Amazon Elastic Block Store (EBS) provides block level storage volumes for use with Amazon EC2 (Elastic Compute Cloud) instances (servers). EBS was introduced for general public by Amazon in 2008. Block level storages can be used to create raw storage volumes which can be attached with the servers. Variety of file systems like NTFS (for windows OS) or ext4 (for Linux OS) can be run on the block level storage. EBS is like a massive SAN (Storage Area Network) under the AWS infrastructure. Delivered storage volume size goes up to TB in size.

13.7.2 Amazon's Simple Storage Service

Simple Storage Service (S3) was introduced by Amazon as a cost-effective web service solution for developers in the year 2006. In S3, files are stored as objects and those objects are stored into the containers called as 'buckets'. Object size can go up to few terabytes and trillions of objects are stored per month as reported by Amazon. S3 can be used together with Amazon's virtual server Elastic Compute Cloud (EC2).

13.7.3 Google's Cloud Storage

The persistence storage attached with Google's cloud server Google Compute Engine (GCE) is the Cloud Storage of Google. There data are stored as objects and objects are stored into containers called as the 'buckets' as well. Objects can be of terabytes in size and does not have a size limit. Billing in Google Cloud Storage is calculated as per storage usages as well as the bandwidth usage on monthly basis.

13.7.4 Rackspace's Cloud Block Storage

Rackspace's Cloud Block Storage is a block-level storage solution and is associated with Rackspace Cloud Server. But users can create or delete multiple storage volumes independent to the cloud servers they are attached with. Storage volume size in Cloud Block Storage may range up to TB. The storage service is charged as per gigabytes of storage used per month.

> *Cloud storage delivered for developers are referred as 'managed' in nature, as they can be managed by the users. Users can divide or format them as needed.*

13.8 POPULAR GENERAL PURPOSE CLOUD STORAGES

There are hundreds of general purpose cloud storage services available for users. This type of storages are used for file hosting purpose in the cloud. Different vendors provide file hosting facility to fulfill storage requirements of consumers who are simple users and their requirements are no way linked with the software development. Few among such popular storage services are mentioned below.

Most of the general purpose cloud storage services provide the applications to access the storage from local computing device. Once someone installs the corresponding app in local device like PC, tablet or mobile it provides a folder always synced to the cloud storage. Any folder or file which is moved into that folder gets automatically synced to the cloud.

13.8.1 Dropbox

Dropbox is a file hosting service offered by Dropbox Inc., United States. The service was officially launched in 2008. Dropbox provides client applications through which the storage can be accessed from different personal devices. It is accessible from Windows, Mac, Linux using desktop applications and also from Android, iOS and the BlackBerry platforms using mobile apps. In the background, Dropbox uses Amazon's S3 storage system to store the files.

13.8.2 Google Drive

This is a popular file hosting service offered by Google. The service was launched in 2012. Google Drive provides file sharing facility with other users. Currently, it provides 15 GB of free storage space for users. Google Drive has the benefit of a built-in office suite where one can edit documents, spreadsheets and presentations. Google Drive client software is available for both desktop platform like Windows, Mac as well as mobile platforms like iOS and Android.

> *Google Drive storage is for general users and Google Cloud Storage is meant for the developers.*

13.8.3 OneDrive

OneDrive is a general purpose cloud storage service provided by Microsoft. The service was first launched in 2007 and was previously known as 'SkyDrive' or 'Windows Live Folders'. OneDrive is built into Windows 8 and 8.1 operating systems. It is also accessible from Mac OS and earlier versions of Windows OS and mobile platforms like Android, iOS and Windows Phone. Apart from file storage, OneDrive offers the facility for document creation and collaboration. OneDrive's biggest strength is that it works closely with Microsoft Office apps such as Word, Excel or PowerPoint.

13.8.4 Box

Box is an online file hosting, sharing and collaboration service. The company Box Inc. is based in California of United States. While Dropbox like services are popular among individuals, Box is popular among business and enterprise users. Box offers 3 types of accounts as Enterprise, Business and Personal. Users can determine how their content can be shared with other users.

13.8.5 Copy

Copy cloud storage service was introduced by corporate IT company Barracuda Networks in 2013. Like other cloud storage services, Copy also has desktop software for Windows, Mac and Linux in addition to mobile apps for iOS and Android. It provides 15 GB of free storage space.

13.8.6 Amazon Cloud Drive

Amazon Cloud Drive is a file hosting service offered by Amazon. The storage can be accessed from different mobile devices and computers. It currently provides 5 GB of free storage space to consumers.

> *Cloud storage delivered for general users are referred as 'unmanaged' as they cannot be managed by users. Such storages are divided or formatted by service providers prior to delivery.*

SUMMARY

❖ Cloud computing is synonymous to high-performance computing. Hence, file system and file processing characteristics of high-performance computing environment are also applicable in cloud computing.

❖ Efficient processing of large data-sets is critical for success of high-performance computing systems. Large and complex data-sets are generated and produced in cloud every now and then.

❖ High-performance processing of large data-sets requires parallel execution of partitioned data across distributed computing nodes. This facility should be enabled with suitable data processing programming models and other supporting file systems.

❖ Several programming models have been developed for high-performance processing of large data-sets. Among them, Google's MapReduce is a well-accepted model for processing massive amounts of unstructured data in parallel across a distributed processing environment.

❖ Several other models have emerged influenced by the MapReduce model. Among them Hadoop, Pig and Hive are a few to mention.

❖ Among the various file systems to support high-performance processing of data, Google File System (GFS) is considered as the pioneer. The open-source Hadoop Distributed File System (HDFS) is inspired by GFS.

- ❖ Storage in cloud is delivered in two categories: for general users and for developers. Storage for general users are delivered as SaaS and for the developers it is delivered as IaaS.
- ❖ For general users, cloud provides ready-to-use storage which is usually managed by the providers. Hence, users can directly use the storage without worrying about any kind of processing of the storage. Such storages are known as 'unmanaged' storage type.
- ❖ Managed storages are raw storages which are built to be managed by the users themselves. Computing developers use such kind of storages.

REVIEW QUESTIONS

Why MapReduce model is considered so important in data-intensive computation?

Data-intensive computation require distributed parallel processing of data for each single problem to deliver high performance. Partitioning large data-sets into smaller pieces, distributed execution of those smaller data-sets, intermediate result generation, accumulating those intermediate results and the processing of those intermediate results for producing final outcome are required for such computations. Earlier all of these were the responsibilities of application developers of data-intensive tasks. A programming model was required which will have all of these attributes inherent into it. MapReduce is such a model and that is why it has attracted the attention of all.

How does 'local storage' of cloud server differ from the 'persistent data storage' available with cloud server?

With every cloud server, a local storage is always attached to facilitate computational tasks and that storage only exists as long as the cloud server exists. This local cloud storage is non-persistent; hence, the users cannot store data in it. Cloud computing also provides persistent data storages with cloud servers. Persistent storages are like storage disks attached with cloud servers those can also exist even after the server is deleted. Amazon Elastic Block Store (EBS), Amazon Simple Storage Service (S3) or Google Cloud Storage are few examples of persistent cloud data storages available with the cloud servers.

How the 'persistent data storage' available with cloud server is different from 'general purpose cloud storage'?

General purpose cloud storages are for general users (persons without having any kind of computing development requirements). Hence, these types of storages are delivered in ready-to-use mode while users can utilize to store their files without worrying about configuring them (like formatting or partitioning). Even to access such storage facility, a user need not to create any cloud server. They can directly avail the facility by requesting for storage space. However, the persistent data storage available with cloud server is delivered in raw format. Users need to divide and format such storages to make it fit for use. But, once the storage is ready, it can be used independently for the cloud servers. The storage can even work after dissolution of its server.

Why are managed and unmanaged cloud storages, called so?

The terms 'managed' and 'unmanaged' are used to refer whether users can manage the storage or not. Storages, over which users get lots of control and are generally configured or managed by the users, are called as 'managed' storage. Developers generally use managed storages. Unmanaged storages are those which users need not to configure or manage. This type of storages is managed by storage providers.

MULTIPLE CHOICE QUESTIONS

1. Cloud storage is built upon

   a) Traditional file system

   b) Cloud native file system

   c) Both a and b

   d) None of these

2. In comparison with traditional storage system, the major difference(s) emerge while building cloud storage is

   a) Supporting scalability

   b) Metering usages

   c) Supporting multi-tenancy

   d) All of these

3. Cloud native storage file systems are actually virtual in nature. Is this true?

   a) Yes

   b) No

4. MapReduce framework was built to efficiently process unstructured data in parallel in

   a) Cloud environment

   b) Centralized environment

   c) Distributed environment

   d) Non-cloud environment

5. Which of the following is an open-source cloud file system?

   a) GFS

   b) HDFS

   c) GlusterFS

   d) KFS

6. Unmanaged cloud storages are actually managed by

   a) Storage provider

   b) Storage consumer

   c) None

   d) Administrator

7. Managed cloud storages are generally used by

   a) Managers

   b) Big enterprises

   c) Application Developers

   d) All of these

8. In unmanaged cloud storage user can install applications of his/her choice.

   a) Yes. Till the space permits.

   b) No. They can install only specific applications.

   c) Yes. If the privilege is given.

   d) No. It comes with pre-installed applications.

9. For file hosting purpose, the type of cloud storage used is

   a) Managed storage

   b) Unmanaged storage

   c) Both a and b

   d) None of these

10. There are cloud storage systems which are used to build cloud service and not offered to consumers as a service

    a) True

    b) False. Cloud storage systems are built to offer as a service to consumers.

11. Mapreduce is a

    a) Storage model

    b) Programming model

    c) File system model

    d) None of these

12. Google Drive is a

    a) General purpose cloud storage

    b) Cloud storage to be used by developers

14 Database Technology

The changing characteristics of data and need for new data processing models as well as file systems in high-performance computing environment have been discussed in previous chapters. The large data-sets produce not only structured data but un-structured data too. Storage requirement for unstructured data is entirely different from that of structured data. There is a need to maintain quicker data storage, search and retrieval as these are basic requirements in high-performance computing.

Cloud computing not only provides support for traditional DBMSs, modern data processing requirements are also catered to as well. This chapter focuses on the characteristics of this new type of databases and discusses how un-structured data are stored in those databases for efficient processing. Apart from these, the chapter also discusses about different forms of database solutions available on the high-performance cloud computing environment.

Data storage and database on the cloud is intimately tied with one another and that provides the scope for suitable solutions to optimize the database performance. This has changed the way how database is managed. Many cloud computing vendors have developed new methods of storing data objects which are different from the traditional methods of storing data.

> *Data storage and database on cloud like high-performance systems are often intimately tied with one another for efficient processing of large volume unstructured data-sets.*

14.1 DATABASE IN CLOUD

Consumers can avail database facility in cloud in two forms. First one is the general database solution that is implemented through installation of some database solution on IaaS (virtual machine delivered as IaaS). The other one is delivered by service providers as database-as-a-service where the vendor fully manages the backend administration jobs like installation, security management and resource assignment tasks.

In the first approach, the users can deploy database applications on cloud virtual machines like any other applications software. Apart from this, the ready-made machine images supplied by the vendors are also available with per-installed and pre-configured databases. For example, Amazon provides ready-made EC2 machine image with pre-installed Oracle Database.

In the Database-as-a-Service (DBaaS) model, the operational burden of provisioning, configuration, backup facilities are managed by the service operators. While the earlier described (first) approach is similar implementation of database solutions over cloud infrastructure where the users used to deploy them over traditional computers, the DBaaS approach provides the actual flavour of cloud computing to database users.

Users can deploy and manage database solutions of their choices over IaaS facility. On the other hand, the Database-as-a-Service is a PaaS offering being delivered by provider.

14.2 DATA MODELS

The traditional database systems with relational models deal with the *structured data*. But, there has been a rapid change in the characteristic of data in last one decade or so. Huge volume of *unstructured data* are being generated and stored every day. The storage and processing requirements of these data are different and it cannot be managed by traditional systems with relational models efficiently.

As a result, new data models have been introduced for use in different database solutions to fulfill the need of unstructured data being apart from continuing with traditional form of database solutions for structured data. Query languages used in these two categories of databases are also different. The data models used in these two categories are as *SQL data model* and *NoSQL data model* respectively.

14.2.1 SQL Model or Relational Model

This is the data model used in traditional database systems that process structured data sets. But this relational data model has a limitation. This model is not made for distributed data storage and thus makes the scaling of a database difficult. Hence relational data models are not natively suited to cloud environment where scaling is an essential attribute. Databases built following this data model is called as relational database or SQL database. Oracle Database, Microsoft SQL Server, Open-source MySQL or Open-source PostgreSQL come under this category.

14.2.2 NoSQL Model or Non-relational Model

Distributed data storage is inherent characteristic of this data model. Thus, this model is suitable for building scalable systems. Databases built following this data model are known as *NoSQL databases*. Such databases are cloud native and able to scale efficiently. NoSQL database is built to serve heavy read-write loads and suitable for retrieval of the storages for unstructured data sets. Amazon SimpleDB, Google Datastore and Apache Cassandra are few examples of NoSQL database systems.

NoSQL data model is more cloud native than relational data models. Relational or SQL data model makes scaling difficult for databases.

14.3 DATABASE-AS-A-SERVICE

Database-as-a-Service (DBaaS) is a cloud service offering which is managed by cloud service providers. DBaaS has all of the characteristics of cloud services like scaling, metered billing capabilities and else. It is offered on a pay-per-usage basis that provides on-demand access to database for the storage of data. Database-as-a-Service allows storing and retrieving of data without having to deal with lower-level database administration functionalities. It provides significant benefits in terms of automated provisioning, monitoring, increased security and management of database in comparison to the traditional architectures.

The DBaaS offering of cloud computing is available to serve the processing requirements of both the structured and unstructured data. For structured data the early DBaaS efforts include Amazon RDS and Microsoft SQL Azure. Example of DBaaS for *unstructured data* include Amazon SimpleDB, Google Datastore and Apache Cassandra.

> Database-as-a-Service comes under Platform-as-a-Service offering category.

14.4 RELATIONAL DBMS IN CLOUD

There are two ways to use RDBMS on cloud. In the first way, the consumers of IaaS service can deploy some traditional relational database (like Oracle or SQL server) on cloud server, where the consumers have full responsibilities of installation and management of such databases. The second way is to use the available ready-to-use relational database services offered by cloud service providers. Such services include Amazon Relational Database Service (Amazon RDS), Google Cloud SQL, Azure SQL Database and others. Two types as mentioned above can be categorized as

- Relational database deployment on cloud
- Relational Database-as-a-Service or fully-managed RDBMS

14.4.1 Relational Database Deployment on Cloud

Users can avail the facility of traditional RDBMS deployment over cloud infrastructure. Even third-party database applications can be deployed over virtual machines in cloud. There are two ways of deploying it. Firstly, the users can install such database applications on cloud servers just like they do it in local computers. Secondly, many cloud services provide ready-made machine images that already include an installation of a database. The major cloud vendors mostly support the common RDBMS applications like Oracle Server, Microsoft's SQL Server or open-source MySQL Server.

Amazon's cloud computing platform provides support for both Microsoft's SQL Server and Oracle Server. In fact, AWS provides an ideal platform for running many other traditional, third-party relational database systems including IBM DB2 on their virtual machines. Users can run their own relational database on Amazon EC2 VM instances. Rackspace also provides deployment support for Oracle Server, SQL Server and MySQL Server. Microsoft Azure supports the deployment option for Oracle database and SQL Server using Azure VM.

When users deploy database on cloud, they get full control over the database administration, including backups and recovery. They can install the database application over operating system of their choice and can also tune the operating system and database parameters according to their requirements.

> *Deploying some relational database on cloud server is the ideal choice for users who require absolute control over the management of the database.*

14.4.2 Relational Database-as-a-Service

Similar to other computing services like machine, storage, network etc., the cloud providers also provide relational DBMS as a service referred as DBaaS. Many cloud service providers offer the customary relational database systems as fully-managed services which provide functionalities similar to what is found in Oracle Server, SQL Server or MySQL Servers. Management of such services is the responsibility of provider who handle the routine database tasks like provisioning, patching, backup, recovery, failure detection and repair. Following section briefly focuses on few such popular services.

> *Relational database management system offerings are fully-managed by cloud providers.*

14.4.2.1 Amazon RDS

Amazon Relational Database Service or Amazon RDS is a relational database service available with AWS. Amazon RDS was first released in 2009 supporting functionalities of open-source MySQL database. Later on, it added capabilities of Oracle Server, Microsoft SQL Server and Open-source PostgreSQL. In 2014, AWS launched a MySQL-compatible relational database called as Amazon Aurora and added it as the fifth database engine available to customers through Amazon RDS. Amazon Aurora provides much better performance than MySQL at lesser price.

Two different pricing options are available with Amazon RDS as reserved pricing and on-demand pricing. These two schemes are known as *Reserved DB Instances* and *On-Demand DB Instances*. Reserved pricing provides the option for one-time payment and offers three different DB Instance types (for light, medium and heavy utilization). This scheme is useful for extensive database use in long run. *On-Demand DB Instances* provide the opportunity of hourly payments with no long-term commitments.

14.4.2.2 Google Cloud SQL

Google Cloud SQL is a MySQL database that lives in Google's cloud and fully managed by Google. It is very simple to use and integrates very well with Google App Engine applications written in Java, Python, PHP and Go. Google Cloud SQL is also accessible through MySQL client and other tools those works with MySQL databases. Google Cloud SQL offers updated releases of MySQL.

Google offers two different billing options for Cloud SQL, namely as *Packages* and *Per Use*. *Packages* option is suitable for users who extensively use the database per month; otherwise hourly-basis billing is preferable which is available in *Per Use* option. In both of the schemes, the billing amount depends mainly on RAM, storage usages and number of I/O operations.

14.4.2.3 Azure SQL Database

Microsoft Azure SQL Database (formerly SQL Azure) is a relational Database-as-a-Service offering functionalities of Microsoft SQL Server. Like Microsoft SQL Server, SQL Database uses T-SQL as the query language. SQL Database is available under three service tiers like basic, standard and premium with different hourly-basis pricing options. The premium tier supports mission-critical, high-transactional volume and many concurrent users whereas the basic tier is for small databases with a single operation at a given point in time.

There are many more such fully-managed relational database services available in the market offered by different providers. But this is still an emerging field and many other companies are in the process of developing their own services with more functionalities.

> Amazon RDS, Google Cloud SQL and Azure SQL Databases deliver RDBMS as-a-Service.

14.5 NON-RELATIONAL DBMS IN CLOUD

Non-relational database system is another unique offering in the field of *data-intensive computing*. Using this database model, the new age non-relational data-sets can be processed more efficiently than the traditional database with relational systems. The new age high-performance computing environments like cloud computing systems are heavily dependent on these non-relational database systems for efficient storage and retrieval of data. This section focuses on the need of such a database, discusses its storage architecture and also briefs few such popular databases.

14.5.1 Emergence of Large Volume of Unstructured Data-sets

Earlier data managed by enterprise applications were structured in nature and less in volume. But with the introduction of web based portals during the end of last century, the nature of web content or data started changing. Volume of data started to grow exponentially and data became unstructured in character. Such data-sets were classified later and their characteristics were identified. This type of data or data-set is referred as 'Big data'.

14.5.1.1 Big data

Big data is used to describe both structured and unstructured data that is massive in volume. It also considers data those are too diverse in nature and highly dynamic (very fast-changing). Differently put, the new age data whose volume, velocity or variety is too great are termed as *Big data*. Three said characteristics of Big data are described below.

Volume: A typical PC probably had 10 gigabytes of storage in the year of 2000. During that time, excessive data volume was a storage issue as storage was not so cheap like today. Today social networking sites use to generate few thousand terabytes of data every day.

Velocity: Data streaming nowadays are happening at unprecedented rate as well as with speed. So things must be dealt in a timely manner. Quick response to customers' action is a business challenge for any organization.

Variety: Data of all formats are important today. Structured or unstructured texts, audio, video, image, 3D data and others are all being produced every day.

The above characteristics cause variability and complexity in terms of managing big data. Variability in the sense that data flow can be highly inconsistent with periodic peaks as they are in social media or in e-commerce portals. The complexity often comes with it when it becomes difficult to connect and correlate data or define their hierarchies.

> It is to be noted that big data is not only about the volume of data; rather it considers other characteristics of new age data, like their variety or speed of generation.

14.5.2 Time Appeared for an Alternative Database Model

Since the emergence of relational database, enterprise applications started using it since 1980s. Those relational database systems were developed to store and process structured data-sets. But the database system started facing challenge as the volume of data started increasing exponentially from the end of the last century and the situation worsened after the introduction of web based social networking and e-commerce portals. Soon, the concept of big data emerged.

Online Transaction Processing (OLTP) applications flooded the web with very high volume of data from the beginning of the current century. These applications needed to function under stiff *latency constraints* to provide consistent performance to a very large number of users as hundreds of millions of clients throughout the world were accessing such applications. These sites were experiencing massive variations in traffic also. Some of these hikes were due to predictable events like New Year, business release or sporting event, but most of others were unpredictable events which becomes more difficult to manage. Data were being accessed more frequently and needed to be processed more intensively.

> Relational databases are appropriate for a wide range of tasks but not for every task.

The basic operations at any database are *read* and *write*. *Read* operations can be scaled by distributing and replicating data to multiple servers. But inconsistency in data may happen when *write* or update operation takes place. And with the new age data, the number of *writers* are often much larger than the number of *readers*, especially in popular social networking sites. One solution to this problem is to exclusively partition the data during distribution. But with that also the distributed unions (of data from database tables) may become slower and harder to implement if the underlying storage architecture is not supported for doing so.

Here, the main problem was that the traditional SQL databases with relational systems do not scale well. Traditional DBMSs can only 'scale up' (vertical scaling) or increase the resources on a central server. But, efficient processing of big data require an excellent 'scale out' (horizontal scaling) capability.

Web applications were moving towards cloud computing model, and it did not take very long to the pioneer of cloud computing services like Google, Amazon, and many other e-commerce and social networking companies as well as technologists to realize that traditional relational databases are no more enough for handling the new age data. They started to look for a suitable database solution.

> Traditional SQL databases do not fit well with the concept of horizontal scaling and horizontal scalability is the only way to scale them indefinitely.

14.5.2.1 Modern Age Database Requirements

Horizontal scaling appeared as one of the necessary attributes of database system to keep pace with the processing needs of large data-sets. It appeared impossible to deliver high-performance without distributing those data among multiple nodes and processing them in parallel. The other major concern was the latency associated with transactions. This *latency* could be reduced by caching frequently-used data in-memory on dedicated servers, instead of fetching them every time required. These facilities had to be incorporated in the new age database systems to reduce the *response time* and enhance the performance of applications. The databases had to be highly-optimized for simple retrieval and appending operations. These things, along with many other issues, worked as the driving forces behind the development of an alternative database system.

14.5.2.2 Role of Cloud Storage System

The characteristics of storage system had changed during this time. From the earlier concern regarding cost of storage space, the cost of storage management was gradually becoming the dominant element of storage systems. That opened the opportunity for replication of files into storage across different geographic locations and hence the uses of distributed file systems became widespread.

In such a scenario, the evolution of storage strategy started introducing many different models of distributed file systems like General Parallel File System (GPFS), Google File System (GFS) or Hadoop Distributed File System (HDFS) and else. All of these works well in high-performance computing environments. Characteristics of such file systems and their storage strategy suited well with cloud's dynamic architecture. This created opportunity of developing *scalable database* systems (over these file systems) to store and manage the modern age data.

> Cloud native databases are facilitated by distributed storage systems and they are closely associated with one another. Hence, the storage and database system often overlaps.

14.5.3 NoSQL DBMS

NoSQL is a class of database management system that does not follow all of the rules of a relational DBMS. The term NoSQL can be interpreted as '*Not Only SQL*' as it is not a replacement but rather it is a complementary addition to RDBMS. This class of database uses some SQL like query languages to make queries but does not use the traditional SQL (structured query language).

The term NoSQL was coined by Carlo Strozzi in the year of 1998 to name the file-based open-source relational database he was going to develop which did not have an SQL interface. However, this initial usage of the term NoSQL is not directly linked with the NoSQL being used at present. The term drew attention in 2009 when Eric Evans (an employee of a cloud hosting company, Rackspace) used it in a conference to represent the surge of developing non-relational distributed databases then.

> NoSQL is not against SQL and it was developed to handle unstructured big data in an efficient way to provide maximum business value.

14.5.3.1 The Evolution

The NoSQL movement slowly started in the early years of current century as the IT industry started to realize the need of new database system in order to support web-based applications. The initial advances got its space when computing majors Google and Amazon published two papers successively in 2006 and 2007.

14.5.3.2 The BigTable Revolution

In 2004, Google employed a team to develop a storage system to manage Big data. *BigTable* is outcome of that. It is a proprietary distributed storage system built by Google on GFS and is in use from 2005. The storage system was built to manage large structured data-sets and was designed to scale to a very large size. It is structured as large table which may be peta-bytes in size and distributed among tens of thousands of machines. BigTable has successfully provided a flexible, high-performance solution for Google products like Google Earth, Google Analytics and Orkut.

Later, this BigTable has had a large impact on NoSQL database design when Google publicly disclosed the details of it in a technical paper in 2006. This opened the scope to the technologists for an Open-source development of BigTable like database. Thus, HBase database developed by Apache Foundation and Cassandra developed at Facebook were surfaced in the market. Meanwhile, during all of these developments, Amazon also published a paper on their Dynamo storage system in 2007 which was also built to address the challenges of working with big data.

> Big Table, although built as storage, resembles database system in many ways. It also shares many implementation strategies of database technologies.

The NoSQL database development process remained closely associated with the developments in the field of *cloud native file systems* (or, cloud storage systems) during those days. Soon, many other players of web services started working on the technology and in a short period of time, starting around the year of 2008, all of these developments became the source of a technology revolutions. The *NoSQL* database became prominent after 2009 as the general terminology 'NoSQL' was adopted to set apart these new databases or more correctly for the file systems.

NoSQL database development has been closely associated with scalable file system development in computing.

14.5.3.3 CAP Theorem

The abbreviation CAP stands for Consistency, Availability and Partition tolerance of data. CAP theorem (also known as Brewer's theorem) says that it is impossible for a distributed computer system to meet all of three aspects of CAP simultaneously. Eric Brewer of University of California, Berkeley presented the theorem in the ACM (Association of Computing Machinery) conference in 2000.

- Consistency: This means that data in the database remains consistent after execution of an operation. For example, once a data is written or updated, all of the future read requests will see that data.
- Availability: It guarantees that the database always remains available without any downtime.
- Partition tolerance: Here the database should be partitioned in such a way that if one part of the database becomes unavailable, other parts remain unaffected and can function properly. This ensures availability of information.

Any database system must follow this 'two-of-three' philosophy. Thus, the relational database which focuses highly on consistency issue sacrifices the 'partition tolerance' attribute of CAP (Figure 14.1). It is already discussed that one of the primary goals of NoSQL systems is to boost horizontal scalability. To scale horizontally, a system needs strong network partition tolerance which needs to give up either 'consistency' or 'availability' attribute of CAP. Thus, all of the NoSQL databases follow either combinations of CP (consistency-partition tolerance) or

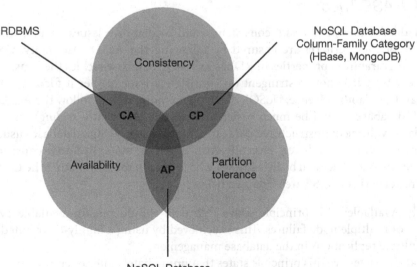

FIG 14.1: 'Two-of-three' combination of CAP philosophy

AP (availability-partition tolerance) from the attributes of the CAP theorem. This means some of the NoSQL databases even drops consistency as an essential attribute. For example, while HBase maintains CP criteria the other popular database Cassandra maintains AP criteria.

> *Some of the NoSQL databases even choose to relax the 'consistency' issue from the CAP criteria and this philosophy suits well in certain distributed applications.*

Different combinations of CAP criteria are to serve different kinds of requirements. Database designers analyze specific data processing requirements before choosing one.

> CA: It is suitable for systems being designed to run over cluster on a single site so that all of the nodes always remain in contact. Hence, the worry of network partitioning problem almost disappears. But, if partition occurs, the system fails.

> CP: This model is tolerant to network partitioning problem, but suitable for systems where 24×7 availability is not a critical issue. Some data may become inaccessible for a while but the rest remains consistent or accurate.

> AP: This model is also tolerant to network partitioning problem as partitions are designed to work independently. 24×7 availability of data is also assured but sometimes some of the data returned may be inaccurate.

> *Partition tolerance is an essential criteria for NoSQL databases as one of their primary goals is the horizontal scalability.*

14.5.3.4 BASE Theorem

Relational database system treats consistency and availability issues as essential criteria. Fulfillments of these criteria are ensured by following the ACID (Atomicity, Consistency, Isolation and Durability) properties in RDBMS. NoSQL database tackles the consistency issue in a different way. It is not so stringent on consistency issue; rather it focuses on partition tolerance and availability. Hence, NoSQL database no more need to follow the ACID rule.

NoSQL database should be much easier to scale out (*horizontal scaling*) and capable of handling large volume of unstructured data. To achieve these, NoSQL databases usually follow BASE principle which stands for 'Basically Available, Soft state, Eventual consistency'. The *BASE theorem* was also defined by Eric Brewer who is known for formulating the *CAP theorem*.

The three criteria of BASE are explained below:

- Basically Available: This principle states that data should remain available even in the presence of multiple node failures. This is achieved by using a highly-distributed approach with multiple replications in the database management.
- Eventual Consistency: This principle states that immediately after operation, data may look like inconsistent but ultimately they should converge to a consistent state in future. For example, two users querying for same data immediately after a transaction (on that data) may get different values. But finally, the consistency will be regained.

- Soft State: The eventual consistency model allows the database to be inconsistent for some time. But to bring it back to consistent state, the system should allow change in state over time even without any input. This is known as Soft state of system.

BASE does not address the consistency issue. The AP region of Figure 14.1 follows the BASE theory. The idea behind this is that data consistency is application developer's problem and should be handled by developer through appropriate programming techniques. Database will no more handle the consistency issue. This philosophy helps to achieve the scalability goal.

> *To satisfy the scalability and data distribution demands in NoSQL, it was no longer possible to meet all the four criteria of ACID simultaneously. Hence, BASE theorem was proposed as an alternative.*

14.5.4 Features of NoSQL Database

NoSQL database introduces many new features in comparison with relational databases. Few of those features oppose relational-DBMS concept. They can be listed as *schema-free*, non-relational, horizontally scalable and distributed.

14.5.4.1 Flexible Schemas

Relational database system cannot address data whose structure is not known in advance. They need to define the schema of the database and tables before storing any data in it. But, with this schema-based design, it becomes difficult to manage agile data sets. When at the middle of the business, it needs to introduce a new field (column) in some table, then it becomes extremely disruptive as that require alteration of the schema. This is a very slow process and involves significant downtime.

NoSQL databases are designed to allow insertion of data without a pre-defined schema. This makes it very easy to incorporate real-time changes in application at the time of requirement as that does not cause service interruption.

> *Unlike relational database, NoSQL database is schema-free.*

14.5.4.2 Non-relational

NoSQL database can manage non-relational data efficiently along with relational data. The relational constraints of RDBMS are not applicable in this database. This makes it easier to manage non-relational data using NoSQL database.

14.5.4.3 Scalability

Relational databases are designed to scale vertically. But *vertical scaling* has its own limitations as it does not allow new servers to be introduced into the system to share the load.

Horizontal scalability is the only way to scale indefinitely and that is also cheaper than vertical scaling. NoSQL database is designed to scale horizontally with minimum effort.

14.5.4.4 Auto-distribution

Distributed relational databases allow fragmentation and distribution of a database across multiple servers. But, that does not happen automatically as it is a manual process to be handled by application making it difficult to manage. On the other hand, the distribution happens automatically in NoSQL databases. Application developers need not to worry about anything. All of these distribution and load balancing acts are automated in the database itself.

> *Distribution and replication of data segments are not inherent features of relational database; these are responsibilities of application developers. In NoSQL, these happen automatically.*

14.5.4.5 Auto-replication

Not only fragmentation and distribution, replication of database fragments are also an automatic process in NoSQL. No external programming is required to replicate fragments across multiple servers. Replication ensures high availability of data and supports recovery.

14.5.4.6 Integrated Caching

NoSQL database often provides integrated caching capability. This feature reduces *latency* and increases *throughput* by keeping frequently-used data in system memory as much as possible. In relational database, a separate caching layer needs to be maintained to achieve this performance goal.

But one thing needs to be added here that although NoSQL database offers many advantages over relational database, it fails to provide the rich reporting and analytical functionality like RDBMS in some specific scenarios.

> *Despite many benefits, NoSQL fails to provide the rich analytical functionality in specific cases as RDBMS serves.*

14.5.5 NoSQL Database Types

There are four different types of NoSQL databases. Each of them is designed to address the need of some particular classes of problems. Various NoSQL database service providers try to offer solution for different types of problems. Following sections describe four different NoSQL database types.

14.5.5.1 Key-Value Database

The Key-Value Database (or KV Store) is the simplest among the various NoSQL databases. It pairs up data with a key and maintains the database like a hash-table where data values are referred by the keys. The main benefit of such pairing makes it easily scalable. However, it is not suitable where queries are based on the value rather than on the key. Amazon's DynamoDB, Azure Table Storage and CouchDB are few popular examples of this type of NoSQL databases.

14.5.5.2 Document-Oriented Database

A Document Oriented Database (or Document Store) is an application where data is stored in documents. It is similar to the Key-Value stores with the values stored in structured documents. The documents are addressed and can be retrieved from the database using key. This key can be a path, a URI or a simple string.

The documents are schema-free and can be of any format as long as the database application can understand its internal structure. Generally document-oriented databases use some of the XML, JSON (JavaScript Object Notation) or Binary JSON (BSON) formats.

One document can be referred by multiple keys and a document can refer to other documents by storing their keys. But each document is treated as stand-alone and there is no constraint to enforce relational integrity. MongoDB, Apache CouchDB, Couchbase are few popular examples of document-oriented databases.

14.5.5.3 Column-Family Database

A Column-Family Database (or *Wide-Column Data Store/Column Store*) stores data grouped in columns. Each column consists of three elements as name, value and a time-stamp. Name is used to refer the column and time-stamp is used to identify actual required content. For example, the time-stamp is useful in finding up-to-date content. A similar type of columns together forms a column family which are often accessed together. A column family can contain virtually unlimited number of columns.

In relational databases, each row is stored as a continuous disk entry. Different rows may get stored in different places on disk. Contrary to this, in column-family database, all of the cells corresponding to a column are stored as a continuous disk entry. This makes the access of data faster. For example, searching of a particular title from a record of million books stored in relational data model is an intense task as that will cause millions of accesses to disk. On the other hand, using column-family data model, the title can be found with single disk access only.

The difference between *column stores* and *key-value stores* is that column stores are optimized to handle data along columns. Column stores show better analytical power and provide improved performance by imposing a certain amount of rigidity to a database schema. In some ways, the column stores are an intermediate solution between traditional RDBMSs and key-value stores. Hadoop's Hbase is the best example of popular column store-based database.

14.5.5.4 Graph Database

In the Graph Database (or *Graph Store*) data is stored as graph structures using nodes and edges. The entities are represented as nodes and the relationship between entities as edges. Graph database follows index-free adjacency where every node directly points to its adjacent nodes. In this set up, the cost of a hop or tour remains same as the number of nodes increases.

This is useful to store information about relationships when number of elements are huge, such as social connections. Twitter uses such database to track who is following whom. Examples of popular graph-based databases include Neo4J, Info-Grid, Infinite Graph and few others.

14.5.6 Selecting the Suitable NoSQL Database Solution

Each of the NoSQL database types has its own strength and weaknesses. They are designed to serve different kind of data storage requirements and hence are not comparable to each other. The 'one-size-fits-all' philosophy of relational databases is not applicable in NoSQL database domain. Here the users have the flexibility of choosing of multiple options after analyzing the requirements of their applications.

Selecting the NoSQL database strategy is not a one-time decision. First, one will have to identify the requirements of an application which are not met by relational database systems. Then suitable NoSQL database solution has to be identified to meet those unfulfilled requirements. Even more than one NoSQL database types may be used to meet all of these necessities.

Sometime a single application may provide optimized performance when more than one NoSQL database types are employed together. In such case, *multi-model NoSQL database* can be used which is designed to support multiple data models from four primary NoSQL data models.

> *The days when one DBMS was used to fit all needs are over. Now, a single application may use several different data stores at the back-end.*

14.5.7 Commercial NoSQL Databases

Commercial NoSQL databases started surfacing two years after the publication of Google's paper on BigTable in 2006 and Amazon's paper on Dynamo in 2007. After these publications, many initiatives were taken up both for *open-source* and *close-source* developments of NoSQL databases. By the end of 2009, there were several releases including BigTable-inspired HBase, Dynamo-inspired Riak and Cassandra. The following section briefs some of the popular NoSQL databases.

14.5.7.1 Apache's HBase

HBase is an Open-source NoSQL database system written in Java. It was developed by Apache Software Foundation as part of their Hadoop project. HBase's design architecture has been inspired by Google's internal storage system BigTable. As Google's BigTable uses GFS, Hadoop's HBase uses HDFS as underlying file system. HBase is a column-oriented database management system.

14.5.7.2 Amazon's DynamoDB

DynamoDB is a key-value NoSQL database developed by Amazon. It derives its name from Dynamo which is Amazon's internal storage system and was launched in 2012. The database service is fully-managed by Amazon and offered as part of the Amazon's Web Services portfolio. DynamoDB is useful specifically for supporting a large volume of concurrent updates and suits well for shopping-cart like operations.

14.5.7.3 Apache's Cassandra

Cassandra is an open-source NoSQL database management system developed in Java. It was initially developed at Facebook and then was released as an open-source project in 2008 with the goal of further advancements. Although Facebook's kingdom was largely dependent on Cassandra, they still released it as an open-source project, possibly having assured on that it might be too late for others to use the technology to knock its castle down. Cassandra became an Apache Incubator project in 2009. Cassandra is a hybrid of column-oriented and key-value data store being suitable to be deployed over both across many commodity servers and cloud infrastructure.

14.5.7.4 Google Cloud Datastore

Cloud Datastore is developed by Google and is available as a fully-managed NoSQL database service. Cloud Datastore is very easy to use and supports SQL-like queries being called as GQL. The Datastore is a NoSQL key-value database where users can store data as key-value pairs. Cloud Datastore also supports ACID transactions using optimistic concurrency control.

14.5.7.5 MongoDB

MongoDB is a popular document-oriented open-source NoSQL database. It is developed by New York City-based MongoDB Inc. and was first released as a product in 2009. It is written in C++, JavaScript and C programming languages and uses GridFS as built-in distributed file system. MongoDB runs well on many cloud based environments including Amazon EC2.

14.5.7.6 Amazon's SimpleDB

SimpleDB is a fully-managed NoSQL data store offered by Amazon. It is a key-value store and actually not a full database implementation. SimpleDB was first announced on December 2007 and works with both Amazon EC2 and Amazon S3.

14.5.7.7 Apache's CouchDB

CouchDB is an open-source document-oriented NoSQL database. CouchDB was first developed in 2005 by a former developer of IBM. Later in 2008, it was adopted as an Apache Incubator project. Soon in 2010, the first stable version of CouchDB was released and it became popular.

14.5.7.8 Neo4j

Neo4j is an open-source graph database. It is developed in Java. Neo4j was developed by Neo Technology of United States and was initially released in 2007. But its stable versions started appearing from the year of 2010.

Apart from these few NoSQL databases as mentioned above, there are numerous of other products available in the market. New developments are happening in this field and many new products are being launched. Database management application giant like Oracle has also launched their own NoSQL database. Hence, much more of new advancements are expected in this domain in coming years.

SUMMARY

❖ Database facility in cloud can be availed in two forms. One is by installing available database applications over cloud servers. The other one is offered by the providers as fully-managed Database-as-a-Service delivery.

❖ Most popular virtual machines provide support for the common RDBMS applications like Oracle Server, Microsoft's SQL Server or open-source MySQL Database.

❖ Amazon RDS, Google Cloud SQL, Azure SQL Database are some popular examples of relational Database-as-a-Service offerings. Such database services are fully-managed by the providers.

❖ New age data are huge in volume, unstructured in nature, come in various formats and are accessed or produced more frequently. Such data sets were identified as Big data.

❖ The data-intensive computing requirements of large volume unstructured data cannot be fulfilled with schematic relational databases. Distribution of data does not happen automatically in them and it becomes the programmer's responsibility. Hence it becomes difficult to develop the scalable applications.

❖ Performance became an issue when such large volumes of data were being accessed frequently from all over the world. Horizontal scaling of the database was the only solution to this problem.

❖ Non-relational database systems (NoSQL database) emerged to fill this gap. NoSQL scales automatically and is able to fulfill the processing and storage requirements of large unstructured data-sets.

❖ NoSQL databases do not follow the ACID properties. They follow BASE theorem.

❖ Four different types of NoSQL databases are present in the market. Each one of them are built to serve specific purposes. One application can use multiple databases if required.

❖ Google made significant contributions in the development of NoSQL database systems as it introduced a data-store called BigTable. Later, many open-source and proprietary NoSQL databases were released by different vendors.

REVIEW QUESTIONS

How is accessing the Azure SQL Database-as-a-Service different from deploying SQL Server Application on Microsoft Azure cloud and using it?

Azure SQL is a database-as-a-Service (DBaaS) facility offered by Microsoft. It is the implementation of Microsoft SQL Server over Azure cloud. This is a fully-managed service which users can access like any other cloud services and the back-end administration tasks like installation, configuration, back-up etc. become the responsibilities of the provider.

The other way of using database facility in cloud is by installing any supported database application over a cloud virtual machine. It is like installing some application in a computer and using it. Thus, the users can install Microsoft SQL Server over Azure Virtual Machine. The difference between two of these can be viewed through cloud service models. Deployment of SQL Server is consumption of IaaS facility where a consumer uses virtual machine infrastructure. But accessing Azure SQL Database is consumption of a PaaS facility.

How is it possible to use databases like Oracle or SQL Server in Amazon RDS?

Amazon RDS is a relational Database-as-a-Service facility being available with AWS. It is not a new database application. Rather, it supports functionalities of other traditional databases like Oracle Server, Microsoft SQL Server, MySQL database and PostgreSQL database. Recently it has also added another database engine designed by Amazon called as Amazon Aurora. The consumers can use any of these database functionalities through Amazon Relational Database Service.

How NoSQL databases survive after sacrificing consistency attribute of CAP theorem?

NoSQL databases like Cassandra, DynamoDB and CouchDB do not consider consistency as an essential attribute. Their internal architecture concentrates on 'AP' attributes of CAP theorem. But that does not mean that these NoSQL databases have totally sacrificed the consistency issue. The real fact is that they have changed the approach of handling the data consistency. Consistency of data in a database system can be maintained in two ways: either by the database system itself which will ensure consistency through its internal mechanism or the responsibility can be passed on to the developers of the databases who must ensure that no inconsistency can occur. Above mentioned NoSQL databases follow this second approach. This releases a lots of burden from the part of database system and performance increases in terms of availability and partition tolerance.

What is the need for NoSQL database in cloud computing system?

Large volume of structured as well as unstructured data are produced in cloud computing environment every day at present. While structured data can be processed efficiently using relational databases, unstructured data-sets do not fit into relational data model. Moreover, the distributed processing of data in multiple nodes is difficult in relational data model which results as the system does not scale well. NoSQL data model has fulfilled all of these requirements and being considered as cloud native.

MULTIPLE CHOICE QUESTIONS

1. Which of the following is not treated as one of the 3-Vs in Big data?

   a) Volume

   b) Velocity

   c) Volatility

   d) Variety

2. NoSQL databases are designed to process

   a) Structured data only

   b) Unstructured data only

   c) Both structured and unstructured data

   d) Big size data

3. Which of the following organizations has the biggest contribution in NoSQL database development?

   a) Apache
   b) Google
   c) Amazon
   d) Facebook

4. When a user deploys some database application over cloud server and uses the database, the user actually consumes which type of cloud service?

   a) DBaaS
   b) SaaS
   c) PaaS
   d) IaaS

5. The performance issue for relational database while volume of data becomes huge basically arises because its architecture does not support

   a) Horizontal scalability
   b) Vertical scalability
   c) BASE theorem
   d) CAP theorem

6. NoSQL databases can scale

   a) Horizontally
   b) Vertically
   c) Both horizontally and vertically
   d) None of these

7. Instead of strictly following ACID properties, many NoSQL databases follow

   a) CAP theorem
   b) BASE theorem
   c) NoSQL theorem
   d) Big data theorem

8. As per BASE theorem, consistency of data may not reflect instantly after transaction

   a) True
   b) False

9. Which among the following goes along the relational DBaaS model?

   a) Amazon RDS
   b) Oracle Server
   c) HBase
   d) Amazon S3

10. NoSQL database Cassandra was initially developed by

    a) Google
    b) Amazon
    c) Apache
    d) Facebook

15 | Content Delivery Network

$\mathbf{I}$n cloud computing everything moves around the globe through a huge network called Internet. All requested services and data from any public cloud are delivered to consumers via Internet. The delivery of the content from the source to the consumer may involve delays as the two may be far apart geographically from one another. This delay in content delivery in cloud computing could increase the response time barrier in acceptance of the technology. This delay may further increase due to heavy traffic over the network. And, studies have shown that delay in response time can cause huge business loss.

Cloud computing is made not only for *network-centric computing* but also for *network-centric content management*. To serve the purpose of instant delivery of content via network to the consumers, technologists have introduced the concept of a dedicated network for faster content delivery. Content generators like cloud service providers can make use of these networks for efficiently delivering their content to millions of consumers across the globe.

15.1 CONTENT DELIVERY IN THE CLOUD

Content is any kind of data ranging from text to audio, image, video and so on. Delivering this content to any location at any time is a critical issue for the success of cloud services. Smooth delivery of content and a positive user experience have always been the prime concern of content makers and *content providers* in world-wide networked environment like cloud computing. The primary objective is to minimize the page (that is the content in a page) load time as studies have shown that even a delay of a second in page loading time can negatively affect customers' experience significantly.

Forecasting any failure in network delivery and overcoming it has always been a challenge for content suppliers and the scenario has turned more critical with the adoption of network-centric cloud computing environment. The network requirements for delivering content have changed extensively during the last decade when large volumes of multimedia content started pouring in and consumers' expectation regarding content availability over Internet shot up.

Computing performance over cloud-based services is very important to encourage cloud service adoption as consumers are accustomed to working on their personal work-stations in traditional way of computing. Thus, fast web-content delivery is essential for producing high-performance computing in cloud and for better *quality of service* (QoS).

Instantaneous delivery of content in cloud is essential for improved user experience.

15.1.1 The Problem

The problem of delivering content in cloud exists due to the distance between the source of the content and the locations of content consumers. In most cases, data centers are the originators of digital content. Cloud service providers set up a limited number of data centers (infrastructure) around the world and store all content in those data centers. Any request from a user for some content may travel a long distance over the network depending on the geographical distance between the data center and the user. Transferring huge content like the high-definition video files far across the network path to the user may cause performance issue.

A user in Delhi may request some content which is available in a server located in London. Then the user's request has to travel thousands of miles through network to reach the destination. For every request, the server in London has to perform some processing and return the requested content. Delay in content delivery is primarily caused by the number of *router hops* (passing of a network packet from one router to another) between source and destination nodes. As the number of hops between client device and server increases it causes the delay between the user request and server response.

To meet the business needs and to fulfill application demands, the cloud-based services require a real-time information delivery system (like live telecasting of events) to respond instantaneously. This is only possible when LAN-like performance can be achieved in network communication for content delivery.

Latency and bandwidth also matter a lot. If too many requests are made for some content on a particular server, then bottleneck problem will generate and a mild congestion at the network path can create problems in latency and packet loss. All of these could act as stumbling blocks for widespread acceptance of cloud services.

> *Cloud computing is basically built upon the Internet, but cloud based services require LAN-like performance in network communication.*

15.1.2 The Solution

Architects have created a new model for content delivery to overcome the above-mentioned problem. Rather than remotely accessing content from data centers, they started treating content management as a set of cached services located in servers near consumers. The basic idea is that instead of accessing data content in cloud centrally stored in a few data centers, it is better to replicate the instances of the data at different locations. It is much faster to access an instance of the replicated set of data that has been stored on a server (apart from centrally located data center) which is close to the user or has a good connection and leading to faster download-time and less vulnerability to network congestion.

A network of such cached servers made for the faster and efficient delivery of content is called *Content Delivery Network* (CDN). Such networks were designed to support the delivery of any volume of growing content without clogging the network. This helps the organizations to scale their applications. CDN played a big role in the emergence of cloud computing which is about delivering everything over the network including data and computing services. And with time the demarcating lines between the cloud and CDN have blurred. A CDN actually drives cloud adoption through enhanced performance, scalability, security and cost savings.

Establishing content delivery network has been one of the major areas of interest in cloud computing.

15.2 CONTENT DELIVERY NETWORK

The CDN is a network of distributed servers containing content replicas that serve by delivering web-content against each request from a suitable content server based in the geographic location of the origin of request and the location of content server. This service is particularly effective in speeding up the delivery of web-content during high traffic in the network.

Alternatively, it can be said that a CDN is a system of inter-connected servers that speedily delivers content to consumers, spread across the world, over the Internet. The fast delivery of content is achieved by duplicating the content on several servers located at different locations and then directing them to users from those servers when required.

The actual or original source of any content is known as *content source* or *origin server*. CDN offers fast and reliable content delivery through low communication band-width channels by caching and replicating content in multiple content servers strategically placed around the globe. These additional content servers, placed at different geographic locations, are known as *edge servers*. A CDN, after receiving the content from an origin server, replicates them to *edge cache servers*. Any request for content automatically gets routed to the closest (in network time, not in miles) servers. In other words, a site visitor from New York can grab the same content from a server in New York that a visitor from Singapore is getting from a server in Singapore.

CDN enables faster delivery of content by caching and replicating content from 'content source' to multiple 'edge servers' or 'cache servers' which are strategically placed around the globe.

During implementation of the technique, CDN places copies of recently used content and created content in edge servers that are closer to the consumers. This network is also called as *edge network* because they cache content geographically to set lower *latency* and maximize *band-width* by delivering content to users who are nearby. When a user requests for some content that is not cached in the nearest server to the request location, the integrated mechanism of CDN delivers the content either from some other nearby server, if available, or from the originating server otherwise. The system also caches the content to the nearest server of the request location for future use.

A CDN operator can have thousands of nodes spread across the world. Each such node is made up of large number of servers. The geographic locations of the nodes are known as the *points of presence* (POP) of that CDN service.

15.2.1 Content Types

Digital content can be categorized into two types, when delivery of the content is concerned: static content and live media. CDN can be used for delivering both static content and live or on-demand streaming media. *Static content* refers to media that generally do not change.

Examples include text documents, HTML pages, images and audio or video files. In CDN, static content can be supported using traditional caching techniques because changes rarely occur in that content.

Live media refers to the content that is generated and delivered in real-time. This happens during *live streaming* of some event, especially in sports. While all CDNs used to provide support for delivery of static content, the live streaming of media is considered to be more challenging.

> *Delivering live streaming media to users around the world is more challenging than the delivery of static content.*

15.2.2 The Policy Decisions

The design of a CDN system from provider's end is driven by policy decisions. The designers of the system define the strategies which are critical for the ability of the system to deliver high quality content in minimum possible time. These *policy decisions* includes the following points:

a. Placement of the edge servers in the network.
b. Content management policy which decides replication management.
c. Content delivery policy which mainly depends on the caching technique.
d. Request routing policy that directs user request for content to make appropriate for the edge server.

The placement locations of edge servers are often determined with the help of heuristic (or exploratory) techniques. In the field of artificial intelligence, *heuristic* refers to search techniques that can solve problems when classical search techniques fail or deliver poor performance. Prior to CDN development, simulated environment is created to find some optimal or near-optimal positions of the edge servers by supplying realistic sample workload patterns to the system. Then the edge servers are strategically placed across the globe according to the solutions obtained.

There are two policies of content management: *full-site replication* and *partial-site replication*. Full-site replication is done when a site is static. Then the entire content of the site is replicated in one or more suitable edge servers from the origin server. The partial-site replication strategy is adopted for sites in which non-static content is embedded. Then the static parts of the web pages are replicated from the origin server to edge servers. Non-static content is referred by those pages and delivered based on some content management strategy.

In caching technique, the cache update policies along with the cache maintenance are important in managing the content over CDN. Proper planning and implementation are required to maintain the consistency and integrity of content at replicas placed at different edge servers. There are different content update policies which are applied on the replicated content, like updates triggered by content change, *on-demand updates* and *periodic updates*. The designers of CDN system uses some of these update policies (or a combination of more than one) in their system.

Through *request-routing*, the user requests are directed to the optimally closest edge server over a CDN that can best serve the request. Here the distance is not measured in miles. The decision combines multiple parameters like type of the requested resource, the location of the user, present state of the network and load of the edge server.

The designers of CDN-system architect the content delivery policies based on real-time conditions and geographic location of the user. The delivery load should remain balanced. Advanced load balancer, like *application delivery controller* (ADC) is used for this load balancing purpose.

> Policy decisions play a major role in the performance of any CDN service.

15.2.3 Push and Pull

In the initial days of CDN, the content delivery was based only on pull technology. Whenever a new content was requested by some consumer, that content used to be pulled from the origin server into some content server near the location of the user. In case of already cached content, the software would check whether it is the latest version, otherwise latest content would be pulled from the origin server. This reposed and speeded up the delivery of the content to that user or users of the nearby geographic locations on later instances.

In *pull* mechanism, latest version of content is not transferred to edge servers automatically. It only happens when request for the content is raised by some user. Only then the updated version of the content is stored on the edge server during delivery of that content.

This mechanism works in caching of web-content during Internet browsing. Once an item of interest is browsed by web a consumer, the browser pulls content from server and cache content by using temporary storage of Internet files. These stored files hold information about previously-visited web pages and files, such as graphics displayed on a page. This mechanism speeds up the page loading process for later time. But *web caching* is only effective when the content of a document does not change. For documents that change frequently, this technique becomes less effective. In such cases, the client needs to check the source content server every time user tries to access the content and pull the updated parts again.

To solve this problem, *push* mechanism is used. With HTTP push, content is automatically distributed or pushed to related edge servers whenever it is added to the origin server or whenever it is updated or changed. This technique is more effective for larger files since such files take more time to be delivered. If local copy or latest versions of such files are not stored in CDN, it would take longer time for end users to download them from the origin.

> In push mechanism, content is automatically transferred to edge servers whenever it is changed. In pull process, latest version of content is only transferred to edge servers when a request is raised for that content.

15.2.4 The Model of CDN

Figure 15.1 represents the content delivery network model. Publisher and subscriber of content are two most important entities of the CDN model. *Publisher* is the supplier or generator of content. They generally tie up with and authorize some CDN operator to deliver their content to subscribers.

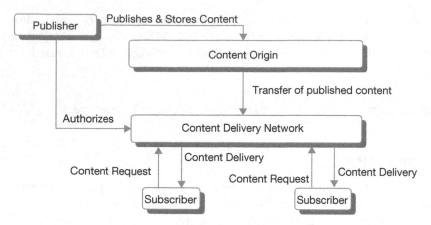

FIG 15.1: The model of Content Delivery Network

The publisher drops the actual copy of the content at the content origin. Then that content is processed by the CDN. Through authorization, the publisher actually permits the CDN operator to take care of the delivery of its content. *Subscribers* or consumers remain unaware about the existence of CDN and requests for any content of interest directly go to the publisher, though the content is ultimately delivered by publisher through CDN.

15.3 HOW THE CDN SERVICE OPERATES

Most CDNs function the way application services are offered by some *application service providers* (ASP) work on the Internet. Content providers, such as e-commerce vendors or media companies, may develop their own CDN infrastructure. Otherwise they rely on some CDN operator for delivering their content to their consumers or end-users. For this, the content provider pays the CDN operator. A CDN operator in turn pays the ISPs, carriers and network operators for availing their infrastructure and services, for hosting servers.

CDN minimizes latency, optimizes delivery speed and maximizes available bandwidth for each client. When request for some content appears, the management system of a CDN calculates and locates the nearest edge server to the requesting source and delivers content from that server. This reduces the travelling distance of content and minimizes the number of hops a data packet makes. Depending on the volume of content to be delivered, the network traffic and number of hops, the network's algorithms select the best routing options aiming to deliver optimum performance and avoid the chokepoints. The process of getting service through a CDN remains transparent to the user. End users never know about the existence of CDN.

> CDN operates independently and content providers or content generators can avail CDN services to deliver their content to consumers.

15.4 EVOLUTION OF CDN

Content delivery networks were actually functioning quietly in the background for a quite long time. It was required since the emergence of Internet to ease the way web content could be delivered to consumers. CDN first emerged towards the end of the last century to enable websites to keep pace with growing Internet usage.

During that period, the CDN was being developed in United States to support growing demand of newspaper like the New York Times for faster delivery of graphics via caches. Players like Limelight and Akamai in particular led the development. That time it was commonly referred as *web acceleration* which used to hoard frequently-requested content in servers closer to the points of consumption.

In the very early days of Internet, web-content was almost entirely static. Hence the service providers (ISP) used to segregate the parts of web pages which would rarely change and cached them out in servers. With the increase in dynamic content, the service providers started pushing the updated dynamic parts of pages on to the caches in real-time scenario.

In the early years of the current century, with the rapid increase in storage capacity and network band-width, web sites started embedding video files. This abruptly increased the amount of data CDNs had to handle. But, then the video content which were being embedded to websites were all pre-recorded and hence were static. Delivery of such videos was not very difficult as these were only large files to be delivered over the network.

But, with time the demand for live video streaming started increasing and this paved the way for second generation of CDN. This time the focus shifted from static video content to dynamic (live) videos. The focus of the new CDN system was on video-on-demand (VoD), audio and video streaming with interactivity amongst the users. Additionally, the second generation CDN focussed on cloud computing and content delivery for mobile users.

> CDN operators, Akami and Limelight, led the development of the technology in initial years.

15.5 ADVANTAGES OF CDN

CDNs facilitate proper distribution and optimized routing service of web-content. CDNs focus on delivering content to end users with higher availability and exorbitant speed. It relieves its customers (the *content producers*) from the burden of content delivery. Hence the content producers can focus on content creation and other concerned activities. The other important benefits of CDN include the following.

15.5.1 Accommodating Heavy Traffic

Network traffic is huge nowadays. Web users expect nearly instantaneous availability of content. And in this competitive business market, delivery speed make a lot of difference. CDN provides mechanism to manage such heavy network traffic efficiently through the distribution of content delivery responsibility among multiple servers spread over the network.

15.5.2 Support for More Simultaneous Users

CDN facilitates cloud service provider or any other content provider to simultaneously support more number of users to consume their services. This is because of the strategically placed servers in CDN which ensure that a network always maintains a very high-data threshold.

15.5.3 Less Load on Servers

Servers cannot deliver high performance when they are over-loaded. Performance and efficiency degrade when they become bogged down during heavy traffic hours. CDN resolves this problem by deploying multiple servers instead of offloading the responsibility of content delivery on to one large server. This ensures that load of delivering content gets distributed and remains balanced.

15.5.4 Faster Content Delivery

Content no more requires to travel very long distances as it is delivered from some server placed near the location of user request. Hence delivery of content becomes faster and high quality content can be transferred with high level of service.

15.5.5 Lower Cost of Delivery

Strategically-placed edge servers in CDN make the content to travel less to reach destination (that is, to the consumers). This decreases the load on network backbones and interconnects with lowering the cost of delivery.

15.5.6 Controlling Asset Delivery

Network load and asset being delivered can be monitored by CDN technology. CDN operators can analyze which content has more demand than others and can also determine the region from where the majority of requests are coming. Depending upon these statistics CDN operators decide where to prioritize extra capacity to ensure smooth running of all systems.

15.5.7 Facilitates Scalability

Deployment of multiple content delivery serves across different geographic locations ultimately spreads the content delivery system. This helps to grow the system horizontally increasing the scalability. Hence performance of the system remains consistent during high demand.

15.5.8 Better Security

In CDN, the content files are replicated in multiple content servers. This makes the recovery of damaged files of a server easier as other copies of the same data are stored in additional servers. Thus CDN protects content from being lost in case of natural disasters or some other calamity.

15.6 DISADVANTAGES OF CDN

CDN provides lots of advantages but it has some drawbacks too. But those drawbacks are not major issues when the benefits are considered. The disadvantages include the following points.

15.6.1 New Points of Failure

The content delivery network system creates a new point of failure along the delivery chain. Any content provider starts to depend heavily on the content delivery network service for content delivery task. If a CDN service provider fails for some reason, the content provider also suffers.

15.6.2 Additional Content Management Task

Content provider who uses outsourced CDN service must manage content through the CDN provider's facility instead of directly managing the same. Any modification of content must follow the CDN service provider's policy. Hence the content providers have to be careful about this additional task.

15.7 CDN SERVICE PROVIDER

CDN services are offered by many vendors, that any content provider can use to deliver content to customers worldwide. Cloud service providers sometimes build up their own CDN infrastructure; otherwise they outsource the content delivery task to some CDN service providers.

CDN service providers are specialists in content delivery and can deliver highest possible performance and quality irrespective of delivery location. Being experts in the content delivery domain, they can deliver better quality of service and their volume of business also reduces the actual cost of content delivery for the content providers.

There are many players in this domain. Akamai, CDNetworks, CloudFront, CloudFlare, CacheFly, MaxCDN, Azure CDN are few instances of these services. The choice of one CDN vendor or service depends on many factors, like the volume of business, performance goal, as well as the location of customers. One CDN service provider may have better service than others in some specific geographical regions. In such case, consumers (the content providers) may decide to use more than one CDN provider's service. This concept is known as *multiple CDN*.

15.7.1 Akamai

Akamai Technologies is a company with its headquarters at Cambridge, United States. They are one of the leading cloud computing services and content delivery network providers. The company primarily develops software for web-content and application delivery. Akamai is a Hawaiian word which means 'intelligent'.

Akamai evolved from a project work at Massachusetts Institute of Technology (MIT) which was trying to optimize the network traffic. The company was formally founded in 1998. Akamai's Intelligent Platform provides a distributed cloud computing environment that is spread worldwide with more than 100,000 servers.

Currently Akamai's content delivery network service is world's largest CDN service. Customers of Akamai include major online players like Facebook, Twitter, ESPN Star (for live streaming of games) and BBC iPlayer (to stream its recorded and live programs) among a substantial list of others. Yahoo also uses Akamai CDN service to deliver content.

15.7.2 Limelight

Like Akamai, Limelight Networks also led the development of CDN from the initial days. The company was founded in 2001 in Arizona, United States as a provider of content delivery network services and has extensive *point-of-presence* (PoP) worldwide. It is a world-wide content caching and delivery system that offers global solutions for delivering high-bandwidth content.

15.7.3 Amazon's CloudFront

CloudFront is a content delivery service offered by Amazon as part of Amazon Web Services (AWS). The service was launched in 2008 and operates on a pay-per-use basis like other services of AWS. CloudFront delivers content through a worldwide network of edge locations. The service operates from more than 50 edge locations spread throughout the world.

CloudFront is proprietary to Amazon.com and hence integrates well with other Amazon Web Services. It works seamlessly with the Amazon Simple Storage Service (Amazon S3) but can be used as stand-alone too. CloudFront CDN service provides very simple-to-use interfaces with which customers can manage it easily.

15.7.4 Azure Content Delivery Network

Microsoft has developed its own content delivery network service known as Azure CDN. It was developed for delivering high-bandwidth content by caching blobs (a collection of binary data stored as a single entity) used by cloud services. Azure CDN was introduced with commercially available Azure platform in 2010. Microsoft's data-centers spread around the world (referred to as endpoints) are used to host this service.

Access to Azure blobs through CDN is preferable over directly accessing them from source containers. CDN delivery of blobs stored in containers has been able through the Microsoft Azure Developer Portal. When request for data is made using the Azure Blob service URL, the data is accessed directly from the Microsoft Azure Blob service. But if request is made using Azure CDN URL, the request is redirected to the CDN end point closest to the request source location and delivery of data becomes faster. The CDN refreshes the cached blob from Azure Blob service once after a certain elapsed time, called as *time-to-live* (TTL).

Time-to-Live is a timestamp attached with data packet limiting the lifespan of the packet in a computer network. This prevents packets to circulate indefinitely, and improves the network performance. The use of TTL in CDN enhances the efficiency and quality of caching.

15.7.5 CDNetworks

CDNetworks enables global cloud acceleration and has been in the CDN business since 2000. Originally founded in Korea in 2000, currently CDNetworks has offices in the Korea, US, China, UK and Japan. It has customers across industries like finance, travel, eCommerce, manufacturing, media and so on.

CDNetworks has developed massive network infrastructure having strong POP (point-of-presence) coverage on all of the continents. Currently it has more than 140 POPs in 6 continents including around 20 in China.

SUMMARY

❖ The performance of the digital content delivery system plays a major role in any web-based service; as well as for cloud computing because the cloud service is generally delivered over the Internet.

❖ Delivery of any content anywhere and anytime upon user request can only be facilitated by establishing a system of inter-connected servers which replicate the content. This network is known as content delivery network or CDN.

❖ Content producers store the main copy of a particular content in one server and that server is known as content source. The additional content servers of a content delivery network are called edge servers.

❖ CDN places content at different edges of the network enabling the content to be delivered from a location close to the user requesting it; thereby lowering the access latency. Thus, this technique speeds up the content delivery.

❖ Content of a webpage can be static or dynamic. Static content can be easily replicated in the edge servers. But fast delivery of content that changes frequently especially live-streaming videos is extremely challenging.

❖ Any content provider, like cloud service providers, can develop its own CDN. Otherwise they can avail the service of any CDN operator by paying for it.

❖ Akamai and Limelight Networks are two CDN service providers who have contributed a lot in the development of the CDN service.

❖ Major cloud service providers like Amazon, Microsoft and Google have their own CDNs.

REVIEW QUESTIONS

How should a content provider select a CDN operator to deliver its content among consumers efficiently?

CDN service providers operate by establishing point of presence (POP) at different geographic locations from where they deliver content to users of surrounding regions so that delivery of content can be fastest. Hence one important parameter for high-performance content delivery is how close the user is to some POPs of the concerned CDN operator.

A content provider will have to survey well before selecting operator for content delivery network services. The basic goal of the content provider is to deliver its content to its customers without any delay. Hence, a content provider should look for a CDN operator which has strong presence (having POPs) around the regions where the content provider has strong customer base.

How is the content delivery network service associated with cloud computing?

In cloud computing, the users avail computing resources and perform all of the computation tasks generally via Internet. Data-intensive computation tasks require high-speed availability of data so that users can experience on-premises like performances. Thus, every cloud service provider needs to use content delivery network service in the background to deliver speedy and high-performing content to consumers.

Like Amazon and Microsoft, is there any CDN service that Google offers to consumers?

No. Google has its own CDN infrastructure that they use to deliver their services worldwide. But, unlike Amazon or Microsoft, Google does not offer CDN service to consumers commercially. The content delivery service of Amazon and Microsoft are known as CloudFront and Azure CDN respectively. Amazon and Microsoft use their own CDN services to deliver content to consumers but these services are also offered independently. Hence any content provider can avail CloudFront or Azure CDN like any other third-party CDN services (like Akamai and CDNetworks) to get relief from the tensions of content delivery.

Google has a robust content delivery infrastructure built upon Google's backbone network that reaches more than 100 countries and has points of presence (POPs) across the globe. But they does not offer this CDN service for others. Google Global Cache (GGC) represents the final tier of Google's content delivery platform and is closest to users. It enables the organizations to deliver Google and YouTube content efficiently. But this service is available by invitation only.

Does CDN help in every kind of cloud services?

No. CDN is a must for cloud services whose consumers are not concentrated around some particular geographic location. Generally, the public cloud services who have consumers across the globe use the CDN. Other cloud services, especially on-premises private cloud services most often need not to take help of CDN as they deliver service to a limited number of consumers.

MULTIPLE CHOICE QUESTIONS

1. Content Delivery Network is developed based upon the principle of

   a) Delivery management
   b) Network planning
   c) Data replication
   d) None of these

2. The additional content servers in CDN placed at different geographic locations are known as

   a) Origin server
   b) Edge server
   c) Content server
   d) Source server

3. Partial-site replication policy is followed in CDN while web pages include

   a) Only dynamic content
   b) Only static content
   c) Static and dynamic content
   d) All of these

4. User-requested content is always delivered to users from the origin server of content.

   a) True
   b) False

5. Content consumers remain unaware about the use of the CDN service by content providers.

a) True

b) False

6. A content provider can use the services of more than one CDN operator to deliver its content.

   a) Not possible

   b) Possible in some cases

   c) Always possible

   d) Depends upon content type

7. The placement of edge servers mainly depend on

   a) Location of content providers

   b) Geographic locations of users

   c) Availability of space

   d) policy of CDN operator

8. Content is automatically distributed to edge servers whenever added to origin server using

a) Push technique

b) Pull technique

c) Both push and pull techniques

d) Distribution technique

9. Which of the following cloud service providers has its own CDN service?

   a) Amazon

   b) Microsoft

   c) Google

   d) All of these

10. The use of content delivery network is required for

    a) Reducing network traffic

    b) Instantaneous delivery of content

    c) Server load balancing

    d) All of these

CHAPTER 16

Security Issues

The introduction of cloud computing creates numerous benefits for consumers of computing services but it also has security concerns associated with it. In addition to most security risks present in the traditional computing environment, cloud computing brings a new set of security issues with it. These issues emerge basically due to the massive sharing of infrastructure and resources which is an inherent feature of the utility service model.

A proper understanding of cloud architecture and appropriate selection of cloud deployment may reduce the security risks to a great extent. It is also important to understand that security maintenance is a combined effort for both the provider and the consumer of cloud. This chapter tries to focus on the security aspects of cloud from different service levels, apart from discussing the cloud security design principles and frameworks.

Cloud-based security systems need to address all the basic needs of an information system like confidentiality, integrity, availability of information, identity management, authentication and authorization. These security requirements are not new, but cloud computing specific standpoint on these issues are essential to analyze as well as implement security in a cloud-based system.

Despite its enormous benefits, security is one critical concern in cloud computing.

16.1 CLOUD SECURITY

For an enterprise, sharing infrastructure in cloud computing environment is like a person going to some public place with valuable belongings. Others with wrong intent may anytime target those valuable belongings. Similarly, moving sensitive files or data out of an enterprise's own network security boundary, in cloud computing, also causes security concerns. Hence, implementation of strong identity management and access control mechanism are important in cloud environment.

Security is developing resistance to damage or protecting a system from any harm. Security is a major concern for any computing system and also for the cloud computing system too. Computing system security means protection of the system itself and also of the data that it stores.

When an IT service consumer, be it an individual or an organization, migrates to cloud computing, especially in public cloud services; much of the computing infrastructure moves into the control of third-party cloud services providers. Shifting consumer's sensitive data into the control of third-party cloud providers increases and complicates the risk landscape as outsourcing makes it harder for the consumer to maintain confidentiality and integrity of sensitive information.

For a business to gain the full advantage from cloud-based computing, reliable security architecture is necessary. It is important to understand how the security as an important aspect of the cloud architecture spans across all of layers of the reference models. Security in cloud ranges from physical (infrastructural) security to application security.

16.1.1 Whose Responsibility Is It?

The security issues associated with cloud computing can be viewed from two angles: as the concerns of cloud providers (providing SaaS, PaaS or IaaS) and the concerns of the service consumers. The provider must ensure security of its own infrastructure as well as of the clients' data and applications. On the other hand, the consumers must verify and make sure that the provider has employed all possible security measures to make the services secure. Experience and expertise of provider plays a significant role in this context.

The relationship between the consumer and the service provider is also important in establishing a robust security system. Provider must establish a trust relationship with its consumers. Both parties should have a clear idea about their own responsibilities towards security management. To understand the risk in terms of how providers implement and manage security, the consumers can employ technical experts.

Ultimately it is the responsibility of the consumers to ensure the safety of their application and data since a larger part of the job moves towards the provider's end and most often (particularly in public cloud) consumers have very little control over the entire environment. For ensuring security of computing environment, it is often up to the consumer to initiate the inquiry that makes the process rolling. The on-premises private cloud deployments, though, decrease the risks associated to some extent.

> Cloud computing demands shared responsibilities to take care of security issues. It should not be left solely under the purview of the cloud provider, the consumers also have major roles to play.

16.1.2 Importance of SLA

Service-level agreements (SLAs) are used in different industries to establish a trust relationship between service providers and consumers. The SLA details the service-level capabilities promised by the providers to be delivered and requirements/expectations stated by consumers. These details are very important as the document establishes a legal binding for both the parties and works as reference in any dispute. Organizations should engage *legal experts* to review the SLA document during contract negotiation and before making the final agreement.

Many security challenges associated with cloud computing can be addressed through management initiatives. Thus, SLA document should include the security issues in adequate detail. Strong security maintenance activities need to define the responsibilities of both service providers and consumers in documented form.

The SLAs between the *cloud service providers* (CSPs) and consumers should have detailed mentioning of the security capabilities of the solutions and the security standards to be maintained by the service providers. Consumers, on the other hand, should provide clear-cut information to the service providers about what they consider as a breach in security.

> *SLA document plays an important role in security management, for consumers moving towards cloud solutions.*

16.1.3 Threat, Vulnerability and Risk

The conventional security concerns like threat, vulnerability and risk also persist in cloud computing system. *Threat* is an event that can cause harm to a system. It can damage the system's reliability and demote confidentiality, availability or integrity of information stored in the system. Threats can be malicious such as deliberate alteration of sensitive data or can be accidental such as unintentional deletion of a file or problem arisen from erroneous calculation.

Vulnerability refers to some weaknesses or flaws in a system (hardware, software or process) that a threat may exploit to damage the system. It refers to security flaws that poses the threat to a system increasing the chance of an attack to be successful. Detection and removal of those weaknesses reduce the vulnerable aspect of a system which in turn reduces impact of threats on the system.

Risk is the ability of a threat to exploit vulnerabilities and thereby causing harm to the system. Risk occurs when threat and vulnerability overlap. It is the prospect of a threat to materialize.

Following are the common threats to any computing system:

- Eavesdropping: This attack captures the data packets during network transmission and looks for sensitive information to create foundation for an attack.
- Fraud: It is materialized through fallacious transactions and misleading alteration of data to make some illegitimate gains.
- Theft: In computing system, theft basically means the stealing of trade secrets or data for gain. It also means unlawful disclosure of information to cause harm.
- Sabotage: This can be performed through various means like disrupting data integrity (referred as data sabotage), delaying production, *denial-of-service* (DoS) attack and so on.
- External attack: Insertion of a *malicious code* or *virus* to an application or system falls under this category of threat.

Security experts have devised many mechanisms to protect information and computing systems from these age-old threats. But cloud computing system has its own characteristic as public utility system having shared resources. Hence, security mechanism in cloud needs to be examined and organized accordingly.

> *Security concerns inherent to any computing system are also present in cloud computing and require a cloud-specific perspective for their resolution.*

16.2 THREATS TO CLOUD SECURITY

To understand the security threats that cloud computing presents, it is important to understand different areas of concern. Many among these threats are not new and were already there with traditional computing environment. But cloud model has its own issue regarding security. The security threat concerns in cloud computing can be categorized in following three sections:

- *Threats to Infrastructure*: Application level, host level or network level infrastructure security threats are no new issues introduced by cloud. The only difference to understand here is the share of responsibilities that both provider and consumer have, to safeguard the system.

    The threats to cloud computing infrastructure have to be studied from different perspective, although almost all of these threats were present in any traditional distributed system also. Virtualization protects the computing infrastructure of cloud to some extent but at the same time it brings new sort of security complexity which should be handled very delicately.
- *Threats to Information*: Apart from conventional threats to information, the cloud computing introduces new security concerns as consumers' (both organization and individual) data stays under the control of third-party cloud provider.
- *Threats to Access Control*: As the *trust boundary* expands beyond organization's own control (especially in public cloud), proper authentication and authorization management for applications in cloud is very vital issue for security.

While discussing about security in cloud computing, one must keep two important and distinguishing points in mind:

- The cloud computing model itself has some unique security concerns associated with it which surfaced due to sharing of infrastructure or multi-tenancy features.
- When cloud is deployed outside the control boundary of consumer organization it brings new set of security concerns. In this regard, public cloud is the most critical case to study.

So, when security of cloud is talked about, it mainly focuses on public cloud deployment which covers all of cloud related security concerns. In the subsequent part, infrastructure security concerns, information security means and access control mechanisms have been discussed.

> Public cloud deployment is the most critical case study to understand security concerns of cloud computing. It covers all possible security threats to the cloud.

16.3 INFRASTRUCTURE SECURITY

Infrastructure security describes the issues related with controlling access to physical resources which support the cloud infrastructure. From consumer's point of view, although infrastructure security may seem to be more closely related to infrastructure-as-a-service (IaaS) or IaaS vendors but the platform-as-a-service (PaaS) and software-as-a-service (SaaS) layers cannot be ignored as they also have some roles to play in securing computing infrastructure.

Infrastructure security can be classified into three categories like network level, host level and service level.

The dynamic nature of the cloud environment sometimes bring challenges in security administration. Security professionals generally set guidelines and rules for security of the computing infrastructure. Many time organizations customize these rules according to their needs and practices. It is important to understand the share of security responsibilities of both service providers as well as the consumers before moving into cloud. Consumers should understand the things needed to be done from their end to secure the systems against physical vulnerabilities.

16.3.1 Network Level Security

The network-level security risks exist for all the cloud computing services (e.g., SaaS, PaaS or IaaS). It is actually not the service being used but rather the cloud deployment type (public, private or hybrid) that determine the level of risk.

There are no new threats, vulnerabilities or risks associated with private clouds apart from those already been there if the organization uses a private extranet in place. An *extranet* is a controlled private network (intranet) that allows access to authorize outside users enabling businesses to exchange information in a secure way. However, in case of public cloud services, use of appropriate network topology is required to satisfy security requirements. Organizations must take care about how their internal network topology will interact with the service provider's network topology.

Ensuring data confidentiality, integrity and availability are the responsibilities of network level infrastructure security arrangement. Data confidentiality risk is generally reduced by using techniques like encryption and digital signatures but data availability problem at the network level causes more difficulty and needs more attention to manage.

If an organization can afford on-premises private cloud to meet their business needs, their network level security risks naturally decreases. Here it should be noted that the network-level security of private cloud deployed as on-premises or at some provider's facility depends on the potential of the infrastructure architect, either be it developed by some third party or the enterprise itself. In case of public cloud though it entirely depends on the provider.

> Most of the network-level security challenges are not new to cloud; rather, these have existed since the early days of Internet. Advanced techniques are always evolving to tackle these issues.

16.3.2 Host Level Security

At cloud service provider's end, the 'host' refers to the physical machines. No new threats occur to the hosts which are specific to cloud computing, rather hypervisor provides added layer of protection. Therefore, weak implementation of access control mechanism to the hypervisor may create trouble for physical hosts. VM escape problem may also cause damage to physical hosts as virtual machines are a little prone to this particular security threat as associated to virtualization technology.

The important point here to be noted against traditional computing is that the cloud ties together the capacity of hundreds of computing nodes. This means that any threat is easy to amplify quickly which is called as *velocity of attack* factor in the cloud. The responsibilities of the host-level security management for different types of consumers of cloud services vary. Following section briefs those share of responsibilities.

For SaaS and PaaS consumers: Service providers would not publicly share details regarding their host platforms like operating systems or security management mechanisms to secure the hosts. Otherwise, hackers may exploit those details to break the security. Hence, for the SaaS and PaaS services, the service providers take the entire responsibility of making the hosts secure.

One difference between PaaS and SaaS consumers arises from the difference in access right to the abstraction layer that covers the OS on which applications they run. This abstraction layer is not accessible by the SaaS consumers but is accessible by the developers who are actually the PaaS consumers. But, the PaaS users cannot access this abstraction layer directly; rather they are given indirect access to the layer through the application program interface (API) of PaaS application.

In general, the security responsibility of hosts in PaaS and SaaS services largely depends on the service providers. This is a big relief for consumers not only from security management headaches but also beneficial from the standpoint of cost.

For IaaS consumers: Unlike PaaS and SaaS, IaaS consumers have the shares of responsibility in securing the host. Service providers use to take care of the security of physical resources through abstraction. But IaaS consumers must take care that no malicious application could try to break it.

> Among service consumers, IaaS consumers have major share of responsibilities for ensuring security of host machines in cloud.

16.3.3 Application Level Security

Both the consumer and service providers have their share of responsibilities of security management at this level so that no application can harm to the infrastructure. For both, it is important to understand their roles in the security management task depending on the contract of service-level agreement.

16.3.3.1 IaaS Application Security

At IaaS level, the users are largely accountable for managing and securing the virtual servers they work with, along with the providers. At this level, the virtual servers (which are delivered by IaaS service providers) are owned by customers, and the IaaS providers blindly serve the applications running over those virtual servers with full trust without verifying any threats. Therefore, the major responsibility of security management of virtual resources at this layer is task of consumers as well. But they use to get guidance and security assistance from service providers. The IaaS providers mainly ensure that any attack to virtual resources can never penetrate into physical resources.

> Security of virtual resources at IaaS level is the responsibility of both provider and consumer.

16.3.3.2 PaaS Application Security

The security issues can be divided into two stages at the PaaS application level:

- Security of the PaaS platform itself and
- Security of consumers' applications deployed on a PaaS application.

PaaS service providers are responsible for securing the platform software stack on which consumers deploy or develop their applications. Security management of these applications deployed on PaaS is consumer's prime responsibility, although PaaS providers take care of any kind of dependencies. In case, some third-party applications are used, the third-party application provider may have share of responsibilities in securing the services. It is liability of consumers to understand dependencies too.

> Security management of PaaS is the responsibility of service provider. Consumers are responsible for the security of applications they install over the platform.

16.3.3.3 SaaS Application Security

In SaaS model, it is the responsibility of the provider to manage the complete set of applications they deliver to consumers. Therefore, the SaaS providers must take suitable measures to make their offering secure so that consumers with ill intention cannot cause harm to them. From the consumer's viewpoint, the use of SaaS reduces lots of tensions. At the SaaS level, consumers are only responsible for the operational security management of the applications which includes user authentication and access control management.

> At SaaS level security management, consumers' responsibility is only limited to operational level of application management.

Figure 16.1 summarizes the whole discussion by showing consumers' responsibility in security management at different levels of cloud applications. Here, the horizontal axis represents three cloud services and the vertical axis represents consumers' responsibility in cloud application security management.

It can be seen from Figure 16.1 that consumers' responsibility for application level security management decreases as they move from IaaS towards SaaS. As discussed earlier, at the SaaS level, consumers' responsibility becomes very limited.

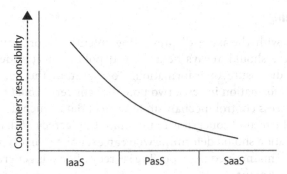

FIG 16.1: Application security responsibility of consumers

> *Security management is a continuous process rather than a periodic activity.*

16.3.4 Safety and Security of the Physical Systems

Apart from the above issues, the IaaS service providers are responsible to take care of some other issues to ensure reliable cloud services. Any general, physical or technical problems may cause the physical servers to go down and hence the cloud service loses its pace as well. This would be a loss of availability of service which harms the business. The following issues should be taken care of to ensure uninterrupted availability of cloud services:

- Facility of uninterruptible power supply (UPS).
- Proper safety measures against fire to minimize the loss in case of disaster.
- Adequate cooling and ventilation facility.
- Stringent restriction on physical access to the servers. Unauthorized persons must not have any access to the area.
- The physical protections listed above should also be maintained for all of the network related devices (such as routers) and cables.

16.4 INFORMATION SECURITY

An information system security policy deals with a number of critical issues and all those are justifiable concerns in cloud also. One concern of the cloud service consumers is related to the unauthorized access to confidential information and the data theft. In cloud computing, there must be a policy for securing data both during transfers between entities or when it is kept in rest.

Three fundamental principles of information security as confidentiality, integrity and availability are important pillars of cloud software security as well. They together are known as the *CIA-triad* and should be managed carefully for security of any information system. Cloud computing systems deal with user's confidential information and the CIA-triad is a vital issue there.

16.4.1 Confidentiality

Confidentiality deals with the issue of preventing intentional or unintentional leakage of sensitive content. There should always be a defined policy for confidentiality maintenance to prevent unlawful disclosure of information. To maintain the confidentiality of stored information (that is, information in rest), two potential concerns must be addressed. The first one is related to the access control mechanism to protect data which deals with authorization and authentication. The second concern is to maintain the secrecy of data. For information in transit, policy specification should determine who can exchange what type of information. The secrecy of data must be maintained here too. The secrecy of data is generally maintained using different encryption techniques.

> *Confidentiality deals with the threat of illegal disclosure of the users' confidential data.*

To maintain *confidentiality of information* and to make a secure cloud system (or any networked computing environment), the following issues should be taken care of with utmost precision.

Encryption: Through encryption, the information is scrambled so that no unauthorized access can interpret it. Only authorized entities can understand it after decryption. Strength of encryption depends on the robustness and quality of the encryption algorithm.

Traffic analysis: For information in transit to maintain confidentiality, the measures should be taken against traffic analysis attack. Traffic analysis investigates for sudden change in traffic activity (like rate, volume, source or destination of traffic) which may indicate as some incident is taking place. Counter-measures against this attack can be taken by masking the source and destination hosts and by maintaining a near-constant rate of traffic flow.

Covert channels: Hackers often try to receive information by establishing secret communication paths known as covert channels. They generally do this by studying the timing of messages passing or through utilizing some vulnerability.

Among these three issues as mentioned above, while the first two matters were present in traditional systems, the problem of covert channel is new to cloud-based systems. A *covert channel* is a path established to illegally pass information between elements of systems. Covert channel exploits weakness of system design and utilizes system resources for (evil) purposes which they (the system) were not intended for. In computing, covert channel poses security threats. Processes can convert any communication path into a covert channel by exploiting the system's security flaws.

Although, virtualization adds protection to the physical resources, a covert channel can break the isolation of the virtualization platform. Dynamic nature of cloud environment also causes the risks related with covert channel problem. Covert channel particularly exploits imperfections in the shared resources of the elastic cloud environment.

Apart from encryption, traffic analysis and covert channel issues as discussed above, protecting *intellectual property* (IP) of information through copyright law is also important in maintaining information confidentiality.

> *Covert channel problem is a new threat to confidentiality in virtualization-based cloud system.*

16.4.2 Integrity

Integrity of information guarantees against intentional or unintentional alteration. Information can be encrypted to maintain confidentiality but it may still get distorted. Loss of integrity in information can happen due to some deliberate attacks to alter it or there can be unintentional modifications where data is accidentally altered. Integrity of information can be protected through strict access-control. Access to information is generally restricted by installing firewalls and intrusion detection systems. A policy must also be there to recover information from detectable errors, such as deletion and modification. Integrity is the protection of information against corruption.

16.4.3 Availability

Availability ensures reliable and timely access to information. It guarantees that information is available when needed. One threat in this regard is network-based attacks like *denial-of-service* attack. A system must implement reliable network security mechanisms for these kind of attacks. The other threat to availability is Cloud Service Providers' (CSPs) own accessibility by denying the legitimate access to computing resources. This problem can be avoided by using backups and redundant systems.

Availability of information in cloud largely depends on the CSP's own availability. Ideally, service of a provider should be up for 99.999% of time. But, hardly any CSP can offer the desired 'five 9s' (that is, 99.999%) of uptime. In general, reputed service providers ensure of delivering 'three 9s' of uptime. For instance, Amazon promises 99.95% of service availability for its virtual machines (EC2) in the service level agreement. From Table 16.1, it emerges that there is a substantial disparity in availability between five 9s and three 9s of service uptime.

16.4.4 Protection of Information from Undesirable Circumstances

Some other practical problems are there concerning the security of information in cloud computing that businesses can never compromise. It is important to have necessary measures in place to tackle situations arising from following circumstances.

Scenario 1: Cloud provider declares the bankruptcy. In such a scenario, a cloud service consumer should have access to data for a specified period of time and there should be some defined policy to address such situations.

Scenario 2: Provider organization is acquired by someone. In case when ownership of the service provider organization changes, the whole applications and data automatically

Table 16.1 Service downtime in different cases of service availability

Service Availability	Total Downtime (HH:MM:SS)		
	Per day	*Per month*	*Per year*
99.999 %	00:00:01	00:00:26	00:05:15
99.99 %	00:00:09	00:04:19	00:52:33
99.9 %	00:01:04	00:43:00	08:38:24
99 %	00:14:24	07:12:00	87:36:00

moves under the control of new organization. A pre-defined policy should be there to save the interest of consumers and it should be ensured that the privacy of consumers' sensitive data is not harmed.

Scenario 3: The cloud service will be discontinued. For such situations, there should be some pre-defined process of shutdown activities. Cloud service consumers should have enough time and facility of retrieving and moving their data to the facility of some other service providers.

The above scenarios are unusual for large and reputed service providers. However, a cloud consumer should consider all of these when placing application and data into the cloud.

> *There are many security challenges in cloud computing. The question is: are the risks associated higher than the risks faced in traditional computing system? In most cases, the answer is No.*

16.5 IDENTITY MANAGEMENT AND ACCESS CONTROL

Identity management and *access control* (often termed as *identification and access management* or *IAM*) are primary functionalities needed for any secure computing system. The benefits of identification and access management are:

- Proper execution of IAM technique improves a system's operational efficiency through automation of user verification process.
- It protects a system and enhances the security of its application and information against harmful attacks.

The IAM processes to support a business roughly comprise of the following activities:

Identification Management: It is the way by which users state their identities to a system. Through the identification, users establish their accountability for any action performed in the system. Identity of user for a system is managed with a user Id or user name which must be unique in the system.

Authentication Management: The verification of a user's identity for a system is known as 'authentication'. It checks the validity of the claimed identity and is commonly implemented by asking for a password during log-in or through fingerprint or retina scan.

Authorization Management: Authorization decides the user's level of access right to functionality or resources of a system and is determined after a system establishes user's identity and authenticity.

Access management: It deals with the execution of organizational policies and pre-stored system privileges in access control when an entity (user or process) requests for some computing resource.

Accountability: Accountability establishes the concept of non-denial of activities where an individual cannot deny the activities he/she has performed in a system. It is the system's capability of identifying a particular individual from his/her actions and behaviours within the system by using audit trails and logs.

Monitoring and auditing: User can monitor, audit and report compliance issues regarding access to resources based on the defined policies of the organization.

16.5.1 IAM in the Cloud

Identity management and *access control* have high value in cloud computing. Since with the adoption of cloud services, an organization's *trust boundary* may move beyond their own control. The boundary extends into the service provider's domain. This loss of control challenges the security of cloud and if it is not controlled appropriately it may get in the way of cloud service adoption. Both the service providers and consumers have roles to play in controlling these means.

Service providers must provide utmost effort towards implementing identity management and access control mechanisms to protect their cloud computing environment from any malicious activities. Specially in public cloud environment this becomes very critical as the entire computing environment resides at some remote place outside the *network boundary* of consumer organization. From consumer organization's end, this loss of network control can be compensated by the implementation of proper user access control techniques, like authentication and authorization.

Identity management in cloud computing requires robust authentication, authorization and access control mechanisms. At present, it is implemented by using modern technologies such as administering the biometrics or smart cards, governing the resource access rights by authorized users and preventing resource access by unauthorized entities.

Organizations can pass on the identification and access management responsibilities to an identity management-as-a-service (IDaaS) provider also. A number of vendors offers cloud-based solutions for identity management services (examples include Symplified, Ping Identity and others).

> Cloud security needs strong identity management and access control mechanisms to compensate the loss of network control .

16.5.2 Exploring Identity Management

User identity is checked by authenticating registered users during sign-in into system. This is generally done by maintaining usernames and passwords of users. Each and every secure computing system or application implement identity management mechanism. But, maintaining multiple usernames and passwords to access different applications, especially in the enterprise applications, reduce productivity and hampers application adoption. SSO and federated identity solve this problem by integrating applications and eliminating the need for multiple usernames and passwords without compromising security.

16.5.2.1 Single Sign-On

Single sign-on (SSO) is a user authentication process that solves the problem of repeated log-in to access different applications where user is individually known to each and every application. It permits a user to access multiple applications where user's identity is enrolled by signing on only once. The applications may belong to different enterprises but should be part of a group. SSO internally authenticates and authorizes the users for all of the applications and eliminates further need for providing identity when they switch applications during a particular session.

16.5.2.2 Federated Identity Management

Federated identity management (FIM) enables the linking and distribution of identity information across different applications within known trust boundaries. It is a kind of agreement that can be made among multiple enterprises to allow the users to use the same identification information to obtain access to the applications of all enterprises in the group. The use of such a system is sometimes called as *identity federation*.

Federated Identity (FID) refers the way of connecting multiple identity management systems of different enterprises together. In FID, a user's credential remains stored at the home organization (the identity provider) only. When the user tries to access service of some other enterprise within the known trust boundary, he need not to provide credentials to the other provider provided he is already logged into application of his own enterprise. Instead, the application of the other enterprise trusts the home organization to validate the credentials.

> In federated identity management system, a user never provides credentials directly to anybody but to the identity provider (the home enterprise).

In order to manage users of distributed applications, through which the organization maintains internal and external supply chain system, the identity federation is an emerging practice. With *federated identity management* system in place, a user of enterprise can interact with external service (like public cloud service, or service of some other enterprise) from his own enterprise's network.

Since federation coupled with well-organized identity and access management can enable efficient access control services, it plays a significant role in bridging enterprises and cloud services and hence it accelerates cloud computing adoption within organizations.

16.5.2.3 Federated Identity Management versus Single Sign-On

Federated system and single sign-on may appear same to the end user but they are different. In both, the user logs-in in some applications and then can access multiple applications or systems without logging in again. However at the background, the SSO and identity federation work entirely in different ways. Table 16.2 represents a comparison between these two.

In federated system, a user of an enterprise gets enrolled in the home application only. That means he/she can only be recognized by the home application. All of other enterprises

Table 16.2 Comparison Between SSO and Federated Identity System

Single Sign-On	Federated Identity System
User can access multiple applications under SSO group by signing in once.	User can access multiple applications under a federation by signing in once.
User needs to enroll themselves uniquely to each of the applications under SSO group.	User enrolls in any one application only under a federation.
User is known by all of the applications.	One user is known by only one application which is the home application of that user.
All of the applications of a SSO group allow a single sign-on of user being done through any of the applications.	Enterprise applications under a federation allow a single sign-on of user done through the home application only.
User credential is checked by all of the applications individually without prompting.	User credential is checked only once by the home application.
Every application under a SSO group checks the user separately.	All of the applications under a federation trust the home application.

under that federation agree to accept the identity and authorization supplied to them from that home application. User need not to get enrolled in those systems (applications) and those applications remain unaware of the end-user's identity. Federated identity systems are based on single credential stored to obtain access to multiple systems.

With SSO, a user needs to enroll uniquely to each of the applications or systems that come under a SSO group but all of the applications of the group agree to rely on a single sign-on. SSO allows the end users to provide their identity and authorization details once during log-on and provide access to all of the applications. The key point of the concept is that although user credentials are stored with multiple applications, they need to provide it once to access all of them during an active session.

In SSO, user has to be enrolled in each and every application to access them. In federated system, users need to enroll only in their home application.

Hence, in federated system, user authentication and authorization are checked only once by the home application and other applications of that federation trusts that. But in SSO, user authentication and authorization are checked by each application without prompting to the user.

16.5.3 Exploring Access Control

Access control is basically a procedure or policy that allows, disallows or limits access of users to a system. Access control is inherently attached with identity management and is necessary to defend the confidentiality, integrity and availability of data.

In cloud computing, the access to the computing environment is determined by the deployment models. While public and community cloud deployments follow shared access policy, the private cloud deployment maintains exclusive access strategy. This thing has been shown in Figure 16.2.

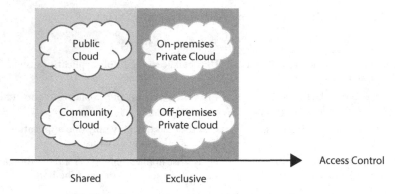

FIG 16.2: Resource access permit in cloud environment

From consumer's perspective, access control in cloud applications needs to be planned based on an organization's security policy. Such policy states management's intention concerning control of access to data and application and identifies people who are authorized to gain the access. There are three important points as, the threats to a system, a system's weakness against those threats and the risk that those threats may happen which are being considered while designing any access control policy or mechanism.

16.5.3.1 Degree of Control

Access control protects information from any unauthorized or unintentional modification. Planning and implementation of access control is a rigorous task and needs budget allocation as per the requirement. The effort and cost of implementing access control have to be decided depending on the merit of the information being protected. Hence, the organizations must estimate the value of their information before deciding how much control on access is required.

The *value of information* is determined through different qualitative and quantitative processes. These processes contain factors such as the effort/value to produce or acquire the information, the worth of the information to an organization and its rivals and the magnitude of the effect on organization's reputation if the information is compromised.

> *Degree of access control must be proportionate to the value of the information being protected.*

16.5.3.2 Models for Access Control

Several access control models are there in practice like *mandatory access control* (MAC), *discretionary access control* (DAC) and *non-discretionary access control*. These models are known as identity-based access control models where the users (and sometimes processes) are called subjects, resources are called objects and they are identified uniquely (generally by unique Ids).

Access control mechanism monitors and controls the access of resources (objects) by users (subjects). This control is governed by some pre-defined access rules which organizations need to define prior to setting up a system or application. The models of access control as mentioned above are distinguished based on these rules.

16.5.3.2.1 Mandatory Access Control

In mandatory access control (MAC), access policies are controlled by a central authority. Here the system (and not the users) specifies the access rule. Subjects are assigned into some classification levels (like management, administrator, official and friendly) and objects are assigned into some protection levels (like top-secret, private, moderate and friendly). In this example, the classification and protection levels are mentioned in descending order of grade in terms of security. A subject can be a group, department, project or process.

When the system makes an access control decision, it tries to match the classification level of the subject with the protection level of the object. If a user has a lower classification level than the protection level of the object he is trying to access, the access will be denied. For instance, if user has classification level administrator and he tries to access an object with a protection level of top-secret, then the user will be denied access because his classification level is lower than the protection level of the object.

Adoption of MAC ensures a safe and secure access control environment but that comes with some cost as well. Since it is controlled from the system level, planning of the access rules requires a considerable amount effort. The MAC model is usually used in environments where the confidentiality is of utmost importance.

16.5.3.2.2 Discretionary Access Control

Discretionary Access Control (DAC) is not so restrictive like MAC as it is more open. In DAC, the access policies are controlled by owner of object. There are no central rules to control access, rather object owners can decide which subjects will be given access of an object. The model is called discretionary as the access permission of objects depends on the discretion of owners. Owner of object has to determine what kind of privileges he/she is going to provide to a user. If appropriate privilege is given, a user in turn will be able to pass on access rights to other users.

Unlike the protection levels of MAC system, DAC-based system maintains a list containing identity of objects and their access permissions. This list is maintained for each and every object separately and is called as *access control list* (ACL). Although DAC is more flexible than MAC, but this approach has some risk associated with it if not planned properly because the users have the privileges of granting access permissions to the objects.

> *Unlike in MAC, where access policies are determined centrally by the system, in DAC, the access policies are determined by the owner of an object.*

16.5.3.2.3 Non-discretionary Access Control

In non-discretionary access control mechanism, the access policies are determined based on user's role. At first, roles are defined according to different possible job profiles or responsibilities in an organization. These roles assign access privileges. Later with each user as added into the system, they are assigned with appropriate roles. Access privilege of user is defined with this role assignment. Here, the assignments of access controls to subjects do not depend on discretionary decisions of the owner of an object, rather it complies with the organization's guidelines.

These access control policies are non-discretionary in the sense that they are imposed on all of the users based on their roles. Among those popular access control methods often been heard in enterprise applications, the *Role-Based Access Control* (RBAC) is actually non-discretionary access control mechanism. Roles in non-DAC differ from groups in MAC in the sense that while a user may belong to multiple groups, he/she can be assigned only a single role within an organization.

> It is called non-discretionary because the access permissions of objects do not depend on the discretion of individual owner of objects.

16.6 CLOUD SECURITY DESIGN PRINCIPLES

The fundamental principles of security design approach of any information system remain valid for cloud computing also. Any software design methodology includes security as a primary objective. But, an intensely-secure cloud system may ultimately deliver poor performance features. Hence, it is necessary to maintain a balance between security and performance. Following section summarizes all of those principles from cloud computing security perspective.

16.6.1 Least Privilege

The *least privilege* principle states that any subject (user or process) should always be assigned minimum required privileges to perform its task. A time limit should also be set to bind the period for which the subject can hold a resource to complete a task. This reduces the opportunity of any malpractice and prevents unauthorized access to sensitive information.

16.6.2 Defense in Depth

The *defense in depth* principle states to architect the protection system having multiple layers. This enhances the safety mechanism. If one layer is breached for security, the subsequent internal layers defend the attack and provide the protection to the system.

16.6.3 Fail Safe

System failure sometimes causes scope for breaching the security. It becomes difficult to strictly maintain all of the access control principles while recovering the system. Attackers may utilize this room. *Fail safe* principle says a system should be safe of any security threats even if it crashes sometime and should ensure that the safety of information is not compromised. From the other angle it can be said that the system recovery from failure should take it to a secure state to prevent any unauthorized access that may happen to the system or to its sensitive information.

16.6.4 Economy of Mechanism

A simple design of security mechanism reduces the chance of going wrong in understanding and implementation. Again in case of error it becomes easier to find and fix it. This is known as *economy of mechanism* which says to keep the security design as small and simple as possible.

16.6.5 Open Design

There have always been debates on the strength and merit of security designs those are kept secret versus the designs those are open. For example in encryption techniques, one opinion says that undisclosed algorithms make it more difficult to break and the other view is to reveal the algorithm for review by others is better option since it creates more chances of uncovering flaws in it. In cloud computing, as a multi-tenant and utility service provider where high security is the key, the *open design* principle suggests to architect such a model where security of the system does not depend on secrecy of its design.

16.6.6 Complete Mediation

Following the *complete mediation* principle ensures a rigorous checking of access controls with every request. Any access by a subject to any object is checked for authority using an effective authorization procedure.

16.6.7 Least Common Mechanism

The *least common mechanism* principle discourages the sharing of similar security mechanisms among different components. When security mechanisms are common among the components, the whole system becomes unsafe if security of any one component is cracked by the hackers.

16.6.8 Separation of privilege

The principle of *separation of privilege* suggests to break a single privilege among multiple independent subjects (component or user) so that more than one authorizations are required to perform an action. This protects the system from someone's evil intention.

16.6.9 Weakest Link

Like the old saying 'a chain is only as strong as its *weakest link*', the security of any system is also as good as its weakest module. Attackers always try to identify the most fragile part of the whole protection system in order to start their activities to dilapidate the system. Thus, the security system should be revised again and again to detect and resolve the weakest parts in the security chain.

16.6.10 Psychological Acceptability

Psychological acceptability states that the accessibility of the system for its authorized users should remain as simple and easier as it was in the absence of the security mechanism. It means that users must not face difficulty in using the system introduced by the complexity of the security mechanisms. Any complexity should remain hidden behind the screen.

> *The motive of building a completely-secure cloud system should not result in poor performance of the system. That is the goal of security design principle in cloud.*

16.7 CLOUD SECURITY MANAGEMENT FRAMEWORKS

In cloud security management, responsibilities of consumers and providers vary depending on the service delivery model and service-level agreement. One should understand the trust boundary of the services in the cloud before planning for its security.

There are industry standard management frameworks that provide guidance to plan for security of cloud systems and govern the processes to protect the assets. Information Technology Infrastructure Library (ITIL) and ISO (International Organization for Standardization) provide such service management frameworks which any mature computing organization may adopt to strengthen their security management systems.

16.7.1 ITIL

Information Technology Infrastructure Library (ITIL) is globally accepted as a security guideline for information technology service management (ITSM). ITIL was introduced by the Central Computer and Telecommunications Agency (CCTA) of United Kingdom to meet the business organization's growing dependence on information technology. ITIL provides guidelines for managing information technology services including cloud computing services. Hewlett-Packard Co. and Microsoft use ITIL as part of their own best-practice frameworks.

16.7.2 ISO 27001/27002

ISO 27001 (also known as ISO/IEC 27001) defines the mandatory requirements for information security management system (ISMS). It was jointly proposed by the International Organization for Standardization (ISO) and the International Electro-technical Commission (IEC). ISO 27001 and 27002 are two complementary directives for management of security of information systems with 27001 focussing on management and 27002 providing necessary controls for 27001.

> *Cloud security management frameworks are basically a blueprint for building a cloud service security program to manage risk and reduce vulnerabilities.*

16.8 SECURITY-AS-A-SERVICE

In the discussion related to security of cloud services, till now it has been focused in two aspects. They are the security mechanism employed by service providers and the security measures recommended for consumers. But, there is another angle to it where organization can outsource the security management responsibilities to some third-party service providers. The provider delivers it as a cloud service known as 'Security-as-a-Service'.

Security-as-a-Service is built, hosted and managed by the third-party service provider. Like any other cloud services, the business model of security-as-a-service is also subscription-based. Following are few services which are usually delivered as part of security-as-a-service.

Email Filtering: Security-as-a-Service primarily protects an organization's incoming mailbox from spam, phishing emails and malware by filtering them from delivered emails. It is also used to filter the outgoing emails from an organization when organizations want to ensure and restrict the un-intentional despatches of any malware-infected emails.

Web Content Filtering: Web traffic filtering facility of security-as-a-service can be utilized to scan web content. An organization's outgoing web content can be diverted through a security-as-a-service provider where content is checked for malware threats or for sensitive information (e.g., banking account related data, intellectual property and others) which a user could send intentionally or unintentionally without approval.

Vulnerability Management: There are security-as-a-service providers who assess and detect vulnerabilities in systems. They also provide remedy for those vulnerabilities and ensure that the system operates securely.

Identity Management: Apart from vulnerability management and data filtering facilities, another offering is delivered as part of security-as-a-service which is identity management-as-a-service. It facilitates user identity management by providing a centralized and trustworthy source of user identities.

SUMMARY

❖ Apart from establishing on-premises private clouds, consumers/enterprises extend their faith to trusted off-premises cloud services to benefit from the economic advantages of utility computing. Responsibility of this trust building process falls on the shoulders of service providers.

❖ Service providers must develop a secure computing environment by taking measures against all possible security threats. Securing the infrastructure, information and implementing strong access control mechanism can guarantee a safe environment.

❖ Security policy is the foundation of any sound security implementation. There should be standard security policies in every organization, specific to its need. The service-level agreement between the provider and consumer plays an important role in the policy implementation.

❖ The service-level agreement should also be comprehensive enough to resolve issues in case of any security dispute.

❖ There are industry standard management frameworks, which provide guidance for robust security management in cloud systems. Information Technology Infrastructure Library (ITIL) and ISO 27001 documentations provide such guidelines.

❖ Establishing the host and network level infrastructure security is provider's responsibility. Consumers are responsible for the security of their applications, that they run on cloud.

❖ Consumer's responsibility increases as they move from SaaS level to PaaS level applications and from PaaS level to IaaS level applications. From a consumer's viewpoint, using SaaS in the cloud minimizes their responsibilities for security management.

❖ Unauthorized access to confidential information and data theft is another major concern of cloud services. Apart from taking care of the conventional CIA-triad for information security, a strong identification and access management (IAM) system should be in place in cloud environment to compensate the loss of network control.

REVIEW QUESTIONS

Where is data stored in the cloud?

In public cloud computing, all of the data are stored at the service provider's end, at the data centers. Major public cloud service providers generally maintain multiple data centers spread over several geographical locations. Hence consumers' data goes in to the storage of some of those data centers. Consumers generally have no knowledge about specific location of their data storage.

For private cloud deployed under an organization's network security boundary, the scenario is a little different. In such cases, stored data remains under the control of the consumer enterprise.

Does cloud security vary with service providers?

Every service provider has their own policy, business goal and technical expertise. Security of cloud service depends on those factors. Hence, security may vary with service provider in cloud. Consumers must keep the reputation of the service provider in mind and examine the security measures employed by them before adopting a cloud service.

Is it safe to store personal data in the cloud?

It is quite similar to ask like 'Is it safe to keep valuables in locker of bank?' People deposit currency and valuables in bank while they trust the banks. This trust/reputation building is the responsibility of the bank and business of the bank also depends on this trust building.

It is same in cloud computing too. Service provider's business depends on this trust relationship. Security of sensitive data is the prime concern in cloud computing. But with reputed vendors, consumers' data are almost safe. And moreover, the vendors works continuously to provide further protection to the stored data at their data centers.

How does the data security issue in cloud compare with that in traditional computing system?

For enterprise level applications, organizations always choose to outsource the job to some outside service-company. Those IT service companies have either managed the stored data themselves or have used storage of some other service providers. Hence the security of enterprise data used to depend on the policy of those IT service companies in traditional computing environment. The risk (regarding data security) associated with cloud computing is no more than those systems. People who managed computing and storage on their own in traditional computing, have the options of private cloud. But again, with reputed cloud service providers, the backup and recovery mechanism promise to be more robust and may return significantly in case of a disaster.

Justify the statement: 'Security of IaaS level resources is the exclusive responsibility of consumer.'

At IaaS level, the providers deliver virtual computing resources to consumers. Consumers become the owner of those virtual resources, like virtual servers. Service providers blindly trust those owners regarding any activity and the safety becomes responsibility of the IaaS consumers.

MULTIPLE CHOICE QUESTIONS

1. In which type of cloud service consumers have most of the security responsibilities?

   a) IaaS

   b) PaaS

   c) SaaS

   d) Same in all of these

2. Which of the following is done through Identity management?

   a) Preventing unauthorized use

   b) controlling access to data in the cloud

   c) Maintaining user roles

   d) All of these

3. Which document works as the reference for both the service provider and consumer in case of any security dispute in cloud?

   a) Project agreement document

   b) Service level agreement

   c) Security agreement document

   d) All of these

4. By running over which application, the PaaS consumers can access the abstraction layer?

   a) Using APIs

   b) Using direct calls

   c) Using programs

   d) None of these

5. From consumer's end, who must review the SLA document before making the final agreement?

   a) Legal expert

   b) Business expert

   c) Technical expert

   d) All of these

6. Who among the following from enterprise's behalf must review the SLA document to ensure security in cloud?

   a) Legal expert

   b) Business expert

   c) Technical expert

   d) All of these

7. Security management responsibilities of SaaS application consumers include managing of

   a) Application security management

   b) Platform security management

   c) Operational security management

   d) All of these

8. Security management responsibilities of PaaS application consumers include managing of

   a) Application security management

   b) Operational security management

   c) Platform security management

   d) Both a and b

9. Covert channel problem is a threat to

   a) Information confidentiality

   b) Integrity of information

c) Information availability

d) All of these

10. Identification and access management plays the vital roles in cloud computing as

a) Anyone can work in cloud.

b) Consumers work outside trusted network boundary.

c) Virtualization brings the vulnerability.

d) All of these

11. Tell the statement if True or False.

'In federated identity system, the user credentials are stored in one application only.'

a) True

b) False

17 Privacy and Compliance Issues

CHAPTER

Security and privacy are often mentioned in the same breath, but they are not similar. It is a fact that both of them are important for trustworthiness of a system. However, when it comes to cloud computing, security tends to draw more attention and concern. But that does not mean that privacy can be compromised in anyway. Privacy maintenance in cloud is mainly the responsibility of service providers but consumers should also be conscious about their own privacy while drafting the service-level agreement (SLA).

Regulatory compliance is another issue that has taken a complicated shape in the context of public cloud computing facility. It often becomes difficult to fulfill all legal compliance requirements in a cloud environment where data centers of a service provider are spread across the globe and more often consumers do not know where (in which country or region) their data are being stored. Cloud consumers must be aware about their responsibilities regarding the information privacy and regulatory compliance maintenance, apart from checking service provider's reputation and approach towards maintenance of these issues.

Apart from these, this chapter discusses GRC (governance, risk and compliance) issue as another important concern of any business and how the issue becomes more prominent with adoption of cloud computing services for businesses. Regular auditing of these issues may help identify any violation. Standard audit frameworks exist, which when adopted for auditing cloud services can help build trust among the consumers.

> A common misconception is that data privacy is a subset of information security. But, security and privacy do not mean the same.

17.1 WHAT IS PRIVACY?

Both security and privacy are interrelated but it is a misconception that privacy is a part of information security. Rather, privacy brings its own set of concerns. Privacy of personal kind of information may be very sensitive and needs special attention.

In line with the concerns about the security of a cloud system, consumers need to be careful about the *privacy* of their data before they use services or enter into a contract with any cloud vendor. Who owns the data? Who has access to it? How many copies are being maintained? Will the data be erased in the event the customer changes the service provider? What is the acceptability level for vendor's use of consumers' cloud-based data for business or other purpose? To build trust among the service consumers and cloud service providers (CSPs), awareness and transparency about these issue is crucial.

The term 'privacy' refers to the right of an individual or organization to keep *proprietary information* or information of personal nature from being disclosed. The information which falls under the jurisdiction of privacy regulations is known as *'personally-identifiable information'* (PII). Examples of such information include names, bank account details, contact details, date of births and even information about one's personal likes or opinions. Basically, any information that can make someone identifiable comes under this category.

The concern about privacy protection is nothing new but with the emergence of *World Wide Web* era, lawmakers have faced significant challenges to preserve privacy. For example, personal information (such as name, date of birth etc.) shared by users in some web portal may be accessed and misused by fraudsters which may lead to *identity theft*.

Like security, the privacy of information has always been a concern in traditional computing systems. IT outsourcing has caused privacy concerns for enterprises for last two decades. And with the appearance of cloud computing, the privacy threats generate more concerns.

> Privacy refers to the right of an individual or organization to 'know what is being known about their personally-identifiable information (PII)'.

17.1.1 Privacy is About PII

In cloud computing, the consumers may use storage or database services of providers to store personal or sensitive data. These data are either stored in files of various formats or are managed by some DBMS applications. The cloud vendors arrange for appropriate protection of all of the users' data as stored in cloud. But this protection is not exactly a privacy concern. This is more about security of data. Vendors employ several mechanisms like *encryption*, access control etc. to ensure security of all of these data.

Regarding security of data, there is no disparities in rules around the globe. Here the one and only rule is that users' or organizations' stored data must remain absolutely secured. And more than by a rule, this requirement is governed by business need of vendors or service providers to build reputation and trust among the consumers in the competitive market.

> Protection of sensitive or business data of the consumers of cloud services is a security concern.

Privacy concern arises only for those kinds of data which have the potential of revealing user's identity. For example, in the banking sector, a bank may reveal how much money transaction has happened through their branches during a span of time. But, individually how much transaction a particular customer has made should not be disclosed. If so, that will fall under privacy breach. Only in case of investigation by some government-authorized body, such data may have to be shared if asked for.

In cloud computing also, such concerns arise. A cloud service provider having online shopping portal, may share its customers' pattern of purchasing articles with the product vendors. The provider may also share the contact details of customers or their bank account details. All of these kinds of personally-identifiable information (PII) which generally remains open among a trusted group of people or organizations (like friends, relatives, colleagues, offices and businesses) only, create the privacy concerns.

> Protection of the personally-identifiable information (PII) of consumers is a privacy concern.

17.2 DISPARITY IN PRIVACY PROTECTION LAWS

Trusted bodies (service providers) are not supposed to share the personally-identifiable information with anyone else without prior permission from the users concerned. But when such violation happens, different legal systems driven by the laws like common law, religious law, civil law etc. across the globe treat that in different ways. The legal jurisdiction generally varies country wise. The common law system is employed in the Australia, Canada, UK and US. Civil law systems are used in France and Germany and in other countries.

In most countries, the data privacy regulations are there to protect PII. Any organization collecting or storing such information must abide by the laws of that country. But, as the concept of privacy and the laws made for privacy protection vary widely among countries, cultures and jurisdictions many nations consider privacy as a basic human right issue, whereas many other countries are not so aggressive in addressing the privacy concerns. Hence, an organization's or a person's right to privacy is limited by laws or privacy policy of their own jurisdictions.

The abbreviation PII mainly comes from US context regarding privacy law and information security. The first two letters of this abbreviation (PII) stands for personal or personally, and identifiable or identifying which results in four different variations of PII. Not all the variations have similar meaning, and the actual definition depends on legal purpose as well as jurisdiction.

In an unusual circumstance, it may happen that a cloud service provider breaches its trust and takes undue advantage of feeble privacy law of some country by revealing some privacy-related information of consumers to give advantage to some other business organization. But, usually this does not happen because that will raise question about the reliability of the cloud service provider and will cause huge business loss for them.

Privacy protection laws are only applicable when PII is involved. Otherwise there can be no privacy harm. But the concern is that there is no uniform definition of PII in information privacy laws of different legal systems. In cloud computing, a consumer going to use some vendor's service should enquire about how the vendor may use their PII and what policies are there to prevent its potential abuses. Every vendor must maintain their own privacy policy. *Privacy policy* of an organization refers to the document that explains how the organization handles any customer's PII.

> The concept of privacy varies widely in different geographical jurisdictions and that causes a major problem for businesses using cloud computing.

17.3 PROTECTION OF PRIVACY

Any information management service that is outsourced brings privacy concerns and so for the cloud computing services as well. Moreover, the business spreading across the globe through cloud service make privacy a critical issue. The privacy in cloud depends mainly on accountability of hosting organization. The basic areas of concerns where organizations should focus are listed below.

Access to data: Who will have access to an organization's data hosted in some cloud service? Cloud vendors must clearly define this explaining those unavoidable situations when such information are required to be shared with authorized legal bodies.

Compliance: Cloud computing services generally spread across large geographical areas by crossing multiple legal jurisdictions. The privacy laws of these regions may not be same.

Consumers must be aware about this fact and must examine legal concerns before moving into cloud with some service vendor.

Storage location: Consumers storing data in cloud through some application or service would not be able to know where the data is actually being stored since it may get stored into data centers of multiple countries or regions. This is important because where (in which country or region) data are located determines the nature (the strictness of the law of concerned country) of the privacy protection law to be applied on those data.

Retention and destruction: How long information can be retained at CSP's end after service contract gets over or what can happen in case consumer moves to cloud service of another vendor? Here the retention policy of the hosting organization plays the main role. Vendors generally replicate cloud storage for safety and recovery purpose. One thing is to verify here whether all of those are really being destroyed or just being made inaccessible to the consumer organization.

Administrative access to consumers' data from provider's end may cause privacy concern if not been controlled appropriately. The accessibility of a client's data by the provider's system engineers must be controlled well. Providers should take care of this so that none of their own employees can collect and pass any data about stored data for targeted advertising or some other purpose. This can be done in many ways such as separation of duties and other means.

Privacy assurances should be mentioned in details in the service-level agreements (SLAs) too. For example, a SLA for a hosted ERP system in cloud may state that the client business enterprise is the sole owner of all of the data and that can never be used or shared by the vendor or cloud service provider with other firms or researchers.

> *Consumers should address all their privacy concerns in the service-level agreements.*

17.4 KEY PRIVACY CONCERNS IN THE CLOUD

Information privacy issue is one of the key concerns for enterprises moving towards cloud, especially in public cloud domain. This is due to disparity in privacy laws. Generally reputed cloud service vendors never compromise regarding privacy issue and protect their consumer's interest with maximum planning and effort. But, problem may arise when a government entity asks for data from service provider while conducting some enquiry. Private clouds being owned and managed on-premises or outsourced to some third party vendor to be developed within the same jurisdiction of the consumer enterprise do not cause this concern so much in general.

One solution to the information privacy problem may be segregation of data according to its sensitivity and storing them separately. Enterprises can keep extremely sensitive data under their own control to ensure security and compliance to government regulations. Hybrid cloud model may work well in this regard where extremely sensitive data are stored in the private cloud part.

> *Consumers may segregate and store sensitive information within their own infrastructure to safeguard the privacy of their information.*

Business organizations who run their business with the help of some outsourced cloud services, remain answerable to all of their stakeholders regarding privacy of their business information.

Organizations must enquire about the matters as mentioned above and should also investigate about CSP's reputation before providing assurance to its stakeholders.

17.5 SECURITY vs PRIVACY

Security and privacy may seem to be related with each other but they are not same despite the fact that in some cases these two concepts use to overlap. The differences need to be understood in order to design new systems that address both. It is possible to have good security control but poor privacy protection in a system. Security is necessary for privacy but privacy alone cannot ensure security.

Following section tries to focus on the contrasts between security and privacy:

■ Security is maintaining *'confidentiality, integrity and availability'* of data which is commonly referred to as the *CIA-triad*. Security provides assurance about the custody or storage of data against unsanctioned access, takes care about reliability and accuracy of data and makes the data available for authorized users whenever they need so.

Privacy, on the other hand, is *'the appropriate use of information'*. Everyone should use any information provided to them only for the intended purpose. For example, the e-commerce services should not reveal its customers' email addresses or any other details to a third party for business or any other purpose. Violating trust by sharing someone's personal information with others without prior approval is the violation of privacy.

> *Security is necessary but not sufficient for addressing privacy. Even the best security control mechanism may not have any impact on privacy protection.*

■ Security is *'being free from danger or threat'*. No one should be able to steal crucial data which may cause threat to business or intellectual property loss. Data preserved as confidential by the organization or user must remain secret forever.

Privacy is *'to be free from being observed or disturbed by others'*. A cloud provider's service may provide fool-proof security but that does not ensure that consumer's privacy is also protected.

'Information privacy' refers to the degree of control customers have over the decisions when, how and to what extent information collected about them can be used or be shared with others. 'Information security' refers customers' ability of securing their data from vulnerabilities and maintaining the integrity of stored data.

> *Privacy without security is not possible. But it is possible to have poor privacy despite having a strong security mechanism in place.*

17.6 THE IMPORTANCE OF PRIVACY POLICY

Every cloud vendors must have a documented privacy policy. The policy document should be able to satisfy all of the privacy-related queries of client organizations. Defining a standard policy and conforming to that will work as trust-builder among cloud service provider and consumers.

Consumers also should thoroughly study such policy documents carefully before subscribing services from vendors.

As there is no parity in *privacy protection laws* across different regions of world, it becomes very difficult for everyone to be sure about privacy of their information stored or shared in cloud. When and which government authorities or other agencies can access all of the data stored under their jurisdiction remain uncertain to the business houses and other cloud service consumers. In such situations, the privacy policy of cloud vendor is the only document that may give some idea about how the cloud provider is complying with various privacy laws and what safety measures they are going to adopt.

Here it should be noted that even if a cloud provider is in full compliance with laws, privacy compromise can still occur. This limitation is inherent to any outsourced information system and not a unique problem of cloud computing. A privacy policy may define the limits a cloud provider is placing on its liability in such an event.

> Apart from privacy protection procedures, a privacy policy should also declare the limitations or bindings of the service provider in privacy maintenance.

17.7 COMPLIANCE

Compliance issue in business arises out of conflicting regulations and laws of different countries or regions. The proliferation of new regulations and standards around the world makes it difficult for the global enterprises to maintain performance objectives, sustain value, protect the organization's reliability and to uphold stakeholders' expectations.

With the adoption of cloud computing, enterprises need to move their application and data from internal infrastructure to cloud provider's infrastructural facility to span the businesses worldwide. Cloud services as well as infrastructure, by its own nature, spread over multiple countries and continents. All of those different regions are likely to have different regulatory requirements. With this, it becomes necessary to observe how all of these overlapping regulatory requirements are being maintained by the service provider in a coherent manner.

Cloud computing does not raise any new compliance issues but it makes existing ones more complex. This is mainly for the reason that data in cloud are stored in multiple locations. Hence, data stored in cloud by one consumer may get stored in multiple other countries those follow different regulatory or legal systems. This increases complexity as overlapping or conflicting regulations become critical for a system to handle. Hence, to comply with all of those overlapping or inter-conflicting regulations and laws, the service providers must attentively design and manage their services and systems.

> Compliance issue arises because of conflicting regulations and laws of different countries or regions around the world.

In general, compliance issues in computing may arise from different viewpoints. Following are the different compliance concerns:

- Regulatory
- Performance

- Security and
- Legal

Among these, performance compliance or security related compliance are technical issues and are not difficult to achieve with proper expertise and effort. But regulatory and legal compliance issues most often appear as main concerns in business arena.

Compliance agreements can be made between a CSP and service consumers through SLA contract. There must be consistency between the requirements of the consumer and assurances provided by the service provider. SLA must address all of the compliance-related issues and whenever some violation is observed, it must be sorted out immediately between those two parties. But, when the regulatory, performance and security issues can be resolved between CSP and consumer, any solution regarding non-compliance of legal issues depends on the jurisdiction of the concerned geographical region.

> The main concern regarding compliance in cloud computing is legal compliance.

17.7.1 It is Not Provider's Responsibility Alone!

Managing compliance issues may seem to be a responsibility solely of the cloud service provider. But, it is not so. Consumers often have roles to play to fulfill all of the compliance requirements. The regulatory needs and performance must be monitored constantly both by the provider and consumers and whenever some problem is observed, both parties have to cooperate with each other to resolve it. Security-related compliance is one issue that must be monitored and addressed by the CSP. Regarding the most critical compliance issues like the legal compliance, both CSP and consumer will have to be very cautious and strategic. For instance, the service providers may choose to store some business organizations' data within their business jurisdictions to avoid compliance related problems or enterprise may select a CSP who provide options for storing data at data centers of consumer's choice.

17.8 GOVERNANCE, RISK AND COMPLIANCE (GRC)

In large enterprises, good governance is treated as a potential measurable commodity. Similarly, the risk management and compliance to the regulations are also very important for organizations to gain confidence of partners and clients. GRC is the umbrella term covering an organization's approaches towards these three areas as governance, risk management and compliance. Being very closely related to one another, organizations prefer to address these issues together in a planned manner to avoid any gap or conflict:

- Governance: It means the approaches or strategies taken by the management body of an organization which governs their policy or business.
- Risk management: Risk may cause adverse effect on business if not dealt with properly. A well-organized risk management strategy is necessary to be there so that organizations can efficiently deal with any such situation.
- Compliance: This is related with any business need to be abided by some standards and regulations. Compliance is the act of following all of the regulations without any miss.

Organization needs to clearly define its principles of governance, determine how it will address risks and uncertainties while emphasizing the importance of remaining in compliance with laws and regulations. Otherwise, in cloud computing arena this may stand as a barrier between providers and service consumers.

Cloud computing presents new set of challenges before GRC maintenance for enterprises. Cloud adoption is a governance decision. All types of cloud deployments have GRC-related concerns associated with them but GRC strategy of public cloud emerges as the major concern. To address this issue of GRC maintenance at cloud computing, the Cloud Security Alliance (CSA) proposed a GRC stack that can inject transparency and confidence in the public cloud.

> *GRC is a term that reflects the way in which organizations adopt an integrated approach towards governance, risk and compliance aspects of their business.*

17.8.1 Steps to Address GRC

GRC is an age-old issue of business. As businesses grow, GRC maintenance becomes a critical task. And for business having global presence GRC issue remains at the center stage of concerns. The issue can be managed well when being addressed in planned manner. Following are the steps to address GRC issue:

Risk assessment: Assessing risks in terms of governance and compliance issues on regular basis is essential.

Key controls: When any potential risk is identified, the key controls associated with the matter have to be recognized and documented for effective solution. For example, security controls are designed to safeguard any weaknesses in the system and the measures to reduce the effect of any attack.

Monitoring: Key controls have to be monitored carefully to find out any defect in the adopted approach for fulfilling compliance requirements.

Reporting: Different functional metrics and *key performance indicators* (KPIs) defined by the organizations have to be reported on regular basis.

Continuous improvement: Whenever some gaps or conflicts are identified during monitoring, necessary corrective measures have to be taken to sort out the fault and improve the processes.

17.8.2 Why GRC has Become so Important

Risk is unavoidable but it can be managed. With appropriate GRC policy and its compliance measures, the businesses can strategically balance risk and opportunity. The term 'GRC' is not new and any organization doing business had to take care about this earlier too. But at present, the issue of GRC has become important for organizations due to several reasons. The main reasons behind this are mentioned below.

Information explosion: The emergence of information technology and advanced network communication system have made it easier to deal with information effectively. The more information a business can gather or store, the more chances would generate of getting competitive advantages. This philosophy has caused the explosion of information. Now how to deal with all of these information securely and maintain their privacy have been the primary concern.

Scores of regulations: There are too many regulatory bodies and rules of the organizations. Any enterprise or business organization must be careful to abide by all of these regulations so that no violations of laws can happen which can cause huge business loss. But the problem is that often these regulations are conflicting in nature.

Globalization of enterprises: Enterprises nowadays have become larger in volume and can easily spread their business all over the globe. As different regulations are applicable in different geographical zones around the world, it has become difficult to monitor and maintain country- or region-specific business laws.

Cloud computing: Cloud computing has several good effects. But, it has made life difficult for enterprises and specially cloud service providers. In a public cloud environment, the provider stores clients' data at several storage locations. These locations generally fall under different legal and regulatory jurisdictions. They remain unknown to the clients and hence clients can never know if any violation of regulations has happened or not.

The four reasons as mentioned above show same *problem of visibility* in each of them. It is simply not possible to monitor all of the regulatory issues without forming proper strategies. The large sizes of businesses and the high speed of the communication have made it difficult to look over these critical issues on regular basis.

Cloud service providers, particularly the public cloud service providers, face lots of challenges in GRC to keep up with the volume of business spread over different countries. Apart from those regulations varying jurisdictions-wise, they have to fulfill the requirements of a diverse client-base. To maintain all of the GRC requirements, it has become essential for CSPs to build a sustainable model.

> GRC issues require caution and a planned approach, particularly in public cloud arena.

17.8.3 Automated GRC Monitoring

To reduce the cost and effort of managing GRC, various GRC monitoring tools have become available in market. Many vendors have come up with specialized software solutions that can automate the activities of GRC monitoring across both physical and virtualized computing environments. These solutions can increase the visibility, transparency and efficiency in GRC monitoring process significantly. These GRC monitoring solutions can keep a watch on all of the flow of activities and can generate reports with GRC summary. But, such solutions have some limitations also while working under the virtualized cloud architecture which enterprises need to take care of their own.

Many reputed vendors offer automated GRC service. ERP solution provider SAP offers a bunch of such GRC solutions to maximize business performance like SAP Process Control solution, SAP Risk Management solution, SAP Fraud Management solution, SAP Access Control solution and others. These solutions automate GRC programs starting from risk management to compliance reporting.

> Information technology-enabled GRC solutions help enterprises bring order in GRC.

17.9 AUDIT AND MONITORING

To maintain operational standards including privacy, security and to maintain compliance requirements, IT organizations exercise two basic methods as system *auditing* and *monitoring*. In cloud computing, these methods can be employed by anyone between customer or provider, depending on architecture and deployment.

- A *system audit* is a regular affair to assess system performance, security controls, information privacy, compliance etc.
- *Monitoring* is also a regular activity that keep track on all activities performed on the system, such as intrusion detection and others.

Audit is basically a function that checks that standard, method or practice is followed. The IT audit perspective helps the organizations to clarify compliance risk and security risk to their systems.

17.9.1 Auditing for Compliance

Auditing is actually done to check and ensure compliance requirements. For fulfillment of compliance issues, an organization should comply with following steps:

- Classify the constraints which bar to go with the compliance standards. Those constraints may be driven by the factors like business objectives, customer contracts, laws and regulations, corporate policies and standards.
- Design and follow procedures and practices to satisfy all of such requirements.
- Check periodically to examine whether there is any violation in following the standards.

Auditing and monitoring are the abilities to observe events, to understand performance and maintain integrity of system. This is often done by recording events into log files and examining those files later. *Logging* is an important function for any system for performance evaluation and security checking.

17.9.2 Internal and External Audit

The auditing processes of information technology (IT) enterprises are divided into two types as *internal audit* and *external audit*. Internal auditing is performed by auditors internally in the organization. They are employees of the organization. The purposes of the internal auditors are to identify the risks whenever they arise related to the performance, security and compliance issues. They also keep a watch on what are being done to mitigate those problems aiming to help the organization perform better. External audit is carried out by professional auditors external to the organization. They are independent body, often being *certified public accountants* (CPAs), and perform an independent auditing of the organization. The shareholders and clients of any organization pay more attention and importance to this external audit report regarding performance, security and compliance of the system.

Table 17.1 Differences between internal and external audit

Internal Audit	External Audit
It is performed by auditors who are employees of the organization.	It is performed by the external professional auditing body.
Auditors generally have much wider authorizations.	Auditors generally have restricted authorizations.
The objective is to identify loopholes in processes for betterment of the organization.	External auditing is done by the organization to build confidence among clients and shareholders.
Audit report is not published outside, it is used only for internal purpose.	Audit report is published outside of the organization.
It can be executed anytime. Generally, it is done on regular basis.	It does not happen too frequently. Generally it occurs once in a year.

17.9.3 Audit Framework

Auditing helps in building trust among a service provider and its clients. If organization can provide the performance and compliance audit reports to its stakeholders on regular basis that develop the confidence among them. There are many standard frameworks according to which organizations prepare their audit reports. Few among those common audit frameworks used by the auditors of IT services are discussed below.

17.9.3.1 SysTrust and WebTrust

SysTrust and WebTrust are two audit frameworks jointly developed by the American Institute of Certified Public Accountants (AICPA) and Canadian Institute of Chartered Accountants (CICA). The frameworks are made to focus on the risks and opportunities associated with information technology and performs audit based on pre-defined set of criteria for security, availability, processing integrity and confidentiality. The service frameworks were designed with a focus on three trust-service principles of security as availability, confidentiality and integrity. These frameworks act well for cloud service providers serving enterprise customers.

17.9.3.2 ISO 27001

ISO 27001 is a standard to provide security to Information Security Management System (ISMS). It was jointly published by the International Organization for Standardization (ISO) and the International Electro-technical Commission (IEC) and also known as ISO/IEC 27001. The framework defines how to address information security and manage risk assessment in any kind of organization.

17.9.4 Auditing the Cloud for Compliance

Cloud customers need assurance and testimony that a provider is strictly maintaining all complicated and conflicting compliance issues. This is very important because any violation to comply regulations and laws may attract huge penalty and also cause severe business losses too.

In outsourced computing services, the *Right to Audit* (RTA) clause is often used in the service-level contracts to ensure that clients can conduct auditing activities on their own. In cloud services also the RTA can be applied. However, due to multi-tenancy and shared resources, performing an audit in cloud is more complex. The CSPs can adopt compliance programs based on standard audit frameworks (such as *ISO/IEC 27001*) and keep assurance certification to develop trusts among their customers.

SUMMARY

- ❖ Like any other outsourced information management service, cloud computing also gives rise to privacy concerns among its consumers.
- ❖ Information security and privacy are two different issues. Security does not ensure privacy.
- ❖ Privacy gets affected when the identity of someone gets revealed to others without his or her permission. The kind of information which can be disclosed is known as personally-identifiable information or PII.
- ❖ To protect privacy of consumers and their business, cloud vendors should ensure that personally-identifiable information is not being shared with others. Every service provider generally maintains some documented privacy policy of its own.
- ❖ The inequality in privacy protection laws among different countries or regions make it challenging for cloud service providers and consumers to maintain the privacy.
- ❖ Compliance of all kinds of business, performance and legal requirements become important issues for cloud service providers. Among these, complying with all legal constraints is another challenge as data in cloud is stored at different locations around the world. These regions have their own separate regulations which are often in conflict with each other.
- ❖ All of the cloud service providers must define their principles with respect to Governance, Risk management and Compliance issues. Together, these three are called as GRC.
- ❖ Periodical auditing and constant monitoring are important in cloud to ensure compliance, performance and security of the system.

REVIEW QUESTIONS

Is it possible to ensure the privacy of information when the information security is maintained properly?

No. Privacy does not get ensured if information security is maintained properly. Information security and privacy are different things altogether. For instance, a consumer who stores data at the facility of some cloud service provider will expect that all of the data will remain secure and no one will be able to access any data without his/her authorization. A reputed cloud service provider leaves no stone unturned to keep the data absolutely secured for their own business interest. But, if somehow any personal detail (PII) of the customer gets reveled to the outer world from the service provider's end beyond interest and without having the permission of the customer, then that will be called as privacy breach. The data may still remain secure but this already has caused the privacy breach.

What is personally-identifiable information in real life?

Information which can be used to identify a person or organization or which can be used to distinguish one person or organization from others, is known as personally-identifiable information (PII). This does not mean information like name, address or unique identification number which can be used for direct identification only. It may also include a combination of multiple information which can indirectly identify an individual or business.

Why is compliance issue such a big worry in cloud computing?

Cloud computing is supported by huge infrastructural setup at the back situated at data centers located at different places around the world. The consumers storing data in the cloud most often do not know in which data centers their data are actually being stored. The data stored at a data center remains under the jurisdiction of the country or region where the data center is located. Hence, data of a client of some country is likely to remain under the jurisdiction of some other legal or regulatory bodies when data are stored in several data centers of different countries. This causes worry about the legal compliance issue in cloud computing as the client remains unsure about whether their business policies are sufficient to fulfill the legal or regulatory requirements of all of those different jurisdictions.

What can a cloud service consumer do to ensure compliance?

A cloud service consumer can seek an information technology audit of the system it is using, by some external professional audit firms. This may help it get a fair idea about compliance issues. To ensure conducting such auditing on their own, consumers can add the Right to Audit (RTA) clause in the SLA which is often used for outsourced IT services. Apart from this, consumers may look for reputed service provider who have data centers in their (consumer's) jurisdiction of business (and offers choice to consumers to select the data centers) before moving into a cloud service. But this solution is not much effective for big businesses who have multi-national presence.

MULTIPLE CHOICE QUESTIONS

1. Information privacy is actually a part of information security.

   a) True
   b) False
   c) Depends on situation
   d) Both of them are same

2. Generally, to store consumers' data in encrypted form in the cloud means to preserve information

   a) Security
   b) Privacy
   c) Both security and privacy
   d) None

3. Which among the following causes challenge to privacy protection in cloud computing?

   a) Lack of awareness
   b) Weak security implementation

c) Different legal systems

d) All of these

4. There can be strong security in a system without any privacy.

a) True

b) False

5. Does the compliance maintenance task is cloud service provider's responsibility alone?

a) Yes

b) No. Clients should also be alerted on this.

6. IT auditing is done to check the

a) Compliance issues

b) Security issues

c) Financial issues

d) Both a and b

7. The IT audit report that is of more value for the cloud consumers is the

a) System audit

b) Internal audit

c) External audit

d) Privacy audit

8. Internal audit for compliance is done by service providers

a) To gain confidence of shareholders

b) To gain confidence of consumers

c) To earn more revenue

d) To improve privacy of the system

9. 'R' in the term GRC represents

a) Reliability

b) Responsiveness

c) Risk

d) Recovery

10. Privacy in information system is to maintain the secrecy of

a) Stored data of clients

b) PII of clients

c) Financial information of clients

d) Name of clients

18 Portability and Interoperability Issues

CHAPTER

Cloud computing is about using services provided by cloud vendors. When consumers invest effort and capital to develop their computing setup on some provider's service, one major concern for them is whether they can move to other cloud service in future, if necessary, with minimal disruption and effort. Can things once built over one cloud service be moved to another cloud service? This question arises since there are possibilities of *vendor-lock-in*, a situation where a consumer using one cloud service cannot easily move to a similar service delivered by a competitor company or service provider. All investments by a consumer may be in stake if computing setup created on one provider's service cannot be moved to other provider's service in future.

An other concern comes in mind when consumers think about linking applications of two different cloud services together or, when it is required to link some on-premises non-cloud or cloud computing setup with a public cloud service. Such linking brings forth the issue of interoperability. Can applications of two different cloud environments be linked in such a way? This concern may worry the consumers.

Consumers should have a clear understanding regarding these issues before moving into cloud. Such understanding enables one to take informed decisions when choices have to be made concerning technology, application or platform.

> Cloud adoption among the consumers also depends on how a cloud environment can address users' concerns regarding portability and interoperability, apart from the issue of security.

18.1 CHALLENGES IN THE CLOUD

Although the cloud service offerings present a simplistic view of computing services to consumers, there are few critical issues to consider while moving into cloud. As already discussed, the prime challenges among these are the challenges associated with information security, privacy and compliance. The other vital challenges are related to issues of:

- Portability and
- Interoperability

These two issues arise while moving a system into cloud. The primary concerns during such initiatives are whether the system components are portable into a new environment or not. And then, there are concerns about the interoperability of the components of the existing system too.

Users may want to move their existing systems (applications and data) to some other cloud service that meet their requirements better or for some other reason. But *vendor-lock-in* may stand as a barrier in the process. Moreover, the cloud computing is in its early age and that's why, probably, the technocrats are thinking about its further developments in the potability and interoperability arena. This chapter explores various aspects of these two issues and discusses how to overcome these barriers in the process of cloud adoption.

18.1.1 Portability

Portability is about the ability to move an entity from one system to another without compromising its usability. In computing, portability can be described as the ability of moving one component from one technological or architectural platform to another. The ported component should remain operational at its full ability.

In cloud computing perspective, portability is about the ability of moving some computing constituent (like virtual machine, development environment or application) from one environment to another. Portability concerns are highest when these two environments are from two different vendors. It is important to note that portability issues at different layers of cloud services are not similar.

> Portability is the ability to run components or systems developed for one cloud provider's environment on some other cloud provider's environment.

18.1.2 Interoperability

In general sense, *interoperability* is referred as a measure of the degree to which dissimilar systems or components can work together successfully. In computing, interoperability can be described as the ability of two or more systems or applications to communicate by exchanging information and deliver expected outcome by processing those exchanged information.

In the cloud computing perspective, interoperability is about communicating between multiple clouds. Clouds can be of different deployments (public, private and hybrid) and/or from different vendors. Diverse systems should be able to understand one another in terms of application, data formats, configurations, service interfaces etc. Only then they will be able to cooperate and interoperate with each other. Like portability, in interoperability too, issues related to different layers of cloud services are not similar.

> Interoperability means being able to seamlessly exchange data or information between systems running in different cloud environments. Interoperability is an enabler for portability.

18.2 THE ISSUES IN TRADITIONAL COMPUTING

It may seem that the problems of *portability* and *interoperability* are new to cloud computing. But the truth is that these problems were present during the earlier days of computing also. Since, the traditional computing environment was much more constrained, there was little scope to deal with these issues. But still few fruitful efforts had been made to address it. In this context, one remarkable development that comes in mind is that the evolution of java platform which could provide application portability.

Unlike in traditional computing, cloud computing customers need not procure any computing facility. They can avail everything on rent which is economical and does not require one time large investment. This provides the option for moving from one cloud service to another.

In traditional computing, it used to take huge investment to build computing infrastructure. Hence, porting of existing systems or applications over some new infrastructure was never an easy decision. Once a setup is created, the customers have little options to change anything. They can do nothing other than continuing with old setup. Otherwise, everything has to be built almost from scratch that is expensive.

Interoperability has always been a need of the computing world. But the issue was overlooked earlier as almost all of the applications used to run in isolation. The need of interoperability mainly emerged with advancements in the field of enterprise applications and it has become a necessity now when enterprises are going to opt for multiple applications from different vendors to run their businesses. Consumers can get maximum benefits when those applications can interoperate.

> *There was limited opportunity for dealing with the issues of portability and interoperability in traditional computing.*

18.3 ADDRESSING PORTABILITY AND INTEROPERABILITY IN CLOUD

Let us consider the mechanism of a hybrid cloud. In hybrid cloud computing environment, a system running on private cloud expands itself into some public cloud when load exceeds the capacity of private cloud. During such situation, these two systems running in two different environments which must recognize each other and work together. For implementation of such a system, two issues become vital.

Firstly, depending on the requirements, at least some portions or the whole system running in the private cloud have to be re-implemented in the public cloud environment. Such re-implementation of a system into new environment depends on the *portability* of the system. All of the functionalities of the existing system should work properly after porting. But what happens when these two cloud environments belong to different service providers?

And secondly, successful porting does not finish the task completely. All of the related components and functionalities of these two running systems (over two different cloud environments) must be able to interoperate. They will call one another, exchange data and make decisions collectively. This is *interoperability*. The question arises here is that to be interoperable, is it at all necessary for two systems to be developed in same technology?

The following discussion provides a simplistic view of the portability and interoperability problems. But, the actual problems related with these two issues are quite diverse in nature and each of them needs to be addressed separately.

18.3.1 Addressing Portability

Portability issues in computing bring the concerns through the following categories:

- Data Portability,
- Application Portability and
- Platform Portability.

18.3.1.1 Data Portability

Data portability issue is the most interesting thing to study among these. This is because the data portability problem remains present at all levels of cloud services but challenges change with the service levels. Thus, portability of data must be addressed separately for SaaS, PaaS and IaaS. Data is generally structured to fit some particular application, platform or storage. Hence, one has to be careful while moving data from one cloud service to another. Use of standard data formats can resolve the problem of data portability.

> *Data portability enables re-usage of data components across different applications and platforms.*

18.3.1.2 Application Portability

Applications often use characteristic-specific to the platform it is built on. Thus it becomes difficult to move an application from its native platform to other. Applications generally communicate with platform through interfaces (APIs) provided by the platform. Hence non-standard platform APIs may make an application rigid or non-portable.

For application portability over cloud, all of the vendors need to agree on a common *application program interface* (API) that will allow applications to be portable across multiple cloud environments. When an application uses features that are specific to a platform and the platform interface is non-standard, then the portability hampers.

Simple Cloud API initiative of Zend Technologies is one such effort to promote application portability in cloud. They started an open-source initiative to create a common set of APIs that will allow applications to be portable. In 2009, Zend Technologies launched the Simple Cloud API to improve portability of PHP applications almost across all of the major cloud computing platforms. It was a collaborative effort supported by many cloud computing vendors like Microsoft, IBM, Rackspace, GoGrid and Nirvanix. Vendors are now supplying adapters which use Simple Cloud API for their cloud application services.

> *Application portability enables the re-use of application components across computing platforms.*

18.3.1.3 Platform Portability

Platform porting is more critical than data or application porting. Porting a platform may mean two different things and they are done in two different ways:

Porting platform environment: This means reusing platform components over the IaaS facilities of different vendors. It deals with platform elements like operating system, web server or database management system. Such portability can be achieved by recompiling the source codes of platform components on every non-cloud infrastructure or IaaS services. This may require rewriting of the hardware-dependent sections of the codes.

Porting machine image: In this case, applications running over the platform are bundled together with platform components. This bundled entity is known as *machine image*. Porting machine image means that the moving of virtual machine instance from one provider's infrastructure to another provider's infrastructure service. This archiving technique requires a standard representation of the machine images that can be deployed in different IaaS environments. Such initiatives have already been started by the technologists and evolution of *Open Virtualization Format* (OVF) is a major development towards this aim. OVF has been discussed later in this chapter.

> Platform porting has two forms: porting of platform components and porting of machine images.

18.3.2 Addressing Interoperability

Implementation of interoperability needs standardization as well as collaboration among computing vendors. The issue brings the concerns divided in following categories:

- Application Interoperability and
- Platform Interoperability

In cloud computing, platform or application components of two environments interact through interfaces or APIs using communication protocols. Applications can interoperate only when they share common process and data models. Thus, the interoperability issue becomes critical when these two different environments (to be interoperated) are from different vendors.

The solution of this problem is to standardize the communicating interfaces. Data format standardization is another requirement in the making of portable application or platform. Additionally, platform interoperability requires standard protocols for service discovery. If cloud services leverage SOA design principles, then interoperability becomes easier while linking applications of two different cloud services.

Efforts have been undertaken for creating *open standards* to boost interoperability in the cloud. The Cloud Computing Interoperability Forum (CCIF) has been formed by various computing and technology organizations such as Intel, Sun and Cisco in order to develop such standards. The Unified Cloud Interface (UCI) is one such initiative from CCIF to create open and standardized cloud interfaces.

Another group named as Open Cloud Standards Incubator (OCSI), working under the Distributed Management Task Force (DMTF), is trying to develop interoperability standards for managing interactions between different cloud systems. The DMTF is an organization that works to develop system management standards to promote IT interoperability. The member companies of DMTF are spread across the globe and represents different sectors of industry including cloud vendors, service providers and telecom companies. Industry leaders like VMware, Microsoft Corporation, Broadcom Corporation, Cisco, Dell, HP, CA Technologies, Intel Corporation, Citrix, IBM, Software AG, Oracle, Red Hat and others are part of DMTF. These companies along with many others companies and working groups regularly contribute in DMTF's initiatives to address the various challenges in the industry.

Various on-going initiatives promise promotion of interoperability in cloud computing in the near future.

18.4 PORTABILITY AND INTEROPERABILITY SCENARIOS

There can be several types of interoperability and portability issues to deal with in cloud computing. This section introduces and explains such scenarios where interoperability and portability issues are like the prime concerns. Different recommendations and remedies have also been discussed to tackle these issues efficiently.

18.4.1 Scenario 1: Customer Switches the Cloud Service Provider

In this scenario (represented in Figure 18.1), consumer of a cloud service wishes to change the service provider. This turns out to be the most crucial case among all. Depending on the type of service, such a situation touches several issues associated both with portability and interoperability.

18.4.1.1 Portability Considerations

Changing SaaS provider means that the switching from one SaaS application to another equivalent SaaS application. Although at SaaS level no application portability issue arises, but data associated with those applications bring portability concerns. *Data portability* arises from three aspects of data like format, extent and semantic. Ideally the format, extent and semantic types of data should be the same for both service A and service B as shown in Figure 18.1. While tools are going to be built or available standard tools are used to make data format transformations, the data extent and semantic issues may stand as barrier in data portability.

At PaaS level, provider's database may be sensitive to the format of data. In such cases, data migration facility has to be examined to check how data is retrieved and loaded. Otherwise, if PaaS uses any common data formats available (like XML) that can eliminate portability concerns.

IaaS, being a low level facility, does not bring any data portability issue since consumer needs to build everything from the scratch. Data files at IaaS level come in binary or object form and are generally stored using common formats. Hence, format of the data files is not a concern for IaaS level porting. But, there may be some concerns regarding the volume of data files.

FIG 18.1: When consumer changes cloud service provider

Switching of SaaS and PaaS providers will bring data portability concerns. Adoption of services with standard data formats or use of some standard data format can resolve data portability problems.

For IaaS or PaaS consumers, *applications portability* is of utmost importance while changing providers. At IaaS level, the question is whether these two providers support same virtual machines and if the virtual machine architectures are similar. A portable machine image format like Open Virtualization Format (OVF) resolves the machine porting problem from one provider to another.

At PaaS level, concern is about operating system and the application development environment. The application development environment may consist of a substantial stack of software with many APIs which are used by the application code. If machine architecture, operating system and/or the development environment are not similar, then applications have to be redesigned which is highly undesirable. Compatible platform elements like web server, database server etc. boost the application portability. Otherwise, if there is any mismatch in OS version or version of the libraries, then the redesigning is required as well. In such scenarios, the rebuilding of the whole application code may be the simpler, less costly and rather preferred approach.

While cloud vendors (till now) provide little scope for PaaS level application portability, consumers' choice towards application development environment may raise the probability of porting their application to some other clouds. This is by adopting open technology-based development environments. Such move certainly raises the number of viable alternatives.

IaaS level application portability is possible when two environments support open standard machine packaging formats. For PaaS level application, it is open technology-based development environment.

18.4.1.2 *Interoperability Considerations*

For SaaS facility, the application used by consumer belongs to or delivered by the service provider. Hence no question arises for the first provider's (provider A) SaaS application to be interoperable with other service provider's (provider B) platform since switching of SaaS service provider means switching of the SaaS application itself. The new provider will have their own version of the SaaS applications.

But the important thing here is that the similarity of the functional interfaces of these two SaaS applications. The interfaces may not be visually identical but for the end user the functional familiarity is important. The other issue may arrive when the SaaS application provides functional APIs to be used by consumer's application. In such scenario, before switching the service provider, consumer must check whether their own application is interoperable with the new set of APIs provided with the new SaaS. Otherwise, if they are not interoperable, then the implementation of any such application, using SaaS APIs, needs to be changed.

For consumers of PaaS and IaaS facilities, switching providers does not bring functional interface-related concerns (like SaaS consumers) since consumers in these cases are supposed to use their own (existing) applications over the new cloud facility. At this level, the main concern arises regarding the APIs those are used by consumer's applications. Provider-supplied APIs should be interoperable with consumer's applications. In PaaS level application porting, adoption of open technology-based application development environment helps to raise the interoperability.

> *The interoperability concerns for SaaS, PaaS or IaaS level application porting to other cloud environment arises due to API interoperability issues.*

18.4.2 Scenario 2: Customer Uses Cloud Services from Multiple Providers Concurrently

Under this scenario (represented in Figure 18.2), there can be two cases. First one, where consumer uses two services of different providers having equivalent functionalities. This is done to increase flexibility in case one of the providers would face some kind of service disruptions. Second one, where two services are to serve different functionalities. This happens since different providers can have expertise on different functional areas and consumer always wants the best service for each required functionalities.

Under this circumstance, all of the recommendations made in Scenario 1 above remain valid. The additional issues are discussed in the following section.

18.4.2.1 Portability Considerations

Data portability in case of equivalent SaaS facilities can be a critical issue since these two services may have to work on same set of data by maintaining duplicate copies through import/export. Even in cases where two SaaS services are not equivalent in functionality, there may arise the need of extracting data from one service to be used by the other service. In such cases, if two providers do not maintain data in same format, extent and semantics, the cloud consumers are left with one option only. Data transformation is the only solution in order to use both cloud services successfully.

> *SaaS offering with standard APIs and data formats can resolve portability and interoperability issues in cloud computing.*

Data portability in IaaS level is of least concern as IaaS service consumers have full control over their data format and use of common data format can resolve the issue there. At PaaS level, data portability depends on the database technologies used by two service providers. In case of different database technologies, data transformation tools may come handy.

FIG 18.2: When consumer uses cloud services from multiple providers together

Application portability concern appears at PaaS level when same application is to be run on both of the platforms. Consumer then would like to deploy same application codes on both platforms. In that case, both service platforms should have support for the technology by which the application is made of. However, PaaS level application portability concern may also arise even in case of different applications are to run on the platforms but customer wants to maintain those using same technology.

At IaaS level, the application portability concerns are less, since customer gets full freedom (in terms of choice of technology) for building applications over it. Only thing is both of the service providers must provide similar virtual machines.

18.4.2.2 Interoperability Considerations

When both of the services deal with equivalent functionalities, it is likely that same customer components will interact with those services. In that case, both services must have same or interoperable interfaces. Otherwise, customer components will have to be modified to operate with both of the services which is not an ideal situation. But, when two services deal with different functionalities, need of interoperable interfaces decreases depending on their degree of dissimilarity.

18.4.3 Scenario 3: Customer Links One Cloud Service to Another Cloud Service

It is also possible to directly link one cloud service with another. In such scenario, one service uses the other service. Such combination is very effective as different vendors may not provide equivalent capabilities on all of the levels of services. Then, the combination of capable services from different providers delivers more effectiveness.

The scenario can be illustrated using a simple example (represented in Figure 18.3). Let a customer is familiar to work under PaaS facility of provider B. But provider A offers a SaaS facility that fulfills maximum of the customers' business needs. Only few advance functionalities for analyzing data are required. Then the customer has the option of separately developing those remaining necessary functionalities and integrating them with the SaaS. The customer develop

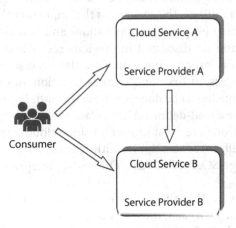

FIG 18.3: When consumer links one cloud service to another cloud service

the additional capabilities by using PaaS service of provider B whereas the newly-developed components can consume data from the SaaS application of A, analyze the data to produce additional statistics and return the result to the SaaS. After integrating these components into the SaaS, the end product is a customized SaaS application running on cloud service A that gets additional statistics from the developed solution over the services of provider B.

18.4.3.1 Portability Considerations

Under this scenario, portability issue does not arise as no entity is effectively being transferred from one cloud service to another.

18.4.3.2 Interoperability Considerations

If first cloud service (service A) is either an IaaS or a PaaS, and the application is developed by the consumer then it is likely that the user has had the full control over the application codes. Thus it becomes easier to utilize the APIs of the second cloud service.

The situation becomes complex when the first cloud service (service A) is a SaaS offering. Then the application is not developed by the customer and to use the APIs of the second cloud service (Service B) the SaaS application must be properly structured. This implementation is generally possible when standardized APIs are used in the applications of both providers and consumers.

Same can be said about the second cloud service. If it is IaaS or PaaS, user will have full control on the APIs to use. If it is SaaS, APIs are directed by the service provider and uses of standardized APIs are essential for interoperability. The use of service-oriented architectural approach in cloud service development eases interoperability issue while integrating services of different cloud vendors.

> *Services developed following SOA paradigm enables interoperability.*

18.4.4 Scenario 4: Customer Links In-house Capabilities with Cloud Services

Capacity of *in-house* computing facilities can be enhanced by linking it with some cloud service. In such scenario, interoperability is the concern as the important thing here is to establish the connections between existing on-premises applications and new cloud deployments. Like any other computing integration (as discussed in previous scenarios), other two aspects as data integration and functionality/process integration are also necessary to deal with in this case.

In the integration process, at first, on-premises functionalities and data will have to be clearly identified. Then same has to be done for the cloud end. For each of these functions and data sources, there must be a well-defined API in place that can be utilized remotely. For SaaS facilities, the API descriptions are most important since cloud part is fully controlled by the provider. The integration effort reduces significantly when both of the on-premises applications and cloud services leverage SOA techniques. Otherwise, integration requires redesigning of applications.

In case of PaaS, the integration effort reduces since the customers tend to control most of the integration requirements. In IaaS, the effort is least as platform services and applications which will run in the cloud service are controlled by the customer.

18.5 MACHINE IMAGING OR VIRTUAL MACHINE IMAGE

The term 'machine image' signifies image of a virtual machine which can be used to launch more instances of that machine. A machine image generally contains an operating system to run the machine, plus common pre-installed applications and tools. Machine image is actually a clone of an entire system contained in a file which can be deployed later. System imaging applications are used to make such images and these can be used to restore a system.

A *machine image* file contains all of necessary software to facilitate the execution or running of intended application. The necessary software stack starts obviously from the operating system and includes other system components. The choice of the OS and the system components largely depend on the type of application or service that the machines run.

18.5.1 Machine Image versus Machine Instance

It is important to understand the difference between the machine image and machine instance. Machine image is like an inactive entity holding template and all of other associated files of a virtual machine from which instances of that machine can be created. Virtual server launched from a machine image is called an *instance* of the image. Any number of machine instances can be launched from one machine image.

Whenever a machine instance is launched from some machine image file, the exact image of the machine (of the moment when the image was created) gets installed onto that new instance's virtual drive and then boots up the instance.

> To draw an analogy with object-oriented programming terminology, machine image can be compared with a class (that contains all the details) whereas the instances are the object instances of that class.

18.5.2 Benefits of Machine Imaging

To use cloud computing of popular vendors, consumers get the opportunity of launching virtual server or machine from pre-configured set of machine images. Consumers can know the specifications and also the cost of running instances from those images. On selection, the deployment is nothing more than the process of starting up a new virtual instance.

Machine imaging technique is very effective in disaster recovery also. If state of a server is stored as an image, then it becomes easier and faster to bring up a server from that backup than to install the stack of software all over again and taking care of all critical configuration issues.

Hence, the two prime benefits of machine images in the cloud computing service are:

- Disciplined deployment and
- Easier disaster recovery

18.5.3 Case Study: Amazon Machine Image

A well-known example of *machine imaging* is the Amazon Machine Image (AMI). AMI is a utility provided by Amazon Web Services to create and store copies of a virtual machine in cloud computing. An AMI is a file system image that contains images of the operating system, all of appropriate device drivers and any applications and state information that a working virtual machine would have.

An Amazon Machine Image (AMI) can be used to instantiate (create) any number of virtual machines within the Amazon Elastic Compute Cloud (EC2). Subscribers of AWS can choose to use from the available list of AMIs provided by Amazon or they can build their own. Many AMIs are available in AWS marketplace too. During creation of an Amazon machine image, it gets encrypted and is stored in Amazon S3.

18.5.4 Case Study: Azure Virtual Machine Image

Virtual machine image in Microsoft Azure cloud is called as *VM image*. A VM image includes the image of operating system as well as the images of all of the disks attached to a virtual machine while creating the image. Azure also offers a gallery of images which can be used to instantiate new virtual machines.

Azure provides an option called as 'Capture' to create new VM image from any machine instance. Clone image of any virtual machine can be created by this 'Capture' option. On creation, the image file is stored as a VHD (Virtual Hard Disk) in user's storage account by default which can later be used to launch new machine instances.

18.6 VIRTUAL APPLIANCE

A *virtual appliance* (VA) is a pre-integrated, self-contained system consisting of a pre-configured Just enough Operating System (JeOS) environment and a single application. The purpose of a virtual appliance is to simplify the delivery and deployment of an application. JeOS refers to a customized operating system that fulfills the needs of a particular application.

In comparison with traditional hardware-based appliance, virtual appliance is a type of software appliance. Most interestingly, it runs on virtual resources or over virtualized environment, instead of physical resources. Virtual appliances are not complete virtual machines, rather pre-configured machine images with minimal stack of software containing necessary components to run one or more applications, but generally it hosts single application.

A software appliance is a software application combined with a JeOS for it to run optimally on a standard physical machine. There are two types of software appliances as *Virtual appliance* and *Live CD appliance*.

JeOS is not a generic, one-size-fits-all type operating system. It includes the minimal part of an operating system required to support the application(s) it hosts. However, it is understandable that virtual appliances are larger than the application themselves as they are bundled with the JeOS on which they are meant to run.

> *Virtual software appliance eliminates the trouble of installing and configuring complex stack of software to run an application.*

18.6.1 Benefits of using Virtual Appliance

Packaged solutions as virtual appliance are very useful as it provides ready-to-use applications. The benefits of virtual appliances are listed below.

- **Simplified deployment:** A virtual appliance encapsulates an application's dependencies in a pre-integrated and self-contained unit. This simplifies application deployment by reducing the tensions of the users about resolving complex compatibility issues.
- **Less volume:** Compared to the total volume of software required to install to run any general application in virtualized environment, the virtual appliance is smaller in size.
- **More security:** Each virtual appliance is typically used to run a single application in isolation. This makes it more secured than running multiple applications under a full general-purpose OS, due to less possibility of undesirable interactions with other applications.

> Virtual appliance is smaller in size, simple to deploy and more secured to use than installing and configuring the same application separately in a fully-configured virtual server.

18.6.2 More into Virtual Appliance

A virtual appliance is actually a container generally for a single application and all of its dependencies, like operating system, runtime, third-party libraries, databases, configuration etc. The virtual appliance container is a type of *VM image* (VMI). In cloud computing paradigm, virtual appliance falls under the Software-as-a-Service (SaaS) category.

There are two types of virtual appliances as closed and open. A *closed virtual appliance* (closed VA) is packaged as a sealed unit. An *open virtual appliance* (open VA) provides the scope of modifications to customers. The developers of such appliances provide an interface for configurations or updates.

> Virtual appliance is a software appliance that installs onto an empty virtual machine.

18.7 DIFFERENCE BETWEEN VIRTUAL MACHINE IMAGE AND VIRTUAL APPLIANCE

Virtual machine image contains the entire image of a virtual system at some instance. It contains the total image of the machine's operating system and integrates images of any other software installed over it.

A *virtual appliance*, on the other hand, is one type of pre-configured virtual machine image, ready to run on a hypervisor. Its primary goal is to run a software application on virtual environment. It is not a complete virtual machine image; rather it contains the minimal required parts of the OS (known as JeOS) and other associated software, along with the application itself so that the application can be executed when the appliance is installed on an empty virtual machine space.

> Both virtual machine image and virtual appliance are installed over empty virtual machine.

Table 18.1   Comparison between Virtual Machine Image and Virtual Appliance

Virtual Machine Image	Virtual Appliance
It contains full image of operating system.	It contains the minimal required part of the OS which is known as just-enough OS.
It may or may not contain any application.	It always contains an application and its dependencies.
It may contain more than one application installed over the OS.	It generally contains only one application installed with per OS image.
Here the primary objective is to launch machine instances over virtual infrastructure.	Here the primary objective is to launch application over virtual infrastructure.
In this image, other software applications can be installed over machine instances created from virtual machine images.	In this image, nothing can be installed over a deployed virtual appliance.
It is the image of a virtual machine stored in archived format as captured at some instance.	Here, it is a type of virtual machine image in customized (and reduced) form.

18.7.1 Issue of Cross-Platform Compatibility

The virtual appliance marketplace can be compared with the apps that mobile stores supply for cell phones. Many mobile apps are available in on-line marketplaces which allow the exchange of ready-made applications. Such marketplace is also there for virtual appliances. Most popular among them is the VMware virtual appliance marketplace.

But there is a compatibility issue. VMware's appliances can run on its own hypervisors or on partner public clouds. Similarly, many other vendors' virtual appliances are made to be run on some other hypervisors. Different formats are used by Citrix's Xen, Microsoft's Hyper-V, VMware's ESXi and Linux based KVM.

> A compatibility issue arises for virtual appliances due to dissimilar formats of the hypervisors.

However, the problem exists as the virtual appliance (or any archived virtual machine instances) which is built on one type of hypervisor will not run on other types of hypervisors. Hence, the virtual appliances are not interoperable in general. To solve this problem, all of the hypervisors (or rather the owners of hypervisors) agreed upon a common format for archiving virtual systems that is Open Virtualization Format (OVF). This enables one vendor's appliance to operate on any hypervisors. Under this mechanism, hypervisors may operate on OVF in two modes as direct support for OVF and by converting the OVF to the product's native format.

Thus, Open Virtualization Format (OVF) has become an *open standard* for packaging and distributing virtual systems as understood by any IaaS offerings. The format has been recognized by International Organization for Standardization (ISO) also. Any individual or computing vendor can develop and distribute virtual appliances as OVF package to publish some virtualized software solutions.

> OVF promotes virtual appliances' portability. It is not tied to any particular hypervisor and is recognized by ISO as common format for archiving virtual appliances.

18.8 OPEN VIRTUALIZATION FORMAT (OVF)

Open Virtualization Format (OVF) is a packaging standard developed by the DMTF as discussed earlier which provides standard packaging format for software solutions based on virtual systems. OVF is designed to resolve the portability issue of packaged virtual systems (like virtual machine images or virtual appliances). Its common packaging format enables cross-platform portability of such systems.

The virtualization standardization initiative led by DMTF is known as the Virtualization Management Initiative (VMAN) project. OVF is result of this initiative and major companies in the field, like Dell, HP, IBM, Microsoft, XenSource, VMware and others have joined forces to make it happen. Immediately after the introduction of OVF specification in February 2009, the hypervisor vendors announced and introduced support for OVF. DMTF is an organization devoted in the development and promotion of interoperable management standards for computing/IT environments. It has numerous member companies and organizations representing varied industries across the globe. The organization was founded during early 1990s with headquarter in United States.

Virtual machine images or virtual appliances can be deployed easily with pre-built configuration using OVF meta-data and can be customized during installation. Sometimes, the multiple virtual machines' images are packaged as one virtual appliance for easy deployment.

With the maturity of cloud computing, clients and consumers have started to prefer to interact with services from different providers. So, OVF has fueled the delivery of applications over cloud computing. OVF standard is now used for packaging applications for cloud platform. The power behind virtual appliances lies in the ability to freely share them among different hypervisors.

> *DMTF, the developer of OVF, is an organization devoted to the development and promotion of interoperable management standards for computing environments.*

18.8.1 OVF Package Details

An *OVF package* consists of one file or set of files into a directory. The directory contains a descriptor file in XML (Extensible Markup Language) format which is called as *OVF descriptor* containing metadata for the OVF package and one or more virtual disk files. The OVF descriptor contains the specifications of the virtual hardware requirements and corresponding references to other virtual disk images in the package. The OVF package also contains operating system details, startup/shutdown actions and other data containing product and licensing information.

From the file system perspective, OVF is not just a single file. It is a collection of files representing everything from virtual machine metadata, virtual disks, certificates etc. These files can be encrypted, digitally signed, compressed and archived.

18.8.2 How OVF Package is Delivered

Appliances in OVF format is generally supplied in two ways as a package of several files or all archived together in a single file. The files of OVF package comes with different extensions.

The textual XML descriptor file comes with .ovf extension. The virtual disk image files may come in various formats like VDI, VMDK, VHD, HDD, QED or QCOW from various vendors. Following list displays the disk image file formats of different vendors:

- VMware's VMDK (Virtual Machine Disk),
- Oracle VirtualBox's VDI (VirtualBox Disk Image),
- Microsoft's VHD (Virtual Hard Disk),
- Parallels' HDD (Hard Disk),
- QED (QEMU enhanced disk) and
- QCOW (QEMU Copy-On-Write).

When supplied as a package, virtual appliance contains the .ovf files and disk image files in some formats and other necessary files. Alternatively, all of the files of OVF packages are packed together in one and as the single OVA (Open Virtualization Appliance) file may be supplied as archive file typically with an .ova extension.

> *Virtual appliances are supplied in two ways. Either, as a package (containing .ovf and other files) or all files archived into a single .ova file.*

SUMMARY

- ❖ Unlike traditional computing, cloud computing shows great promises towards addressing the issues of portability and interoperability.

- ❖ The pay-per-use model of cloud computing opens up the option of moving from one cloud service to another without tensions about previous capital investments. Only thing that is required for such movement is the portability of components which have been developed and used over the period.

- ❖ Interoperability issue comes next as components of two different cloud environments must recognize and operate with each other to get the benefit of cloud services of different providers.

- ❖ Portability and interoperability needs are not similar at different layers of cloud services. Hence they have to be addressed separately.

- ❖ Porting of one vendor's software system or data to some other vendor's cloud environment is a critical issue that vendors are working upon to resolve. Use of some common and standard set of API and data formats across various cloud platforms may resolve this problem.

- ❖ Machine imaging is a technique to capture a virtual machine's current state, with all applications and data, which is used to create a replica of that machine later.

- ❖ Machine imaging technique helps in quicker deployment of virtual systems. The biggest benefit of machine imaging technique becomes evident during disaster recovery.

- ❖ A virtual appliance is a kind of machine image normally created for a single application. It is a self-sufficient system that contains all the dependencies to run an application including minimal required components of the operating system.

❖ Virtual appliance does not need any pre-configured virtual machine, rather it can be directly installed on any virtualized environment (that is hypervisor) just like an application.

❖ While virtual appliance is a remarkable idea, its portability over different cloud services has been a matter of concern.

❖ Major software companies have agreed upon a common packaging standard called Open Virtualization Format (OVF), which is used to distribute virtual appliances across different virtualized platforms to overcome the portability issue.

REVIEW QUESTIONS

Why is the cloud computing community so concerned about portability issue?

As cloud computing services are gaining popularity, an obvious concern for technologists as well as the consumers is the vendor lock-in problem. Services of one cloud vendor cannot run on other cloud environments. The problem arises when someone develops a critical application that locks him to a particular vendor. Cloud computing can have significant economic benefits but if cloud service consumers need to depend on the mercy of a vendor's facilities and pricing strategy, that may become a concern.

Are the portability and interoperability problems new in cloud?

Portability and interoperability problems are nothing new to cloud computing. They were very much in traditional computing environment. For example, an application developed for Windows environment may not run in Mac or Unix environment. Java platform provides a solution towards portability through java virtual machine (JVM) in traditional computing by generating machine (hardware) independent application codes. Otherwise, the portability and interoperability issues were received less attention in traditional computing.

How is cloud computing going to benefit from the open format of virtualization?

In cloud computing, consumers ultimately use virtualized computing resources. Hypervisor is an integral part of virtualization. Different cloud vendors use different hypervisors. For example, Amazon uses Zen hypervisor whereas Google uses KVM. Appliance of one cloud vendor will only run on other vendor's cloud service when there is some open format of virtualization which all of the vendors adhere to. Open virtualization format is outcome of one such effort.

Why will anyone move to cloud if such portability and interoperability issues exist?

As we know that the traditional computing did not provide any solution to these issues. Apart from offering various new age benefits, cloud computing has created scope for greater flexibility and business collaboration. Thus the necessity of application portability and interoperability are being felt. Technologists and cloud vendors are not only trying to resolve the portability issue in cloud computing staying limited to the application area, they are also trying to build portable platform environment. This will make the technology more attractive and flexible for consumers.

Does the Installation of an application on a virtual machine create a virtual appliance?

No. Installation of software application on virtual machine does not create a virtual appliance. Virtual appliance itself is a complete solution which combines just enough operating system (JeOS), other dependencies and the application together. Such appliances are self-sufficient and can be installed on virtualized environment independently.

Can a virtual appliance include two or more applications?

Ideally each virtual appliance is made for a single application. This is because virtual appliances are nothing but self-sufficient pre-configured solution for installing and running applications in virtualized environments by users. So, in order to use some application generally a user will search for the corresponding virtual appliance. But, there is no restriction in combining two or more applications in one virtual appliance.

Can a machine image be called a virtual appliance?

The term 'appliance' in 'virtual appliance' generally represents some applications. In the making of virtual appliance, it packs the application into a self-contained package containing the minimal OS and other dependencies to run the application on virtualized environment independently. Machine imaging captures a particular state of a virtual machine. It contains the full operating system (unlike JeOS in virtual appliance) and may or may not include any applications. While in virtual appliance the one and only focus is the application (and how to make it functional), machine image rather focuses on to hold the full state of a virtual machine.

Why is OVF important for independent software vendors?

OVF is a common packaging format to distribute virtual appliances. Independent software vendors (ISVs) who develop virtual appliances do not want to make their product as vendor-locked. They market their solutions with the hope to make their appliances popular among consumers of various (vendors') cloud services. OVF provides them the scope to distribute their applications in such a way that it can be installed on many virtualized environments or on cloud infrastructure of different vendors.

MULTIPLE CHOICE QUESTIONS

1. Portability enables the components to
   a) Communicate with other components
   b) Move in other environments
   c) Become light weight
   d) None of these

2. The interoperability is not applicable on which of the following?
   a) Application
   b) Application platform
   c) Data
   d) None of these

3. Portability and interoperability can be achieved by standardizing the format(s) of
   a) APIs
   b) Data
   c) Communication protocols
   d) All of these

4. Tell if the statement is 'true' or 'false'.
   'IaaS stores raw data files. Portability is not applicable on the IaaS level data.'
   a) True
   b) False

5. Machine imaging helps in

   a) Hardening security of VM

   b) recovering easier disaster Deploying of VM easily

   c) Both a and b

6. JeOS is a part of

   a) Virtual appliance

   b) Machine image

   c) Both a and b

   d) None of these

7. Virtual appliance is one kind of software appliance. This statement is

   a) True

   b) False

8. Virtual appliances are useful because they provide

   a) More security

   b) Ease of installation

   c) Liberty from complex configuration

   d) All of these

9. Each virtual appliance is generally made to distribute

   a) One single application

   b) At least two applications

   c) Any number of applications

   d) None of these

10. Virtual appliances are distributed in which of these common packaging formats?

    a) Open virtual format

    b) Open volatile format

    c) Open virtualization format

    d) None of these

11. OVF descriptor that contains metadata related to the OVF package is a

    a) UVI file

    b) XML file

    c) VMDK file

    d) HTML file

12. Formats of virtual disk images created by different machine virtualization vendors are

    a) Same

    b) Different

13. Which server virtualization vendor uses VMDK as format for capturing virtual disk images?

    a) Oracle

    b) Microsoft

    c) Google

    d) VMware

14. The OVA (Open Virtualization Appliance) format for supplying OVF package in a single archive file is a

    a) Zip file

    b) Tar file

    c) Rar file

    d) Zipx file

15. Use of some standard and common APIs by all cloud service vendors will increase

    a) Application portability

    b) Application standard

    c) Cost benefits of business

    d) All of these

16. The development of Open-source Simple Cloud API to improve portability of cloud applications was an initiative taken by

    a) Rackspace

    b) Distributed Management Task Force (DMTF)

    c) Cloud Security Alliance

    d) Zend Technologies

17. The Simple Cloud API was developed to improve portability

    a) PHP applications
    b) Java applications
    c) Cloud applications
    d) All applications

18. Bundling virtual appliance in OVF package format helps

    a) To harden the security of VM
    b) To increase application portability
    c) To increase portability of platform
    d) To market them easily

19. Which among the following organizations works towards promotion of interoperable standards for cloud applications?

    a) VMware
    b) Distributed Management Task Force (DMTF)
    c) Citrix
    d) Cloud Security Alliance

20. The data, application or platform portability problems faced in cloud environment.

    a) It was not there in traditional environment
    b) It is an unique problem for cloud
    c) It was there in traditional environment also
    d) The platform portability problem is new to cloud.

19 Cloud Management and a Programming Model Case Study

Cloud computing does not imply any single technology. In short, a combination of multiple methodologies defines its architecture. The management of various aspects associated with this computing facility thus becomes very important case for successful outcome during its real-life implementations. Be it business delivery, or technical foundation of system development, the 'service' takes center stage in cloud computing. Consequently, cloud service management has become another important issue to be discussed in a new context.

Most management activities in cloud are automated and SLA-driven. The service level agreement (SLA) thus plays an important role in the success of cloud computing. This chapter represents the lifecycle of SLA, apart from discussing the lifecycle of cloud service. Cloud management standards, tools and responsibilities of providers and consumers have also been discussed.

This chapter also focuses on various programming models which are implemented on cloud. For this purpose a case study is represented with Aneka cloud platform which has a special feature of supporting multiple programming models. In this context, the chapter tries to revisit the cloud computing architecture once more and represents its design characteristics and few non-functional features as well from different angles.

19.1 CLOUD ARCHITECTURE: REVISITED

In very broad sense, the cloud computing system can be viewed as composition of two elements:

- *Client application* at the front end
- The *cloud* as the back end.

This is a very simple description as the backend comprises of several layers and abstractions. In most cases, the 'client application' at the *frontend* is a web browser through which cloud service interfaces (i.e. the portals) are accessed. Consumers can access the backend 'cloud' from any simple electronic device capable of running web browsers. Only prerequisite is the availability of network or Internet service. Quality of cloud service accessibility often depends on the speed of the network. But with advancements in the field of internet technology, speed is the least worrying factor nowadays.

At the *backend*, the 'cloud' resides at some remote location generally being managed by some service providers. Reputed providers develop cloud service infrastructure at their own data centers. A provider can have multiple data centers at different geographic locations. As shown in Figure 19.1, this backend part can be seen as composition of two broad components: a cloud building platform and the cloud services. Cloud computing services (which attract the

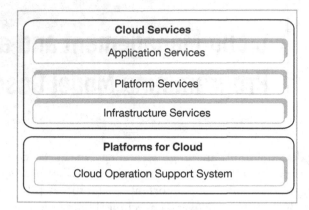

FIG 19.1: An architectural model of cloud computing

maximum interest of learners of this subject) are built over a stage that can be called as the platform for cloud. This platform provides the supporting system for cloud operations.

The *platform for cloud* computing operations is generally built over large distributed homogeneous/heterogeneous computing environments. This underlying layer provides the support system on which different cloud computing facilities are developed to be delivered over internetwork/Internet. Apart from computing devices, this layer (the platform for cloud) also includes supporting facilities like the power supply system, cooling system, physical security of infrastructure and others. The host operating system (operating system that activates the physical systems at data centers) and hypervisors stay at the top of this layer.

Cloud service layer mainly comprises of three categories of computing services as infrastructure service, platform service and application service. Among three of these, the infrastructure service is most interesting. Although, at data centers cloud infrastructure services are built using actual physical computing resources, consumers get access to these resources in virtual form through IaaS facility.

> *Cloud architectures at data center can be portrayed as a combination of two layers: 1) the underlying infrastructure for cloud service development, and 2) the layers of services developed over the infrastructure.*

19.2 REVIEWING DESIGN CHARACTERISTICS

The power of cloud computing system is often considered the outcome of combination of *dynamic-elastic infrastructure* and *flexible-composable application architecture*. In a sense, the application part gathers its strength from the dynamic nature of underlying computing infrastructure.

The dynamic infrastructure is built by the systematic application of techniques like resource pooling, resource sharing, resource virtualization, dynamic resource provisioning and load balancing. Flexible system design helps to easily incorporate horizontal scaling into the system which is a major strength of cloud computing system. Scalable system resources provide the elasticity to the system. Among all techniques mentioned here, resource virtualization has

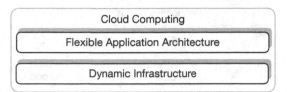

FIG 19.2: Cloud Design Characteristics

brought a revolution in computing and it plays a vital role in the making of the dynamic nature of cloud system.

The application architecture of cloud system being built over the dynamic infrastructure, has introduced flexibility by adhering service orientation standards. The usage of service oriented architecture (SOA) principles in application development facilitates two most important features of system design: *loose coupling* among the components and *composability*. Loose coupling makes the applications flexible and it becomes easier to incorporate changes, like converting functional or business requirements with time. On the other hand, *composable service components* can be put together in order to easily develop any business functionality. As these services are replaceable and reusable, they can provide immense flexibility to an application.

> Cloud computing infrastructure is dynamic and elastic in nature. Cloud application architecture is flexible and composable.

19.3 CLOUD COMPUTING IN A NUTSHELL

Cloud computing basically provides three unique deployment options namely the private, public and hybrid deployments. A fourth deployment option is also available as an extension of private deployment, namely community deployment. At service delivery end, it has three categories as IaaS, PaaS and SaaS. Any other specialized service delivered by cloud providers must have to be a part of one of these three services. Each of these three deployments is capable of delivering all of the categories of cloud services. The scenario has been demonstrated distinctly in Figure 19.3.

As shown in Figure 19.3, the level of abstraction intensifies as one moves upwards along the service levels. At SaaS level, the degree of abstraction is the highest and almost everything remains transparent to consumers (as they need not have any technical knowledge of the underlying system). It is quite understandable that the *flexibility of purpose* is inversely associated with the *level of abstraction*. At IaaS level, the consumers get full freedom (flexibility of purpose) for choosing and composing the system to meet their purposes. Moving upwards along the service levels, the options keep reducing due to choices opted for in underlying layers.

> Cloud consumers' flexibility of purpose fulfillment decreases as one moves upwards along the layers of service abstraction.

Among the deployment models, the public cloud deployment is the most economical for consumers. Public cloud facility generally hosts a large numbers of consumers and sharing (as well as multi-tenancy) of resources among them makes the service offering possible at cheaper rates.

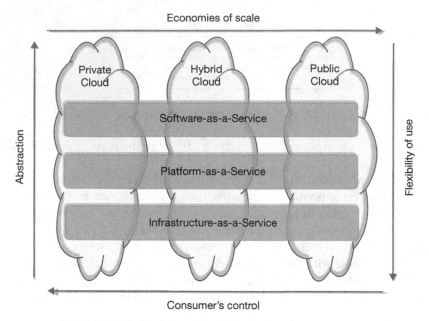

FIG 19.3: A single window view of cloud computing environment

Any enterprise can maintain its own private cloud deployment for security purpose, but it may become expensive on several occasions, or the procured or reserved resources may remain idle on other occasions. Hybrid cloud provides a middle path in such situations, where enterprises can maintain a smaller private cloud to store the core or essential parts of their applications as well as data and expand into the public cloud facility when the demand grows.

Consumers have very little to do in the governance of the public cloud. Almost everything is controlled by the service providers. The governance option maximizes in private cloud deployment models for customers. There they can decide and control different attributes of services. Ultimately, the *governance* option is inversely associated *economies of scale*. This is justified as the cost of cloud computing increases for consumers with degrees of ownership and controls over cloud resources.

> *The cost of cloud is directly-related with consumers' control over the cloud environment.*

19.4 MIGRATION INTO CLOUD

There can be business needs as well as technological reasons behind the migration into cloud computing. Consumers may choose to migrate their in-houses or outsourcing (non-cloud computing) facilities into cloud. Migration may happen at various levels of computing and depending on them the migration into cloud can be done in IaaS, PaaS or SaaS offerings. Among them, generally the migration of traditional application into SaaS is the most common and important concern for enterprises.

The application migration can happen in various forms. First, the entire application may be imported to cloud in its original form. Second, some minor changes may have to be incorporated in the code of an application in order to make it adaptable before migrating into cloud. Third, the application may require re-designing and re-implementation. Thus, it may need re-coding of the application again from the scratch. And finally, the whole architecture may require changing. Besides these, for any form of application migration, all of its usages have to be migrated into the cloud which will in turn need suitable adaptations and modifications. In brief, the migration of an application from non-cloud environment into cloud can happen in one of the five above mentioned forms: application, code, design, architecture and usage.

19.4.1 Phases of Migration

Migration into cloud must follow a structured and integrated approach. Technologists have recommended a few sequential phases for migrating the applications to cloud. The seven phases have been identified in this process are mentioned below:

1. Assessment: The first step in assessment is the study on return on investment (ROI). Complexity of migration is another matter for consideration here. The assessment may involve with some issues at the application, code, design and architecture level.
2. Isolation: Traditional applications must be isolated from their environmental (that is the computing system environment) dependencies.
3. Mapping: Features are identified to be moved into cloud and those need to be retained as in earlier environments.
4. Rebuilding: The part which moves into cloud may need to be re-coded, re-designed or re-created as per the requirements.
5. Augmentation: This feature in cloud computing service (contrary to non-cloud system) is used to increase the efficiency and capacity of the applications.
6. Testing: Testing of the new form of the application is carried out before moving it into the cloud.
7. Optimization: Depending on the result of testing, some optimizations may be needed. This phase may go in an iterative way as long as the migration is successful.

A well planned migration into cloud provides significant advantages and opens up doors for new opportunities. It cuts down *capital expenses* (Capex) for computation and also reduces *operational expenses* (Opex).

19.5 ASSET MANAGEMENT IN CLOUD

Cloud computing has made the asset management task very simple for the consumers of computing. The task of managing computing assets has mostly been transferred to the service provider's end. Organizations can meet the growing needs of their businesses more readily being empowered by the agile nature of cloud computing.

Capacity expansion or provisioning is no more a tension for the consumers as any type of computing asset procurement is possible through a few clicks. Any reputed cloud system enables the consumers to very easily keep a track on the type, volume and cost of acquired computing assets. This saves a great deal of time, effort and helps to make up-to-the-moment data available round the clock.

19.6 CLOUD SERVICE MANAGEMENT

NIST documents on cloud computing classifies the cloud service management related functionalities into three parts: 1) *business support,* 2) *provisioning and configuration* and 3) *portability and interoperability.* Figure 19.4 represents the entire idea in detail.

In business support, issues like establishing contracts with customers, determining pricing rules, accounting and billing, are generally addressed. Provisioning and configuration category addresses the issues of cloud service requirements like resource arrangement, metering and SLA management. The third category of cloud service management activities deals with portability of data and system, as well as the interoperability of services. From Figure 19.4, it can be noticed that the service interoperability can be achieved through implementation of unified management interfaces.

> NIST has classified the cloud service management activities into three categories.

19.6.1 Business Support

Business Support functionalities of cloud service managements take care of the business-related service dealings with the clients. These include the following client-facing business operations:

1. *Customer management:* This includes activities like opening and closing customer accounts, providing points-of-contact to each customer, administration of user profiles and resolving customer issues and problems and so on.

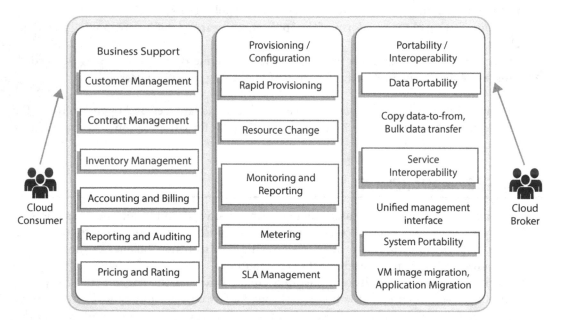

FIG 19.4: Three perspectives of cloud service management[8]

2. *Contract management*: Managing service contracts with customers may include the negotiation, initiation and termination of the contracts.

3. *Inventory Management*: This works to register the service or deals with the *service catalog management* where all the service providers are listed.

4. *Accounting and Billing*: Activities that come under this head are related to the management of customers' billing, like preparing and sending billing statements, processing received payments, tracking invoices and so on.

5. *Reporting and Auditing*: Auditing user operations and generating necessary reports also plays a part in business support activities.

6. *Pricing and Rating*: Activities under this head include determining the pricing of different cloud services after proper analysis, rating customers and plotting pricing rules based on customer's profile and so forth.

19.6.2 Provisioning and Configuration

Provisioning and configuration activities can be considered the core of all cloud service management activities by the providers. Activities like SLA management and/or metering of services also fall in this section.

1. *Rapid provisioning*: This activity takes care of the automatic and rapid deployment of cloud systems depending on the consumer's request.

2. *Resource changing*: This happens when replacement of existing physical resource component is required for repairing or up-gradation. Necessary adjustments in the configuration are also required when physical nodes are introduced into the cloud.

3. *Monitoring and Reporting*: This activity includes the monitoring of cloud operations, monitoring virtual resources and generating reports about the system performance.

4. *Metering*: Metering is one of the basic attributes of cloud computing. Metering of different types of resources (like storage, bandwidth, processing etc.) at different levels of cloud services are managed under this head.

5. *SLA management*: This takes care of different aspects of SLA contract made between the providers and consumers like its definitions, continuous monitoring on the feasibility of the agreements and ensuring the enforcement of SLAs according to defined policies.

19.6.3 Portability and Interoperability

Portability and interoperability issues are big concerns for customers moving into the cloud environment. The requirements related with portability and interoperability vary with different cloud service models. Hence, the management of these operations need special attention and expertise, as the cloud computing world has not progressed much in the resolution of portability and interoperability issues.

Portability is related with data, application and platform in order to move entities from one cloud service to another. Interoperability becomes a necessity while the consumers try to establish connection between applications of two different cloud services. Currently a section of the cloud computing developers' community is working to resolve the portability and interoperability issues through the methods of standardizations. But this needs participation from all concerned sections.

19.7 CLOUD MANAGEMENT TOOLS

Use of an appropriate cloud management tool can enhance different performance attributes like effectiveness, security or flexibility in a cloud computing environment. Computing vendors are developing administration and management tools designed for the efficient operation and delivery of cloud services.

The age-old network management solutions had their focus on vital system attributes like Fault, Configuration, Accounting, Performance and Security. These attributes are often expressed with the acronym 'FCAPS'. The attributes of network management solutions remain relevant in cloud management systems as well. Solutions are generally developed to address one or more of these areas together. Cloud management operations include the following activities:

- Resource configuration,
- Resource provisioning,
- Policy management,
- Performance monitoring,
- Cost monitoring,
- Performance optimization, and
- Security management.

Service vendors generally have their own *cloud management solutions* through which they administrate their cloud from the data centers. Many of the vendors who were involved in developing network management products over the years have turned their focus towards securing and managing the cloud environment. Cloud vendors along with these companies offer a wide variety of cloud management solutions to consumers. Each of these solutions focuses on a different set of cloud features and has its unique strength. For instance, VMware's vRealize Business is a resource utilization and cost monitoring tool. Dell Cloud Manager helps to enhance the agility and governance over cloud.

Thus, there is no single 'best solution' that consumers can use for managing their clouds. Rather, the choice of the 'best fit' cloud management tool should depend upon the requirements of business. But, consumers would face trouble when such solutions indicate the vendor specific properties. Various initiatives have come up to develop vendor neutral cloud management solutions. Use of open standard interfaces is a way to solve the problem.

There are several vendor neutral solutions available in the market. Dell Cloud Manager is one such solution that is offered as SaaS to manage cloud infrastructure including the provisioning, management and automation of applications and can also be deployed as on-premises software to control any types of cloud deployments. It can work with multiple public clouds including AWS, VMware and Microsoft Azure and can even manage open-source environments such as OpenStack. VMware's vRealize Business tool can be used with various public, private and hybrid clouds. The Cloudyn is another solution which is customized for AWS, Microsoft Azure, Google and OpenStack deployments. Other notable cloud management solutions are offered by BMC Software, CA Technologies, IBM, HP, Red Hat and other renowned names as well.

Vendor-neutral cloud management solutions can be used to manage various public, private and hybrid clouds.

19.8 CLOUD MANAGEMENT STANDARDS

Different service providers develop cloud services using different technologies to provide desired flexibility and performance. Management of such clouds with common tools was not possible without a common cloud management standard. It was realized soon and various initiatives had been taken for development of such standards to address known challenges of cloud management. Meanwhile, the Distributed Management Task Force (DMTF) came up with the standards which alleviated the tasks of the cloud managements.

The Cloud Management Working Group of DMTF was engaged to create a model to standardize the operations of the cloud service lifecycle. To simplify the process of cloud system management, DMTF introduced an open-standard interface specification known as 'Cloud Infrastructure Management Interface (CIMI)' happened to be applied specifically in the IaaS space.

The objective of CIMI is to standardize the management process of any cloud infrastructure. By eliminating the use of vendor-specific proprietary interfaces for cloud development, it has been possible to develop a common cloud administration or management tool that can be used to manage any cloud infrastructure from any vendor.

CIMI provides standard APIs for managing cloud infrastructure. This enables the development of vendor independent cloud management tools.

DMTF's cloud work also includes the emergence of Open Virtualization Format (OVF) to package and distribute virtual systems over different environments. OVF simplifies the process of machine lifecycle management by providing an open and portable standard for software to run in virtual machines. It has been adopted as American National Standard Institute (ANSI) standard in 2010 and as an international standard by the International Organization for Standardization (ISO) in 2011. The acceptance of OVF as standard for packaging virtual system has promised to simplify the virtual machine lifecycle management.

Other DMTF efforts in cloud computing arena include the contributions from the Software Entitlement Working Group to address the challenges of software license management in cloud systems and virtual environments. These initiatives try to trace and identify licensed software products across different deployments.

19.9 SHARE OF MANAGEMENT RESPONSIBILITIES

The shares of cloud management responsibilities are different for service consumers and service providers at all levels of service delivery. In SaaS model, consumers can access applications through application interface and they (the consumers) have almost no responsibility in

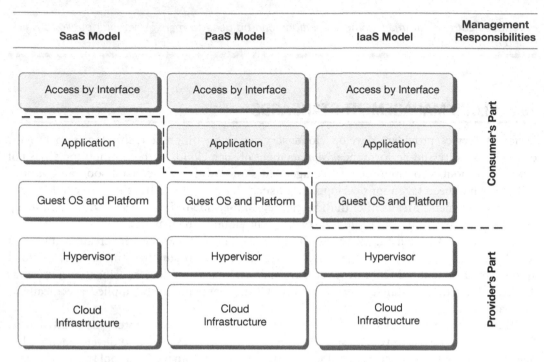

FIG 19.5: Share of responsibilities between service provider and service consumer

managing any part of cloud services. But, responsibilities of managing services are being increased for the consumers as they are going to move towards PaaS and IaaS models. In case of IaaS, consumer's responsibilities of managing services are highest in the cloud service hierarchy.

At SaaS level, the applications are managed by the SaaS providers who are actually PaaS consumers. Service providers manage everything including guest OS, platform and application. Consumers simply access applications generally through web interfaces and have no role to play in cloud service management.

At PaaS level, the service providers manage everything except the end application. In this case, it is the PaaS provider's responsibility (who is also the IaaS consumer) to manage everything up to the PaaS service and takes care of all middleware facilities like web servers, database server, libraries and things like Java virtual machines.

At IaaS level, the consumer's responsibility starts form installing the guest OS from a list of OS supported by the IaaS offering. IaaS provider manages the whole hardware (servers, storage and networks) and takes care of activities related with the layers of the host OS, hypervisor and also manages the system attributes like security, load balancing and so on.

IaaS consumers have the maximum system management responsibilities among all cloud service consumers as they get full control of everything over the cloud infrastructure facility.

19.10 CLOUD SERVICE LIFECYCLE

Lifecycle of cloud services has different stages. A defined lifecycle helps to manage the dynamic nature of the cloud environment. When users or businesses feel the need for some service and ask for it or the service providers identify the requirements for some service themselves that initiates the service lifecycle, as the cloud developers tend to start the development of those services. Different phases of the service lifecycle are shown in Figure 19.6.

■ Phase 1: For creation of services, at first, the service templates are to be defined properly. So, in initial phase, new service templates are created or existing templates are modified or deleted. Service instances are then created from the service templates later (during Phase 3).
■ Phase 2: This phase is about to develop understanding and managing relationship with consumers with reference to a service. This is usually done through an SLA (Service-Level Agreement) contract.
■ Phase 3: In this phase, actual services are created, deleted or modified as per the SLA definition or service contract made in Phase 2. This also includes planning for deployment

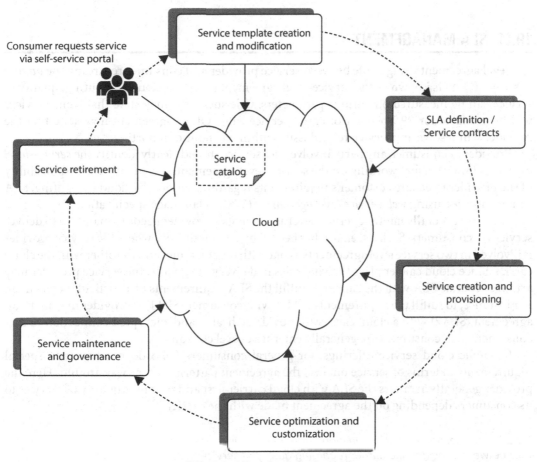

FIG 19.6: Lifecycle of cloud service

of service instances on the cloud and run-time management of those instances which needs resource provisioning (for execution of the services).

- Phase 4: The main job during this phase is to perform service optimization wherever feasible and service customization wherever necessary after studying the service performances. This can be done by modifying values of certain attributes.

- Phase 5: This is a critical phase after creation (i.e. instantiation) of a service. During this phase, resources and components must be kept under close monitoring to avoid violation of any service agreements including security. Managing the operation of instances, routine maintenance, reporting activities and billing functions are also parts of this phase.

- Phase 6: The last phase deals with service retirement issues. Consumers can request for migration of the system or service contract termination. Other issues like, archiving and data protection are also parts of this phase. The retirement phase is very important as the goal of cloud computing is always to lower resource wastage and optimal use of resources.

> The cloud service lifecycle starts with service template creation and ends with the service termination.

19.11 SLA MANAGEMENT

The legal agreement being made between service provider and consumer regarding the *quality of service* (QoS) is known as the service-level agreement (SLA). In cloud computing, quality of service can be measured on various parameters. One such SLA may state that some services will be available for 99.9 percent of entire service time. Other agreement may state that the provider will resolve any service related issue within one hour of reporting.

Provider or consumer, any party involves in a service should clearly identify the *service-level objectives* (SLOs) before working on the service-level agreement. It is mainly the responsibility of the provider to ensure customer's requirements regarding service. In cloud computing, SLA can be modeled using *web-service level agreement* (WSLA) language specification.

There are generally multiple service level agreements a provider needs to maintain to deliver services to consumers. Such a scenario has been shown in Figure 19.7 where the service provider is involved in two service level agreements as one with the consumer and the other with the cloud carrier. Since cloud carrier plays the vital roles in delivery of services, the service provider may arrange separate SLA with the carrier to fulfill the SLA requirements of a particular consumer. For instance, to fulfill the requirements of SLA with consumer (SLA1), a provider may make an agreement (SLA2) with a cloud carrier to provide dedicated and encrypted connection to that consumer. Such consumers are generally enterprise-level consumers.

In public cloud service offerings, for general consumers (who do not have any special requirements in terms of service quality) the agreement pattern is other way around. Here the provider generally arranges the SLA with cloud carrier first and promises quality of services to its consumers depending on the agreement made with the carrier.

> SLA is a legal agreement and in cloud computing, it is made between provider and consumer or between provider and carrier regarding quality of services.

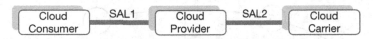

FIG 19.7: Implementation of SLA[9]

19.11.1 Types of SLA

From the perspectives of application hosting by consumers into cloud, SLA can be divided in two parts where one part assures infrastructural service quality and the other does the application.

- Infrastructure SLA and
- Application SLA

Infrastructure SLA deals with infrastructure-related issues like network connectivity, server availability, packet loss issues etc. For example, one Infrastructure SLA statement may state that packet loss will not exceed 1 percent in one calendar month or data center network availability will be at least 99.99 percent of the entire duration in one calendar month.

Application SLA deals with different performance metrics of applications to maintain the desired *quality of services*. It may address issues like latency of web server, latency of database server, application response time and others.

19.11.2 SLA Lifecycle

In the process of establishing and maintaining the agreement on terms and conditions, each SLA passes through a lifecycle consisting of a sequence of phases. Figure 19.8 shows the phases in the lifecycle of SLA which are listed below:

1. *Contract definition*: Service providers define SLAs corresponding to their service offerings by using the standard templates. Customized SLAs for individual customers or enterprises, if required in future, are derived from these base SLA templates.
2. *Publishing and discovery*: The base service offerings of service providers are published and the appropriate promotion is done so that consumers become aware about those services. Consumers must find those services on searching the service catalog along with other competitive offerings. Consumers can then shortlist the most appropriate one and later on, go after further negotiation for any necessary customization with the corresponding provider.
3. *Negotiation*: Once the customer shortlists service and corresponding service provider, the SLA terms and conditions are the next important things to be mutually agreed upon before signing the final service contract. For a standard service offering, this phase is automated. For customizable service offerings, this phase is manual and negotiable. In this case, the consumers should have clear idea about their requirements and service providers must analyze the service needs of the consumers. At the end of this phase, a mutually agreed SLA is prepared and is signed by both parties.
4. *Operationalization*: A SLA in operation may involve three different activities like

   SLA monitoring,
   SLA accounting and
   SLA enforcement.

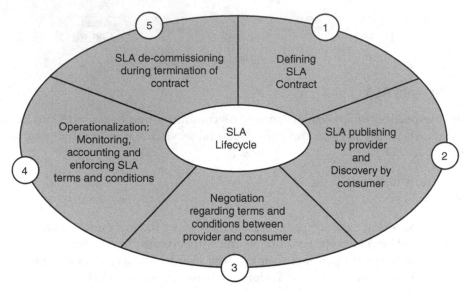

FIG 19.8: SLA lifecycle

SLA monitoring is done by consumer party to measure and monitor performance parameters and determine deviations, if any. In SLA accounting phase, the frequency and duration of deviation is reported to the provider along with the report of penalties to be paid for the SLA violations. SLA enforcement activities involve appropriate actions taken by consumer to ensure no further SLA violations by informing the provider and by claiming penalties, if necessary.

5. *De-commissioning*: Need of this phase appears when relationship between service consumer and service provider is to be terminated. The terms and conditions of any contract termination should be specified in SLA document to make the end of agreement complying all of its legal bindings.

> SLA lifecycle management process passes through five phases.

19.12 DISASTER RECOVERY IN CLOUD

Natural disaster or accidental incidents may cause damage to physical computing resources anytime. Contrary to traditional computing approach, disaster or damages of computing devices at clients' location can no more cause much harm in cloud computing model. Moreover, the planning and protection system of cloud data centers can provide safety in case of disaster as discrete silos are avoided in cloud model and different data centers of a vendor spread over different geographic locations remain well-connected through network.

Disaster recovery planning involves decisions on two key factors: recovery point objective (RPO) and recovery time objective (RTO). The *recovery point objective* determines or refers to the maximum volume of data which can be compromised in case of disaster. Here, the volume is denoted in terms of storage duration like number of hours or days. For instance, if it is decided that data which is already eight hours old cannot be compromised, then there should be a plan to create backup at not more than eight hours' interval.

The *recovery time objective* determines the acceptable system downtime in case of disaster. If this downtime is determined as six hours, then system must have to become operational within six hours after breaking down for any reason.

> Recovery point objective and recovery time objective are two key factors in disaster recovery planning in computing.

19.12.1 Data Recovery Strategies

A disaster recovery plan should meet the desired RPO and RTO needs. Effective disaster recovery mechanism in cloud depends on data backup policy, geographical data redundancy strategy and organizational data redundancy decision.

A. *Backups and data retention*: Recovery of data depends on the quality and frequency of back-ups. Every service provider has their own back-up strategy and back-up file retention policy. Table 19.1 illustrates the categories of data that cloud or any web environment uses to deal with and approaches towards their back-up policies.

   Hence, it is evident that back-up and recovery of persistent data are the main measures in cases of disasters. Persistent data are generally stored in databases and thus database back-up policy and its related solutions play important role in this regard.

B. *Geographic redundancy*: Geographic redundancy of data increases the chances of surviving during disaster. But geographic redundancy requires physical infrastructure setup which may be expensive on the other hand. In cloud computing, this becomes easy as geographic distribution is almost inherent in cloud.

C. *Organizational redundancy*: Natural disaster or accidental damages to data are relatively rare event. But, business disaster is a scenario which can throw even very big organizations

Table 19.1 Data types and their back-up strategies

Type of Data	Description	Back-up Strategies
Fixed data	This is cloud-specific data (like operating system and utility software) and has no connection with clients' transactions.	There is no need to maintain backup for this data.
Transient data	Such data need not survive when system restarts and is stored in caches. Application state does not depend on this data.	There is no need to maintain backup for this data.
Configuration data	It hold system or application specific configurations that need to survive when system restarts.	These Back-ups should be maintained at semi-regular interval.
Persistent data	This type of data is related to day-to-day transactions generated from user application. They change and get updated regularly.	Back up at regular intervals are required for this data.

out of business. If a reputed cloud service provider shuts it cloud computing business, the data stored in it may be at stake. For this unexpected situation, it is a good idea to maintain another set of back-up with some alternative service provider(s).

> *Cloud consumer's planning regarding data backup, geographical data redundancy and organizational data redundancy are the critical factors for recovery of data in case of any disaster.*

19.13 'INTERCLOUD' OR CLOUD FEDERATION

The term 'InterCloud' represents the idea of 'cloud of clouds'. The term was introduced in 2007 to symbolize the data centers of future. The concept was emerged to counter the fact that no cloud has infinite physical resources and when one saturates, requests may be sent to other inter-related clouds for necessary support.

The concept is similar to the way how Internet works. Internet is built over the 'network of internetworks' where traffic from one network/internetwork boundary travels outside its own area to reach the destination. This is done by using appropriate networking protocol. In the same fashion, 'InterCloud' concept states that clouds should interrelate through communication protocol. The protocol implementation must include appropriate node discovery mechanism, fault tolerance and authentication techniques.

InterCloud concept is also known as *federated cloud* or *federation of clouds* or *cloud federation*. Such federations are only possible when clouds share similar architecture and interfaces (APIs). A cloud federation is formed not to enable users to move their applications form one cloud to another; rather it provides flexibility for moving workloads whenever it is needed.

> *InterCloud is the idea of forming a 'cloud of clouds'.*

19.14 CLOUD PROGRAMMING: A CASE STUDY WITH ANEKA

Aneka is an outcome of efforts in the field of distributed and grid computing from the University of Melbourne, Australia. It offers PaaS facility in cloud computing. 'Aneka' is a Sanskrit term meaning 'many in one'. The uniqueness of the solution is its support for multiple programming models like *task programming, thread programming* and *MapReduce programming*. This section discusses these programming models with references to their implementations by Aneka cloud.

Each of the three programming models supported by Aneka has three main elements as 'Executors', 'Schedulers' and 'WorkUnits'. Apart from this there is a 'Manager'. The 'WorkUnit' is a logical entity that defines the size or unit of an executable module that can be handled by Aneka. Figure 19.9 is going to explain the component structure of Aneka execution model.

The 'Scheduler' arranges the execution of work units comprising an application, distributes them to multiple executing nodes ('Executors'), receives the result and sends it to users. The 'Manager' is a client component that communicates with the Aneka system on behalf of the client system.

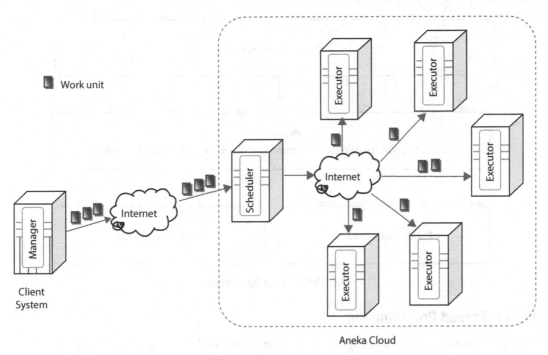

Work unit

Client System

Aneka Cloud

FIG 19.9: Aneka component model

Aneka has been commercialized by Manjrasoft, an Australian company which was formed to commercialize the grid and cloud computing software technologies developed at research lab of University of Melbourne. Manjrasoft first released the beta version of Aneka in 2009.

Aneka, which means 'many-in-one', is named so because it supports multiple programming models like task programming, thread programming and MapReduce programming.

Aneka is built over Microsoft .NET framework and provides run-time and set of API for developing .NET applications over it. Aneka works as a workload management and distribution platform that empowers (speeds up) applications over Microsoft .NET framework environment. Aneka has special ability of being deployed on third-party IaaS as it supports provisioning of resources on public cloud like Amazon EC2, Microsoft Azure, GoGrid and several other private clouds. This helps in building hybrid application with very minimal programming efforts.

Aneka basically comprises two key components:

- Tools for rapid application development and software development kit (SDK) containing application program interfaces (APIs) and
- A run-time engine to manage deployment and execution of applications.

The following section discusses about three programming models supported by Aneka in brief.

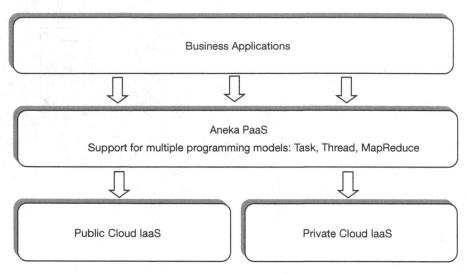

FIG 19.10: Aneka PaaS model

19.14.1 Thread Programming

High performance computation system focuses on delivering better output during computation. High throughput in computation is achieved by allowing concurrency through multi-processing and multi-threading. A process represents a program in execution. In multi-processing, multiple processes are executed in parallel at a single machine. Such system is meant to support multi-tasking. On the other hand, a thread represents a single flow of control within a process. A system supports multi-threading when it can execute different threads in parallel within a process.

19.14.1.1 Multi-threading in Aneka

For high-end requirements, performance of executing multi-threaded applications on a single multi-core system (systems having two or more processing units, known as cores and which is generally attached as a single component) becomes insufficient. In such cases, the distributed execution of application is the only solution. For this purpose, an application can be decomposed into several units.

In Aneka, *multi-thread programming* is implemented over cloud, using *Thread Programming* Model. In this model, threads are treated as distributed threads being known as *Aneka thread*. Aneka threads follow the principle of local threads which can be executed over distributed system architecture. Aneka schedules the executions of threads efficiently while creation and control of the threads is the responsibility of the application developer.

APIs for Aneka thread programming imitate the .NET-based thread class library. Hence it becomes effortless to port .NET-based multi-threaded application on Aneka as the transition between a .NET thread and an Aneka thread is almost transparent. .NET applications need not be fully rewritten to be ported in Aneka platform, rather only a replacement of the class System. Threading.Thread by AnekaApplication does the trick.

In *Aneka Thread* Programming model, the work units are represented as Aneka threads. Programmatically, the concept is implemented by using the template class *AnekaApplication*<AnekaThread and ThreadManager>. The 'AnekaApplication' class type is used for all distributed applications using Thread Programming model in Aneka. A Configuration class also defines the application's interaction with the cloud middleware.

> In Aneka Thread Programming model, an application is treated as a collection of threads called Aneka threads which can be executed remotely over distributed environments.

19.14.2 Task Programming

Thread programming provides parallelism in execution and can run in a single system having a distributed system architecture. Many such programming models are available which tie the power of multiple computing systems together. Task programming model was designed to be executed over clusters and architectural distribution is inherent in it. This programming model provides an attractive solution for executing high-performance distributed applications.

In *task programming* model, any application is considered as collection of tasks which are independent of each other and can be executed in any order. Task is defined by every operating system in its design. All the present-day OSs support multi-tasking activity where multiple tasks can be executed concurrently.

A task is a combination of one or more programs constituting a computing unit of application. The computing unit must represent a component of the application that can be executed independently in isolation. Additionally, an application is a collection of multiple tasks. Task generally takes input files and produces output file(s) as outcomes.

Depending on various characteristics and requirements of applications, task computing can be segregated in two primary categories: High-Performance Computing and High-Throughput Computing. Each category has some specific infrastructural requirements.

High-Performance Computing (HPC) is the use of task programming model for executing applications needing high computing power over a relatively shorter period of time. HPC combines tasks in tightly-coupled manner and hence requires very low latency in network communication to minimize data exchange time. Thus low-latency network is a requirement for HPC model. Traditionally, the clusters are designed to support HPC applications.

High-Throughput Computing (HTC) is the use of task programming model for executing applications which needs the high computing power over a longer period of time. HTC applications generally constitutes of large number of independent tasks which run for long time (for several weeks or months). Such tasks need not to communicate during execution and can be easily scheduled over a distributed system architecture. Traditionally, the computing grids which are composed of heterogeneous resources supports HTC applications very well.

There is another category in task computing called as *Many Task Computing* (MTC) that combines HPC and HTC both. Tasks under MTC model are loosely coupled but communication-intensive. Cloud infrastructural model is most suitable to support MTC.

19.14.2.1 *Task Programming in Aneka*

Aneka task programming model offers the support for developing distributed applications over Aneka platform without any difficulty. Aneka tasks are implemented through APIs which are packed into 'ITask' (Aneka.Tasks.ITask) interface. Tasks created at local nodes can be passed

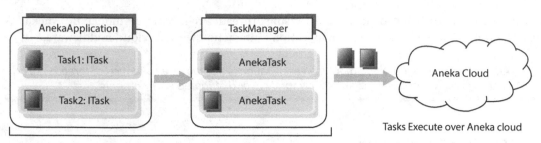

Aneka Tasks created through programming

FIG 19.11: Aneka Task Programming model

over to Aneka cloud where supports for execution of Aneka tasks are implemented. Figure 19.11 describes the scenario.

The 'AnekaApplication' class which is specialized for handling tasks bundles together the tasks created through 'ITask' interface and all of their dependencies (like library and data files). The other client side component 'TaskManager' warps and represents the tasks to the cloud, 'AnekaTask' submits tasks to Aneka cloud, monitors execution and accepts the returned result. In Aneka cloud, there are four services which coordinate the entire task execution activities, namely as 'MembershipCatalogue', 'TaskScheduler', 'ExecutionService', and 'StorageService'. Among these, 'TaskScheduler' schedules the execution of tasks among the resources.

> *Tasks are created by developers using Aneka-supplied interface and classes and then handed over to Aneka cloud for execution.*

19.14.3 MapReduce Programming

Several applications today produce huge volume of data that need to be stored and processed efficiently. This is a challenging task and is known as *data-intensive computing*. In cloud computing environment, data-intensive computing happens in many domains for business analysis or scientific simulation purposes.

MapReduce is a programming model introduced by Google to process large volume of data. It works by representing the computational task using two functions as map and reduce. Underlying storage infrastructure is of distributed nature in this model and data is generally presented as a key-value pair.

The job of 'Map' function is to filter and sort data into queues. For example, name of students can be sorted using their surnames. One queue is maintained for each distinct surname. 'Reduce' function performs summary operation. For example, a summary may show number of students under every different surname. Hence it can be observed that, MapReduce operation takes key-value pair as input and produces lists.

19.14.3.1 *MapReduce Programming in Aneka*

MapReduce operation executes in two phases. First, multiple 'Map' operations run in parallel independently. In second phase, 'Reduce' operations operate on output produced in first phase.

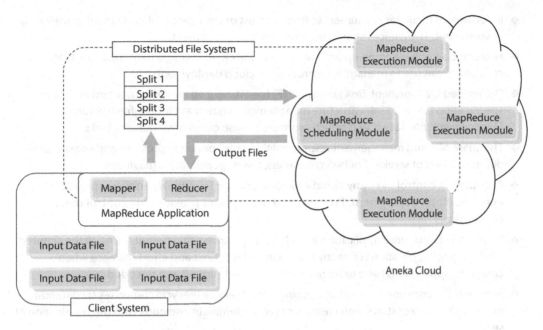

FIG 19.12: Aneka MapReduce Programming Model

MapReduce in Aneka has been implemented following its implementation in Hadoop (a Java-based open-source programming framework). Figure 19.12 represents the model in Aneka.

The *Mapper* and *Reducer* correspond to the class implementations of map and reduce operations respectively. Mapper and Reducer class are extended from Aneka MapReduce API. The run-time implementation comprises of three modules as

- A supporting distributed file system,
- MapReduce Scheduling module and
- MapReduce Execution Module.

Local data files from client's MapReduce application is submitted along with MapReduce job. Thereafter, the process remains transparent and output is returned to client.

> *Aneka PaaS consumers have the options of developing applications following Thread model, Task model or MapReduce model, as Aneka supports all of them.*

SUMMARY

- ❖ Cloud service management activities are classified in three parts by NIST as business support, provisioning-configuration, and portability-interoperability.
- ❖ Vendors offer various cloud management tools for consumers. These tools focus on different aspects of cloud management like resource provisioning, policy management, performance monitoring etc.

❖ It becomes difficult for consumers to find one best or complete tool for managing their cloud environment. The choices should be driven by the requirements.

❖ Few companies have come up with vendor-neutral cloud management solutions that consumers can use to manage infrastructure in cloud deployments.

❖ Distributed Management Task Force (DMTF) has introduced an open-standard interface specification for cloud infrastructure management (known as Cloud Infrastructure Management Interface (CIMI)) which promises to ease cloud management tasks.

❖ The share of cloud management responsibilities varies between provider and consumer at different levels of service. For IaaS consumers, the responsibility is maximum.

❖ Consumer's control over any cloud environment is minimum when they operate in public cloud deployment. Private cloud deployment provides full control to its consumers.

❖ Migration of enterprise application into cloud may happen in different forms. In the simplest form, original application is directly moved into cloud. Cost and effort increase when complete applications have to be re-architected, re-designed and re-coded.

❖ Service is the core unit of cloud computing. Cloud service lifecycle comprises six different phases. The process starts with creation of service template and ends with the termination of services.

❖ The SLAs play an important role in cloud service management. SLAs go through five phases in their lifecycle.

❖ Providers can maintain two types of SLAs with consumers. One is related to infrastructure related issues and the other one concerns the quality of the hosted application.

❖ Programming over any cloud environment is empowered by each cloud's support, with its enriched set of unique functionalities.

❖ Aneka is a PaaS facility that has a special feature for providing support to three different programming models: task programming, thread programming and MapReduce programming.

REVIEW QUESTIONS

How are vendor-neutral cloud infrastructure management solutions possible?

One application can establish communication with other applications through appropriate API calls only. The first application should have knowledge about second applications' APIs so that those can be invoked with their names by passing suitable set of parameters. Since different cloud vendors develop clouds in different technologies and using their own standards, their API specifications vary. Distributed Management Task Force (DMTF) has proposed standard API specification for cloud infrastructure management. When all of the cloud vendors follow this specification, any third party management solution can access them and thus vendor-neutral cloud management solution becomes a reality. Dell Cloud Manager is one such solution that can be used to manage different public cloud deployments.

What is the significance of SLA management in managing cloud services?

SLA clearly defines the requirements of consumers. Service providers can understand consumer's requirements from the specifications in these SLAs. Resource requirements and configuration-related issues to maintain quality of service being delivered to consumers largely depend on the terms of SLAs. Thus, management of the SLA becomes an important part of cloud service management for conflict-free delivery of cloud services. According to NIST description, SLA management is a part of provisioning and configuration management of cloud services.

How does the flexibility of using cloud service decrease as consumers move up along service layers?

At SaaS level, each SaaS delivers one application. For multiple applications, consumers have no other choice but to opt for different corresponding SaaS. A PaaS consumer in such scenario has the liberty of installing multiple supported applications over a platform as one platform can incorporate multiple application run-times. Even, they have the liberty of installing operating system of their choice and run-times (for applications) over the OS. The IaaS consumers remain one step ahead. They can start from selecting an appropriate computing system architecture. Thus, the flexibility of using any cloud service decreases as consumers move upward along the service layers.

How can the 'InterCloud' concept bring a revolution in computing?

Cloud computing has brought revolution but it is yet to reach its goal. In present-day scenario, multiple vendors are offering cloud services being built-in either as proprietary or based on open technology. But those services are not connected with each other. InterCloud or cloud federation concept talks about establishing connection and communication among different cloud services from different providers. The idea is adopted from networking system where network of internetworks built and owned by different vendors eventually build the world wide internet system.

How is the disaster recovery planning associated with recovery point objective?

Keeping apart the disasters, even a small network interruption can cause loss of data on transition. Or storage failure can cause data loss if back-up is not ready. Hence, data becomes safe only when it is ready with well-planned backups. But backup is not created instantly with generation and primary storage of new data. Backup is taken periodically. What transpires if any disaster happens at the middle of such a period? The data generated since the last back-up point gets lost. There is no way of recovering this data.

System designers must take a strategic decision on how much of such data can be compromised in case of disasters. The volume of such data is measured in time. For example, designers of some system may decide that it is permissible to loss one business day's data at the most. In such cases, periodic backup must happen at each twenty-four hours' interval. This fact is known as recovery point objective (RPO) in disaster-recovery planning.

Why low-latency network communication is required for High-Performance Computing?

High-Performance Computing (HPC) facility is built over distributed computing environments. Requirement of such system is to generate very high computing power for a relatively shorter period of time. During such cases of high-performance computing, tasks execute in parallel at distributed computing nodes and maintain direct communication with each other. This needs a high-speed network communication path with very low latency so that computation does not get disrupted due to slow network communication.

MULTIPLE CHOICE QUESTIONS

1. Which of the cloud deployments provides most economical services?

   a) Public cloud

   b) Hybrid cloud

   c) Private cloud

   d) None of these

2. Metering falls under which category of cloud service management?

   a) Business support

   b) Provisioning and configuration

   c) Portability and interoperability

   d) None of these

3. Billing falls under which category of cloud service management?

   a) Business support

   b) Provisioning and configuration

   c) Portability and interoperability

   d) None of these

4. Vendor-neutral cloud infrastructure management tool can be possible through the standardizations of

   a) Cloud services

   b) Cloud providers

   c) Infrastructure management APIs

   d) All of these

5. CIMI-specified standardized APIs are associated with which level of services?

   a) IaaS

   b) PaaS

   c) SaaS

   d) IDaaS

6. Service management responsibility of consumer is least at the layer of

   a) IaaS

   b) PaaS

   c) SaaS

   d) DBaaS

7. The number of phases present in cloud lifecycle management is

   a) 5

   b) 6

   c) 4

   d) 10

8. The number of phases present in SLA lifecycle management is

   a) 3

   b) 4

   c) 5

   d) 6

9. Data backup for recovery in cases of disaster should be maintained for which type(s) of data?

   a) Fixed data

   b) Transient data

   c) Configuration data

   d) Persistent data

10. Which among the following models is not a supported programming model of Aneka cloud?

    a) MapReduce programming

    b) Filter programming

    c) Task programming

    d) Thread programming

CHAPTER 20 | Popular Cloud Services

Computing as a utility service has been a long desired dream in the field of computing. Although the basic idea about cloud computing was introduced many years back, it could not become a reality due to several technological constraints. Later on, technologists succeeded in overcome these technical constraints one after another, and with time computing technology started advancing at a steady pace. The economical and other advantages of cloud computing were visible to everyone including business houses and once all of the required technologies were in place, the computing vendors jumped into the development of cloud services.

In last ten years, many companies have been successful in offering cloud services in different types, sizes and shapes. List of such companies include the major technology vendors like Microsoft, Amazon and Google whose cloud services have gained a major share in the market. These providers along with many other large and middle size vendors and research institutes have developed and offered a number of service plans suitable for both individual consumers and businesses.

Cloud computing is the future of computing in forthcoming years. Cloud services are rapidly gaining more and more appreciation globally and the expansion of cloud service industry is evident. It provides swift availability of enterprise-quality resource and high-performance computing services that can significantly improve business productivity. This chapter focuses on some very popular public cloud services presented by computing majors who also have contributed immensely in the development of IaaS, PaaS and SaaS.

20.1 AMAZON WEB SERVICES

Amazon.com, Inc. is an American electronic-commerce company with headquarters in Washington, United States. The company started as an online bookstore but later expanded its business in different domains. Amazon has emerged as a front-runner among the providers of public cloud services. Among the business domain of different cloud services, Amazon is considered as a market leader in Infrastructure-as-a-Service. The suite of cloud computing services offered by Amazon is known as Amazon web services (AWS).

Amazon Web Services is currently the leading IaaS offering in the market. AWS is offered through the web and has been built strictly based on SOA standards following SOAP, HTTP, REST protocols. It also uses open-source operating system and application servers.

Like other major cloud service providers in the market, Amazon Web Services offer various solutions under the following categories:

- Compute,
- Storage and content delivery,

- Application platform,
- Database, and
- Networking.

Succeeding sections focus on few among the popular services of AWS:

- Elastic Compute Cloud (EC2): To create virtual servers in cloud.
- Simple Storage System (S3) and Elastic Block Store (EBS): Data storage in cloud.
- Elastic Beanstalk: An application development and deployment platform.
- Relational Database Service (RDS), DynamoDB and SimpleDB: For database management.
- CloudFront: Content delivery (CDN) service.

Amazon is a pioneer and market-leader in the area of Infrastructure-as-a-Service (IaaS).

20.1.1 Amazon Elastic Compute Cloud

Amazon Elastic Compute Cloud (EC2) is the main component of Amazon's cloud computing platform. This service provides the facility of launching virtual servers in Amazon cloud. These servers come with the option of different operating systems like Windows and a variety of Linux which runs over Xen hypervisor. Users can launch and manage their own servers with specific configurations as required.

For convenience of users, AWS maintains a collection of machine prototypes which can be used to create virtual servers. It actually stores some standard configurations of virtual machines those are often required in different usage cases. These prototypes are called as *Amazon Machine Image* (AMI) and the virtual servers launched using theses prototypes are called instances of machine images or *Amazon Machine Instances*. So, AMIs can be treated as instance types.

Amazon EC2 uses Xen hypervisor for its virtualization technology.

AMI provides a wide collection of instance types comprising varying combinations of processor, memory, storage and networking capacity. Depending on requirements, customers can choose the most appropriate combination for their applications. The varieties of instance types are classified into several groups depending on their configuration profile and utility. Following are those groups or families of instance types:

- General purpose instance: This set of instance types are made to serve general requirements. These are not for specialized utilities like processor-intensive or memory-intensive applications. It maintains a balance between processor, memory, storage and network resources and comes handy for a lot of common applications including many ERP applications. Instances under this family comes in multiple categories which are made to serve different purposes. Currently there are three categories namely as M3 M4 and T2. M3 and M4 instances are fixed-performance instances whereas T2 instances are burstable performance instances. Burstable Performance Instances maintain a minimum level of processor performance with the ability of bursting above the baseline.
- Compute optimized instance: This family of instance types are suitable for applications that needs high-computing power. These instances create servers with higher power of

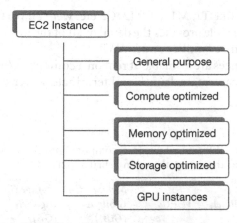

FIG 20.1: AWS VM instance types under pre-defined category

processor compared to memory. Instances under this family come under two categories called as C3 and C4.

- Memory optimized instance: This family of instances is optimized for memory-intensive applications like larger deployments of enterprise applications or high-performance databases. From business perspective, this family of instances provides lowest cost memory. All of memory-optimized instances fall under R3 category.
- Storage optimized instance: This family is optimized for applications with high-storage capacity and I/O performance. It is suitable for data warehousing, Hadoop and NoSQL databases which benefit from very high random I/O performance. Instance types under this family come in two categories as High I/O Instances (I2) and Dense-storage Instances (D2).
- GPU instance: For applications with high-graphical requirements like video streaming or 3D game streaming, the GPU instance family comes handy. Instances under this family are identified by the category called as G2.

> *Amazon Machine Images (AMIs) are pre-configured templates for machine instances from which virtual servers can be created.*

Table 20.1 Present generation instance families and instance types of AWS (as per data gathered in February, 2016)

Instance Family	Instance Types
General purpose	t2.nano | t2.micro | t2.small | t2.medium | t2.large | m3.medium | m3.large | m3.xlarge | m3.2xlarge | m4.large | m4.xlarge | m4.2xlarge
Compute optimized	c3.large | c3.xlarge | c3.2xlarge | c3.4xlarge | c3.8xlarge | c4.large | c4.xlarge | c4.2xlarge | c4.4xlarge | c4.8xlarge
Memory optimized	r3.large | r3.xlarge | r3.2xlarge | r3.4xlarge | r3.8xlarge
Storage optimized	i2.xlarge | i2.2xlarge | i2.4xlarge | i2.8xlarge | d2.xlarge | d2.2xlarge | d2.4xlarge | d2.8xlarge
GPU instances	g2.2xlarge | g2.8xlarge

The missing instance types like T1, M1, C1, M2, C2 etc. were all parts of earlier generation of instance families. Following table provides the detail of all of the instance types available under the present generation instance families under AWS.

Amazon Machine Instances are available at rent on a computing/hour basis. After selecting the appropriate AMI, user can create, launch and terminate server instances as needed while

Table 20.2　Specification of AWS general purpose, compute optimized and memory optimized instances (as per the data gathered in February, 2016)

Instance Family	Instance Model	vCPU	Memory (in Gibibyte (GiB))	Storage (in Gigabyte (GB))	Networking Performance
General purpose	t2.nano	1	0.5	EBS	Low
	t2.micro	1	1	EBS	Low to Moderate
	t2.small	1	2	EBS	Low to Moderate
	t2.medium	2	4	EBS	Low to Moderate
	t2.large	2	8	EBS	Low to Moderate
	m4.large	2	8	EBS	Moderate
	m4.xlarge	4	16	EBS	High
	m4.2xlarge	8	32	EBS	High
	m4.4xlarge	16	64	EBS	High
	m4.10xlarge	40	160	EBS	10 Gigabit
	m3.medium	1	3.75	SSD	Moderate
	m3.large	2	7.5	SSD	Moderate
	m3.xlarge	4	15	SSD	High
	m3.2xlarge	8	30	SSD	High
Compute optimized	c4.large	2	3.75	EBS	Moderate
	c4.xlarge	4	7.5	EBS	High
	c4.2xlarge	8	15	EBS	High
	c4.4xlarge	16	30	EBS	High
	c4.8xlarge	36	60	EBS	10 Gigabit
	c3.large	2	3.75	SSD	Moderate
	c3.xlarge	4	7.5	SSD	Moderate
	c3.2xlarge	8	15	SSD	High
	c3.4xlarge	16	30	SSD	High
	c3.8xlarge	32	60	SSD	10 Gigabit
Memory optimized	r3.xlarge	4	30.5	SSD	Moderate
	r3.2xlarge	8	61	SSD	High
	r3.4xlarge	16	122	SSD	High
	r3.8xlarge	32	244	SSD	10 Gigabit

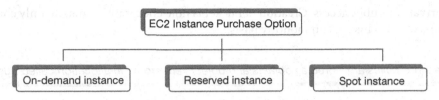

FIG 20.2: Options for AWS EC2 instance purchase

paying by the hour for active servers. The term *elastic* refers to high scalability of EC2 instances which provides the *flexibility* of resizing the capacity as needed through simple web interfaces.

There are three ways customers can consume and pay for AWS EC2 instances as on-demand, reserved and spot. In on-demand scheme, the consumers only pay as per the specified hourly rate for the instance used. Under reserved scheme, AWS offers significant discount over the on-demand instance pricing. In spot-pricing scheme, the consumers have the options of setting a maximum price tag for some instances. AWS delivers the instances to those consumers at that tagged price (or on lower price rate when demand is very low) on supply and demand basis. When resource demand grows too high automatically the spot price of instances increase and the instances are shut down so that a consumer never pays more than his/her tag price.

20.1.2 Amazon Storage Systems

All Amazon machine instances come with a certain amount of temporal storage for computation. This storage is non-persistent and only exists as long as the machine instance is alive. This storage joins the pool of AWS storage system on termination of machine instance. Therefore, to store data permanently, some persistent storage system has to be used.

> *Storage provisioned with AMI instances are non-persistent. It only exists as long as the machine instance is alive.*

To fulfill this need of persistent storage with cloud services, Amazon provides two choices as Amazon EBS volumes or Amazon S3. Users can choose them depending upon their application requirement.

20.1.2.1 *Amazon Simple Storage System (Amazon S3)*

The Amazon S3 is scalable and persistent storage system and delivered as a low-cost web service. To store durable data and to install applications, users of AWS can utilize this storage service. Like other services of AWS, S3 also provides a simple web-service interface. It can be used independently from other Amazon cloud services. Even, the applications as hosted in some local (non-cloud) servers under consumer's own infrastructure can use Amazon S3 service to store data.

In S3, any types of files are stored as objects and those objects are stored into containers called as buckets. The maximum size of an object in S3 can be of 5 terabytes (5 TB). In a single upload though maximum 5 GB of data can be uploaded. For objects larger than this, users will have to use multiple upload capability of AWS. Subscribers have the option of storing their data as private or public access. Creation of bucket is non-chargeable. Amazon only charges for storing objects into buckets on monthly basis.

> In Amazon S3, files are stored as objects and objects are stored in a location called bucket.

According to Amazon, S3 gives access to the same highly-scalable, reliable and secure infrastructure that Amazon uses to run with its own global network of web services. Amazon EC2 uses S3 to store Amazon Machine Images. The service has been developed to provide 99.99 percent availability and 99.999999999 percent durability of objects. Amazon even presents the agreement offering credits to its consumers if availability of S3 service falls below 99.9 percent.

20.1.2.2 Amazon Elastic Block Store (Amazon EBS)

Amazon Elastic Block Storage (Amazon EBS) is a persistent storage designed specifically to be used with Amazon EC2 instances. EBS provides raw block devices which is used to create disk volume that can be attached to EC2 instance. EBS volumes are like raw unformatted disk drives that can be formatted using any file system of consumer's choice (such as *ext3* or *NTFS*).

EBS cannot function independently like S3. It can be used only with EC2 instances but data is stored persistently independent to the life of instances. A volume can be attached to only one EC2 instance and cannot be shared between instances. But, multiple volumes can be attached to a single EC2 instance. The size of EBS volume ranges from 1 GB to 1 TB. Though EC2 does not impose any limitation on the number of volumes that can be attached to an instance, it depends on the operating system being used for the same. For security of data, there is option of launching the ESB volumes as encrypted volumes where all of the data are automatically stored in encrypted form.

EBS is extremely reliable and provides high-operational performance with high-speed data access and availability. ESB can be used to install relational databases (like Oracle, Microsoft SQL Server or MySQL), NoSQL databases, enterprise applications (like SAP, Oracle) and so on.

20.1.2.3 Amazon S3 versus Amazon EBS

Simple Storage Service (S3) and Elastic Block Store (EBS) are two storage services offered by Amazon. But they are not same and are to serve different purposes. EBS is meant to be used with EC2 (Elastic Computing Cloud) instances and is not accessible unless attached to some EC2 instance. On the other hand, S3 is not dependent on EC2. S3 storage can be accessed through any applications using HTTP protocol or with the open-source BitTorrent protocol.

Amazon S3 storage cannot be directly accessed. Some software or application is required to access S3 since it communicates through web service interfaces (REST, SOAP and BitTorrent). With EBS, once a volume is mounted on an EC2 instance, it can be accessed just like a disk partition.

The storage in ESB is counted on volumes whereas in S3 it is bucket where objects are stored. The two systems differ on many other parameters if performance is measured. But these cannot be treated as advantages or disadvantages as these two systems are made to serve different purposes.

The file storage services S3 and EBS are made to serve different purposes.

20.1.3 AWS Elastic Beanstalk

AWS Elastic Beanstalk is Amazon's PaaS (Platform-as-a-Service) offering. Users can develop applications on Beanstalk and also include them into different AWS services like Amazon EC2, Amazon S3 etc. Elastic Beanstalk automatically manages issues like load balancing, scaling, capacity provisioning of deployed applications and others.

Integrated development environment like Microsoft Visual Studio or Eclipse can be used in Elastic Beanstalk. AWS Beanstalk provides support for a host of applications including .NET, Java, PHP, Node.js, Python, Ruby, Go and Docker. Although the non-web applications can also be deployed but Elastic Beanstalk is ideal for web applications.

Elastic Beanstalk follows the open-architecture way. An open-architecture means that applications not written for the web can also be deployed on the Elastic Beanstalk.

20.1.4 Database Services of AWS

Amazon Web Services provides the facility for database management in cloud. Amazon's database service offers fully-managed relational and NoSQL databases. As a fully-managed service, the responsibility of managing the service is carried by the service provider. In relational database category, Amazon offers Amazon Relational Database Service (Amazon RDS) and in non-relational category, it offers two services as SimpleDB and DynamoDB. Amazon RDS, SimpleDB and DynamoDB, all of them are cloud services and fall under the category of Database-as-a-Service (DBaaS) offering.

Apart from using Amazon's own database services through AWS, consumers have the option of installing their own choice of DBMS on EC2 instance. In this case, the database will require an EBS volume to get installed and store data persistently.

20.1.4.1 *Amazon Relational Database Service (Amazon RDS)*

Amazon Relational Database Service (Amazon RDS) is the RDBMS offering as cloud service from Amazon. Like other Amazon cloud services, it also provides web interfaces to easily manage the relational database in the cloud. As a fully-managed service, it relieves consumers from several tensions by allowing them to focus more on higher-value application development. Amazon RDS supports MySQL, PostgreSQL, Oracle and Microsoft SQL Server database engines. Moreover, the consumers can use almost all of the capabilities of a familiar MySQL, Oracle, Microsoft SQL Servers or PostgreSQL database engines. Hence, the users familiar with those databases easily feel comfortable with Amazon RDS.

Amazon imposes hourly charges for the RDS service. The service is offered into two schemes as on-demand scheme and reserved scheme. The on-demand service scheme named as on-demand DB instances is charged based on hourly usage. The other scheme called as reserved DB instance provides the option of reserving DB instances for longer period through one-time payment. This provides a significant discount on the hourly charge for instances.

RDS provides the facility of automated *point-in-time back-up* for data stored in it. In addition to this back-up, RDS supports to create database snapshots which can store the full database system including the schemas in its current state. Additionally, using the CloudWatch tool of AWS the database usage can be monitored as well.

> Amazon RDS is a distributed relational database service. Almost all database tools that come with popular databases like MySQL, Oracle or Microsoft SQL Servers, are also available in RDS.

20.1.4.2 SimpleDB

SimpleDB is Amazon's offer of a fully-managed non-relational data store. Being non-relational one, it is free from restrictions of relational database and is optimized for flexibility and high-availability. SimpleDB is delivered as web service and can be used with EC2 instances. The data requires no schema and the database is very simple to use. Like other DBaaS offerings, SimpleDB is also a distributed database service and is automatically replicated at different geographical locations to provide high availability and to become fault-tolerant.

SimpleDB is primarily a NoSQL key-value store and provides many useful query functionalities. A simple and SQL-like query language is used here to write the queries. There are no base fees for its usage. Amazon charges the consumers on resource consumption basis through monthly billing. Amazon also offers a free usage plan up to a certain amount of data storage.

> SimpleDB is a fully-managed NoSQL database service suitable for smaller work loads.

20.1.4.3 DynamoDB

DynamoDB is Amazon's offer of another fully-managed NoSQL database service. It is suitable to work with large volume of data and provides very fast and predictable performance. High performance makes it fit for many data-intensive applications like critical games and other complex applications. It provides seamless scalability and guarantees latency of milliseconds in single-digit.

For DynamoDB, Amazon does not charge consumers on storage-usage basis. It allows the developers to purchase a service based on throughput which is the capacity of its read/write operations per seconds. Different usage plans are offered including a free plan allowing a certain million database operations per month.

> DynamoDB is fully-managed, NoSQL database service designed for high-performance database and hence suitable for heavier work loads.

20.1.4.4 SimpleDB versus DynamoDB

Both SimpleDB and DynamoDB are key-value paired NoSQL database services offered by Amazon but they are made to serve different purposes. DynamoDB is designed to provide the facility of high-performance database. It is suitable for applications targeting high traffic in data store. SimpleDB on the other hand can provide better performance than DynamoDB being employed with smaller work load.

SimpleDB is more simple and flexible than DynamoDB. This is primarily because DynamoDB is not so flexible on indexing like SimpleDB. DynamoDB indexing fields have to be defined manually at the beginning and cannot be modified later. This limits the future change whereas SimpleDB automatically manages indexes depending on suitability.

Although, the SimpleDB has some limitations relating scalability but it is very good for smaller workloads requiring flexibility of query. So, in comparison, ultimately there is a tradeoff between simplicity/flexibility and performance/scalability and the choice between these two Amazon NoSQL databases (SimpleDB and DynamoDB) depends on application requirements.

> Amazon RDS, SimpleDB and DynamoDB, are fully-managed and distributed databases delivered as Database-as-a-Service (DBaaS) offerings.

Table 20.3 tries to elaborate the different uses of AWS database services. It notes down various scenarios regarding consumer's database service requirement and suggests the preferred solution to fulfill those requirements.

20.1.5 Amazon CDN Service: CloudFront

CloudFront is a content delivery network (CDN) service and an IaaS offering from Amazon. Amazon had developed a global edge network to build this CDN facility. Any request for content from consumers is automatically routed to the nearest edge location so that it can be delivered in least time and can provide the experience of best-possible performance.

Table 20.3 Databases solutions on AWS

Consumer's Requirement	Preferred Solution
The relational database service with minimal overhead regarding administration is required	Amazon Relational Database Service (RDS), a fully-managed relational DBMS which offers a choice of MySQL, Oracle, SQL Server or PostgreSQL database engines.
A NoSQL database service with high scalability is required.	Amazon DynamoDB, a fully-managed NoSQL database service which offers very high-scalability and performance too.
A NoSQL database service is required for application to deal with huge volume of data.	Amazon DynamoDB is the perfect solution as it is good fit to manage high-volume of data efficiently.
A NoSQL database service is required to manage low volume of data.	Amazon SimpleDB, a fully managed NoSQL database service which is made to deal with low volume of data efficiently.
A highly-flexible NoSQL database service is required.	Amazon SimpleDB is very flexible with its structure to become the option for this.
It requires such self-chosen database systems which can be managed by themselves .	Customers can install their self chosen DBMS on Amazon EC2 Instance with EBS as storage.

The CloudFront CDN service works in collaboration with other Amazon Web Services and gives consumers a low-latency service through which they can easily distribute their content to end users. Like other AWS offerings, CloudFront also has a simple web-service interface.

To lower the latency during the delivery of large and popular content, CloudFront caches copies of static content close to viewers so that it can be transferred very fast. There are no monthly rentals for using this service and consumers only need to pay for content actually delivered through the service. CloudFront competes with other larger CDN services such as Akamai and Limelight Networks.

> *Amazon CloudFront is a cloud service for content delivery.*

20.1.6 Amazon Message Queuing Service: SQS

Amazon Simple Queue Service (SQS) is a fully-managed message queuing service to store messages as they travel between computing nodes. Message queues play important roles while messages are passed among components of distributed application. Message queuing service is a SaaS facility. Usage of SQS offloads the administrative burden of managing messages from application developers. SQS makes it simple to build advanced message-based applications easily without worrying about storing and managing messages.

It is highly-scalable and can grow as per demand to achieve increasing level of throughput. Hence applications can use the service without worrying about the performance factors. SQS can even hold messages when some targeted applications are not available and thus they start to decouple different components of cloud application.

20.2 MICROSOFT AZURE

Microsoft's business in cloud service offerings spans all over application, platform and infrastructure. Microsoft treats its cloud services as complementary to its other traditional applications. They offer hosted services (in the cloud) combined with locally-running software.

Microsoft had initially named its cloud services as software plus services (software + services). Through that initiative, Microsoft provided traditional software integrated with a suite of cloud hosted services to offer additional flexibility to the users and enterprises. Later on Microsoft renamed the service as Windows Azure. It was again renamed to Microsoft Azure on 2014. Following section briefly focuses on different components of Microsoft Azure's offerings.

> *The term 'azure' signifies deep blue color, like the color of the clear sky, onto which one can paint the clouds.*

20.2.1 Azure Virtual Machine

Microsoft's cloud service Azure uses a special operating system called as Microsoft Azure and runs a layer called as 'Fabric Controller' over it which manages computing and storage resources of clusters at Microsoft's data center. Users can create virtual machines over this layer using Azure Virtual Machines to use scalable computing infrastructure on-demand. Fabric Controller manages the scaling.

The operating system of this is also called as "cloud layer". It is built over Windows server system and combines a customized version of Hyper-V being known as the Microsoft Azure Hypervisor.

Microsoft offers the options of choosing between Windows and Linux operating systems at the time of launching the virtual machines in Azure. Azure provides per-minute billing system for their virtual machines. Azure Virtual Machine with Windows OS runs all Microsoft enterprise applications with outstanding ease and also supports a full range of Linux distributions like Red Hat, Ubuntu and SUSE.

Virtual machines in Azure are offered in two categories as basic tier and standard tier. The basic tier provides economical option for development or testing purpose where features like load balancing or scaling are not required. Standard tier provides all of the advanced features.

Virtual machines of different sizes are offered under several series like A, D, DS, G etc. Consumers can launch machines from the list of available choices to fulfill various requirements. Pre-configured machines are designed to meet the needs of compute-intensive application, network-intensive application, better local disk performance, high memory demand and so on.

Table 20.4 shows the available options and specifications of the general purposed azure virtual machines under basic tier. These machines are the most economical among all.

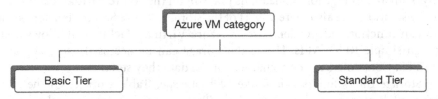

FIG 20.3: Azure virtual machine tiers

Table 20.4 Specification of Azure general purposed compute: Basic tier and Standard tier (as per data gathered in February, 2016)

VM Category	Instance	Cores	Memory (RAM)	Disk Size
Basic tier	A0	1	0.75 GB	20 GB
	A1	1	1.75 GB	40 GB
	A2	2	3.5 GB	60 GB
	A3	4	7 GB	120 GB
	A4	8	14 GB	240 GB
Standard tier	A0	1	0.75 GB	20 GB
	A1	1	1.75 GB	70 GB
	A2	2	3.5 GB	135 GB
	A3	4	7 GB	285 GB
	A4	8	14 GB	605 GB
	A5	2	14 GB	135 GB
	A6	4	28 GB	285 GB
	A7	8	56 GB	605 GB

20.2.2 Azure Platform

Azure does not offer IaaS and PaaS facilities separately. These two services are delivered together. Taken together as a unit, Microsoft Azure service can be viewed as a Platform-as-a-Service (PaaS) offering. Azure offers application server along with the necessary storage, networking and other computing infrastructure for building and running applications.

Azure has the cloud-enabled version of the integrated .NET Framework on its virtualized infrastructure which developers can use in Windows-based application development. Users can host their applications on Azure. Microsoft has also added a number of services interoperated with Azure, including SQL Azure (a version of SQL Server), SharePoint Services, Azure Dynamic CRM and so on.

> Microsoft Azure provides both IaaS as well as PaaS offerings together. Azure Platform is comparable with Google's App Engine.

20.2.3 Azure Storage

Azure Storage is the storage home for Azure Virtual Machines. It provides scalable, durable and highly-available storage for applications that run on the Azure Virtual Machines. Back-up and recovery solutions are also there as part of the storage. Azure Storage is a persistent storage space and can function independently from Azure Virtual Machines. It allows access to its data through simple REST APIs. Hence the storage can be accessed using applications via HTTP/HTTPS. Consumers are only charged for the data they store.

Azure Storage offers four services like Blob storage, Table storage, Queue storage and File storage. Blob storage is for storing files. Table storage is for non-relational datasets. Queue storage facilitates the communication between components of cloud services by storing large number of messages. File storage is the legacy Windows storage to store folders/files which can be shared among multiple applications. Currently, Azure allows a user to hold upto five storage accounts. Blob, Table and Queue storages are integral parts of every Azure storage account whereas file storage is optional and becomes available only on-request. Figure 20.4 shows the storage structure of Azure Storage.

20.2.3.1 Blob Storage

Among these four types, blob storage is the most significant one. To store large volume of unstructured text or binary data, Azure uses blob storage. The term 'blob' stands for

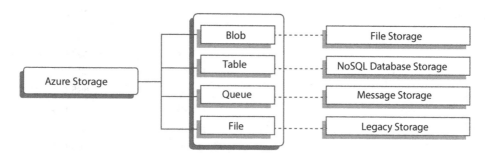

FIG 20.4: The Azure Storage concept

'Binary Large Object' and it typically stores the images, audio, other multimedia content and binary executable files. Blobs are stored into containers and a storage account can contain any number of containers. Currently, the maximum capacity of a storage account is 500 TB and any number of blobs can be stored into a container up to that of 500 TB limit.

> Blob Storage enables applications running on Azure to store large amount of unstructured data.

20.2.3.2 Table Storage

Table Storage is Microsoft's offering as a NoSQL key-attribute data store. It is schema-less and ideal for storing large volume of non-relational data. Different rows within a table can have different structures. It also provides the facility of storing simple relational data. It is very simple to use and has automatic scalability capacity to meet the application demand. Table Storage allows the access from inside and outside of the Azure cloud.

Entities are stored into Table Storage. Entities are actually collection of properties and their values. Any number of entities can be stored into a table and a storage account may contain any number of tables. Entities under a storage account may consume up to 200 TB space.

> Table Storage is the NoSQL data-store offered by Microsoft Azure.

20.2.4 Azure Database Services

Like other major players, Microsoft also offers database services as part of their Azure cloud service offerings. Following section discusses few of these services in brief.

20.2.4.1 Azure SQL Database

Microsoft Azure SQL Database (formally known as SQL Azure database) is the relational data store of the Microsoft Azure platform. It is a fully-managed database service that extends the power of Microsoft SQL Server capabilities to the cloud. It is easily scalable, simple-to-use and offers low cost service under different service tiers (Basic, Standard or Premium).

Azure SQL provides predictable performance and the levels of performance are expressed in database throughput units (DTUs). SQL Azure Database can be accessed through applications running on Azure Virtual Machines or on local server at consumer's end.

> Azure SQL is a relational database service and comparable to Amazon RDS and Google SQL.

20.2.4.2 DocumentDB

DocumentDB is Microsoft's NoSQL database offering to work in cloud. DocumentDB is a fully-managed JSON document database service. It processes schema-free NoSQL document databases as a Big Data solution. DocumentDB supports SQL syntax to query JSON documents. In DocumentDB, the users can define functions at the server side using java script too. DocumentDB presently supplies SDKs for .NET, JavaScript, Java, Node.js and Python.

20.2.4.3 HDInsight Service

HDInsight is an implementation of Hadoop as offered by Microsoft which represents Apache Hadoop solution in the Azure cloud. Apache Hadoop is an open-source software that enables the storage and analysis of Big Data (large unstructured or semi-structured datasets). HDInsight uses Azure Blob storage as the default storage.

Offered by Microsoft Azure as a PaaS (Platform-as-a-Service), Azure HDInsight provides a facility of the Apache Hadoop data processing platform. HDInsight also provides the capabilities to import or export data from or to an Azure SQL database by using a Sqoop connector. HDInsight also include Apache HBase, a columnar NoSQL database which runs on the Hadoop Distributed File System (HDFS) in order to enable the processing of non-relational data.

> *Azure HDInsight is a Big Data solution powered by Apache Hadoop.*

Microsoft is not the first to offer Hadoop as a cloud service, Amazon Web Services also offers the Hadoop. HDInsight offers programming capabilities to developers with a choice of languages including .NET and Java.

20.2.5 Azure Content Delivery Network

The Azure Content Delivery Network (CDN) offers solutions for easy delivery of high-bandwidth content which are hosted in Azure. It provides high performance in content delivery. The Azure CDN caches Azure blobs and static content at strategically-placed locations. Once the CDN is enabled on some of the Azure storage accounts, all of their publicly accessible blobs become available to CDN.

> *Microsoft Azure CDN is comparable to Amazon CloudFront.*

20.2.6 Microsoft's SaaS Offerings

There is a number of Software-as-a-Service (SaaS) offerings from Microsoft. But Microsoft does not offer them as part of Azure cloud. Those services are available separately. Such services include office suite, online storage facility and others.

20.2.6.1 Office 365

Office 365 is the most attractive SaaS offering of Microsoft. It is actually the cloud version of the traditional Microsoft Office suite with few additional services like Outlook, Skype and OneDrive. The service was first launched in 2011. It is a subscription-based service and users can access Office 365 from anywhere using a variety of devices.

20.2.6.2 OneDrive

OneDrive (previously named as Microsoft SkyDrive) is free online storage where general users can store their files and access those from anywhere. It is a file-hosting service. OneDrive is included in Office 365 offerings. Any kind of data can be stored in OneDrive including photos, videos and documents. OneDrive provides 5 GB of free storage to users and 1 TB of storage with an Office 365 subscription. Using the OneDrive desktop app users can synchronize their files to personal devices automatically. Office 2013 onwards Microsoft offers the facility of working on Word, Excel and other Office documents directly on OneDrive.

20.2.6.3 SharePoint Online

SharePoint Online is Microsoft's offering for highly-secure collaboration at a central location online. Employees of enterprises or project groups of organizations get a flexible way to manage information, workflow and collaborate effectively. It has been built based on the concepts of Microsoft SharePoint Server 2010 that facilitates on-premises secure collaboration. Consumers can subscribe SharePoint Online in the cloud as a standalone offering or as part of an Office 365 suite.

> Microsoft OneDrive service is comparable to Google Drive.

20.3 GOOGLE CLOUD

Google initially built its empire based on the search engine business over Internet which has always been highly regarded. Later on Google expanded its domain of activities and among few other new things, they started developing cloud services. Currently, almost all of the products of Google are delivered as cloud services. Google's cloud service is built upon its data centers spread across the globe.

Google is presently one among the leaders in the cloud computing market and offers a vast collection of web-based applications as cloud services. Presently Google divides its cloud services under the following categories as Compute, Storage, Networking, Database, Services and Management. The last two categories are new in Google compared to AWS. 'Services' offer facility like text translation and 'Management' offer monitoring service among others.

> Like Amazon, Google also offers cloud services for computing, storage, networking and database.

Following section discusses different Google cloud services. But, unlike the preceding discussion on Amazon Web Services and Microsoft Azure, the organization of topics follows a separate manner. Services have been arranged based on their service category like IaaS, PaaS and SaaS.

20.3.1 Google's IaaS Offerings

Google's Infrastructure-as-a-Service (IaaS) offering include two popular services as Google Compute Engine and Google Cloud Storage. Both of the offerings have been briefly discussed here.

20.3.1.1 Google Compute Engine (GCE)

Google ventured into Infrastructure-as-a-Service (IaaS) after gaining success in SaaS and PaaS markets and the GCE is the outcome of that effort. Developers can run large-scale distributed applications on virtual machines hosted on Google's infrastructure by using GCE.

GCE uses KVM (Kernel-based Virtual Machine) as the hypervisor and supports guest machines to run Linux as operating system. Instances can use different popular distributions of Linux using a standard image provided by Google Compute Engine or a modified version of one of these images as customized by customer.

> Google Compute Engine (GCE) is comparable to Amazon EC2.

Google provides both pre-defined and custom-configured machines. Pre-standardized machines are divided into different categories from which users can select as per the requirements. Presently (as on February, 2016), the available machine categories offered by GCE are as following:

- Standard Machine,
- High Memory Machine,
- High CPU Machine,
- Shared Core Machine, and
- Custom Machine Types.

Shared-core machine type becomes cost-effective where small amount of resources are required. The instance types under each machine category specify the number of virtual processors and size of memory among other features. In Table 20.5, one such specification of instances under standard category is displayed.

When the pre-defined machine types do not match with requirements, then consumers have the option of building custom-defined machine. There one can specify the memory and CPU needs.

Machines under GCE offering are charged per minutes basis after first 10 minutes. For usage of less than 10 minutes, consumers need to pay the charge for 10 minutes. Apart from machine instances, Google separately charges its customers for network usages, load balancing, persistence disk usages etc.

20.3.1.2 Google Cloud Storage

Google Cloud Storage is an Infrastructure-as-a-Service (IaaS) offering from Google and comparable to Amazon S3. The storage can be accessed through simple APIs or can be used with Google Compute Engine, App Engine and so on.

Data in Google Cloud Storage are stored as objects. Each object has two parts like data and metadata. These objects are stored into containers called as *buckets*. Buckets are used to organize data and to specify access control on that data. Buckets are stored as part of a project. One bucket cannot be shared among multiple projects. Unlike directories or folders, buckets in a project cannot be organized in nested manner. There is no limit on the number of buckets a project can contain. A consumer can be part of one project or multiple projects.

Table 20.5 Specification of GCE pre-defined machine types (as per data gathered in February, 2016)

Machine Type	Instance type	Virtual CPUs	Memory	Pricing Model
Standard	n1-standard-1	1	3.75 GB	Per minute
	n1-standard-2	2	7.5 GB	Per minute
	n1-standard-4	4	15 GB	Per minute
	n1-standard-8	8	30 GB	Per minute
	n1-standard-16	16	60 GB	Per minute
	n1-standard-32	32	120 GB	Per minute
High-memory	n1-highmem-2	2	13 GB	Per minute
	n1-highmem-4	4	26 GB	Per minute
	n1-highmem-8	8	52 GB	Per minute
	n1-highmem-16	16	104 GB	Per minute
	n1-highmem-32	32	208 GB	Per minute
High-CPU	n1-highcpu-2	2	1.80 GB	Per minute
	n1-highcpu-4	4	3.60 GB	Per minute
	n1-highcpu-8	8	7.20 GB	Per minute
	n1-highcpu-16	16	14.4 GB	Per minute
	n1-highcpu-32	32	28.8 GB	Per minute
Shared-core	f1-micro	1	0.60 GB	Per minute
	g1-small	1	1.70 GB	Per minute

> *Google Cloud Storage is comparable to Amazon S3.*

20.3.2 Google's PaaS Offering

The PaaS facility offered by Google is called as Google App Engine (GAE). Google also offers a number of database services as part of their cloud offering.

20.3.2.1 Google App Engine

App Engine (GAE) is Google's offering as Platform-as–a-Service (PaaS) facility. In this area, Google is one among the market leaders. On GAE, applications can be developed in high-level programming languages by using Google App Engine Framework. The frameworks ease the development efforts required to build an application. GAE allows developers to create and deploy web applications without worrying about necessary managing tasks to run their applications. GAE also provides facility for cloud-based web hosting services on Google's infrastructure.

Google App Engine provides several high-level programming language run-times like Java runtime, Python runtime and PHP runtime with necessary libraries for application developments. GAE provides a persistent storage facility with it and applications deployed over App Engine are easy to scale when traffic or data storage needs the growth. GAE also has auto load balancing feature.

> Google provides Software Development Kits (SDKs) for all supported languages to develop applications over App Engine platform.

Like other cloud platform services, there are some limitations from developer's point of view though. Applications developed on App Engine must comply with Google's infrastructure. User's programs communicate with GAE APIs and uses objects and properties from the App Engine framework. This narrows the range of application types that can be developed and run on GAE. Again it may become difficult to port application to another platform since it may be dependent on some unique GAE feature.

Apart from this limitation, the Google App Engine provides a low-cost and flexible option for developers to build applications that can run on the Google's cloud infrastructure. There are no set-up costs and consumers only pay for what they use. Moreover, to encourage to write applications using GAE, Google allows free application development and deployment up to a certain level of resource consumption for the developers.

> Developers can use App Engine's APIs to build and host SaaS applications.

20.3.2.2 Database Services

Google has its own database service offerings. Google offers the following database services as part of their cloud services.

20.3.2.2.1 Cloud SQL

Google Cloud SQL offers a fully-managed database solution MySQL which is the most popular open-source database. This Database-as-a-Service (DBaaS) allows users to use a relational database that is highly scalable. Users can concentrate more on database design and application development since other database management activities are managed by Google.

Google Cloud SQL integrates well with Google App Engine and very easy to use. It provides most of the features of MySQL and is ideal for small or medium size applications. It also presents a set of tools enabling users to easily move data in and out of the cloud.

> Cloud SQL is a Database-as-a-Service offering from Google and is comparable to Amazon's RDS.

20.3.2.2.2 Cloud Datastore

Google Cloud Datastore is a fully-managed, schema-less NoSQL data store for storing non-relational data. Cloud Data store is very easy-to-use and supports SQL-like queries being called as GQL. The Datastore is a NoSQL key/value store, where users can store data as key/

value pairs. Cloud Datastore also supports ACID transactions for concurrency control. Although Cloud SQL and Datastore are totally different, many applications require to use both of them together.

> Google's Cloud Datastore is comparable to Amazon's DynamoDB and SimpleDB offerings.

20.3.2.2.3 BigQuery

BigQuery is Google's offering that provides facility of analyzing *Big Data* in the cloud. *Big Data* refers to a massive volume of both structured and unstructured data which is so large that it becomes difficult to process it using traditional database management tools and software techniques. BigQuery enables for interactive analysis of massive datasets having billions of rows in real time using SQL-like queries.

BigQuery is easy to use and provides an interactive user interface through which queries can be run. To analyze huge volume of data, users can upload it into the BigQuery facility and then can query it interactively or programmatically. Internally, Google uses a query system known as Dremel which has extraordinary query performance and analysis capabilities.

It should be noted that BigQuery is not a database. It is a tool for analyzing vast quantity of data quickly but data cannot be modified or inserted using BigQuery. The popular Indian online travel agency RedBus uses BigQuery to analyze the customers' travel pattern, so that they can identify the popular destinations and routes.

> BigQuery is not a database service. It is a tool for quick exploration and examination of Big Data in the cloud using SQL-like queries and can analyze terabytes of datasets in seconds.

20.3.3 Google's SaaS Offerings

Google offers a number of applications through its Software as a Service (SaaS). Most of those services have become part of people's day-to-day activities. It features several applications with similar functionality to traditional office suites. Among many services they offer, cloud-based word processing (Google Docs), email service (Gmail), or calendar/scheduling service (Google Calendar) are to mention a few. These SaaS facilities from Google are offered under 'G Suite' and are popularly known as 'Google Apps'.

> Google provides an extensive set of very popular applications for general public, delivered as SaaS.

20.3.3.1 Gmail

This is a popular SaaS offering from Google. Gmail is offered under the communicate section of 'G Suite' (formerly know as 'Google Apps for Work'). Other offerings under this communicate suite include Calendar and Google+. Gmail is a free service and apart from personal use Gmail offers services for enterprise users too.

20.3.3.2 Docs

Google Docs is a SaaS offering for managing documents. It comes under the collaborative application suit offered by Google which resembles traditional office suites and provides functionalities to create text documents, spreadsheets and presentations over the cloud using any web-browser. The features of Google's collaborative suite are almost similar to those present in traditional Microsoft Office suite. Like other offering under this collaborative suite (namely Sheets, Forms, Slides), Google Docs is also free for anyone to use and allows multiple users to edit and update same document which is very useful feature in this age of global collaboration.

20.3.3.3 Google Drive

This is Google's SaaS offerings for general users to store file. It is basically built for the users of 'G Suite' to enable them for storing data in cloud seamlessly. Users can access their stored data from anywhere and share it with other Google Drive users. It acts as the default storage for Gmail or Google Docs. It also provides easy and simple way of transferring data from user's own computer to the cloud.

> *Google Drive storage is for normal users and Google Cloud Storage is for the developers.*

20.4 A COMPARISON AMONG AWS, AZURE AND GOOGLE CLOUD

AWS, Azure and Google Cloud almost offer similar type of capabilities. But there are many differentiating factors also. Table 20.6 represents a comparative review of these popular cloud services on various aspects.

Table 20.6 Comparison among AWS, Azure and Google Cloud

	Amazon Web Services (AWS)	Microsoft Azure	Google Cloud
Vendor	Amazon	Microsoft	Google
Hypervisor used in building the cloud	Xen Hypervisor	Microsoft Azure Hypervisor	KVM (Kernel-based Virtual Machine)
Internal Load balancing	Available	Available	Available
Internal auto-scaling	Available	Available	Available
Provisioning	Instant provisioning	Instant provisioning	Instant provisioning
Name of the Virtual Machine Service Offering	Elastic Compute Cloud (EC2)	Azure Virtual Machine	Google Compute Engine (GCE)
VM Types	Pre-defined VM type	Pre-defined VM type	Pre-defined VM type and Custom VM type

	Amazon Web Services (AWS)	Microsoft Azure	Google Cloud
VM Subscription Options	■ On-demand, ■ Reserved and ■ Spot	■ On-demand and ■ Reserved	■ On-demand
OS options for Virtual Server	Windows and Linux	Windows and Linux	Windows and Linux
VM Billing Plan	Per-hour billing and Fixed hourly rate	Per-minute billing and Fixed hourly rate	Per-minute billing
Name of the Application Platform Offering	Elastic Beanstalk	Azure	Google App Engine
Supported Runtimes	■ .NET ■ Java ■ PHP ■ Python ■ Ruby ■ Node.js ■ Go ■ Docker	■ .NET ■ Java ■ PHP ■ Python ■ Ruby ■ Node.js	■ Java ■ PHP ■ Python ■ Go
Storage Service Offering	Simple Storage System (S3), Elastic Block Store (EBS)	Azure Storage	Google Cloud Storage
Native Relational Database Service	Relational Database Service (RDS)	Azure SQL Database	Cloud SQL
Big Data Solution/ NoSQL DBMS Offering	DynamoDB and SimpleDB	DocumentDB	Cloud Datastore
Big Data Analytics Tool	Elastic MapReduce (Amazon EMR)	HDInsight	BigQuery
CDN Offering	CloudFront	Azure Content Delivery Network	No offering. Google is partnered with CDN service provider named as 'Fastly'.
Consumer Identity and Access Management Service	AWS Identity and Access Management	Azure Active Directory B2C	Google Cloud IAM

SUMMARY

❖ There are scores of vendors of different sizes who offer cloud services today. Amazon.com, Microsoft and Google are current market leaders, who are battling to capture more market shares.

❖ The IaaS, PaaS and SaaS services offered by these companies have already gained significant popularity among enterprises, institutes and general users.

❖ Amazon Web Services, Microsoft Azure and Google Cloud are the names of cloud service offering from three big vendors.

❖ These cloud service vendors offer services to fulfill various needs of computing, including compute, storage, networking, content delivery, application platform, relational database system, Big Data solution etc.

❖ Amazon Elastic Compute Cloud (EC2), Azure Virtual Machine and Google Compute Engine (GCE) are the services for launching VMs in these three cloud services respectively.

❖ The PaaS offering from Amazon, Microsoft and Google are named as Elastic Beanstalk, Azure and Google App Engine. All these vendors provide runtime support for different platforms like Java, PHP and Python. Support for .NET, Ruby and Node.js is provided by Elastic Beanstalk and Azure.

❖ Microsoft and Google also provide many SaaS offerings, which have gained popularity among consumers. Google's email service (Gmail), Google's storage services (Google Drive and OneDrive) and Microsoft's Office 365 are names of a few among them.

REVIEW QUESTIONS

What is the difference between on-demand and reserved VM subscription plans offered by cloud service providers?

On-demand VM subscription model is the general subscription model of cloud computing where payment is made purely based on the usage basis. When consumer does not use the service he/she need not to pay anything. There is no prior agreement of service use.

In reserved VM subscription model, consumers commit to use VM for certain amount of time or amounting certain volume of resource consumption within a specific period. For instance, a consumer may reserve a VM for 100 hours to be used along next entire month. In this model, the providers often offer discounts in rates.

Why is Microsoft Azure known as PaaS cloud offering in general?

Microsoft Azure develops and delivers both IaaS and PaaS facilities, but does not offer IaaS facility separately to consumers. Rather, both IaaS and PaaS services are delivered together. This is why Microsoft Azure is generally known as PaaS cloud offering.

What is the difference between storage services offered as IaaS and SaaS?

Storage services in cloud are offered in two different forms as IaaS and as SaaS. Azure Storage and Google Cloud Storage are IaaS offerings whereas OneDrive and Google Drive are SaaS offerings from Microsoft and Google respectively. In IaaS, storages are delivered in raw form. Consumers need to manage the storage starting from partitioning and formatting of the space. Storages in SaaS form are readily available for use and consumers have no control over the management of the storage apart from storing, replacing or deleting files.

How does pricing and purchasing work in GCE?

Charges in Google Compute Engine are determined based on combined usage of compute instance, storage and network. Virtual machines in Google are charged per-minute basis and it needs a minimum 10 minutes of use. Storage cost is determined based on the volume of data stored in the storage attached with the VM. Network usage cost is calculated based on the volume of data transferred to and from a virtual machine.

Who are the market leaders among public cloud service providers?

According to the research and analyst firm Gartner's report, Amazon had the maximum market share among all of the IaaS providers in 2015. Microsoft Azure comes on the second place. Comparatively the late entrant in the cloud computing market, Google emerges as a distant third after those two. Apart from these giants IBM SoftLayer and VMware's vCloud Air also scores well. In the enterprise PaaS service markets, Salesforce and Microsoft have been categorized as the market leaders.

MULTIPLE CHOICE QUESTIONS

1. Amazon Web Services is which type of cloud computing distribution model?
   a) IaaS
   b) PaaS
   c) SaaS
   d) All of these

2. Azure is which type of cloud computing distribution model?
   a) IaaS
   b) PaaS
   c) SaaS
   d) All of these

3. Google's cloud service offering for launching virtual machine is
   a) Elastic Compute Cloud
   b) Azure VM
   c) Compute Engine
   d) App Engine

4. Microsoft's cloud service offering for Big Data solution is
   a) DynamoDB
   b) DocumentDB
   c) BigQuery
   d) SimpleDB

5. The service offered by Azure cloud for Big Data analysis is,
   a) HDInsight
   b) Elastic MapReduce
   c) BigQuery
   d) None of these

6. OneDrive storage facility offered by Microsoft Azure is a
   a) IaaS
   b) PaaS
   c) SaaS
   d) None of these

7. Which hypervisor is used by AWS for its data center resource visualization?
   a) Hyper-V
   b) KVM
   c) VMware's ESX
   d) Xen

8. Which of the storage services of Google is comparable with Azure OneDrive?
   a) Google Cloud Storage
   b) Google Drive
   c) Google Cloud Data store
   d) All of these

9. Google Cloud Storage and Google Drive are respectively

   a) IaaS and IaaS
   b) IaaS and PaaS
   c) SaaS and IaaS
   d) IaaS and SaaS

10. Which among the storages of AWS is the home for general purpose EC2 instances?

    a) Solid-state device
    b) Simple Storage System
    c) Elastic Block Storage
    d) All of these

11. Azure Hypervisor is a customized version of which among the following?

    a) Hyper-V
    b) Xen
    c) VMware's ESX
    d) KVM

21 | Mobile Cloud Computing and The Internet of Things

The introduction of cloud computing has revolutionized the way of computing as it was being done. The impact of cloud computing technology has reached every corner of the world. It has introduced a new era where innovative technological advancements are emerging based on the strength and utility of cloud computing. Cloud computing may take some time to attain its full maturity but it has appeared as the biggest thing after the Internet. With its fast adoption in different domains and businesses, researchers are working on several issues of cloud computing. This concluding chapter of the book discusses such topics.

This chapter briefly introduces two topics which are emerging as subjects of attraction after cloud computing. Mobile cloud computing is a technology that has opened the scope for overcoming the limitations of mobile computing through effective utilization of cloud computing. This makes mobile computing attractive and more useful for users, especially for billions of smart phone users.

The most remarkable happening in the connectivity domain, after cloud computing is the 'internet of things'. It promises to bring a revolution in human civilization by connecting living and non-living objects, and simplifying the act of collecting different information about them. All these digital innovations are propelling us towards a smarter planet.

21.1 MOBILE CLOUD COMPUTING

Mobile cloud computing (MCC) refers to the computing facility introduced by combining three fascinating technologies together: mobile computing, cloud computing and wireless communication. The emergence of MCC is followed by the explosive growth in uses of mobile devices, especially smart phones where cloud computing acts as a potential technology enabler for mobile services. The actual objective of MCC is to provide rich experience to users by offering cutting edge applications over a variety of mobile devices.

The popularity of mobile devices which facilitates trouble-free communication and instant availability of information has made them an integral part of modern age human civilization. As a consequence, mobile cloud computing has emerged as an advanced step in the process of enriching mobile computing.

21.1.1 Mobile Computing

In simple words, *mobile computing* is a technology where computing-capable devices can transmit data without being connected to any device or network physically, even when in transit. The technology is the convergence of mobile computing devices and mobile communication technology.

Mobile computing devices refer to light-weight, portable computing devices capable of running local stand-alone as well as web-based applications. They generally come with a full character key-set. Such devices are battery-powered and enabled for wireless communication. Examples of mobile computing devices include laptop, notebook, tablet and mobile phone.

Mobile communication technology includes issues like establishing ad-hoc network, protocols for communication, format of data, network bandwidth and so on. Mobile communication infrastructure is built on *radio wave transmission* through towers installed around the world. Development of mobile applications differ from conventional computing applications in the absence of fixed network since location and connectivity issues are critical factors to be considered every time a task is to be executed.

Mobile computing devices are the next step in the development of computing devices and have emerged in the evolution process after portable computing devices. Earlier, *stationary computing devices* were made to work at a fixed location and later *portable computing devices* were developed to work at different locations but in stationary mode. It was not possible to compute (rather to communicate) during transit. Mobile computing overcomes the constraints of stationary or portable commutating and allows to work during movement.

> Mobile computing is referred to as the human-computer interaction where a computing device can transmit data over wireless network and can be operated normally during movement.

21.1.2 Limitations of Mobile Computing

Mobile computing is not as simple as conventional stationary computing. But with time and technological advancements, peoples' expectations and requirements from mobile computing have increased. With the emergence of smart mobile devices like smart phones, users can now access and use high-quality mobile applications. This introduces performance concerns for resource-constrained mobile devices.

This performance criterion can be achieved by producing highly-configured mobile devices which increases the cost. But, mobile devices have their own limitations as they have to be lightweight and small enough to make themselves portable. This limits many attributes of mobile computing devices like processing capability, storage capacity and battery lifetime. Thus, the following issues restrict the growth of mobile computing capability after a point:

- Resource constrained mobile devices are incapable of executing high-performing resource-intensive tasks,
- They have limitations in data storage capacity, and
- Extensive execution of *process-intensive tasks* cause quicker drainage of battery power.

Apart from this, there is *vendor-lock-in* problem as well. For example, when someone purchases a smart phone, he/she becomes bound to a particular platform (like Symbian, Android, Windows etc.) offered by the provider. They cannot use applications exclusively made for some other platforms.

While sustained developments in the field of wireless communication technology have almost eliminated an important hurdle of mobile computing and made way for seamless and speedy mobile communication, technologists have also addressed the processing performance issue through a technique called *task offloading*.

21.1.3 Offloading of Tasks

The solution to the processing performance problem is to offload the execution of application to some resource-heavy non-mobile computing system(s) which remain connected with the mobile device through wireless network. Such technique may also solve the data storage issue. This not only resolves the application performance and data storage issues but the energy issue also as processing of tasks consume battery power heavily.

This idea was introduced during the beginning of the current century when mobile computing devices, especially mobiles phones were rapidly gaining popularity. The computing systems having rich resources used in the offloading process were referred as *surrogate systems*. The main objective behind this was to augment the computing capabilities of mobile devices by conserving mobile energy (battery power) and extending storage and enhancing data security.

With this mechanism, the mobile devices mainly play the roles of human-computer interfacing with less processing burden. Lesser processing obligation improves energy conservation in mobile devices which is a critical factor in mobile computing technology. Moreover, with the offloading of tasks to surrogate devices and by transmitting data to and from those computers, the mobile devices can deliver far better performance to customers.

While offloading of processing tasks improves performance of mobile applications, sometimes this may pose threats for the safety and reliability of the applications as well as data in the absence of proper authentication or due to the lack of supervision of surrogate systems. Initially the process of offloading used to be happen from mobile devices to some stationary computer connected through network or Internet. But this had limited utility. Later on, the idea of *resource augmentation* arrived with the advent of more developed computing models.

> Resource-constrained mobile devices can deliver better application performance through task offloading technique, where processing of tasks is performed on some external system.

21.1.4 Integration of Cloud Computing into Mobile Computing

With continuous progress in the field of communication, mobile communication technology has overcome the barrier of network bandwidth and range issues. Introduction of technologies like GPRS and EDGE, 3G and 4G networks have created opportunities for high speed service delivery. As a consequence, higher quality of application performance has become an automatic expectation of the users.

In cloud computing model, computing takes place at a cloud data center which are then consumed by users remotely. Due to its elastic feature, cloud computing can supply as much resources as required; hence there is no question of resource shortage for processing of resource-centric applications. Moreover, the architecture of cloud computing enables it to provide high-performance computational delivery by using easily available and cheaper commodity hardware. This reduces the computational cost and makes cloud computing cost-effective.

Another attractive feature of cloud computing is that it delivers different computational facilities as utility services in an on-demand mode. Application can be run on cloud from any location over the Internet without any concern about resources. Cloud provider ensures consistent performance of application irrespective of the number of concurrent users of the application at any moment.

As a result, cloud computing has emerged as the best option for *offloading* the processing of mobile applications to meet the expectations of current-age smartphone users. The critical and heavier parts of an application can be offloaded to some reputed cloud services (for execution) which ensures consistent application performance.

The integration of cloud computing into mobile computing helps to overcome several performance-related limitations. Mobile applications can now avail almost unlimited pool of resources at minimal cost due to the utility-service delivery model of cloud computing. The elastic nature of cloud computing ensures rapid provisioning (and de-provisioning too) of resources which enhances application performance. Apart from data processing, cloud computing also offers attractive data storage facility.

> *Mobile cloud computing enables mobile computing to take full advantage of cloud computing.*

21.1.5 Benefits of Mobile Cloud Computing

Through the integration of cloud computing in mobile computing, it enjoys all the advantages of cloud computing. This integration also provides many other advantages by overcoming limitations of mobile computing. Following section discusses these advantages.

Extended life of battery: *Mobile computing devices* are integral parts of mobile computing. These are battery-powered devices and so the life of the battery is a major concern for mobile computing. By offloading tasks and executing them on some cloud server, prolonged execution of applications can be avoided inside mobile devices which preserves battery power.

Improved processing performance: *Offloading* of application processing tasks from resource-constrained mobile devices to resource-rich cloud servers automatically improves the user experience. Application performance hardly depends on the local (mobile) devices anymore.

Enhanced storage capacity: Cloud provides the unlimited storage. Hence mobile computing users are no more restricted by the local storage capacity of mobile devices. MCC users can store and access any volume of data in cloud storages.

Improved reliability: Reputed cloud services deliver reliable services through dynamic resource management and improved application security. MCC inherits this reliability of service.

Enhanced data security: Data is more secure in cloud rather than the local mobile computing devices. This is because data is replicated over multiple locations which almost eliminate the chance of any data loss.

Relief from vendor-lock-in: With mobile cloud computing, the computing device can act as viewing or interfacing device where the users can connect to a large pool of cloud services and use various types of applications. Availability of application no more depends on the platform of local device only.

Apart from these, MCC gets all of other advantages of cloud computing like scalability, dynamic provisioning, ease of collaboration etc. All of these capabilities enable MCC users to run highly-accessed mobile commerce applications or play resource-centric gaming without any performance or data storage issues.

21.2 INTERNET OF THINGS

Internet of Things (IoT) is the next big happening in the field of computing, after cloud computing. In a very simple sense, the *internet of things* can be referred to as the network of any type of real world things with computing in some form as embedded into them. Here the term 'thing' refers to any device or object which have electronic chips (generally very small, low-power, battery-powered wireless sensors) attached with network interfaces that enable them to communicate with each other. Such devices or objects include mechanical devices, electrical appliances, automobiles, different sensors, non-living objects like cars or televisions, living objects like human or animals and also full-fledged computing devices. Whenever computing in some form along with communication capability is implemented in these objects, they turn capable of becoming the parts of some IoT.

Being the next major development after cloud computing, IoT often operates using cloud-based applications to interpret real-time data. Cloud-connected dashboards are used to control the items (chips or sensors) connected through an IoT. But the concept of IoT is influenced by and has emerged from the combination of two other innovative developments in the field of computing: smart objects and fog computing.

21.2.1 Smart Objects

'Smart objects' are some sort of objects which can interact with other smart objects as well as with human beings. Any non-smart physical object can be turned into smart physical objects by embedding an electronic chip with power source in addition to some computing and/or sensing and data transmission capability. Apart from this, smart physical objects can interact with smart virtual objects also, which are represented by software applications running in any core of a computing environment. A smart object generally holds a set of application logic that enables it to analyze specific conditions and interact with others through network communication.

The interaction activities of the smart objects are either scheduled or triggered by the events like changes in physical property or environmental condition or other attributes. The triggering effect may be caused by many factors like speed of movement, location of object, time of happening, temperature and others.

> *Smart objects are any mobile or stationary objects embedded with an electronic chip, thereby being enabled for sensing, processing and communication.*

21.2.2 Fog Computing

In meteorological meaning, fog refers to the presence of cloud closer to the ground. In a similar way, *fog computing* extends the concept of cloud computing where apart from the cloud servers, computational tasks also take place among the edge computing devices in a collaborative manner. Here the *edge computing device* generally refers to any mobile computing device. Countless data and application processing tasks are produced from such devices every day and it is not always an efficient approach to transmit and then process everything in a cloud. Rather, the *end devices* (*edge devices*) situated at the edges of network can be assigned many of these processing tasks. This approach is particularly useful for mobile computing devices and works well for systems with a large number of nodes (devices).

Fog computing can improve processing efficiency by eliminating the need for back-and-forth communication with cloud which may cause transmission delay. If an *edge computing device* can fulfill its processing needs from other nearby edge computing devices, then it can deliver better performance. Fog computing has got its specific name because this approach extends the concept of cloud computing towards the edges (or closer to the ground level) of the network.

> The term 'fog' in fog computing refers to the idea of transferring cloud computing-like effects closer to the data sources at the surface level.

21.2.3 Unique Identification of 'Things'

Each and every 'thing' in an IoT should be assigned an unique identifiers (IP address) and should have the ability of transferring data over network without any human interaction. For example, a person can have an implanted heart monitoring system or a sensor implanted in a car may alert the driver about air-pressure of tires or animals with biochip transponders implanted into them which may pass-on information about their where-abouts. All of these devices are accessible remotely, creating scope for integration of the physical world into computer-based systems.

Another important factor that has contributed to the emergence of IoT is the introduction of IPv6 standard of IP addressing. Huge number of IP addresses need to be included in a large number of objects to become part of IoT. This would not be possible using the capacity of IP addresses available under IPv4 standard. The address space expansion through introduction of IPv6 promises to uniquely identify each and every object and particle on earth (or even beyond the earth) with unique IP addresses. In other words, it is now possible to assign unique IP address to each and every 'thing' on the planet using IPv6.

> With full-fledged implementation of IoT, all the manufacturers will now have to play the role of computing providers as well.

21.2.4 Benefits of IoT

The world has progressed through advancements in computation and communication technologies. But the data collection process mostly remains manual, dependent on human beings. This way, the accuracy and quantity of collected data about 'real world things' depends on the persons entering or capturing the data. If data can be collected or gathered from the 'real world things' automatically without human intervention it would increase availability and accuracy of data with minimal effort by saving labour and reducing time wastage. Once the IoT concept gets implemented comprising of all of relevant 'things' of the world, each 'thing' will know everything about all other 'things' that are required to be known. IoT enables visibility or accessibility of objects which were once considered to be offline.

The other major advantage of IoT is the real-time availability of information about all these things whenever it is needed. These advancements can make the world smarter and facilitate the management of things effortlessly. Concepts like smart home or smart city are based on this idea. For instance, when a smart car enters a smart city it can instantly get the traffic-related information regarding all routes leading to its destination. This helps the car (or the driver of the car) to take the most convenient route and thus the traffic flow of the city is optimized.

The term 'internet of things' was first coined by a British man in 1999 on the pretext of describing the network of objects connected through radio-frequency identification (RFID). The ubiquitous and high-speed availability of Internet, wireless communication technology like Wi-Fi, production of network-enabled sensors and decreasing technology cost makes IoT a feasible idea. According to the analyst firm Gartner, there will be more than approximately 20 billion connected devices by 2020. Major computing vendors like Amazon, Google, Microsoft and Cisco have already started to launch IoT services. They allow consumers' connect their devices in the IoT service to serve a range of purposes.

SUMMARY

❖ Mobile computing is a technology which has become an essential part of daily life. Billions of mobile computing devices are being used across the world and with the emergence of smart mobile computing devices like smart phone, users' requirements have gained pace.

❖ Mobile computing devices have a major constraint: their limited resource capacity.

❖ Many limitations of mobile computing can be eliminated by integrating cloud computing into it. This combined technology is called mobile cloud computing (MCC).

❖ In mobile cloud computing, users of mobile computing enjoy all facilities and advantages of cloud computing. They can access any platform or application by connecting to different cloud services from their mobile devices.

❖ In this approach, a mobile device can act as computing interface where it uses resources from the cloud and this resolves the resource limitation problem.

❖ MCC also resolves the vendor-lock-in problem of mobile devices, in which users used to be restricted within the application or platform tied to a procured mobile device.

❖ When mobile computing devices build a network among themselves and utilize each other's unutilized resources to fulfill computing requirements instead of offloading application processing loads into cloud servers, the technique is called 'fog computing'.

❖ Smart objects are sort of real-life objects which have some computing and network communication capability. Generally such objects have electronic chips integrated into them.

❖ Internet of Things (IoT) is a revolutionary idea that combines fog computing idea and the concept of smart object.

❖ Any real-life living or non-living thing can become a part of IoT by embedding a sensor or processing chip into themselves along with data transfer capability.

❖ IoT simplifies information collection mechanism and helps to make the environment smarter.

❖ Through IoT, an object can automatically and instantly collect information about other objects in the network. This enables an object to behave intelligently without any human intervention.

REVIEW QUESTIONS

What are the limitations of mobile computing?

Mobile computing is the technique where computing is performed during movement. The first issue in such mechanism is the access to network or Internet as mobile computing devices cannot be restricted from movement by connecting them with network through cable. Hence wireless network communication is the only way out. Although introduction of 3G and 4G networks have created opportunities for high-speed communication, wireless communication during movement may often raise bandwidth issue. The second issue is related to the limitation of resources in such computing systems as portability becomes important for mobile devices. The third problem arises due to vendor-lock-in where a computing device supports some limited platform as well as application.

How does mobile cloud computing help to overcome the limitations of mobile computing?

Through mobile cloud computing, mobile computing users can avail all of the facilities of cloud computing. First of all this frees them from vendor-lock-in problem. Access to facilities (like application, platform etc.) are no more restricted by the specification of mobile computing device. Users can access various cloud services where the mobile device plays the simplified role of human-computer interfaces.

    Integration of cloud computing into mobile computing has also eliminated the mobile device's resource limitation problem. Any type of computing tasks can be offloaded to resource-rich cloud servers which can provide the scalability features. Thus, the mobile computing can serve high-performance applications to users without any glitch.

Why is Fog Computing called so?

In cloud computing, tasks are performed in cloud servers instead of processing them in users' own computing devices. This helps to overcome several constraints like having limitation in resources of end devices and others. Any device can access any volume and type of computing facility by connecting to cloud. In fog computing, end computing device distributes (or, offloads) load among other nearby end computing devices when they are free. This way, every end devices can satisfy their computing needs through resource augmentation into other end devices without reaching to the cloud. With this technique, cloud computing-like effect is transferred towards the ground or end or edge of network. That is why it is called as fog computing.

Why is Internet of Things (IoT) being considered such a happening topic?

There is countless numbers of real-life things in this world. We need to continuously collect information about many among them. Most of those data are collected manually. This is a cumbersome job and manual data collection may cause erroneous entry. IoT talks about connecting these real-life objects with each other through the network so that they can gather information about each other that they want to know. This is possible by enhancing real-life things or objects with computing and network communication having enabled with the electronic chips. This will ease the handling of many complicated real-life situations very smoothly which ultimately will lead towards a smart environment.

MULTIPLE CHOICE QUESTIONS

1. Which among the following stands as limitation(s) for mobile computing?

   a) Processing capability
   b) Storage capacity
   c) Battery power
   d) All of these

2. Through which technique, the energy conservation can be done in mobile computing?

   a) Task offloading
   b) Data offloading
   c) Communication offloading
   d) None of these

3. Which among the following cannot be considered as a limitation of mobile computing?

   a) Resource at computing device
   b) Network bandwidth
   c) Mobility of computing device
   d) Power of battery

4. The resource-rich computing system used for augmenting resources of mobile computing device is referred as

   a) Master system
   b) Surrogate system
   c) Secondary system
   d) Server system

5. In mobile-cloud computing, which among the following is used in the resource augmentation process?

   a) Any non-mobile system
   b) Mobile cloud server
   c) Cloud server
   d) None of these

6. Mobile cloud computing solves which of the following limitation(s) of traditional mobile computing?

   a) Resource limitation
   b) Vendor-lock-in
   c) Energy limitation
   d) All of these

7. When task offloading from one end device to other end devices is done instead of cloud that is called as

   a) Mobile computing
   b) Fog computing
   c) Internet of Things
   d) Traditional computing

8. Which among the following is an essential attribute of smart object?

   a) High-end processing capability
   b) Large storage capability
   c) Fast communication capability
   d) None of these

9. Which among the following contributes most in the emergence of IoT?

   a) Cloud computing
   b) Fog computing
   c) Smart object
   d) All of these

10. Smart objects need to have physical existence. This statement is:

    a) True
    b) False

11. Which IP addressing standard is suitable for uniquely identifying objects in IoT?

    a) IPv4
    b) IPv6
    c) Any IP standard
    d) None of these

I Hot Research Topics

A lot of research is happening in and around the field of cloud computing in order to achieve more efficient solutions to different issues and to gain optimal results from them. This section introduces a few, among many, hot research topics related to the wide domain of cloud computing.

A.1 OPTIMAL MANAGEMENT OF CLOUD RESOURCE

Resource management in cloud computing is the prime responsibility of the IaaS cloud service providers who build and manage the data centers. IaaS cloud provider has two major resource management objectives. First, to make the environment reliable as well as robust for optimal and efficient utilization of the data center infrastructure. The second is related to the SLA, which defines the relation with the consumer party.

The first objective deals with issues like load balancing, fault tolerance, energy conservation etc. Here, the load should be distributed in a way that in a data center, the utilization rate remains in balance among resources of a similar type. To make a system fault tolerant, the allocation of the resources should happen in a way that the effect of the failure of some resource component remains insignificant. Energy conservation is another important issue while managing resources at a data center. Optimal energy use reduces computing cost and it should also be minimized to reduce the carbon footprint.

A cloud provider may opt for a number of approaches to handle these issues. It can optimize these parameters by taking a combined approach, or it can work on every metric individually. The cloud provider may use some consistent set of combinations and/or may also decide to employ varied performance goals for individual operational situations. For instance, energy minimization may be a higher priority during low-load conditions, while the service performance may be the higher priority during high load. A balance should be maintained among all these choices without affecting the user expectations. Finding out an optimal balancing point between performance and energy conservation is a critical concern of the research in such cases.

For resource management objectives related to the Service Level Agreements (SLA), the cloud providers generally adopt an approach called *service differentiation*. In this approach, different levels of service performances are delivered to different consumers depending on the service level agreements made with them. Thus, the performance–energy balancing point, as discussed above, would vary depending on the SLA related to them.

Resource scheduling has an important role in the resource management processes. The global scheduling of resources is about dealing with the entire set of physical and virtual resources together in a cloud environment. Various techniques and frameworks have been proposed for the same. Most of these proposals use centralized resource controllers where the controllers have the full control over all resource components. But to incorporate system scaling, proper capacity planning has to be done to maintain sets of extra resources in addition to estimated demand. In order to implement effective scaling even in a small cloud environment, there has to be a minimum number of resource components and that number generally counts in thousands. Optimal organization of resource controllers is another area of work for researchers. Among different organization being studied, a hierarchical arrangement of resource controllers has shown effective results to implement the scaling mechanism.

Virtual machine's (VM) placement and provisioning is another important issue in this regard. A request for VM from the cloud user ultimately cascades to the physical machines. Initially in VM placement approach, the static shares of resources from physical machines were allotted for the VMs. Since then, many variants of this approach have been proposed. The advanced solution proposes to allocate resources in a dynamic order from the resource pool. All these allocations are usually managed at the hypervisor level. More advanced solutions propose live migration of VMs into another physical machine when required. But, the live migration has some overhead concerns. Hence, appropriate planning and study is required before employing the VM placement approach.

A.2 LOAD BALANCING ALGORITHM

Balancing of loads among similar type of nodes at cloud data center is a critical and important task in the success of cloud computing. Load balancing serves multiple purposes. Each of these contributes in building a high performance system. The goals of load balancing include the following:

- Improving the overall system performance,
- Maintaining stability of system,
- Building a fault tolerant system, and
- Simplifying the future modification of the system.

Static load balancing allocates the loads among all the nodes (VMs) of a data center after estimating the resource requirement for a task during the time of its compilation. This causes a problem, as this approach does not constantly monitor the nodes in order to track the statistics of their performances. Hence, this approach is not suitable for a system where the resource requirement of tasks may change abruptly with time (after being assigned to some node for execution).

Dynamic load balancing approach is more pertinent for cloud computing like environment where resource requirements of the tasks (and thus the load on nodes) vary highly with time, since it (the load balancer) can make changes in the distribution of workload of a task during its (the task) runtime. But careful implementation of this algorithm is required because the dynamic approach creates additional overheads for continuous accumulation and maintenance of load information (or knowledge) of nodes across the network.

Dynamic load balancing approach maintains and uses a knowledge-base about current state of each and every node load at a data center. In simplified form, a load balancer assigns incoming load to the least loaded node (that is, the node with least number of tasks assigned to it). But this method often creates problems because an under-loaded node may become over-loaded very soon as the balancer does not consider the execution time of the tasks.

One solution to this problem is to model the *foraging behaviour* of honey bees in load balancing. This approach was introduced after detailed study of the behaviour of honey bees in finding their food sources. The special bees called scout bees leave a bee hive searching for food sources. They come back after finding one and convey the message to others with a dance called vibration or *waggle dance*. This dance indicates the different attributes of the food source like its distance from the bee hive, its quality, quantity and else. Few forager bees then follow the scout bees to the food sources in order to collect the food. After collecting food, they all return back to the hive and again convey a message to others about the current status of the food source through the same type of vibration or waggle dance. They even intimate whether any more food is left (and/or how much if any).

The food searching behaviour of honey bees has been adopted in the load balancing activity at cloud data centers. An algorithm has been derived through a detailed study of the behaviour of honey bees in finding their food resources. The returning of removed tasks from nodes (before or after completion) can be considered similar to bees' returning from the places of the food sources. They indicate the number of different priority tasks and load on respective nodes to all other waiting tasks. This behaviour for returning tasks help other tasks choose the nodes based on their load and priority. Whenever a task with some priority has to be submitted for execution to some node, the load balancer looks for the suitable node with minimum number of higher priority tasks so that the particular task can be executed at the earliest. In this approach, the stipulated tasks are treated as the bees and nodes are treated as the food sources. Assigning a task to some node is done in a fashion similar to honey bee searching for a food source.

Loading a node with tasks (that is consumption of resources at the node) is similar to diminishing of food sources by the honey bees. When exhausted, tasks from a node are assigned to other under-loaded nodes which is similar to a foraging bee finding a new food source. The message conveyed by a task while returning from a node is similar to the typical waggle dance of a honey bee when it returns from a food source. The message provides a clear idea to the other waiting tasks about the load status of nodes just like the prospect of the food sources.

Use of 'honey bee' approach in load balancing is suitable for dynamic distribution of loads. In this approach, collective decisions are made through feedback cycles based on positive and negative signalling. This approach suggests a type of neighbourhood search in combination with random searching technique and can be used for both functional optimization and combinative optimization problems.

A.3 ENERGY EFFICIENT MOBILE CLOUD COMPUTING

'Green Mobile Cloud Computing (MCC)' is one important issues nowadays, concept as discussed under green computing. The objective of green MCC is to reduce the power exhaustion of mobile devices. To achieve this goal, the offloading of computational tasks from mobile computing devices to the cloud is an attractive and automatic feature of this concept.

Offloading augments mobile computing device's capability by shifting the tasks to more resourceful systems. It may sound familiar, but this technique is not similar to the traditional client-server systems where majority of processing happens at the server end. Unlike client-server system, in MCC, tasks are offloaded outside the user's own computing environment to some system, generally not identified by the user.

But this offloading decision-making is a critical issue in mobile computing, as it may not always provide better performance compared to local processing of applications if it is not implemented carefully. For an instance, the local execution of small codes generally shows better performance in terms of energy saving, in comparison to offloaded execution of the same. This is due to the reason that offloading activity of a small coding module may not conserve much energy, or may even consume more energy than required to execute it locally in the mobile computing device. Hence, it is a critical issue for mobile application developers to determine which part of the application should be processed locally and which part is to be offloaded into the cloud.

There is no standard rule for making this critical decision. Researchers are working on this issue as energy conservation is a vital issue in mobile computing as well as mobile cloud computing. This not only promotes green computing, but also increases the utility of a mobile device by preserving battery power for a longer period of time.

The trade-off is between computation and data transmission costs in terms of the energy conservation at the mobile device end. The computational cost or the energy requirement for computation is proportional to the processing time. On the other hand, the energy expenditure for transmitting programming module for offloading depends on the size of the transmitted data.

Experiments have shown that offloading consumes less power compared to local processing when the size of the code module is relatively large. This difference or gap in power consumption slowly decreases as the size of code module reduces. And after a point, for relatively smaller code modules, the results of observation switche places. That is, the module transmission then starts consuming more energy compared to processing it locally.

One such experiment has shown that for a certain size of code module, offloading can save almost fifty percent of the battery power (over processing it locally). However, this efficiency reduces to thirty percent when the size of the code module is halved. And when the code is further halfed, offloading consumes more battery power than local processing. It is interesting to note that the energy requirement depends on other factors (like processor speed, speed of the network transmission etc.) apart from the size of the code module and thus a different experiment may even yield a slightly different result.

Partitioning of an application is a critical task for designers to determine which parts to process locally and which parts to be offloaded. This partitioning is generally done by dividing an application into multiple smaller modules after conducting a careful study. These modules are then studied for their respective energy requirements and depending on the findings of the study, it is decided whether to opt for local processing or enlist for offloading.

Heuristic algorithms can be applied to determine optimal partitioning and distribution to minimize the processing cost. Generally such decisions are made prior to the compilation of an application. But processing or offloading time varies depending on several current parameters of a system. Consequently, the a priori decision may result in erroneous offloading decisions. Again run-time decision making regarding offloading slows down the process. Hence, there is another trade-off about design-time and run-time decision making regarding the offloading.

Bibliography

Amazon. 2013. 'Auto Scaling Developer Guide (API Version 2011-01-01)'. Accessed on November 18, 2016. https://aws.amazon.com/archives/Amazon-EC2.

Amazon. 2015a. 'Overview of Amazon Web Services (AWS Whitepaper).' Accessed on November 17, 2016. https://aws.amazon.com/whitepapers/overview-of-amazon-web-services/.

_____ 2015b. 'Amazon CloudFront'. Accessed November 19, 2016. https://aws.amazon.com/cloudfront/details/.

_____ 2015c. 'Amazon DynamoDB'. Accessed November 21, 2016. http://docs.aws.amazon.com/amazondynamodb/latest/developerguide/Introduction.html.

_____ 2015d. Amazon SimpleDB. Accessed November 25, 2016. https://aws.amazon.com/simpledb/details/.

_____ 2016a. 'Amazon EC2'. Accessed February 10, 2016. https://aws.amazon.com/ec2/instance-types/.

_____ 2016b. 'Amazon RDS'. Accessed February 18, 2016. https://aws.amazon.com/rds/details/.

_____ 2016c. 'Amazon EBS'. Accessed February 20, 2016. https://aws.amazon.com/ebs/details/.

_____ 2016d. 'Amazon S3'. Accessed February 20, 2016. https://aws.amazon.com/s3/details/.

_____ 2016e. 'Amazon SQS'. Accessed February 22, 2016. https://aws.amazon.com/sqs/.

_____ 2016f. 'Amazon SimpleDB'. Accessed November 28, 2016. https://aws.amazon.com/simpledb/faqs/.

Antonopoulos, Nikos, and Lee Gillam. 2010. *Cloud Computing: Principles, Systems and Applications.* London: Springer Science & Business Media.

Armbrust, Michael, Armando Fox, Rean Griffith, Anthony D. Joseph, Randy Katz, Andy Konwinski, Gunho Lee, David Patterson, Ariel Rabkin, Ion Stoica, and Matei Zaharia. 2009. 'Above the Clouds: A Berkeley View of Cloud Computing.' Technical Report No. UCB/EECS-2009-28. Berkeley: University of California.

Arora, Pankaj, Raj Biyani, and Salil Dave. 2012. *To the Cloud: Cloud Powering an Enterprise.* New York: McGraw Hill Professional.

Babu, Dhinesh L.D., and P. Venkata Krishna. 2013. 'Honey bee behavior inspired load balancing of tasks in cloud computing environments.' *Applied Soft Computing.* Volume 13. Issue 5: 2292–2303.

Buyya, Rajkumar, Christian Vecchiola, and S ThamaraiSelvi. 2013. *Mastering Cloud Computing.* New Delhi: Tata McGraw-Hill Education.

Buyya, Rajkumar, James Broberg, and Andrzej M. Goscinski. 2010. *Cloud Computing: Principles and Paradigms.* Indianapolis: John Wiley & Sons.

Chee, Brian J.S., and Curtis Franklin Jr. 2010. *Cloud Computing: Technologies and Strategies of the Ubiquitous Data Center.* Boca Raton: CRC Press.

CISCO. 2015. 'Fog Computing and the Internet of Things: Extend the Cloud to Where the Things Are'. Accessed on September 22, 2016. https://www.cisco.com/c/dam/en_us/solutions/trends/iot/docs/computing-overview.pdf.

Cloud Council. 2014. 'Interoperability and Portability for Cloud Computing: A Guide.' Accessed on September 23, 2016. www.cloud-council.org/CSCC-Cloud-Interoperability-and-Portability.pdf.

Dikmans, Lonneke, and Ronald van Luttikhuizen. 2012. *SOA Made Simple*. Birmingham: Packt Publishing.

Dinh, Hoang T., Chonho Lee, Dusit Niyato, and Ping Wang. 2011. 'A survey of mobile cloud computing: architecture, applications, and approaches.'*Wireless Communications and Mobile Computing*. Volume 13. Issue 18: 1587–1611. Indianapolis: John Wiley & Sons Ltd.

Elser, Amy. 2012. *Guide to Reliable Distributed Systems: Building High-Assurance Applications and Cloud-Hosted Services*. London: Springer Science & Business Media.

Erl, Thomas. 2005. *Service-Oriented Architecture: Concepts, Technology, and Design*. Upper Saddle River: Pretince Hall.

Erl, Thomas, Ricardo Puttini, and Zaigham Mahmood. 2013. *Cloud Computing: Concepts, Technology & Architecture*. Upper Saddle River: Prentice Hall.

Erl, Thomas, Wajid Khattak, and Paul Buhler. 2015. *Big Data Fundamentals: Concepts, Drivers & Techniques*. Crawfordsville: Prentice Hall.

Fang, Yiqiu, Fei Wang, and Junwei Ge. 2010. 'A Task Scheduling Algorithm Based on Load Balancing in Cloud Computing.' *Lecture Notes in Computer Science*. Volume 6318: 271–277. London: Springer.

Foster, Ian, Yong Zhao, Ioan Raicu, and Shiyong Lu. 2009. 'Cloud Computing and Grid Computing 360-Degree Compared.' IEEE Xplore. Originally published in proceedings of the Grid Computing Environments Workshop (GCE), 2008. Accessed on November 23, 2016. doi: 10.1109/GCE.2008.4738445.

Furht, Borko, and Armando Escalante. 2010. *Handbook of Cloud Computing*. London: Springer Science & Business Media.

Ghemawat, Sanjay, Howard Gobioff, and Shun-Tak Leung. 2003. 'The Google File System.' Published in 19th ACM Symposium on Operating Systems Principles,Lake George, NY, October 19–22.

Gong, Zhenhuan, Xiaohui Gu, and John Wilkes. 2010. 'PRESS: PRedictive Elastic ReSource Scaling for cloud systems.' Proceedings of the International Conference on Network and Service Management (CNSM). IEEE: 9–16.

Google. 2016a. 'Google Compute Engine'. Accessed February 19, 2016. https://cloud.google.com/compute/pricing.

_____ 2016b. 'Google Compute Engine'. Accessed February 19, 2016. https://en.wikipedia.org/wiki/Google_Compute_Engine.

_____ 2016c. 'Google BigQuery'. Accessed March 22, 2016. https://cloud.google.com/bigquery/what-is-bigquery.

Hagen, William Von. 2008. *Professional Xen Virtualization*. Indianapolis: John Wiley & Sons.

Halpert, Ben. 2011. *Auditing Cloud Computing: A Security and Privacy Guide*. Indianapolis: John Wiley & Sons

Held, Gilbert.2010. *A Practical Guide to Content Delivery Networks*. Boca Raton: CRC Press.

Hurwitz, Judith, Robin Bloor, Marcia Kaufman, and Fern Halper. 2010. *Cloud Computing For Dummies.* Indianapolis: John Wiley & Sons.

IBM. 2005. 'An architectural blueprint for autonomic computing'. Accessed on Octobeer 09, 2016. www-03.ibm.com/autonomic/pdfs/AC%20Blueprint%20White%20Paper%20V7.pdf.

———. 2015a. 'The Internet of Things in the Cognitive Era: Realizing the future and full potential of connected devices.'Accessed on October 10, 2016. http://www-01.ibm.com/common/ssi/cgi-bin/ssialias?htmlfid=WWW12366USEN.

———. 2015b. 'Apache Hadoop'. Accessed October 12, 2016. https://www-01.ibm.com/software/data/infosphere/hadoop/hdfs/.

Isom, Pamela K., Kerrie Holley. 2012. *Is Your Company Ready for Cloud: Choosing the Best Cloud Adoption Strategy for Your Business.* Upper Saddle River: IBM Press, Pearson Plc.

ISO. 2016. 'ISO 27001'. Accessed March 14, 2016. http://www.iso.org/iso/iso27001.

Josuttis, Nicolai M. 2007. *SOA in Practice.* Sebastopol: O'Reilly Media, Inc.

Krutz, Ronald L., and Russell Dean Vines. 2010. *Cloud Security: A Comprehensive Guide to Secure Cloud Computing.* Indianapolis: John Wiley & Sons.

Linthicum, David S. 2009. *Cloud Computing and SOA Convergence in Your Enterprise: A Step-by-Step Guide.* Boston: Pearson Education.

Mahmood, Zaigham. 2013. *Cloud Computing: Methods and Practical Approaches.* London: Springer Science & Business Media.

Manjrasoft. 2016. 'Aneka'. Accessed on April 23, 2016. http://www.manjrasoft.com/aneka_architecture.html.

Mather, Tim, Subra Kumaraswamy, and Shahed Latif. 2009.*Cloud Security and Privacy: An Enterprise Perspective on Risks and Compliance.* Sebastopol: O'Reilly Media, Inc.

Mayer-Schönberger, Viktor, and Kenneth Cukier. 2013. *Big Data: A Revolution That Will Transform How We Live, Work, and Think.* Boston: Houghton Mifflin Harcourt.

Microsoft. 2015a. 'Azure Content Delivery Network'. Accessed October 17, 2016. https://docs.microsoft.com/en-us/azure/cdn/cdn-overview.

———. 2015b. 'Azure DocumentDB'. Accessed December 01, 2016. https://azure.microsoft.com/en-in/services/documentdb/.

———. 2016a. 'Azure General Purpose Compute'. Accessed February 10, 2016. https://azure.microsoft.com/en-us/pricing/details/virtual-machines/linux/.

———. 2016b. 'Azure Virtual Machine Image'. Accessed February 22, 2016. https://docs.microsoft.com/en-us/azure/virtual-machines/virtual-machines-windows-about?toc=%2fazure%2fvirtual-machines%2fwindows%2ftoc.json.

Moyer, Christopher M. 2011. *Building Applications in the Cloud: Concepts, Patterns, and Projects.* Boston: Pearson Education.

NCSU. 2015. 'Apache VCL'. Accessed December 18, 2016. https://vcl.ncsu.edu/open-source-apache-vcl-project/.

Neo4j. 2016. 'Graph Database'. Accessed January 06, 2016. https://neo4j.com/developer/graph-database/.

Nimbus. 2016. Accessed January 24, 2016. http://www.nimbusproject.org/about/.

NIST Special Publication. 2011a. *NIST Cloud Computing Reference Architecture.*National Institute of Standards and Technology.NIST SP: 500-292.

———. 2011b. *The NIST Definition of Cloud Computing.* National Institute of Standards and Technology.NIST SP: 800-145.

Opengroup. 2009. 'Jericho Forum Position Paper: Cloud Cube Model: Selecting Cloud Formations for Secure Collaboration, Version 1.0'. Accessed on November 25, 2015. https://collaboration.opengroup.org/jericho/cloud_cube_model_v1.0.pdf

OpenNebula. 2016. 'OpenNebula Technology'. Accessed January 30, 2016. https://opennebula.org/about/technology/.

Oracle. 2012. 'Oracle White Paper:Oracle Information Architecture: An Architect's Guide to Big Data.' Accessed on February 12, 2016. http://www.oracle.com/technetwork/oea-big-data-guide-1522052.pdf.

_____ 2013. 'Oracle White Paper:Big Data for the Enterprise.' Accessed on February 13, 2016. http://www.oracle.com/us/products/database/big-data-for-enterprise-519135.pdf.

Pathan, Mukaddim, Ramesh K. Sitaraman, and Dom Robinson. 2014. *Advanced Content Delivery, Streaming, and Cloud Services*. Indianapolis: John Wiley & Sons.

Pearson, Siani, and George Yee. 2012. *Privacy and Security for Cloud Computing*. London: Springer Science & Business Media.

Reese, George. 2009.*Cloud Application Architectures: Building Applications and Infrastructure in the Cloud*. Sebastopol: O'Reilly Media, Inc.

Rimal, Bhaskar Prasad, Eunmi Choi, and Ian Lumb. 'A Taxonomy and Survey of Cloud Computing Systems.'2009. Proceedings of the Fifth International Joint Conference on INC, IMS and IDC.IEEE Computer Society:44–51.

Ruest, Danielle, and Nelson Ruest. 2009. *Virtualization: A Beginner's Guide*. New York: Tata McGraw-Hill Education.

Sanaei, Zohreh, SaeidAbolfazli, Abdullah Gani, and RajkumarBuyya. 2014. 'Heterogeneity in Mobile Cloud Computing: Taxonomy and Open Challenges.' *IEEE Communications Surveys & Tutorials*.Volume 16. Issue 1: 369–392.

SAS70. 2016a. 'SysTrust'. Accessed March 12, 2016. http://sas70.com/FAQRetrieve.aspx?ID=33287.

_____ 2016b. 'WebTrust'. Accessed March 12, 2016. http://sas70.com/FAQRetrieve.aspx?ID=33288.

Shen, Zhiming, Sethuraman Subbiah, XiaohuiGu, and John Wilkes. 2011. 'CloudScale: Elastic Resource Scaling for Multi-Tenant Cloud Systems.' SOCC '11 Proceedings of the 2nd ACM Symposium on Cloud Computing, Cascais, Portugal, October 26–28.Shroff, Gautam. 2010. *Enterprise Cloud Computing: Technology, Architecture, Applications*. London: Cambridge University Press.

Sosinsky, Barrie. 2010. *Cloud Computing Bible*. Indianapolis: John Wiley & Sons.

Vecchiola, Christian, Xingchen Chu, and Rajkumar Buyya. 2009. 'Aneka: A software platform for .NET cloud computing.'*Advances in Parallel Computing*. Amsterdam:IOS Press.

Velte, Toby, and Anthony Velte, Robert Elsenpeter. 2009. *Cloud Computing: A Practical Approach*. New York: McGraw Hill Professional.

Wikipedia. 2015a. 'CDNetworks'. Accessed October 10, 2016. https://en.wikipedia.org/wiki/CDNetworks.

_____ 2015b. 'CDNetworks'. Accessed October 10, 2016. https://en.wikipedia.org/wiki/CDNetworks.

_____ 2015c. 'CDNetworks'. Accessed October 10, 2016. https://en.wikipedia.org/wiki/CDNetworks.

_____ 2015d. 'Apache Hadoop'. Accessed October 12, 2016. https://en.wikipedia.org/wiki/Apache_Hadoop.

_____ 2015e. 'Apache HBase'. Accessed October 15, 2016. https://en.wikipedia.org/wiki/Apache_HBase.

_____ 2015f. 'CDNetworks'. Accessed October 10, 2016. https://en.wikipedia.org/wiki/CDNetworks.

_____ 2015g. 'Google File System'. Accessed November 02, 2016. https://en.wikipedia.org/wiki/Google_File_System.

_____ 2015h. 'Gluster File System'. Accessed November 05, 2016. https://en.wikipedia.org/wiki/GlusterFS.

_____ 2015i. 'Eucalyptus'. Accessed December 28, 2016. https://en.wikipedia.org/wiki/Eucalyptus_(software).

_____ 2015j. 'CouchDB'. Accessed November 15, 2016. https://en.wikipedia.org/wiki/CouchDB.

_____ 2015k. 'MongoDB'. Accessed November 20, 2016. https://en.wikipedia.org/wiki/MongoDB.

_____ 2016a. 'Neo4j'. Accessed January 06, 2016. https://en.wikipedia.org/wiki/Neo4j.

_____ 2016b. 'OneDrive'. Accessed January 11, 2016. https://en.wikipedia.org/wiki/OneDrive.

_____ 2016c. 'Dropbox'. Accessed January 14, 2016. https://en.wikipedia.org/wiki/Dropbox_(service).

_____ 2016d. 'Google Drive'. Accessed January 14, 2016. https://en.wikipedia.org/wiki/Google_Drive.

_____ 2016e. 'Apache Cassandra'. Accessed January 15, 2016. https://en.wikipedia.org/wiki/Apache_Cassandra.

_____ 2016f. 'Limelight Networks'. Accessed January 16, 2016. https://en.wikipedia.org/wiki/Limelight_Networks.

_____ 2016g. 'OpenStack'. Accessed January 28, 2016. https://en.wikipedia.org/wiki/OpenStack.

_____ 2016h. 'OpenNebula'. Accessed January 30, 2016. https://en.wikipedia.org/wiki/OpenNebula.

_____ 2016i. 'Azure SQL Database'. Accessed March 17, 2016. https://en.wikipedia.org/wiki/Microsoft_Azure_SQL_Database.

_____ 2016j. 'Aneka'. Accessed April 24, 2016. https://en.wikipedia.org/wiki/Aneka.

_____ 2016k. 'Fog Computing'. Accessed May 09, 2016. https://en.wikipedia.org/wiki/Fog_computing.

Wilder, Bill. 2012. *Cloud Architecture Patterns*. Sebastopol: O'Reilly Media, Inc.

Williams, Bill. 2012. *The Economics of Cloud Computing: An Overview for Decision Makers*. Indianapolis: Cisco Press.

Zhang, X. W., A. Kunjithapatham, S. Jeong, and S. Gibbs. 2011. 'Towards an elastic application model for augmenting the computing capabilities of mobile devices with cloud computing.' *Mobile Networks & Applications* Volume 16. No 3: Pages 270–284.

Endnote

1. NIST Special Publication 800-145. Reprinted courtesy of the National Institute of Standards and Technology, U.S. Department of Commerce. Not copyrightable in the United States.
2. Figure 1. NIST Special Publication 500-292. Reprinted courtesy of the National Institute of Standards and Technology, U.S. Department of Commerce. Not copyrightable in the United States.
3. NIST Special Publication 500-292. Reprinted courtesy of the National Institute of Standards and Technology, U.S. Department of Commerce. Not copyrightable in the United States.
4. Figure 2. NIST Special Publication 500-292. Reprinted courtesy of the National Institute of Standards and Technology, U.S. Department of Commerce. Not copyrightable in the United States.
5. Figure 3. NIST Special Publication 500-292. Reprinted courtesy of the National Institute of Standards and Technology, U.S. Department of Commerce. Not copyrightable in the United States.
6. Figure 15. NIST Special Publication 500-292. Reprinted courtesy of the National Institute of Standards and Technology, U.S. Department of Commerce. Not copyrightable in the United States.
7. Jericho Forum Position Paper; Cloud Cube Model: Selecting Cloud Formations for Secure Collaboration; version 1.0; @The Open Group
8. Figure 16. NIST Special Publication 500-292. Reprinted courtesy of the National Institute of Standards and Technology, U.S. Department of Commerce. Not copyrightable in the United States.
9. Figure 4. NIST Special Publication 500-292. Reprinted courtesy of the National Institute of Standards and Technology, U.S. Department of Commerce. Not copyrightable in the United States.

Index

Printed in the United States
by Baker & Taylor Publisher Services